Representing Victims of Sexual and Spousal Abuse

Representing Victims of Sexual and Spousal Abuse

Nathalie Des Rosiers

Louise Langevin

A Quicklaw Company

REPRESENTING VICTIMS OF SEXUAL AND SPOUSAL ABUSE
© Irwin Law Inc., 2002

Published in 2002 by
Irwin Law Inc.
Suite 930, Box 235
One First Canadian Place
Toronto, ON
M5X 1C8

ISBN: 1-55221-047-2

National Library of Canada Cataloguing in Publication Data

Des Rosiers, Nathalie, 1959-
  Representing victims of sexual and spousal abuse

Translation of: L'indemnisation des victimes de violence sexuelle
  et conjugale.
Includes bibliographical references and index.
ISBN 1-55221-047-2

  1. Damages—Quebec (Province) 2. Reparation—Quebec
(Province) 3. Victims of family violence—Legal status, laws, etc.—
Quebec (Province) 4. Sexual abuse victims—Legal status, laws,
etc.—Quebec (Province) 5. Abused wives—Legal status, laws, etc.—
Quebec (Province) 6. Appellate Procedure—Quebec (Province)
I. Langevin, Louise, 1959- II. Title.

KEQ473.D4713 2002   346.71403'3   C2001-904066-0

The Publisher acknowledges the financial support of the Government of Canada through the Book Publishing Industry Development Program (BPIDP) for our publishing activities.

Printed and bound in Canada

1 2 3 4 5   06 05 04 03 02

#54.95

Summary Table of Contents

Detailed Table of Contents

Acknowledgments

Many resources are needed to create and translate a monograph. We would like to express our gratitude to the Department of Canadian Heritage for giving us a grant under the Administration of Justice in the Two Official Languages (AJTOL) program, without which we would not have been able to translate *L'indemnisation des victimes de violence sexuelle et conjugale*, which was originally published in 1998 by Éditions Yvon Blais. We would also like to thank Claire Morency, director general of the Fondation du Barreau du Québec. Without her sponsorship and assistance the AJTOL grant would not have been possible.

Translation is not an easy task. We cannot thank Bettina Karpel and Joani Tannenbaum enough for their professionalism and intellectual rigour in translating our work. They were able to convey civil law notions precisely and eloquently in English.

We would also like to thank all the research assistants for the work they contributed during the creation of the French version of our work: Thierry Dorval, Jacinthe Bourdages, Monica Song, Mona Nandy, Catherine Lawrence, Roland Hanel, Véronique Abele, Josée Patoine, and Susan Norman. Marlène Cadorette, Kim Holas, Natalie L'Heureux, and Viet Nguyen helped us update both versions. Thanks also go to our colleagues Claude Belleau, Marie-Claire Belleau, Daniel Gardner, Ghislain Otis, Nathalie Vézina, Constance Backhouse, Craig Brown, and Bruce Feldthusen for their feedback on earlier versions of our work and recommended avenues of research, as well as Christine Gauthier, from the Crime Victims Compensation Office.

We wish to acknowledge the contributions of the library staff at our respective universities—Marianne Welsch, Debbie Grey, Barb Fetchison, and Suzanne Drapeau—as well as Nicole Moisan for her secretarial help. We also thank Jeffrey Miller of Irwin Law for his technical support and Barbara Tessman for her helpful comments on the manuscript. We are grateful to the Faculty of Law and the Bureau de la recherche subventionnée at Université Laval and to the Law Foundation and the University of Western Ontario for their financial and technical support. The original French version was financed by a grant under the Strategic Theme Program on Women and Change, received in 1994 from the Social Sciences and Humanities Research Council of Canada.

Lastly, we thank our spouses, Gregory Ste. Marie and André Fortin, for their encouragement and support.

Introduction
Representing Victims of Sexual and Spousal Abuse

In recent years, some victims of sexual and spousal abuse in Canada have sought compensation before the civil courts. These civil proceedings are evidence of a growing social awareness and condemnation of violence against women and children. The laws on civil liability and torts must be able to respond adequately to the expectations of people seeking such redress.

The objectives contemplated in our original work in French were based on this conclusion. Our first objective was to provide replies to the many questions raised by the recent emergence of this remedy in Quebec civil law. The development of this remedy presented, and still presents, serious challenges to our legal system: among the considerations to be addressed are specific substantive questions relating to prescription, assessment of damages, and the scope of liability for others. Certain aspects of this remedy—for example, evidence of past, intimate, hidden acts—have created tension in a procedural system originally defined within a different context. We therefore attempted to identify potential problems as well as corresponding solutions.

Both the French version and the English translation address the needs of diverse legal communities. Given that our book is the sole study undertaken in the area of civil remedy for victims of sexual and spousal abuse both in Canada and internationally, we felt that an English translation was indispensable if we were to reach Canadian common law jurists. Such jurists can benefit from our solutions: although our work is based on the Quebec law of civil liability, this law resembles torts. Case law has a large role to play in the Quebec law of civil liability, and the Supreme Court of Canada rulings in torts are often applied in Quebec civil law.[1] The English

---

1. Here we refer, among others, to the trilogy on damages, *Andrews* v. *Grand and Toy, Alberta Ltd.*, [1978] 2 S.C.R. 229; *Thornton* v. *Prince George School Board*, [1978] 2 S.C.R. 267; *Arnold* v. *Teno*, [1978] 2 S.C.R. 287.

translation also contemplates non-francophone civilian jurists since the basic principles of Quebec civil liability are inspired largely by French civil law and this field of law derives from Roman-Germanic law. Moreover, it has been demonstrated that civil law is the most widely used legal system in the world.[2] In this era of globalization and the creation of a free trade zone in the Americas, we hope to reach all jurists in the Americas.

We have adopted an egalitarian and comparative law approach in both the French and English versions. This approach requires explanation. An egalitarian approach was used to analyse substantive and procedural issues. Such an approach holds that all citizens, if they so desire, are entitled to seek compensation under the law for damages suffered due to a fault.

Occasionally, we have been asked what motivated us to research court claims for compensation by survivors of sexual and spousal abuse. We were told that this was unnecessary, that it was perhaps unwise to encourage victims to go before civil courts that were traditionally unreceptive to the notion of compensating women, and that this remedy could be damaging to the victims. Our reply to these criticisms is egalitarian based.[3] First, we note that the reluctance with which spousal and sexual abuse is submitted to the legal system is not new.[4] It is reminiscent of the dichotomy between the private and public spheres, which has often been denounced by feminists.[5] In our opinion, the legal system must respond to the needs of all, not just some, citizens. If the civil legal system offers solutions, albeit often inadequate ones, to problems born of exces-

---

2.   See http://www.uottawa.ca/academic/droitcivil/world-legal-systems/index.html (date of access: 23 April 2001).

3.   The British Columbia Law Institute adopted the same attitude on this question in the report by the Project Committee on Civil Remedies for Sexual Assault, *Civil Remedies for Sexual Assault*, Vancouver, June 2001.

4.   See, among others, the judge's comments in *Kelly* v. *Communauté des Soeurs de la Charité de Québec*, J.E. 95-1875 (Que. Sup. Ct.) (appeal dropped 8 February 1996), where the plaintiff, one of the "Duplessis orphans," made a motion to launch a class action suit. The judge stated: "We are stretching the limits of a remedy offered under the law. Maybe one or the other party is knocking on the wrong door by turning to the courts. But it is a right that the Court respects" (at 27 [our translation]).

5.   See Michelle Boivin, "Le féminisme en capsule: un aperçu critique du droit," (1992) 5 *Revue Femmes et Droit* 357; Susan Boyd, ed., *Challenging the Public/Private Divide: Feminism, Law, and Public Policy* (Toronto: University of Toronto Press, 1997).

sively violent sports or medical negligence, for example, then why should it not address problems predominantly affecting women? Understood this way, our approach is gender-based. Sexual and spousal abuse is a fault committed against women, and they are entitled to be compensated for the consequences of this abuse.

Another issue that needs to be addressed when the topic of remedy is considered concerns the therapeutic benefit of exercising a right of reparation.[6] Although exercising a right in law is not beneficial for everyone, it is for some.[7] For others, it is unavoidable, because they have financial needs that can be satisfied only through compensation. It is our intention to propose solutions that would minimize, to the extent possible, the negative effects this remedy might have on participants. In our opinion, an approach that minimizes negative effects should help those who must proceed before the courts and those who chose to do so. In the end, of course, it is the victim who decides whether and how to pursue redress. We simply aim to clarify the issues related to that decision.

As is usual in Quebec law, our work draws on various jurisprudential and doctrinal resources, including Quebec private law, French law, and Canadian common law. There are two reasons why we draw on all these sources. First, few decisions on this matter are rendered or reported in Quebec.[8] This can be explained on several grounds. The paucity of decisions is due in part to the novelty of such actions, the short prescription periods, the possibility of out-of-court settlements, the fact that complainants consider the compensation offered under the *Crime Victims Compensation Act*[9] to be fair, the legal culture, and the approach favoured by organizations offer-

---

6.   See, among others, the following judgments that have recognized the therapeutic benefits of legal action: *M.M.* v. *S.V.*, J.E. 99-375 (Que. Sup. Ct.); *Leroux* v. *Montréal (Communauté urbaine de)*, [1997] R.J.Q. 1970 (Que. Sup. Ct.).
7.   On this subject, see the results of a preliminary study on the psychological impact of civil proceedings for sexual violence: Nathalie Des Rosiers, Bruce Feldthusen, and Olena Hankivsky, "Legal Compensation for Sexual Violence: Therapeutic Consequences and Consequences for the Judicial System," (1998) 4 *Psychology, Public Policy and Law* 433; Bruce Feldthusen, Olena Hankivsky, and Lorraine Greaves, "Therapeutic Consequences of Civil Actions for Damages and Compensation Claims by Victims of Sexual Abuse," (2000) 12 *Canadian Journal of Women and the Law* 67.
8.   See below, note 8, chap. 3. See also Louise Langevin, "L'accès des femmes au système judiciaire: les poursuites civiles pour violence sexuelle et conjugale au Québec," (1999) 19 *Les cahiers de la femme* 86.
9.   See "State Indemnification Plans," below, §§360ff.

ing assistance to victims of sexual and spousal abuse. In addition, Quebec doctrine has shown little interest in this subject. As for French law, the French civil courts do not, in practice, address the issue of sexual violence; victims are permitted to participate as plaintiffs in the criminal trial and possibly receive compensation.[10] We do, however, refer to French civil law when interpreting important principles of civil liability. Accordingly, it seemed logical to turn to common law sources.

Our goal in using Canadian common law cases is twofold. First, we transpose the factual situations to Quebec and examine the civilian response to the legal issues raised, thereby avoiding the natural tendency to adopt solutions offered by common law jurisprudence instead of reflecting on those offered by Quebec civil law. Where the civil law appears inappropriate or is silent, we suggest innovative solutions. Second, we examine the sometimes inappropriate legal approach adopted by the common law courts towards victims of sexual and spousal abuse and at times offer comments so that Quebec courts can avoid taking a similar route. Comparative law is thus important in the analysis of civil proceedings for sexual and spousal abuse, an area that is currently evolving.

* * *

A few words about terminology and procedure. Given that the victims are most often young girls and women and that the aggressors are almost exclusively men, we use the feminine pronoun when referring to the plaintiff and the masculine pronoun to refer to the defendant.[11] We also identify the plaintiff as "survivor" or "victim," although we are aware that the latter term can be criticized for perpetuating the victimization suffered by women who are, in fact, attempting to put the pieces of their lives back together. More commonly, these women see themselves as survivors who have managed to overcome traumatic events.

---

10.   Sec. 3 and 4 (1) *Code de procédure pénale*, see Philippe Malaurie and Laurent Aynès, *Cours de droit civil, Les obligations*, vol. 6 (Paris: Éditions Cujas, 1995), no. 231ff., pp. 133ff.

11.   See Part I, below, §4.

For simplicity's sake, we refer only to official case law reporters in the footnotes. Where the decision was unreported, we provide the *Quick Law* reference.

The present study is up to date to 1 September 2000.

Nathalie Des Rosiers   Louise Langevin

Part I
The Client

1. *Introduction* – A certain type of preparation is needed to represent the legal interests of a child victim or an adult survivor of sexual abuse, a battered woman, or the parents of a sexually abused
child.[1] To ensure the therapeutic rehabilitation of these types of
clients, an attorney must know how to identify and minimize the
dangers within the judicial system.[2] This task can be facilitated
through a better understanding of the social problems and the psychological dynamics affecting the victim, and through some reflection on the best way to manage the attorney–client relationship in
these types of cases. The purpose of Part I of this book is, first, to
describe the context and impact of sexual and spousal abuse and,
second, to reflect upon the attorney's role in the development and
progress of a civil suit.

---

1. See Kimberly A. Crnich, "Redressing the Undressing: A Primer on the
    Representation of Adult Survivors of Childhood Sexual Abuse," (1992) 14
    Women's Rights Law Reporter 65.
2. For a legal approach that attempts to eliminate the non-therapeutic effects of
    the legal process on participants, see David B. Wexler and Bruce J. Winnick,
    Law in a Therapeutic Key (Durham, NC: Carolina Academic Press, 1996).

1

Chapter 1

Towards a Better Understanding
of the Client

2. *Framework* – Sexual and spousal abuse are significant social problems. In a 1993 statistical survey on the issue of violence against women that continues to be cited as the most complete in its field,[3] Statistics Canada concluded that 51 per cent of women had experienced at least one incident of physical or sexual abuse after the age of sixteen. Other statistics relating to the rate of sexual abuse of children indicate that one out of every two girls and one out of every three boys have had unwanted sexual contact.[4] Many ana-

---

3.   See Holly Johnson and Vincent F. Sacco, "Researching Violence against Women: Statistics Canada's National Survey," (1995) 37 *Canadian Journal of Criminology* 281 at 293. See Julian V. Roberts, "Sexual Assault in Canada: Recent Statistical Trends," (1996) 21 *Queen's L. J.* 395 at 399. There appears to be a gap between disclosure of abuse to public authorities and its prevalence in society: for a discussion on this point, see Jacqueline Oxman-Martinez, William S. Rowe, Silvia Straka, and Yves Thibault, "La baisse de l'incidence et le dévoilement tardif dans les cas d'enfants victimes d'abus sexuels," (1997) 18 *Revue québécoise de psychologie* 77 at 79.

4.   See *Report of the Committee on Sexual Offences against Children and Youths* (Ottawa: Justice Canada, 1984) at 175–6 (hereinafter *Badgley Report*), cited by Nicholas Bala, "False Memory 'Syndrome': Backlash or Bona Fide Defence?" (1996) 21 *Queen's L. J.* 423 at 427; Yves-Hiram L. Haesevoets, *L'enfant victime d'inceste: de la séduction traumatique à la violence sexuelle* (Paris and Brussels: DeBoeck Université, 1997) at 22; Peter G. Jaffe, Nancy K.D. Lemon, Jack Sander, and David Wolfe, *Working Together to End Domestic Violence* (Tampa, FL: Mancorp Publishing, 1996) at 23. However, there is uncertainty as to the exact calculation of the rate of sexual abuse of children. See Oxman-Martinez et al., note 3 above, which refers to a study by David Finkelhor, "Epidemiological Factors in the Clinical Identification of Child Sexual Abuse," (1993) 18 *Child Abuse and Neglect* 409. Finkelhor claims that rates vary according to the quality of the study (i.e., the better the study, the higher the rate). He concludes that one in four adult women and one in ten adult men were abused as children. There is a recent decline in the number of cases disclosed to the authorities: David Finkelhor and T. Felix, "Decline in Sexual Abuse Cases," paper presented at the 5th International Family Violence Research Conference (1997), quoted by Oxman-Martinez et al., above, note 3.

lysts have considered the sources of sexual and spousal abuse, the effects of this abuse, and the means to stop it.[5] Our approach is intended to provide a brief introduction to this important knowledge. We have attempted to summarize some of the current debates within the fields under consideration and have provided readers with other bibliographical sources. In order to provide attorneys with a context for the approach they should adopt, we begin with an examination of the problem of sexual abuse and then focus on spousal abuse.

I.   THE PROBLEM OF SEXUAL ABUSE

3. *Definition of Sexual Abuse* – We define sexual abuse as unwanted touching of a sexual nature. With adults, the absence of consent to the touching is an essential element. With children, the question of consent must take into account the potential for the adult to exploit his relationship of power over the child. In general, we assume that a child under fourteen years of age cannot give valid consent to sexual touching.[6] As for a child over the age of fourteen, the validity of the child's consent must be analysed in light of the relationship of power between the child and the aggressor. Our examination will address the issue of the sexual abuse of children both within and outside the family. We will also touch upon the topics of sexual abuse perpetrated against adolescents and adults.

4. *The Feminization of the Problem* – Sexual abuse is perpetrated against men as well as women. However, the majority of sexual abuse is directed towards women.[7] Although child sexual abuse affects many young boys, the majority of victims are young girls.[8]

---

5.   See, among others, Haesevoets, above, note 4; Hubert Van Gijseghem, ed., *L'enfant mis à nu. L'allégation d'abus sexuel: La recherche de la vérité* (Montreal: Méridien, 1992); Jaffe et al., above, note 4; Donald G. Dutton, *The Domestic Assault of Women. Psychological and Criminal Justice Perspectives* (Vancouver: UBC Press, 1995); Judith Lewis Herman, *Trauma and Recovery* (New York: Basic Books, 1992); Murray A. Straus and Richard Gelles, "Determinants of Violence in the Family: Toward a Theoretical Integration," in Wesley R. Burr, Rueben Hill, E. Ivan Nye, and Ira L. Reiss, eds., *Contemporary Theoriries about the Family: Research-Based Theories*, vol. 1 (New York: Free Press, 1979) at 549; Kersti Yllo, "The Status of Women, Marital Equality, and Violence against Wives," (1984) 5 *Journal of Family Issues* 307.

6.   See below at §160.

7.   See Jaffe et al., above, note 4 at 20; Haesevoets, above, note 4 at 22.

8.   Ibid.

Similarly, one can assume that, regardless of whether the victim is a young boy or girl, the vast majority of aggressors are men.[9] Thus, statistically, it is appropriate to define the aggressor as a male and the victim as a female. Nonetheless, a large part of our analysis also applies to situations in which young boys have been sexually abused. Therefore, we would ask readers to apply the same reasoning, with the necessary modifications to suit the situation.

Although there are links between sexual abuse perpetrated against children and that suffered by adult women,[10] we will first consider these types of abuse separately in terms of their context and their consequences for their victims. We begin with an examination of the contexts in which child sexual abuse occurs, and then discuss the impact of such abuse on children.

A. Sexual Abuse of Children

1. *The Contexts*

5. *Three Contexts Considered* – Child sexual abuse is not limited to situations in which children are kidnapped by strangers, although this is still a real danger. Child sexual abuse is often experienced within the family, or it is suffered at the hands of a person in a position of authority who has been entrusted by the family with the "education" of the child. In these latter two cases, the abuse may be kept secret by the social institutions, such as a religious institution or sports organization. We will examine these three different contexts: sexual abuse within the family, sexual abuse perpetrated by educators (in the broadest sense of the word), and sexual abuse by strangers.

a) *Sexual Abuse within the Family*

By referring to the literature on this topic, we will attempt to describe certain characteristics of incestuous families, of the aggressors, and of the interaction between the family, the victim, and the aggressor. Yet, this general description cannot replace careful attention to the actual situation experienced by individual survivors: each family is different, and each case of sexual abuse has its own story, which deserves to be heard.

---

9.   Ibid.
10.   Post-traumatic stress disorder is the term applied to describe the psychological effects for both groups. See below at §51.

6. *Members of the Family Who Are Aggressors: A Caution* – We include in this category of aggressors not only fathers and stepfathers but also brothers, uncles, and grandfathers. It should be noted that any attempt to develop a profile of a "sexual aggressor" must be treated with great caution.[11] We do not want to suggest that there is one profile of a sexual aggressor who targets children and that the absence or existence of traits within this profile are determining factors as to whether or not a defendant is liable.[12] Nonetheless, we cannot ignore the development of certain scientific knowledge that has helped to provide a better understanding of the context for such sexual abuse. It is with this perspective in mind that we offer the following comments.

7. *The Potential Categories* – Some psychologists[13] have placed aggressors in two categories: the sexually fixated aggressor and the sexually regressed aggressor. The *sexually fixated aggressor*, or pedophile, is sexually attracted by children, usually boys.[14] His attack is planned, premeditated, and results from his immature development. He will most likely be the "stranger" who abuses. By contrast, the *sexually regressed aggressor* usually attacks female children within his family. He views them as adults, not as children. His attempts are often impulsive and sporadic, and are a pathological response to stress in his life. Yves-Hiram Haesevoets states that the sexually regressed aggressor often takes advantage of a child's specific vulnerability or insecurity or her desire for affection.[15]

8. *The Aggressor's Reaction to Disclosure* – The manner in which aggressors react to disclosure provides a measure of the problem that faces victims. Generally, the aggressor will first deny the abuse. After this initial period of denial, the aggressor will perhaps

---

11.   See Luc Morin, "Les profils en matière d'allégations d'abus sexuels: une invitation à la prudence," (1993) 23 *Revue de Droit de l'Université de Sherbrooke* 415.

12.   See *Protection de la jeunesse – 539*, [1992] R.J.Q. 1144, J.E. 92-696 (Que. trib. jeun.), in which the court ruled as inadmissible evidence the lack of personality traits compatible with a sexual aggressor profile. The father, who had been accused of abusing his child, attempted to present such evidence in order to exculpate himself.

13.   See Thom L. McGuire and Faye E. Grant, *Understanding Child Sexual Abuse: Therapeutic Guidelines for Professionals Dealing with Children* (Toronto: Butterworths, 1991) at 5.

14.   See Morin, above, note 11 at 420.

15.   See Haesevoets, above, note 4 at 151–2.

try to rationalize his behaviour, by saying, for example, that he wanted to introduce the child to sexual relations in a positive way. He might then try to minimize the whole situation by denying the frequency of the abuse, or he might project his guilt onto others by blaming the child for having seduced him or by blaming his wife.[16]

9. *The Incestuous Family* – Abuse within the family is not limited to a particular social class—both affluent and less affluent families are affected.[17] That said, there are certain family dynamics that seem to present a greater risk of abuse. These often include an all-powerful father who does not accept challenges from anyone in the family, and a wife/mother who is often absent, either physically or functionally.[18] A mother's absence and the lack of protection afforded by her can be traumatic for a young victim of abuse—she resents her mother, and the relationship between them is strained. The reaction of the family—especially the mother— at the time of disclosure of the abuse can have a serious effect on the victim's rehabilitation. A child who is not believed will have more difficulty overcoming the effects of the sexual abuse.[19]

10. *Silence* – The aggressor's denial following disclosure poses risks for the young victim. The denial automatically pits the victim against her family members, who may hesitate to confront the aggressor because of his economic or even physical power. This is why victims usually keep silent about the sexual abuse perpetrated against them by members of their family. They know they will be blamed, possibly even disowned,[20] by their family at the very

---

16. See McGuire and Grant, above, note 13 at 6–8; Haesevoets, above, note 4 at 153–4.
17. See Groth, *Men Who Rape,* cited by McGuire and Grant, above, note 13 at 6–8. See also the case of *G.K.* v. *D.K.,* [1994] O.J. No. 1680 (Ont. Gen. Div.) (Q.L.), in which the father, a professor of pharmacology, was sued by his daughter for damages due to sexual abuse. The plaintiff is a dentist.
18. See Judith Herman, *Father–Daughter Incest* (Cambridge: Harvard University Press, 1981) at 71, 77; Haesevoets, above, note 4 at 56. See also the case of *D.A.A.* v. *D.K.B.,* [1995] O.J. No. 3901 (Ont. Gen. Div.) (Q.L.), in which the mother, an alcoholic, was unable to protect the child and in which the child took on a "parental" role.
19. See Louise Dezwirez Sas and Alison Hatch Cunningham, *Tipping the Balance to Tell the Secret: Public Discovery of Child Sexual Abuse* (London, ON: London Family Court Clinic, ON, 1995). This point is also made by Oxman-Martinez et al., above, note 3 at 78.
20. See Elly Danica, *Don't: A Woman's Word* (Charlottetown, PEI: Gynergy Books, 1988).

moment when they most need support. The aggressor may have convinced the victim that she is responsible for the sexual relationship or that no one will believe her,[21] or she may be afraid of him because he has threatened her.[22] Such victims often suffer the abuse in silence. Moreover, an initial disclosure marked by a lack of sympathy towards the child, or a refusal to believe her, will plunge the young victim further into silence.[23] It is this silence, towards which the aggressor and even the family have worked, that the justice system threatens. The public proceedings usually "upset" the family balance.[24] Some family members may refuse to believe that one of their relatives is guilty of such actions. Others may have suffered the same abuse but are unable to face this reality. Still others may feel guilty for having suspected something, but having said nothing.[25] Given such likely reactions, the attorney must be well prepared in order to support the client.

Victims who have suffered sexual abuse within the family will feel a great deal of hesitancy and anxiety when talking about the abuse. This is also true when the disclosure of sexual abuse involves, not the family equilibrium, but the "social equilibrium"—that is, when the abuse is perpetrated by educators.

b)   Sexual Abuse Perpetrated by "Educators"

11. *Introduction* – In this section, we use the word "educator" in its broadest sense to include babysitters, teachers, priests and other spiritual educators, sports coaches, guidance counsellors, and those in charge of cultural associations (such as choirmasters) and social organizations (such as scout leaders) to which children belong. All of these people share several characteristics: they are in a position of authority with respect to the child and are often entrusted by the parents or by society[26] with the task of "improving" the child. This

21.   See Sylvia Fraser, *My Father's House: A Memoir of Incest and of Healing* (New York: Harper and Row, Perennial Library, 1987).
22.   See Haesevoets, above, note 4 at 113.
23.   See Dezwirez Sas, above, note 19.
24.   See the eloquent description of family dynamics in cases of incest, in Haesevoets, above note 4 at 56.
25.   See Crnich, above note 1 at 70.
26.   This is, among others, the case with physicians and psychologists treating patients. Their position of authority with respect to their patients requires them to abstain from having sexual relations with them. See Suzanne Richer, "Une dialectique de mise en oeuvre de la politique de tolérance zéro en matière d'inconduite sexuelle professionnelle," (1994) 2 *Revue d'études juridiques* 71;

responsibility places them in a relationship of trust with regards to the child and the child's parents, such that the sexual act is a breach of trust both in terms of the parents and the child.

12. *Social Pressure* – Given that the abuse occurs outside the family, one might think that the child would more easily confide in a family member. However, society may place so much value on the aggressor's position of authority that a child may think that her parents will support the aggressor rather than her. This is often the case with representatives of the religious orders, with teachers, and with sports coaches, among others.[27] Moreover, as in abuse within the family, the aggressor may have convinced the child that she was responsible for the relationship.

13. *Psychological Abuse* – Sexual abuse is often accompanied by insults and threats. In many cases, the adult will exploit his knowledge of a child's weaknesses in order to buy the child's silence about the abuse. Sometimes, sexual abuse also involves physical abuse and is cruel. It is played out as a relationship based on power rather than love.

14. *Institutionalized Abuse* – The shroud of secrecy surrounding sexual abuse may be even harder to lift when the abuse seems to have an institutional character—that is, when the child sees the abuse being tolerated, even approved, by persons in a position of authority who participate in the abuse through their silence. Such institutionalized abuse occurred in places such as reform schools[28] and schools and establishments for the handicapped[29]. In such cases, the

---

Patricia Hughes, "Women, Sexual Abuse by Professionals, and the Law: Changing Parameters," (1996) 21 *Queen's L.J.* 297; see also, for an example of the application of the professional rules of conduct: *Sirois* v. *Psychologues (Ordre professionnel des)*, [1996] D.D.O.P. 319 (Professions Tribunal).

27.   See Gordon Kirke, *Players First* (Willowdale, ON, August 1997) (report prepared for the Canadian Hockey League).

28.   See the compensation agreements for victims of abuse in the Ontario and New Brunswick reform schools: Susan M. Vella, "Balancing Power with Responsibility: Institutional Liability in Sexual Assault Claims," in *Sexual Assault, the Civil Remedy* (Toronto: Department of Continuing Legal Education, Law Society of Upper Canada, 1993). For a review of governmental responses to institutional abuse, see Ronda Bessner, *Institutional Abuse in Canada*, background study paper for the Law Commission of Canada, available on the Internet at www.lcc.gc.ca (date of access: 5 June 2001). The final report of the Commission, *Restoring Dignity: Responding to Institutional Child Abuse* (2000) is also available at the same site.

29.   See the report of the Quebec Ombudsman, *The "Children of Duplessis": A Time*

child's prolonged silence or even her denial of reality results from her vulnerability in the face of authority. The sexual trauma may cause the child to be ashamed and, therefore, hesitant to state publicly that she is a victim. In a homophobic society, where disclosure is especially difficult, young boys are particularly prone to experience this sense of shame.

15. *Racism and Abuse* – Finally, institutionalized abuse can take a racist form. Children of Aboriginal or Black descent who have been in reform schools often report sexual abuse of a particularly cruel nature perpetrated against them. The history of residential schools for Aboriginal children points to the racism underlying the physical and sexual abuse that took place in these institutions.[30]

c)   *Sexual Abuse Perpetrated by Strangers*

Secrecy is the common element in child sexual abuse, regardless of whether the perpetrator is a family member or an educator. This element of secrecy can also exist in cases of abuse by a pedophile who is a stranger to the child.

16. *A Rare Occurrence* – The kidnapping of children and their subsequent sexual exploitation continue to be a nightmare for all parents. Although such abuse is statistically less likely to occur than abuse by a relative or educator,[31] it receives disproportionate media attention. The aggressor in this type of abuse usually acts in accordance with a plan, and may use violence in order to achieve his end. He may also attempt to gain the child's trust by using toys, candy, and other lures. The aggressor's manipulation of the child's trust may cause the child to feel some guilt about the sexual abuse.

---

for *Solidarity* (Discussion and Consultation Paper for Decision-Making Purposes) (Quebec: National Assembly, 22 January 1997).

30.   See Agnes Grant, *No End of Grief: Indian Residential Schools in Canada* (Winnipeg: Pemmican Publications, 1996) at 221–3; Elizabeth Furniss, *Victims of Benevolence: Discipline and Death at the Williams Lake Indian Residential School, 1891–1920* (Williams Lake, B.C.: Cariboo Tribal Council, 1992) at 2. The Final Report of the Law Commission of Canada, *Restoring Dignity*, gives a history of the government policies on residential schools; see Law Commission of Canada, above note 28. See also Canada, Royal Commission on Aboriginal Peoples, *Report of the Royal Commission on Aboriginal Peoples*, vol. 1, ch. 10 (Ottawa: Minister of Supply and Services Canada, 1996).

31.   See Haesevoets, above, note 4 at 23. See also Johnson and Sacco, above, note 3 at 293, who note that only 23 per cent of abuse is committed by strangers.

2.   The Impact on the Client

The impact of sexual abuse on children is a complex matter. The following is a partial list of the symptoms that have been documented through psychological research. Here, again, it is imperative that one listen to the manner in which the victim herself views the effects of the abuse.

We will begin with a description of the symptoms identified in children who have been victims of sexual abuse. We then will consider the "diagnoses" associated with child sexual abuse.

a)   The Symptoms

17. *Types of After-Effects* – The after-effects of sexual abuse can manifest themselves in several ways: anxiety, remorse, shame, lack of self-respect, and feelings of inferiority. Other consequences often associated with sexual abuse include depression; self-mutilation; tendencies toward suicide, bulimia, anorexia, or insomnia; involvement in fringe activities; and alcoholism and drug abuse.[32]

18. *Aggravating Factors* – The effects will depend on several factors: the nature of the abuse, the frequency and duration of the relationship between the victim and the aggressor, the child's level of development, the gender of the child and the aggressor, the age difference, the degree of secrecy and dependence, and the results of the disclosure efforts.[33] Clearly, each victim has her own particular internal strengths and weaknesses that increase or decrease the intensity of her reaction to the abuse. Victims of multiple occurrences of abuse (by several aggressors) often suffer greater trauma than other victims. Research suggests that victims of sexual abuse are less able to avoid subsequent abuse by different perpetrators.[34]

19. *The Importance of the Relationship of Power between the Child and the Adult* – Filiation is not a determining factor with regards to

---

32.   For a list of other symptoms, see David Finkelhor, *A Sourcebook on Child Sexual Abuse* (New York: Sage Publications, 1986) at 143–79; Haesevoets, above, note 4 at 110–20. See also Claudia Tremblay and Ann Carson-Tempier, "Évaluation et traitement des jeunes enfants victimes d'abus sexuel," (1997) 18 *Revue québécoise de psychologie* 189.

33.   See Haesevoets, above, note 4 at 101–4.

34.   See Diana Russell, *The Secret Trauma: Incest in the Lives of Girls and Women* (New York: Basic Books, 1986) at 158ff.

the severity of the effects of sexual abuse. Abuse at the hands of an uncle or a stepfather can be as traumatic as abuse by a biological father. The effects will depend upon the relationship of power between the child and the adult. Yet, the feelings of betrayal may be greater when the sexual abuse is perpetrated by the child's biological parent. The fact that the victim is economically dependent upon the aggressor and the fact that the abuse involves violence can also be aggravating factors.

20. *The Dynamics of the Symptoms of Sexual Abuse in Children* – Finkelhor and Browne[35] classify symptoms of sexual abuse into four dynamics. Their approach is used to educate those who want to help abuse survivors. It is useful for gaining an overall understanding of the complexity of the effects of sexual abuse. It would seem that the cumulative presence of the four dynamics distinguishes child sexual abuse from other traumatic events that affect children. These four dynamics are: 1) the dynamic of traumatic sexualization; 2) the dynamic of betrayal; 3) the dynamic of powerlessness; and 4) the dynamic of stigmatization.

21. *Traumatic Sexualization* – Traumatic sexualization relates to the abnormal development of a child who learns sexual behaviour too early. For example, when the child receives affection, gifts, or other benefits in exchange for sexual contact, she develops the idea that she can offer herself sexually to satisfy her other emotional and material needs. Thus, abused children misconstrue society's standards and morals regarding sexual behaviour. The child believes that she can receive love and affection only if she offers her body. In a homophobic society, the trauma suffered by boys who have had homosexual relations may create confusion regarding their sexual identity.[36]

22. *Betrayal* – Feelings of betrayal result from the child's realization that someone, upon whom she is fully dependent, has hurt and abused her. The child feels betrayed not only by the aggressor, but

35.   See David Finkelhor and A. Browne, "The Traumatic Impact of Child Sexual Abuse: A Conceptualization," (1985) 55 *American Journal of Orthopsychiatry* 530, cited by Haesevoets, above, note 4 at 106–8. For an illustration of how Finkelhor and Browne's conceptualization has been applied, see Jacynthe Lambert and Pierrette Simard, "L'art-thérapie, approche auprès des femmes adultes victimes d'agression à caractère sexuel durant l'enfance ou l'adolescence," (1997) 18 *Revue québécoise de psychologie* 203.
36.   See Jaffe et al., above, note 4 at 55.

also by other members of her family or by members of society who have participated in the abuse through their silence. The extent of the betrayal felt will also depend upon the family's reaction when the abuse is disclosed. A child who is not believed, or who is blamed, will feel an even greater sense of betrayal. Thus, the adult's reaction to the child's account is crucial to the child's therapy.[37] The symptoms associated with the dynamic of betrayal include extreme dependency on others and an inability to judge the character of others. Victims of sexual abuse tend to continue in abusive relationships or in relationships without any future. The dynamic of betrayal may also explain feelings of social isolation and mistrust of others.[38]

23. *Powerlessness* – The feeling of powerlessness is characteristic of child sexual abuse: the child does not know how to escape the situation and must suffer without much in the way of hope.[39] The symptoms associated with these feelings of powerlessness include a lack of self-esteem and difficulty fitting into society. The victim sees herself as an object, rather than as a person with rights.

24. *Stigmatization* – Stigmatization refers to the psychological effects on a child who has been exposed to sexuality too early. The feeling of social isolation often contributes to the development of a double identity. Some victims even develop several personalities in order to survive the abuse:[40] the young girl, who is able to live within society, and her alter ego, who must secretly accept the aggressor's abuse.[41] These personalities often play a protective role or allow the hate the child feels against the aggressor to express itself despite societal norms. Drug abuse and alcoholism are often part of the search for a double identity that allows the victim temporarily to escape the reality of the sexual abuse.

25. *The Link between Child Sexual Abuse and Adult Sexual Abuse* – One of the troubling aspects of research into child sexual abuse is the apparent link between abuse suffered as a child and abuse suffered as an adult. The effect of early abuse on a child's self-esteem

---

37. See Dezwirez Sas, above, note 19.
38. For a list and an analysis of the symptoms of prolonged sexual abuse, see Herman, above, note 5 at 86–95.
39. See Haesevoets, above, note 4 at 107.
40. See the criticism by Herman regarding the excessive use of this diagnosis for survivors of sexual abuse, above, note 5 at 123–4.
41. See the account of Fraser, above, note 21.

will often cause her to choose abusive partners. A child's feelings of guilt may lead her to believe that abuse is her lot in life, that exploitation is the path leading to love. There is another disturbing link between abuse suffered as a child and abuse repeated at the adult stage: aggressors often were victimized themselves when they were children. Children learn about relationships between couples at a very young age, by observing and assimilating the type of relationship they see between their parents. Thus, children exposed to spousal and sexual abuse are more likely than others to repeat such patterns in their intimate relationships.[42]

b)   The "Diagnoses"

Research on the effects of sexual abuse has led to more systematic examination, the conclusions to which are often expressed in terms of "diagnoses."

26. *Introduction* – Any reference to "diagnoses" must be a cautious one. There is a danger that, because her story does not fit neatly within the phenomenology presented by the "experts," the diagnosis will define the survivor's experience and deprive her of her story.[43] The purpose of our descriptions of the various diagnoses is not to replace or shape the survivor's story. It is simply to present the jargon used by professionals who treat survivors. We will examine the accommodation syndrome in children, post-traumatic stress disorder, and the issue of false memory syndrome.

i)   The Accommodation Syndrome in Children

27. *Definition* – The accommodation syndrome, originally defined by Summit,[44] explains the child's inability to escape the abusive situa-

---

42.   See Jaffe et al., above, note 4 at 56. See also Edem F. Avakame, "International Transmission of Violence and Psychological Aggression against Wives," (1998) 30 *Can. Journ. of Behavioural Science* 193 at 199, and Robert T. Muller and Terry Diamond, "Father and Mother Physical Abuse and Child Aggressive Behaviour in Two Generations," (1999) 31 *Can. Journ. of Behavioural Science* 221, which point out that violence inflicted by fathers may have a greater impact on children than that inflicted by mothers because it is often associated with power and authority.

43.   This criticism has been levelled against battered woman syndrome: see, among others, Elizabeth Comack, *Feminist Engagement with the Law: The Legal Recognition of the Battered Woman Syndrome*, CRIAW Document No. 31 (Ottawa: Canadian Research Institute for the Advancement of Women, 1993).

44.   Roland C. Summit, "The Child Sexual Abuse Accommodation Syndrome,"

tion. As explained by Haesevoets, "Unbeknownst to the child, she becomes somewhat accustomed to the abuse and develops survival strategies."[45]

28. *Phases of Development of the Syndrome* – Summit identified five chronological phases of development of the accommodation syndrome, which Haesevoets describes as follows.[46] First, in the secrecy or non-disclosure phase, the child wants to keep silent about the situation. The child sees silence as a source of safety and stability for her family. In the second phase, the child feels helpless and vulnerable, and manifests signs of social maladjustment related to her confusion over the roles being imposed upon her. In the third phase, the child begins to re-create a pleasant, although unrealistic, image of her abusive parent. She blames herself for the negative aspects of their relationship and becomes more anxious and further removed from reality.[47] The fourth phase is characterized by an ambivalent attempt to disclose the abuse: the allegations are vague and hesitant, and are unlikely to be understood or taken seriously. Finally, in the fifth phase, which results from the fruitlessness to her disclosure, the child retracts her confession and resumes her submissive behaviour, thereby restoring the unhealthy family equilibrium.

29. *Application of the Syndrome* – The child's reaction, as described by Summit and Haesevoets, also corresponds to clinical reports on this topic. The accommodation syndrome is all the more relevant when a child has been abused by a family member.[48] However, certain analogies can be drawn to abuse perpetrated by educators, as described above.[49] In certain cases, the attachment to the aggressor-educator is such that it approaches the attachment in a parent–child relationship. This is true, for example, when the educator assumes a parental role because the child lives at school or has been neglected by her own parents.

The accommodation syndrome explains the conflicted reaction of a child faced with a sexual relationship imposed by an adult. The

---

(1983) 7 *Child Abuse and Neglect* 177, cited by Haesevoets, above, note 4 at 86–8.

45.   Haesevoets, above, note 4 at 86 (our translation).
46.   Ibid. at 86–7.
47.   For an example of detachment from reality, see the story of Sylvia Fraser, above, note 21.
48.   In fact, Haesevoets applies it only to cases of incest. See above, note 4.
49.   Above, at §§12–15.

abuse will also produce effects once the child becomes an adult; psychiatric literature has identified this as post-traumatic stress disorder.

ii)   Post-Traumatic Stress Disorder

30. *Description* – Adults who suffered sexual abuse during their childhood usually experience difficulties in their intimate relationships; they tend to let themselves be led into abusive relationships or show a mistrust of others. Drug abuse, alcoholism, and prostitution often result from childhood sexual abuse. The victims often have flashbacks and nightmares and suffer from bulimia, anorexia, or phobias. They may be afraid of the dark or be unable to tolerate physical proximity to others. Psychiatrists and psychologists classify these symptoms as post-traumatic stress disorder.[50]

31. *A Diagnosis Recognized by the Courts* – The Supreme Court of Canada recognized post-traumatic stress disorder in the matter of *M.(K.)* v. *M.(H.)*.[51] La Forest, J. cited the definition of post-traumatic stress disorder provided by the author Lamm: "Many victims of incest abuse exhibit signs of Post-Traumatic Stress Disorder ('PTSD'), a condition characterized by avoidance and denial that is associated with survivors of acute traumatic events such as prisoners of war and concentration camp victims. Like others suffering from PTSD, incest victims frequently experience flashbacks and nightmares well into their adulthood."[52]

32. *A Necessary Diagnosis?* – The courts have recognized that many symptoms associated with post-traumatic stress disorder are comparable to those underlying other "diagnoses" that relate not to

---

50.   See American Psychiatric Association, *Diagnostic and Statistical Manual of Mental Disorders*, 3rd ed. (Washington, D.C.: American Psychiatric Association, 1987). This diagnosis has appeared in the manual since the beginning of the 1980s. See Roger K. Pitman, Linda Stout Saunders, and Scott P. Orr, "Psychophysiologic Testing for Post-Traumatic Stress Disorder," *Trial* (April 1994) 22.

51.   [1992] 3 S.C.R. 6.

52.   Ibid. at 36, citing Jocelyn B. Lamm, "Easing Access to the Courts for Incest Victims: Toward an Equitable Application of the Delayed Discovery Rule," (1991) 100 *Yale L. J.* 2189 at 2194–5.

traumatic events but, rather, to personality disorders.[53] Before making a finding of abuse, some courts[54] require that an expert identify the plaintiff as suffering from post-traumatic stress disorder and not from a personality disorder.

33. *A Diagnosis Which Has Been Criticized* – In her book *Trauma and Recovery*, Judith Lewis Herman explains that, although the diagnosis of post-traumatic stress disorder can be useful, it may result in a partial explanation of the patient's symptoms.[55] According to Herman, post-traumatic stress disorder was conceived to explain a person's reaction to a single traumatic event, not to a prolonged history of trauma. In this regard, post-traumatic stress disorder is more appropriate for describing the effects of an isolated occurrence of sexual assault, rather than the effects of a history of incest, prolonged sexual exploitation, or even spousal abuse. Like some other authors, Herman suggests that the term "complex post-traumatic stress disorder" better describes the impact of prolonged trauma in which the victim's personality is affected.[56]

34. *A Measurable Diagnosis?* – Normally, proof of the diagnosis of post-traumatic stress disorder is provided through the testimony of a psychiatrist or expert psychologist who has examined the victim. A recently developed test seeks to determine, in a more "objective" manner, whether or not the victim is suffering from the disorder. This test, known as script-driven imagery,[57] consists of asking the participant to relate several events in her life. Using this information, the psychologist develops a series of thirty-second scripts that are read to the victim, who must try to imagine the event as realistically as possible. When the scripts are read, the psychologist measures the victim's physical reactions, such as heart rate, changes in skin tone, perspiration, and muscular tension. The rate of manifestation of physical symptoms is calculated for each event and is com-

---

53. For example, borderline personality disorder. See Lewis Herman, above, note 5 at 123–4, where she criticizes the application of a diagnosis of borderline personality disorder to survivors of sexual and spousal abuse. She notes, among other things, the pejorative nature of this label and its "catch-all" character, which she believes to be of the same type as the diagnosis of "hysteria," which was often attributed to women at the beginning of the twentieth century.
54. See *A.D.C.* v. *J.H.P.*, [1996] B.C.J. No. 741 (B.C. S.C.) (Q.L.).
55. See Lewis Herman, above, note 5 at 118–19.
56. Ibid.
57. This name was popularized by the psychologist Peter Lang. See Pitman, Stout Saunders, and Orr, above, note 50.

pared to statistical sources to determine whether a given event causes sufficient physiological responses to constitute post-traumatic stress disorder. This test, which has a current error rate of 18 per cent, does not seem to have been used often before the courts. However, certain attorneys and psychiatrists have proposed that it be used.[58]

35. *A Diagnosis Evolving over Time* – Numerous studies are being carried out on the impact of abuse, so it would be foolhardy to propose a complete explanation of the symptoms experienced by survivors of sexual abuse. One must proceed cautiously in applying new techniques for quantifying post-traumatic stress disorder and even in describing the disorder. The same problems exist with respect to the third "diagnosis": false memory syndrome.

iii)   The Issue of False Memory Syndrome

36. *The Problem Defined* – The recent emergence of the theory of false memory syndrome[59] is an attempt to reopen the debate regarding the admissibility of evidence of repressed memories of traumatic events.[60] The theory holds that such memories are implanted by the therapist. Although the defendant alleges that the memories are false, they certainly do not appear that way to the victim, who believes she is telling the truth.

In essence, the debate within the scientific community[61] centres on two questions. First, can memories of traumatic events, such

---

58.   Ibid.
59.   The term comes from the name of an American foundation that attempts to bring together parents falsely accused of sexual abuse by their children.
60.   See Bala, above, note 4 at 124.
61.   James W.W. Neeb and Shelly J. Harper, *Civil Action for Childhood Sexual Abuse* (Toronto: Butterworths, 1994) at 47–55, indicate that the debate arises from a difference in opinion between cognitive research psychologists, who take the position that memory repression has never been proven, and clinicians, who tend to accept the recovery of forgotten memories because they treat patients whose stories of abuse seem plausible and who present such symptoms. Bruce Feldthusen, "The Canadian Experiment with the Civil Action for Sexual Battery," in Nicholas J. Mullany, ed., *Torts in the Nineties* (North Ryde, Australia: LBC Information Services, 1997), 279, describes the dispute in corporate terms: psychiatrists and psychologists are opposed to the invasion of their market by therapists, who have a different allegiance and may lack a university education.

as sexual abuse, be repressed? Second, can therapy restore the repressed memories, or does the therapy "create" the memories?

37. *A Problem of Limited Significance* – Before we summarize the debate on these two questions, which have divided the scientific community, it would be useful to point out that the issue is of somewhat limited practical importance. False memory syndrome does not affect problems of delayed discovery of a link between the traumatic event and its psychological consequences.[62] In other words, when the victim only partly remembers the event, and realizes its meaning only later on,[63] false memory syndrome does not come into play. The theory of false memory syndrome raises doubts as to the validity of fully repressed memories that surface with the help of therapy.

38. *An American Rather than a Canadian or Quebec Problem?* – It should also be noted that the issue of false memory syndrome may have resulted from American jurisprudential debates regarding the prescription of actions. During the 1980s, the American courts tended to extend prescription periods only when the plaintiff alleged that she had "forgotten" the abuse.[64] Unlike the 1992 Supreme Court of Canada ruling in *M.(K.)* v. *M.(H.)*[65], the American courts, for the most part, did not recognize that the prescription period might be extended due to the failure to discover the link between the injury and the abuse. To a certain extent, victims' need to allege the repression or forgetting of memories was at the origin of the false memory syndrome movement, which began towards the

---

62. See "Extinctive Prescription," below, at §§126ff.
63. See *M. (K.)* v. *M. (H.)*, above, note 51. See also *S.M.* v. *D.D.R.*, [1994] B.C.J. No. 2243 (B.C. S.C.) (Q.L.), in which the court refused to consider the applicability of false memory syndrome when the plaintiff recalled certain traumatic events before beginning hypnosis therapy. Nevertheless, the plaintiff lost the case because she was unable to identify a specific trait of the defendant's genitals.
64. For a review of the American jurisprudence during the 1980's, see Nathalie Des Rosiers, "Limitation Periods and Civil Remedies for Childhood Sexual Abuse," (1992) 9 *Canadian Family Law Quarterly* 43 at 53–6. At that time, the courts placed the victims into two categories: those victims who had "forgotten" the abuse, and those who remembered the abuse but had been unable to take action more promptly. Victims in the first category were more likely than victims in the second category to obtain relief from the rules on prescription of actions. This point is also made by Susan Vella, "Recovered Traumatic Memory in Historical Childhood Sexual Abuse Cases: Credibility on Trial," (1998) 32 *University of British Columbia Law Review* 91.
65. Above, note 51.

end of the 1980s.[66] The fact remains that the false memory syndrome movement has symbolically challenged the civil litigation process. Although this theory, even if adopted, will not affect the validity of numerous allegations of sexual abuse, the movement has somewhat discredited the litigation process. Consequently, we must examine the movement's claims to the effect that it is almost impossible for someone to repress memories of traumatic events and that it is the therapist who creates these memories.

39. *Trauma and Repression of Memories* – Even those researchers who are the most sceptical regarding the reliability of repressed memories admit the possibility that trauma may lead to memory repression.[67] Yet, they consider this to be a rare phenomenon. Several other researchers have suggested that repression is a fairly common phenomenon experienced by survivors of extreme trauma, including Holocaust survivors, torture victims, and sexual abuse survivors.[68] The problem that arises in resolving this dispute is one of evidence: experts are unable to agree on the type of scientific studies that could demonstrate whether or not the repression of memories of traumatic events is authentic.[69]

The best-known study that tends to show that repression exists has been criticized by supporters of the false memory syndrome. In this study, Linda Williams tracked down women who were known to have suffered sexual abuse when they were children, more than twenty years earlier. When questioned, these women did not always mention the sexual abuse they had suffered, particularly when the abuse had been perpetrated by a close relative.[70] Researchers disagree on the reason for this omission: did they repress these memories, or did they simply experience so many

---

66. Professor Bala traces the development of the movement at the end of the 1980s and the beginning of the 1990s, above, note 4 at 426–30.

67. See Joel Paris, "A Critical Review of Recovered Memories in Psychotherapy: Part I – Trauma and Memory," (1996) 41 *Can. J. Psychiatry* 201; Jan G. Ahrens, "Recovered Memories," (1995–6) 34 *University of Louisville Journal of Family Law* 382.

68. See Herman, above, note 5 at 86–95.

69. See Ahrens, above, note 67 at 384; Gary M. Ernsdorff and Elizabeth F. Loftus, "Symposium on Scientific Evidence, Let Sleeping Memories Lie? Words of Caution about Tolling the Statute of Limitations in Cases of Memory Repression," (1993) 84 *J.Crim. L. & Criminology* 129, 134.

70. See L.M. Williams, "Recall of Childhood Trauma: A Prospective Study of Women's Memories of Child Sexual Abuse," (1994) 62 *J. of Consulting & Clinical Psych.*, 1167, cited by Bala, above, note 4 at 433.

other traumas that the childhood sexual abuse was no longer as important or traumatic? Or were they too embarrassed to confide in the researchers?

Yet, other anecdotal evidence seems to indicate that repression of traumatic memories is possible. A young man spontaneously—that is, without the help of therapy—remembered sexual abuse he suffered as a child at the hands of a priest. After he made an appeal in the newspapers, other survivors of sexual abuse at the hands of the same priest spoke up, and the young man is now in a position to corroborate his repressed memories.[71] It seems clear that repressed memories can exist, but the debate continues regarding the clues that would allow us to better identify potential cases of repressed memories. We must also consider the second theme proposed by the false memory syndrome movement—that psychotherapy or hypnosis is unreliable for retrieving memories that have been repressed in one's subconscious.

40. *The Memory Retrieval Process* – It is well known that memory is a faculty that forgets. The memory-retrieval process is very complex and has often been shown to be unreliable.[72] Nevertheless, courts of law continue to rely upon the testimony of eye witnesses, probably for lack of better methods. As Corbett, J. stated in the case of *Colquhoun* v. *Colquhoun*:[73]

> All witnesses rely on memory when giving evidence. Giving evidence necessarily involves re-counting or memory retrieval. It is common knowledge that memory involves a reconstructive process and the capacity to recollect may vary with physical capacity, age, conditions at the time of the original event, and the length of time between the original event and the remembering. Judges routinely instruct juries that it is proper to consider human factors which may affect the giving of perfectly honest evidence when weighing testimony and determining credibility. These factors include errors in memory because of conditions affecting recall at the time of the original event or occasion, memory capacity of the witness, and conditions which may affect memory capacity.

---

71. See Bala, above, note 4 at 434–5.
72. See Elizabeth Loftus, "The Reality of Repressed Memories," (1993) 48 *American Psychologist* 518. Loftus is an expert in the field of memory research. She generally shares the point of view of the false memory syndrome movement.
73. (1994), 114 D.L.R. (4th) 151 at 168, [1994] O.J. No. 681 (Ont. Gen. Div.), online: QL (OJ).

Supporters of the false memory syndrome claim that the resurfacing of memories is not a guarantee that the memories are true; that, in fact, it is unlikely that these memories are accurate; and that they are more likely the fruits of therapist-assisted reconstruction.

41. *The Role of Therapy in Retrieving Repressed Memories* – The false memory syndrome movement probably made its mark with its criticism of therapeutic techniques. The criticism focused in particular on aggressive therapy in which the therapist attributes all psychological problems to past sexual abuse, even if no allegation to that effect has yet surfaced. The movement also seriously questioned the usefulness of hypnosis and truth serums (a substance containing sodium amytal[74]) as well as popular psychology self-help books.[75] In essence, the movement has managed to create a new ethic for therapy with regards to allegations of repressed sexual abuse. As a result, therapists are more aware of their potential influence on a patient. However, overall, the movement's analysis deals only with rather limited elements of the problem of childhood sexual abuse. Its strongest conclusions suggest caution in cases in which, first, the memories are the product of aggressive therapy, second, the memories relate back to very early childhood (before the age of three or four), and, third, the memories tell of satanic rites or abuse by multiple aggressors.[76]

42. *False Memory Syndrome in the Canadian Legal System* – The attitude of the Canadian civil courts of common law with respect to the syndrome has been to consider the theory as one of the elements to be taken into account in assessing a witness's testimony. As Corbett, J. stated in the case of *Colquhoun* v. *Colquhoun*:

> There is a popular trend whereby some seek to characterize memories revived by a therapist as inherently unreliable or as part of a false memory syndrome. Such an approach is neither appropriate nor helpful. The existing techniques for assessing credibility at trial continue to be apt to determine the reliability of memory. Therapeutically

---

74.   See Ahrens, above, note 67 at 387.
75.   See Bala, above, note 4 at 429, citing the criticism levelled by Loftus, above, notes 69 and 72, against the American book *Courage to Heal*, which asked readers identifying with the symptoms, which were rather broadly defined, to consider themselves victims of sexual abuse.
76.   See Bala, above, note 4; Ahrens, above, note 67. See also *T.K.S.* v. *E.B.S.*, [1995] B.C.J. No. 1542 (B.C. C.A.) (Q.L.).

revived memory is not inherently or facially suspect. Rather, it is one factor, among many, which bears on the reliability of memory and, in some circumstances, must be assessed with care.[77]

This measured approach is the one generally endorsed in Canada.[78]

43. *Conclusion* – The issue of the reliability of memories of sexual abuse that resurface after many years will continue to perplex researchers for the foreseeable future. In the meanwhile, it is important that attorneys and judges, who may be faced with decisions that cannot await the outcome of this debate, not exaggerate the contribution of false memory syndrome to scientific knowledge. In fact, the issue of false memory syndrome arises only in certain cases of child sexual abuse, namely those in which the abuse has been erased from the conscious mind. At the very most, false memory syndrome requires that prudence be applied when dealing with memories that have been repressed from very early childhood (before the age of three or four) or when dealing with memories that give rise to scepticism because they were revived through the use of more or less reliable therapeutic techniques or because they describe abuse out of the ordinary.

B.   Sexual Abuse Perpetrated against Adults

Sexual abuse does not stop at the age of eighteen—the age of majority. It also affects adults, and different types of problems may arise within the context of sexual abuse perpetrated against adults. In order to gain a better understanding of the impact that such abuse can have on its victims, we will begin with an examination of the social context of sexual abuse perpetrated against adults.

1.   The Contexts

44. *Statistics* – The most revealing statistic regarding abuse perpetrated against adult women indicates that the vast majority of incidents of abuse are committed by people known to the victim.[79] This

---

77.   See above, note 73 at 168.
78.   See to that effect Bala, above, note 4, and Vella, above, note 64. Again, the debate is less settled in the American literature: Robert T. Reagan, "Scientific Consensus on Memory Repression and Recovery," (1999) 51 *Rutgers L. R.* 275.
79.   Statistics Canada's *Violence against Women Survey*, whose results are discussed by Johnson and Sacco, above, note 3, indicates that sexual and physi-

is particularly true in terms of women who are abused during a date.

45. *Date Rape* – Date rape is generally defined as unwanted sexual touching without physical violence, between persons who are acquainted.[80] Assessing consent of the partners is the determining criterion in deciding whether or not there was abuse. The issue of consent and the limits in understanding the act of consenting have been the focus of much discussion among feminists.

46. *Understanding Women's Consent* – Why is it that some men do not give any thought to the wishes of their partners? Perhaps some men's view of intercourse as "conquest" leads them to disregard signs of non-consent. This phenomenon may be exacerbated by the difficulty that women and young girls have in making themselves heard in a world that often imposes silence upon them. If the media ignore women and represent them only as sexual objects, it is possible that men will not hear language that does not convey a sexual message, language that says "no."[81]

47. *The Link between Sexual Abuse and Gender Inequality* – Many researchers are of the opinion that one cannot truly understand the widespread phenomenon of sexual abuse without understanding the context of gender inequality. According to Catharine MacKinnon and Andrea Dworkin, women cannot truly give free and informed consent to heterosexual sexual relations.[82] Others have taken a less radical approach, recommending that the legal model regarding consent to sexual relations be modified and that economic and political inequality be taken into account when determining consent.[83]

---

cal abuse committed by strangers accounts for only 23 per cent of all identified cases.

80. See Lois Pineau, "Date Rape: A Feminist Analysis," (1989) 8 *Law and Philosophy* 217; David Adams, "Date Rape and Erotic Discourse," in Leslie Francis, ed., *Date Rape: Feminism, Philosophy, and the Law* (University Park, PA: Pennsylvania State University Press, 1996).

81. See Jaffe et al., above, note 4 at 47–9.

82. See Catharine MacKinnon, "Feminism, Marxism, Method and the State: An Agenda for Theory," (1983) 8 *Signs* 635 at 638; Andrea Dworkin, *Intercourse* (New York: Free Press, 1987) at 76–7. For a presentation of the opinions of these authors, see Ngaire Naffine, *Feminism and Criminology* (Philadelphia: Temple University Press, 1996) at 100–2.

83. As regards consent, see below, at §§159ff.

48. *The Legal Model of Consent* – In order to understand the phenomenon of sexual abuse by persons who are close to the victim, one
must consider the fact that our society accepts a certain type of
seduction model and that we look at amorous relationships in a particular way. The seduction model presupposes acceptance of natural
male aggression and natural female reluctance.[84] Based on this,
Pineau suggests that the law has defined amorous relationships on
a contractual basis that takes into account the reality of male
aggressiveness–female passivity. For example, a woman who uses
sexual behaviour to encourage a man to believe that the contract
(intercourse) will be consummated must suffer the consequences of
her implicit promise. This contractual model in some ways accepts
and endorses not only the supposedly uncontrollable nature of
men's sexual drive but also women's concomitant responsibility to
avoid subjecting themselves to the inevitable. In Pineau's opinion,
this approach is unhealthy because it ignores women as agents of
their own sexuality and reduces the role of communication in relationships. Instead, the author favours a model in which sexuality is
communicative. This model would require proof of communication
in connection with the progression of the sexual act.[85]

The issues surrounding consent and the psychological model
most likely to reduce sexual abuse are still controversial.[86] They are
particularly relevant when sexual abuse occurs in marital situations.

49. *Abuse and Power in Marital Relationships* –Sexual abuse can be
a component of spousal abuse. Many battered women are also raped
by their spouses: sex is an instrument of subordination, especially
when it is humiliating or painful. In abusive marital relations, too,
the prevalence of the contractual model of amorous relationships,
which Pineau has denounced, is particularly evident. The contractual model explains our reluctance to conclude that consent is
absent when a person has already said "yes": if marriage is a contract, does it not infer implicit consent to sexual relations? This was

---

84.   See Pineau, above, note 80 at 9, 13–17.
85.   On this topic, see the policy of Antioch College in the United States, which
       requires a student to obtain verbal consent from another student if the sexual
       contact was not begun simultaneously. Verbal consent must be obtained at
       every stage as the sexual intimacy "progresses." See "The Antioch Policy,
       Appendices," in Francis, above, note 80.
86.   Adams, above, note 80, has criticized Pineau's approach.

the case for a very long time in our legislation,[87] given that
Canadian criminal law defined rape as an offence requiring that the
victim not be the aggressor's spouse. While legislative amendments
abolished this requirement, attitudes have not necessarily shifted
in concert with these amendments. Issues of power and control figure prominently in discussions of spousal sexual abuse, as well as
non-sexual abuse. Although these issues are discussed below in the
section on spousal abuse,[88] it should be noted that the remarks are
equally applicable to spousal sexual abuse.

2.   *The Impact on the Client*

50. *Individual Impact* – Each victim reacts differently to sexual
abuse. Although certain types of emotional response frequently
arise from sexual abuse, their intensity and manifestations vary.
Often, every aspect of the victim's past and present life is affected
by the abuse: her whole life story has been influenced by the abuse.
The manner in which the abuse was perpetrated, and the reaction
of the victim's relatives to the abuse, can have varying aggravating
effects on the victim's symptoms.

51. *Post-Traumatic Stress Disorder* – As in the case of child sexual
abuse, a diagnosis of post-traumatic stress disorder can be made
when assessing the effects of adult sexual abuse.[89] Post-traumatic
stress disorder allows us to identify a host of symptoms, including
nightmares and flashbacks, appetite loss or eating disorders, feelings of hatred of and resentment towards the aggressor, loss of self-
esteem, and, sometimes, suicidal thoughts, self-destructive
behaviour (through the use of alcohol or drugs), or sexual dysfunc-
tion.[90] Sexual abuse, particularly when it is perpetrated within an
intimate relationship, also creates complex feelings of guilt; the victim may berate herself for having mistakenly chosen or loved someone who has hurt her.

---

87.   For a history of the provisions defining sexual abuse, see William A. Schabas,
      Les infractions d'ordre sexuel (Cowansville, QC: Les Éditions Yvon Blais, 1995)
      at 24.
88.   See below, at §§58–9.
89.   See Herman, above, note 5; see also, above, §§30ff, in the discussion of post-
      traumatic stress disorder.
90.   See Herman, above, note 5 at 86–95; see also Pat Gilmartin, *Rape, Incest, and
      Child Sexual Assault: Consequences and Recovery* (New York: Garland
      Publishing, 1994) at 104–12.

Certain aspects of the symptoms of post-traumatic stress disorder may affect the legal process. Here we discuss several such symptoms: nightmares and flashbacks, fear, and resentment.

52. *Nightmares and Flashbacks* – The phenomenon of nightmares and flashbacks is a well-known consequence of sexual and physical abuse. However, relatively little has been documented regarding the phenomenon's economic impact. We know that nightmares can prevent a person from sleeping and can thereby reduce productivity and energy levels. However, we have yet to measure properly the day to day impact of flashbacks, which not only interrupt the flow of the victim's thought processes, but also cause constant stress. Disturbing images are often triggered by trivial details of the victim's daily life, and survivors must possess a great deal of self-control to avoid tensing up, fleeing, or becoming paralysed after a flashback episode. The courts will have to consider how to quantify the impact of this source of constant stress.[91]

53. *Fear* – Abuse at the hands of a stranger can result in a visceral fear that paralyses the victim. Fear may justify a move or the installation of a security system, but it is difficult to measure its impact on a person's productivity or ability to earn a living. Thus, fear is an emotion whose day-to-day repercussions may have an economic impact that must be assessed.

54. *Resentment* – It is normal for a victim to feel resentment, hatred, and even rage towards her aggressor. However, the outward manifestation of such emotions does not fit well with the image, favoured by the court system, of a poised and reasonable plaintiff. One popular strategy on the part of aggressors consists of attempting to direct the court's attention to the plaintiff's grounds for revenge rather than the commission of the abusive acts. It is important to properly inform the court that it is normal for a victim to seek revenge against and feel hatred towards the aggressor.

Sexual abuse is a complex phenomenon whose disclosure creates particular challenges for the court system. The same is true of spousal abuse.

---

91.   See "Evaluating Injury," below, at §§290ff.

II. THE PROBLEM OF SPOUSAL ABUSE

As in the preceding sections on child sexual abuse and sexual abuse against adults, we present the social context for spousal abuse and its impact on the client.

A. The Context

55. *The Scope of the Problem* – Statistics reveal that a significant proportion of women are abused by their spouses.[92] Although spousal abuse is not limited to any one social class, many authors have noted that the economic effects of a husband's unemployment, in particular, can increase the risk of abuse.[93]

56. *The Intensity of the Problem* – More than 40 per cent of the cases of spousal abuse can be categorized as severe abuse—that is, abuse that results in physical after-effects.[94] Even more frightening is the link between spousal abuse and the mortality rate of abused spouses, whether death results from the injuries suffered within the marital relationship or from a deliberate murder following the departure of the victim. The moment of a woman's departure from the marital home is the most dangerous. It appears that violent men view the breaking of the cycle of dependency by women as an attack on their ego, with the result that they lose all control over their emotions.[95] Many violent attacks and murder-suicides take place under such circumstances.

57. *Violence That Is Also Psychological* – Abuse can also be psychological. Insults often accompany beatings or can be a prelude to an explosion of violence.[96] Abuse must be examined within its entire context. Repeated insults that belittle the victim contribute to the psychological impact of the abuse. The aggressor may harass the victim over the telephone at work or purposefully keep his spouse

---

92.   See Jaffe et al., note 4 at 10–20.
93.   Ibid.; see also Johnson and Sacco, above, note 3 at 293; Rhonda L. Lenton, "Power versus Feminist Theories of Wife Abuse," (1995) 37 *Can. J. Crimin.* 305 at 313–14.
94.   See Johnson and Sacco, above, note 3 at 293.
95.   See, among others, ibid., at 293; Margo Wilson, Holly Johnson, and Martin Daly, "Lethal and Nonlethal Violence Against Wives," (1995) 37 *Can. J. Crimin.* 331 at 340.
96.   See Lenore E. Walker, *The Battered Woman* (New York: Harper and Row, 1979).

isolated from her family or friends.[97] The loss of a victim's self-esteem results as much from being subjected to what are often public humiliations through insults and abusive language as it does from the feeling of powerlessness with respect to the abuse.

58. *Violence That Is Also Economic* – A man's desire to dominate his wife often expresses itself through economic control. The husband may prevent his wife from working, oblige her to guarantee his debts, or require her to account for each and every one of her expenses.[98] The creation and continuation of this economic dependency often constitutes the major obstacle facing an abused woman who wants to put an end to her relationship. Seizing financial control allows the aggressor to obtain what he often desires—a stranglehold on his wife.

59. *Profile of an Aggressor* – Although there is no socio-economic profile of an aggressor, his psychological profile often shows a desire to control his wife's actions. It may very well be that he was physically abused as a child or that he witnessed physical or sexual abuse within his family. Aggressors usually have difficulty giving verbal expression to their feelings of frustration.[99] As a result, their means of resolving conflicts with their spouses becomes more and more violent. The abuser's continued inability to express his frustration, and his need to assert his control and power over his wife, perpetuates and escalates the cycle of violence.

60. *Alcohol as a Factor* – There seems to be some correlation between spousal abuse and the consumption of alcohol.

---

97.   See Frederica L. Lehrman, "Strategies for Interviewing Domestic Violence Clients," *Trial* (February 1995) 38. See also Benoît Roy and Gilles Rondeau, "Le contrôle exercé sur la conjointe: comparaison de quatre groupes d'hommes," (1997) 30 *Criminologie* 47–65, where it is noted at 47: "As the level of psychological and physical abuse increased, so did the desire to dominate and isolate women."

98.   Lehrman, ibid. at 40. On the particular experience of immigrant women on this issue, see: Baukje Miedma and Sandra Wachholz, "A Complex Web: Access to Justice for Abused Immigrant Women in New Brunswick," (1999) 19 *Can. Woman Studies* 175, and Susan McDonald, "Not in the Numbers: Domestic Violence and Immigrant Women," (1999) 19 *Canadian Woman Studies* 163.

99.   See Dutton, above, note 5 at 121–60, where he describes the diverse personality types of aggressors. See also Pierre Turcotte, "Intervention de groupe auprès des conjoints violents et logique du contrôle social," (1997) 48 *Service Social* 228, where the author comments that in order to rehabilitate the perpetrator, the very nature of masculine identity norms must be addressed.

Nonetheless, statisticians have hesitated to draw firm conclusions on this matter. Citing alcohol as a factor in spousal abuse cannot explain the fact that many men who consume alcohol do not abuse their wives and, inversely, that certain men who are sober do abuse their wives.[100]

61. *The Cycle of Violence* – Most studies of spousal abuse have noted a cyclical aspect to the abuse. Lenore Walker[101] describes three phases of abuse. The first phase is marked by increased tension: insults, intentional cruelty, and physical maltreatment. The aggressor expresses dissatisfaction and hostility. The woman tries to appease him; she attempts to please him and to avoid aggravating him. She often manages to curtail her husband's anger, thereby confirming her unrealistic belief that she can control him. The second phase comprises the abuse itself. The third phase consists of a period of contrition on the part of the abusive spouse. This contrition is often accompanied by displays of love and repentance.

62. *The Issue of Provocation* – Sometimes, the woman takes it upon herself to provoke the inevitable eruption of anger in order to have some control over its time and place. This provocation is often incorrectly interpreted as an indication of masochism.[102] In fact, it allows the woman to survive. She can take better measures to minimize the injuries and pain if she knows when and where the abuse will be perpetrated. It is important to debunk the myth of female masochism, which results from a poor interpretation of the dynamics of the abuse and its impact on the victim. The impact of this interpretation will be the focus of our examination in the next section.

B. The Impact on the Client

63. *Introduction* – Victims of sexual abuse suffer significant physical after-effects that are often a source of embarrassment and anxiety for the victim, who must find a way to hide the bruises from her children and neighbours. The abuse can also have paralysing effects on the victim. This paralysis, as well as the victim's unrealistic hope

---

100. See Dutton, above, note 5 at 123.
101. Lenore E. Walker, *The Battered Woman Syndrome* (New York: Springer, 1984).
102. See Jaffe et al., above, note 4.

that she can improve the situation, often prevents her from leaving her abusive spouse.

64. *The Unrealistic Hope That Things Will Change* – When the aggressor makes excuses, tries to help his victim, treats her kindly and with remorse, and even showers her with gifts, she may believe—and want to believe—that he will never allow himself to be violent again. This unrealistic hope that a couple's relationship will change often characterizes what is known as battered woman syndrome.

65. *Definition of the Battered Woman Syndrome* – Battered woman syndrome is generally associated with the paralysis of a wife who has been the victim of spousal abuse, and with her dependence upon, and inability to leave, her abusive spouse. Battered women lose their ability to make decisions, to assert themselves, and to see themselves as people with inalienable rights. Their ability to earn a living is compromised by feelings of powerlessness, guilt, and marginalization.

66. *An Often Poorly Used Syndrome* – Battered woman syndrome has been criticized for attempting to characterize all battered women and thus discounting those women who do not behave in the prescribed way.[103] Despite this criticism, is it important to understand fully the value of the model presented by the syndrome. The syndrome is not intended to determine whether or not abuse exists within a relationship. Thus, it would be wrong to compare a woman's reaction to the model in order to determine whether or not abuse exists. Many women, perhaps those who are better off economically, do not react to physical abuse in the manner described by Walker. They simply leave their violent spouses. This does not mean that they have not been victims of abuse. The battered woman syndrome serves to explain why certain women remain in violent relationships and how they can reasonably perceive and predict danger to their lives even when the battering has not yet recurred.[104] In fact, it is within the context of assessing self-defence that the syndrome has been recognized in Canadian jurisprudence.

---

103. See Melanie Frager Griffith, "Battered Woman Syndrome: A Tool for Batterers?" (1995) 64 *Fordham Law Review* 141.

104. Professor Walker provides a very clear explanation of why the testimony of an expert witness regarding battered woman syndrome may, nevertheless, be useful before the courts: "There is a fundamental difference between the way women tell of their battering experiences and what is permitted under the

67. *Judicial Recognition* – Battered woman syndrome was recognized by the Supreme Court of Canada, in a criminal context, in the matter of *R. v. Lavallée.*[105] *Lavallée* recognized the existence and validity of the syndrome. This recognition may serve to explain, for instance, a delay between the occurrence of the abuse and the civil suit. Judicial recognition of the syndrome may also be useful for an understanding of the perverse nature of the abuse and the resulting damage to the victim's self-esteem.

68. *Conclusion* – Notwithstanding the above observations, one must remember that sexual or spousal abuse affects each victim differently. An understanding of the common after-effects of abuse may help an attorney gain a better understanding of a client, but it should never replace careful attention to the client's own story.

---

male-identified rules of evidence. Women tend to tell of the events in question rooted in their context, by weaving a tale of patterns of events and feelings in the context of how they happened. Rules of evidence call for the recitation of discrete events separated from feelings or opinions. Facts out of context may be acceptable, but they do not convey the battered woman's experience. Expert witnesses can tie together what the current evidentiary rules do not allow the defendant to say. Until feminist legal scholars argue for and attain reform in the rules of evidence, a battered woman will be constrained from putting her case in front of the trier of fact." See Lenore E. Walker, "A Response to Elizabeth M. Schneider's Describing and Changing: Women's Self-Defense Work and the Problem of Expert Testimony on Battering," (1986) 9 *Women's Rts. L. Rep.* 223–4, cited by Melanie Frager Griffith, above, note 103 at 157.

105.   [1990] 1 S.C.R. 852.

Chapter 2

Towards a Better Representation
of the Client

69. *Introduction.* —Each attorney has an individual style, and each approaches the representation of clients with a particular personality and personal history. The purpose of this chapter is not to suggest "the best" way to represent survivors of abuse, but simply to offer suggestions in light of the past experience of attorneys and judges in this particular field. We will begin with an examination of certain aspects of the attorney–client relationship that can present challenges within the context of representing victims or survivors of sexual or spousal abuse. Then we will extend the scope of our examination to include other means of support that a victim should consider before instituting civil proceedings.

I.   THE ATTORNEY–CLIENT RELATIONSHIP

70. *The Issue of Power in the Attorney–Client Relationship* – The power relationship between an attorney and client is one that merits attention. Victims of abuse have differing needs and do not all react the same way. Their dealings with professionals may have been marked by betrayal. Attorneys must be ready to deal with these issues. Moreover, given that sexual and spousal abuse is often experienced as a situation of intense powerlessness, it is important to minimize, to the extent possible, the imbalance of power in the relationship between an attorney and client. The most practical way of showing respect for a client is to share information in a meaningful way. The plaintiff will have greater confidence in the judicial process if she works in concert with her attorney in developing strategies.

71. *Confidentiality* – It is crucial that the client feel comfortable enough with her attorney to be able to tell her story. Thus, it is essential to provide an explanation of the attorney–client privilege

33

at the very start of the relationship.[1] Confidentiality is a particularly important aspect of this relationship, because the client will have to reveal intimate details about her life. It may be necessary to provide a detailed explanation of the way in which the law firm operates as regards access to files by persons other than the attorney; it may even be necessary to modify usual practices in order to reassure the client.

72. *Clarifying the Objectives of the Civil Suit* – In civil litigation for sexual and spousal abuse, in particular, the client's objectives in instituting proceedings may be more symbolic than financial.[2] These multiple objectives may affect strategy regarding the use of expert witnesses; for example, the courts are often poorly informed and more likely to put faith in the testimony of experts than that of witnesses. Yet, a victim may refuse to put her therapist in the "star witness" role—it is often important for the victim to be the one who tells her story. Therefore, it is essential for lawyer and client to discuss in detail the role of experts and the strategy regarding their testimony. It may prove useful to think of the expert's role as that of an interpreter who provides the judge with a translation of the client's complex feelings in language that is more accessible to a person who may never have experienced abuse and whose vocabulary and understanding are shaped by a sense of security.[3]

73. *Careful and Attentive Listening* – A client's history may evoke strong emotions in her attorney. Clearly, it is crucial that attorneys avoid taking on their clients' stories as their own and putting themselves in the victims' place. At times, particularly if the attorney has never experienced sexual abuse, it may be unwise for the attorney to indicate that she or he "understands" the victim's feelings. The complex nature of the survivor's emotions adds to the difficulty of representing a victim of sexual abuse. The relationship between the victim, her aggressor, and her family may not have been entirely

---

1. See Loretta P. Merritt, "Civil Sexual Assault: Representing the Plaintiff/ Victim," in *Litigating for Physically and Sexually Abused Women: Practical Insights and an Up-to-Date Review of the Legal Issues* (Toronto: Canadian Institute, 1994) at 2.

2. For the results of a survey of sexual abuse survivors that shows the importance of the objective of rehabilitation for the victim, see Nathalie Des Rosiers, Bruce Feldthusen, and Oleana Hankivsky, "Legal Compensation for Sexual Violence: Therapeutic Consequences and Consequences for the Judicial System," (1998) 4:1 *Psychology, Public Policy and Law* 433.

3. For a more detailed discussion of this concept, see ibid.

negative. Therefore, it may be dangerous for the attorney to paint for the court a totally depressing picture of her client's childhood or life.

74. *The Client Interview* – A victim may not always know how to explain her symptoms or the actions of her aggressor. In such cases it is helpful for an attorney to have a general understanding of the behaviour of aggressors and the effects of sexual abuse; such knowledge may contribute to the interview with the victim. The attorney can ask specific questions to properly identify the type of abuse: for example, was the victim slapped or punched in the face? In order to determine the sequence of events, the attorney can use calendars or refer to holidays, birthdays, or seasons. It is important not to focus too much on lapses of memory regarding the frequency of the abuse or the time when it occurred. During the interview it is more important to listen to the story than to prepare answers to the cross-examination.

75. *The Need for an Empathic and Supportive Approach* – The attorney–client interview may be the first time that the client has had to describe the abuse to someone other than her therapist. It is essential that the attorney adopt an approach that encourages the victim and, above all, does not cast doubt on her story. The interview can be very traumatic for the client. It is possible that the language used by the attorney to obtain the client's trust is the same as that used by the aggressor to ensure the victim's submission. The client may have flashbacks and react negatively. The fact that the client may seem, during the first interview, to be a "bad witness" certainly does not mean that this will always be the case. Victims can learn to control their symptoms and the emergence of their other personalities. They merely need time and support.

In order to achieve the objective of providing psychological support to a client, the attorney should make use of the resources within her community.

II. Recourse to Other Types of Support

76. *Limits of the Assistance Provided by an Attorney* – Representing victims of sexual abuse is demanding. It is of the utmost importance that attorneys acknowledge that they cannot be the only source of support to their clients during the litigation process. Attorneys must familiarize themselves with the social services within the com-

munity and direct their client towards these services. This support
may take several forms: therapeutic, domestic, and social.

77. *The Need for Therapeutic Assistance* – Certain attorneys insist
that their clients see a therapist as a condition of taking on their
case. Some clients may resist such a suggestion because they have
had more than enough therapy or because their past experience has
left them disgusted with the therapeutic approach. A client's decision whether or not to have therapy is a personal decision that must
be respected. However, the client must have a clear understanding
of the advantage of having good therapeutic support. Moreover, it is
important that the attorney ensure that the client who decides not
to see a therapist has other sources of support.

78. *The Quality of the Therapy* – Attorneys must also be confident
about the quality of the therapy with which their clients are
involved. For the purposes of civil suits, three elements are key to
effective therapy. First, the client must be able to communicate with
her therapist. For reasons that are attributable to neither the client
nor the therapist, the patient–therapist relationship may not work.
In this regard, the patient–therapist relationship is not that different from the attorney–client relationship: it is based on a true sense
of trust, which cannot be created through logic alone. It is only
within an atmosphere of trust that the client will be able to communicate effectively with the therapist. Second, the therapist
should have specific training and experience in the treatment of
sexual abuse victims.[4] The attorney should also ensure that the
therapist is "available"—that she will be able to offer her services
particularly during the difficult moments of the hearing and the
examination on discovery.[5] Ideally, the therapist should have some
experience with providing therapeutic support within the context of
judicial proceedings, given that these proceedings create stress
within the therapeutic process. Finally, civil suits often turn into
trials of the therapy applied to the victim, particularly since the

---

4.   See Kathy A. Tatone, "Sexual Abuse Litigation: Opportunities and Obstacles,"
       Trial (February 1995) 66. On this point, see the case of proceedings instituted
       against a therapist for having provoked a relapse in the patient within the
       scope of treatment following sexual abuse: *S.T.* v. *Gaskell*, [1997] O.J. No.
       2029 (Ont. Gen. Div.) (Q.L.). The action was dismissed due to lack of evidence
       of an accepted standard of conduct for the treatment of victims of sexual
       abuse.
5.   Tatone, ibid. at 68.

advent of the false memory syndrome movement.[6] Therapies based upon truth serum or hypnosis will undoubtedly come under criticism, especially if they give rise to new memories of abuse. Even overly aggressive therapy, which suggests to the patient that she was the victim of sexual abuse without such memories having surfaced prior to the therapy, will expose the therapist to a vigorous cross-examination. However, the choice of the type of therapy has but one purpose and but one yardstick for measuring success: the therapy must suit the patient. Therefore, the attorney must respect the client's choice of therapy and, if necessary, explain this choice at a later date.

79. *Attendance at the Hearing* – Within this context, it may be important to ask the client, in advance, who will be able to accompany her during examinations on discovery and during the hearing. The emotional and practical support provided by a companion can greatly facilitate the litigation process.

80. *Self-Help Groups* – Many sexual abuse support centres organize self-help groups, which may provide a very positive experience for a client. The group may provide relatively easy access to non-hierarchical and practical support. It should be noted that, within the evidence disclosure process, certain common law courts have permitted access to the names of members of self-help groups. We believe that Quebec law, because of its focus on the protection of privacy,[7] will continue to deny access to lists of potential witnesses.

81. *Family Support* – Clearly, a revelation of past sexual abuse has an enormous impact on a family and its interrelationships. The reaction of the victim's relatives is often unpredictable: some members may become the victim's closest allies and provide her with comfort and immeasurable symbolic support. Others may completely reject the disclosure process and blame—or even abandon—the plaintiff.[8] Loss of family may be the price the victim pays for public proceedings. This must not be weighed lightly by the victim in her decision to institute a civil action.

---

6.   Above, at §§36ff.
7.   Below, at §436.
8.   See Tatone, above, note 4 at 66; Kimberly A. Crnich, "Redressing the Undressing: A Primer on the Representation of Adult Survivors of Childhood Sexual Abuse," (1992) 14 *Women's Rights Law Reporter* 65 at 78.

82. *The Support of Friends* – Friends can also have varying reactions to public proceedings. In cases of past childhood sexual abuse, the victim's spouse may feel threatened by the public disclosure of intimate details about his life. Friends may feel sympathetic but be unwilling to testify. Many people do not look favourably upon recourse to the courts to resolve matters of family abuse, especially if the matter is considered to be ancient history. Clients may find themselves contending with this attitude.

83. *Support for the Attorney* – Representing survivors of sexual and spousal abuse can impose exceptional stress on an attorney, particularly if the litigation process is drawn out. Many psychologists use the term secondary trauma to describe the psychological impact of listening to, and absorbing, stories of abuse. To ensure that they are able to serve their clients properly, attorneys should make certain that their own support systems are in place.

84. *Conclusion* – In cases of sexual or spousal abuse, the demands of the attorney–client relationship present challenges for both the client and her attorney. All judicial proceedings involve some stress, particularly when the issues at hand involve intimate matters. In our opinion, it is of utmost importance that the representation of a client follow the path she has chosen. We must understand that not all victims want to avail themselves of their right to take action in response to the abuse they have suffered. Here, again, it is important to respect the client's choice.

* * *

The purpose of these introductory chapters has been to present the specific context in which victims of sexual or spousal abuse live and to offer suggestions regarding their representation within the judicial system. We will now examine the actual civil proceedings instituted in response to sexual or spousal abuse. In Chapter 3, we examine the conditions for the remedy. Given that the proceedings must be instituted within a certain time period, which can be a problem for a plaintiff in an abuse case, we will first examine the issue of prescription periods. In Chapter 4, we consider the various avenues available to a victim: remedy under the *Charter of Human Rights and Freedoms*, remedy based on the *Civil Code of Québec*, and compensation pursuant to a governmental plan. We will carry out a detailed analysis of the various conditions applicable to such remedies.

In Part III, we examine the implementation of the remedy. In Chapter 5, we consider trial preparation: the appropriate moment to institute proceedings, drafting the declaration, procedures for disclosure of evidence, and out-of-court settlements. Chapter 6, on the trial context, examines the means for protecting the plaintiff's identity and the means of proof. Finally, Chapter 7 examines the response of defendants, namely, actions for defamation instituted against the victim and actions for defamation in respect of the written pleadings and the allegations contained therein.

Part II
The Conditions for Remedy

In this part, we will examine the issue of extinctive prescription and then consider the various remedies available to victims of sexual or spousal abuse.

Chapter 3

Extinctive Prescription

85. *The Problem* – As already discussed,[1] victims of sexual and spousal abuse may try to forget their traumatic sexual experiences, they may often be unable to see themselves as victims, or they may simply be unable to talk about their experiences.[2] Consequently, many years may pass until they realize the damage they have suffered or confide in someone about it. If they do manage to get help and institute proceedings before the civil courts, they face the obstacle of extinctive prescription,[3] among others. The *Civil Code of Québec* (art. 2925 C.C.Q.) standardized the former prescription periods[4] by establishing a three-year extinctive prescription period for

---

1. See Part I above.
2. See Nathalie Des Rosiers, "Limitation Periods and Civil Remedies for Childhood Sexual Abuse," (1992) 9 *Canadian Family Law Quarterly* 43; see also the opinion of Mr. Justice La Forest in *M. (K.)* v. *M. (H.)*, [1992] 3 S.C.R. 6. See, for example, *M.T.* v. *J.L.*, [1998] B.C.J. No. 1459 (B.C. S.C.) (Q.L.), in which the plaintiff, who was fifty-five years old, waited forty-five years after the end of the sexual abuse before instituting a civil action against her father. The plaintiff was able to institute the proceedings, notwithstanding the years that had elapsed, because the British Columbia statute on limitations removes all prescription periods in matters of sexual abuse committed against minors. See *Limitation Act*, R.S.B.C. 1996, c. 266, s. 3(4)(k).
3. Although the problem of extinctive prescription has arisen most often in cases of sexual offences perpetrated against children, it may also prevent adult victims of sexual or spousal abuse from instituting civil proceedings. Therefore, this chapter is applicable to all victims who are subject to prescriptive time periods.
4. In matters of extracontractual liability, the *Civil Code of Lower Canada* provided for several extinctive prescription periods, including a period of one year for bodily injuries (art. 2262 (2) C.C.L.C.), a general two-year period for offences (art. 2261 (2) C.C.L.C.) and a three-year period for medical liability (art. 2260a C.C.L.C.). The standardization of the extinctive prescription periods was also among the objectives of the Civil Code Revision Office [hereinafter CCRO]. See CCRO, *Report on the Québec Civil Code*, vol. 2, *Commentaries* (Quebec: Éditeur officiel, 1977) at 934. However, for injuries that appear gradually, the CCRO had suggested a deadline of ten years from the event having caused the injury. Fortunately for the victims under discus-

personal actions. However, there are certain exceptions. For example, prescription does not run between spouses while they are cohabiting (art. 2906 C.C.Q.). As for minors, article 2905 C.C.Q. stipulates that prescription runs against them, except when they institute proceedings against their representatives—that is, people who have parental authority over them.[5]

86. *A Serious Obstacle* – As recognized by the Supreme Court in the matter of *M. (K.)* v. *M. (H.)*,[6] a decision that we will examine below, short prescription periods constitute a serious obstacle to fair compensation for victims of sexual and spousal abuse.[7] A blind and strict application of prescription periods would make it almost

---

sion in this book, the proposal was not retained in the *Civil Code of Québec*. See CCRO, *Report on the Québec Civil Code*, vol. 1, *Draft Civil Code* (Quebec: Éditeur officiel, 1977), Book 7, art. 51.

5.   Art. 2905, para. 2 C.C.Q. "Nor does it run against a minor or a person of full age under curatorship or tutorship with respect to remedies he may have against his representative or against the person entrusted with his custody." Pursuant to the *Civil Code of Lower Canada*, minors benefited from the general rule of suspension of prescription. Art. 2232 (2) C.C.L.C. See François Frenette, "De la prescription," in *La réforme du Code civil*, vol. 3 (Quebec: Presses de l'Université Laval, 1993) No. 26 at 574. Thus, prescription will run against a minor who wants to institute proceedings against a person who is not her representative, such as an uncle having committed incest. However, given that such victims often establish the link of causality between the fault and their injury only after several years of therapy once they have become adults, prescription may be suspended in such cases, because it was impossible for the victim to act and because the injury appeared gradually. See below, at §120ff.

6.   Above, note 2 at 17.

7.   As regards the negative impact of short prescription periods, see the analysis presented by Janet Mosher, "Challenging Limitation Periods: Civil Claims by Adult Survivors of Incest," (1994) 44 *Univ. of T. L. J.* 169; Des Rosiers, above, note 2; Nathalie Des Rosiers, "Les recours des victimes d'inceste," in Pierre Legrand, ed., *Common Law, d'un siècle l'autre* (Cowansville, QC: Les Éditions Yvon Blais, 1992) at 153. Much has also been written in American doctrine regarding this major obstacle. See, among others, Carol W. Napier, "Civil Incest Suits: Getting beyond the Statute of Limitations," (1990) 68 *Wash. U. L.Q.* 995; Melissa G. Salten, "Statutes of Limitations in Civil Incest Suits: Preserving the Victim's Remedy," (1984–5) 7 *Harv. Women's L. J.* 189; Carolyn B. Handles, "Civil Claims of Adults Molested as Children: Maturation of Harm and the Statute of Limitations Hurdle," (1987) 15 *Fordham Urban L. J.* 709; Rebecca L. Thomas, "Adult Survivors of Childhood Sexual Abuse and Statutes of Limitations: A Call for Legislative Action," (1991) 26 *Wake Forest Law Rev.* 1245; Ann Marie Hagen, "Tolling the Statute of Limitations for Adult Survivors of Childhood Sexual Abuse," (1991) 76 *Iowa L. R.* 355.

impossible to institute any civil proceedings for injuries resulting from spousal abuse or sexual offences perpetrated against children. This explains, in part, why such proceedings are rare in Quebec.[8]

---

8.   As regards the small number of Quebec decisions on this topic, see Louise
      Langevin, "L'accès des femmes au système judiciaire: Les poursuites civiles
      pour violence sexuelle et conjugale au Québec," (1999) 19 *Cahiers de la femme*
      86. The following are the decisions that we have identified on this subject: *Pie*
      v. *Thibert*, [1976] C.S. 180 (Que. Sup. Ct.) (gang rape); *Diamond* v. *Bikadoroff*,
      [1976] C.A. 695 (Que. C.A.) (sexual touching of a patient by a psychiatrist—
      dismissed because the prescription period had expired); *Labonté* v. *Bélanger*,
      J.E. 78-119 (Que. Sup. Ct.) (sexual assault on young girls prescription);
      Beaumont-Butcher v. *Butcher*, [1982] C.S. 893 (Que. Sup. Ct.) (spousal abuse);
      Lacombe v. *D'Avril*, [1983] C.S. 592 (Que. Sup. Ct.) (spousal abuse); *Gosselin*
      v. *Fournier*, [1985] C.S. 481 (Que. Sup. Ct.) (sexual touching of a student by a
      teacher); *Rousseau* v. *Quessy*, [1986] R.R.A. 222 (Que. Sup. Ct.) (sexual assault
      on a waitress by a customer); *Jacques* v. *Tremblay*, J.E. 89-734 (Que. Sup. Ct.)
      (threats made by the defendant against the plaintiff, who had filed a com-
      plaint for sexual assault on her daughter); *Goodwin* v. *Commission scolaire
      Laurenval*, [1991] R.R.A. 673 (Que. Sup. Ct.) (sexual touching of a student by
      a janitor); *Lakatos* v. *Sary*, J.E. 92-6 (Que. Sup. Ct.) (spousal abuse); *Gagnon*
      v. *Béchard*, J.E. 89-590 (Que. Sup. Ct.), rev'd [1993] R.J.Q. 2019 (Que. C.A.)
      (sexual touching of children by their babysitter—appeal allowed on an issue of
      prescription, no decision on the merits); *Bosquet* v. *Zahas* (25 January 1994),
      Montreal 500-05-013873-896 (Que. Sup. Ct.) (spousal abuse); *Bérubé* v.
      Bilodeau, J.E. 95-1244 (C.Q.) (spousal abuse); *Côte* v. *Beaulieu* (22 August
      1995) 150-05-000250-920 (Que. Sup. Ct.) (spousal abuse); *Larocque* v. *Côte*,
      [1996] R.J.Q. 1930 (Que. Sup. Ct.) (sexual assault on a soldier by colleagues);
      Walker v. *Singer*, [1996] R.R.A. 175 (Que. Sup. Ct.) (action for defamation fol-
      lowing a complaint of sexual assault); *Pelletier* v. *Émery*, J.E. 97-1360 (Que.
      Sup. Ct.) (harassment by an ex-husband); *A.A.* v. *B.*, [1998] R.J.Q. 3117 (Que.
      Sup. Ct.) (victim of incest); *Roberge* v. *Carrier*, AZ-98026065, 98 B.E. 86 (Que.
      Sup. Ct.) (spousal abuse); *G.B.* v. *A.B.*, [1999] J.Q. No. 5129 (Que. C.A.) (Q.L.),
      rev'g [1998] J.Q. No. 1588 (Que. Sup. Ct.) (Q.L.) (sexual assault on a child—
      had allowed a motion to dismiss on the ground of prescription); *Major* v.
      Surette, [1999] J.Q. No. 5060 (C.Q.) (Q.L.) (spousal abuse); *Lapointe* v.
      Lapointe, succession, [1999] J.Q. No. 385 (C.Q.) (Q.L.) (incest—dismissed for
      reasons of prescription, among other reasons); *T.L.* v. *M.L.*, [1999] J.Q. No.
      5783 (Que. Sup. Ct.) (Q.L.) (spousal abuse, action for damages within the scope
      of a divorce); *Marcoux* v. *Légaré*, J.E. 2000-960 (C.Q.), AZ-00021467 (on
      appeal: C.A.Q. 200-09-003076-004) (spousal abuse); *Lavallée* v. *Massé*, AZ-
      00036289 (C.Q.) (sexual assault). From among these cases, two were dis-
      missed due to prescription: *Diamond* v. *Bikadoroff* and *Labonté* v. *Bélanger*.
      Moreover, other decisions dealing with the dismissal of employees as a result
      of sexual assault show that the victims who complained to the police or to
      other authorities did not institute civil proceedings. See, for example,
      *Association des bibliothécaires et des professeurs de l'Université de Moncton et
      Université de Moncton*, [1999] R.J.D.T. 1457 (Arbitration Trib.), D.T.E. 99T-
      848; *Syndicat national du transport écolier Saguenay - Lac St-Jean et
      Compagnie d'autobus xxx ltée*, D.T.E. 99T-1149 (Arbitration Trib.).

Such a situation contributes to denying women the protection of their fundamental rights.

In this chapter, we examine the foundations of extinctive prescription and the mechanisms for easing its application—namely, the impossibility for a victim to act and the progressive appearance of the damage. We will then apply these mechanisms to proceedings instituted by victims of sexual and spousal abuse.

I.   THE GENERAL PRINCIPLES OF EXTINCTIVE PRESCRIPTION

Before adapting the concept of prescription to suit the reality facing victims of sexual and spousal abuse, it is necessary to understand the foundations of prescription and examine the mechanisms for easing its application. Indeed, prescription periods would be a source of inequity if such tempering mechanisms were not available to suspend them.

A.   The Foundations of Extinctive Prescription

87. *Protection of Public Order* – Both Quebec[9] and French[10] doctrine justify extinctive prescription on grounds of public order. According to the French authors the Mazeauds, "it is in the interest of public order for obligations to be eliminated after the creditor fails to act for a long period."[11] Thus, prescription "appears, firstly, as an institution intended to create security in legal relationships."[12] Prescription periods are intended to protect the public order, because they prevent the erosion of evidence, ensure security in

---

9.   See Jean-Louis Baudouin and Pierre-Gabriel Jobin, *Les obligations*, 5th ed. (Cowansville, QC: Les Éditions Yvon Blais, 1998) No. 1005 at 792; Wilbrod Rodys, *Traité de droit civil du Québec*, t. 15 (Montreal: Wilson and Lafleur, 1958) at 31–2.

10.   When presenting the draft title relating to prescription in the French Civil Code, Bigot de Préameneu stated to the French legislature: "Of all the civil law institutions, prescription is the most necessary for social order" (our translation). See Henri Mazeaud, Léon Mazeaud, and Jean Mazeaud, *Leçons de droit civil*, t. 2, vol. 1, 8th ed., by François Chabas (Paris: Montchrestien, 1991) No. 1166 at 1206.

11.   Ibid., No. 1166 at 1206 (our translation).

12.   Ibid. (our translation). On this topic, see *Gauthier* v. *Brome Lake (Town)*, [1998] 2 S.C.R. 3.

legal relationships, and protect defendants against the failure of a plaintiff to institute proceedings diligently.[13]

88. *The Effect of Time* – Prescription periods tend to limit the effect of erosion on memory and on the probative value of evidence. Evidence, including corroborating evidence, can disappear with the passage of time, and witnesses can die. Prescription runs in order to avoid such situations and thereby ensure better administration of justice.

89. *The Defendant's Peace of Mind* – Prescription periods are intended to provide defendants with a certain peace of mind, removing the sword of Damocles hanging over them from belated proceedings. Indeed, a creditor's failure to act can lead to a presumption of payment: if the creditor has not acted, he has probably been paid.[14] Thus, a defendant must be notified as soon as possible if he will be the subject of legal proceedings.

90. *The Plaintiff's Failure to Act Diligently* – A plaintiff's belated proceedings may take the defendant by surprise; the defendant has not prepared any evidence, while the plaintiff has had the benefit of a longer period of time within which to build up a file and prepare evidence. Thus, prescription periods are intended to avoid the element of surprise resulting from belated proceedings.

B. Mechanisms for Easing the Application of Extinctive Prescription

91. *Protection of Public Order* – Although public order provides an argument in favour of prescription periods, it also provides support

---

13. These three arguments were raised in *M. (K.)* v. *M .(H.)*, above, note 2, which we will consider below, at §§136 ff. They also provided the inspiration for the Quebec legislature at the time the extinctive prescription periods were standardized within the scope of the reform of the *Civil Code*: "The adaptation of extinctive prescription periods to the actual time frames is based, in part, on the interest which individuals and firms have in establishing stability and diligence in their current affairs; it is also based upon the value of evidence and its possible deterioration." Ministère de la Justice, *Commentaires du ministre de la Justice*, *Le Code civil du Québec*, t. 2 (Quebec: Publications du Québec, 1993) art. 2925 C.C.Q. at 1836 9 (hereinafter *Commentaires du ministre de la Justice*) (our translation).

14. Mazeaud, above, note 10, No. 1167 at 1207.

for mechanisms to temper the application of such periods.[15] Indeed, if such mechanisms did not exist, certain people would be denied access to the justice system. Thus, certain events may delay the starting point for prescription periods: prescription may be suspended due to the victim's impossibility to act; alternatively, it may begin to run only when the damage appears for the very fist time. We will now examine the scope of application of these two tempering mechanisms.

1. The Impossibility to Act

92. *A Cause of Suspension* – The impossibility to act constitutes a cause of suspension of prescription (art. 2904 C.C.Q.)[16] that can arise at the time the prescription begins to run or once it has already begun to run. As indicated in the jurisprudence, the absolute impossibility to act has been equated with superior force and has been interpreted very strictly. However, in order for this tempering mechanism to be truly effective, the courts must recognize the existence of a psychological impossibility to act, as the Supreme Court did in *Gauthier* v. *Brome Lake (Town)*.[17]

a) The Criterion of Superior Force

Although both the French and Quebec courts have equated the impossibility to act with superior force, the Supreme Court has now laid to rest this overly restrictive interpretation.

93. *The Napoleonic Code* – In France, the drafters of the Civil Code used clear language in article 2251 C.N.[18] to limit the causes of sus-

---

15.   This is why we do not believe that these mechanisms should be analysed as "obstacles" or "limits" to prescription.

16.   There is a distinction between the suspension of prescription and the interruption thereof. "[Suspension] consists of events which serve only to stop [prescription] for a certain period of time, such that when the cause of the suspension ends, all of the prescription time acquired prior to the suspension still exists and must be added to the prescription time yet to run." Louis Baudouin, *Le droit civil de la province de Québec* (Montreal: Wilson and Lafleur, 1953) at 480 (our translation). "Interruption destroys the prescription time which has already run and, as regards the person who was about to prescribe, that person loses the benefit of the time elapsed until then." Pierre Martineau, *La prescription* (Montreal: Presses de l'Université de Montréal, 1977) at 324 (our translation). Art. 2903 C.C.Q.

17.   Above note 12.

18.   Art. 2251 C.N.: "Prescription runs against all persons, unless they are under some exception established by law" (our translation). As regards the history of

pension of prescription to those expressly set forth at law, thereby removing the discretion the courts had enjoyed. Nonetheless, the courts slowly reintroduced the maxim: *Contra non valentem agere non currit praescriptio* (No prescription runs against a person unable to bring an action).[19] This type of suspension of prescription was applied to causes that did not relate to personal attributes (the Napoleonic Code provides for suspension for minors, for interdicted persons, and between spouses), but rather to events constituting superior force.[20] Thus, prescription was suspended in cases where the creditor was able to prove that it was absolutely impossible for him to act—a situation that was equated to superior force.

94. *The Civil Code of Lower Canada* – In contrast to the Napoleonic Code, the *Civil Code of Lower Canada*, in article 2232, expressly provided for the impossibility in fact or in law to act. The framers of the 1866 Civil Code added this rule to counterbalance the inflexible language of article 2251 of the Napoleonic Code, which, for its part, had established an exhaustive list of what constituted the impossibility to act[21] in response to the broad interpretation that had earlier been applied by the courts. Although this exception of the impossibility in fact or in law to act was included to allow a broader application than had been the case in France, it would seem that the Quebec courts were rather strict in their interpretation. Indeed, the authors Mignault[22] and Rodys[23] confirmed that kidnapping constituted the only practical application of the absolute impossibility to act. Thus, as in France, the Quebec courts equated this cause of suspension of prescription with superior force.

---

this article, see Mazeaud, above, note 10, Nos. 1162ff at 1203ff.; John W. Durnford, "Some Aspects of the Suspension and of the Starting Point of Prescription," (1963) *Thémis* 245 at 266. See Jean Carbonnier, "La règle *Contra non valentem agere non currit praescriptio*," (1937) *Revue critique de législation et de jurisprudence* 155.

19. See Henry Campbell Black, *Black's Law Dictionary*, 5th ed. (St Paul, MN: West Publishing, 1979) at 296.

20. Mazeaud, above, note 10 at No. 1183; *Juris-classeur civil*, art. 2251–9, fasc. H, by J.J. Taisne, Nos. 97–122.

21. See *Civil Code of Lower Canada: Report of the Commissioners for the Codification of the Laws of Lower Canada relating to Civil Matters* (Quebec: G.F. Desbarats, 1865) at 425; Rodys, above note 9 at 195; Martineau, above, note 16 at 216, 217; Mazeaud, above, note 10, No. 1181 at 1217.

22. Pierre Basile Mignault, *Le droit civil canadien*, t. 9 (Montreal: Wilson and Lafleur, 1916) at 453.

23. Above, note 9 at 195.

95. *A Strict Interpretation* – Left to the appreciation of the judge of first instance,[24] the grounds for the impossibility to act have been interpreted strictly under the *Civil Code of Lower Canada*,[25] as confirmed by Mr. Justice Lamer:

> I am nonetheless of the opinion that care must be taken not to relax the computing of deadlines, substantive as well as procedural, to the point that they become almost inoperative, for such clauses serve the ends of justice as they are designed to provide special protection for certain rights which under certain conditions the legislator wishes to give priority, be that to the detriment of the rights of others, by providing them protection from litigants who act belatedly.
>
> . . . Accordingly, the concept of it being "absolutely impossible . . . in fact to act", provided for in art. 2232 of the Civil Code, should not be unduly extended as a basis for a suspension of deadlines.[26]

96. *Acceptable Grounds* – The courts have applied the impossibility to act to only a few situations. They have recognized an absolute impossibility to act when the plaintiff was unaware of the defendant's identity;[27] when the defendant hid a fact from the creditor, thereby preventing the creditor from instituting proceedings;[28] when it was impossible for the plaintiff to exercise a remedy (because the plaintiff had been kidnapped, had gone off to war, or was unconscious);[29] when the plaintiff was unaware of the damage (because the damage had not yet appeared); or when the plaintiff was unaware that he or she had been a victim (the owner of a house who was unaware that the house had been sold by the municipality for unpaid taxes, because he had not received the notices).[30]

---

24.   See, among others, *Joy Oil Ltd.* v. *McColl Frontenac Oil Co. Ltd.*, [1943] S.C.R. 127 at 142.
25.   See Martineau, above, note 16 at 215ff, 254ff; Durnford, above, note 18.
26.   *Oznaga* v. *Société d'exploitation des loteries et des courses du Québec*, [1981] 2 S.C.R. 113 at 126.
27.   See, among others, *Alain* v. *Fonds d'indemnisation des victimes des accidents d'automobile*, [1976] R.P. 329 (Que. C.A.).
28.   See *Oznaga* v. *Société d'exploitation des loteries et des courses du Québec*, above, note 26; *Schaum* v. *Bourne*, J.E. 85-1093 (Que. Sup. Ct.); *Bank of Montreal* v. *Bail Ltée*, [1992] 2 S.C.R. 554; *Joy Oil Ltd.* v. *McColl Frontenac Oil Co. Ltd.*, above, note 24. See also *M. (K.)* v. *M. (H.)*, above, note 2.
29.   See *Semmelaack* v. *Ferguson* (1941), 48 R.L. 163 (Que. Sup. Ct.).
30.   See *Boutin* v. *Corporation municipale de Saint-Donat*, [1976] C.S. 52 (Que. Sup. Ct.).

97. *Unacceptable Grounds* – However, none of the following have been accepted as grounds for the impossibility to act: lack of awareness of the extent of the damages;[31] difficulties in searching for and collecting evidence;[32] or lack of awareness of one's rights, unless it resulted from the fault of the other party.[33]

98. *The Children of Duplessis* – The experience before the courts of the "children of Duplessis" provides a good illustration of the strict attitude adopted by the courts towards the suspension of prescription. The "children of Duplessis"—orphans who, from 1935 to 1964, were placed in psychiatric hospitals solely because they were orphans and minors—filed a motion to authorize the bringing of a class action against the nuns who administered the establishments. Among other things, they reproached the nuns for the physical and emotional abuse they had suffered, their lack of education, the errors committed in diagnosing them, and the failure of the nuns to act.[34] The judge rejected the motion because, among other reasons, the remedy was prescribed. Based upon the opinion of the religious community's expert—who testified that he considered that the applicant had been in a position to understand for quite some time what had happened to her and, therefore, to take the appropriate measures—the judge rejected the applicant's argument that it had been impossible for her to act. According to this judgment, then, in order to prevent the extinction of their rights of action, these people would have had to institute proceedings in the 1960s. This opinion completely ignores the taboos and silence surrounding the treatment they suffered, as well as their difficulty, as victims, in recognizing the fault committed against them.[35]

---

31.   See *Richer* v. *Larivière*, J.E. 82-697 (Que. Sup. Ct.).
32.   See *Grégoire* v. *Fédération québécoise de la montagne*, [1981] C.S. 238 (Que. Sup. Ct.), [1986] R.R.A. 174 (Que. C.A.).
33.   See *Champs* v. *Labelle (Corporation municipale de)*, [1991] R.J.Q. 2313 (Que. Sup. Ct.).
34.   See *Kelly* v. *Communauté des Soeurs de la charité de Québec*, J.E. 95-1875 (Que. Sup. Ct.) (appeal discontinued 8 February 1996). See also *Sylvestre* v. *Communauté des Soeurs de la charité*, J.E. 96-1736 (Que. Sup. Ct.).
35.   See the report of the Quebec Ombudsman, *The "Children of Duplessis": A Time for Solidarity* (Discussion and Consultation Paper for Decision-Making Purposes) (Quebec: National Assembly, 22 January 1997). See also Law Commission of Canada, *Restoring Dignity: Responding to Child Abuse in Canadian Institutions* (Ottawa: Law Commission of Canada, March 2000).

99. *The Matter of* Gauthier v. Brome Lake (Town) – The matter of
Gauthier v. *Brome Lake (Town)*[36] marks a major turning point in
Quebec law regarding the interpretation of the concept of impossibility to act. Although the Superior Court and the Court of Appeal
had relied on superior force as the evaluation criterion, the
Supreme Court refused to follow this trend and, instead, opted for a
broader interpretation of the notion of impossibility to act. The facts
and the reasoning of the courts were as follows.

100. *A Long Night of Torture* – On 1 March 1982, the plaintiff,
Gauthier, was arrested by police officers from the Town of Brome
Lake and was taken in for questioning regarding the theft of a safe.
At that time, no formal charges were laid against him. He was driven to the police station, and thus began a night of torture that is
almost unimaginable within a society that was on the threshold of
adopting the *Canadian Charter of Rights and Freedoms.*[37] At no
time did the police officers tell him the reasons for his arrest or
inform him of his right to an attorney. The plaintiff, dressed only
lightly and covered with scratches and bruises after five hours of
torture, was tied to a metal pole in an isolated location and left outside for an hour and a half in –25° C temperatures. He was released
nineteen hours after his arrest and had to spend a number of days
in the hospital due to the severity of his injuries. Following these
events, he left for Vancouver, where, for the next six months, he was
completely terrorized and unable to work.

101. *Cooperation with Law Enforcement Authorities* – In 1985,
while the plaintiff was living in Yellowknife, a representative of the
Quebec Police Commission contacted him and convinced him to testify under police protection at the commission's inquiry into the
actions of the Brome Lake police department, including the events
that took place during the night of 1 March 1982. In 1986, Gauthier
testified at the preliminary inquiry against the two police officers,
Mario Beaumont and Alyre Thireau; subsequently, he testified at
their criminal trial in 1988. The police officers were sentenced to
one month and three months in prison, respectively, and to a fine.

---

36.   J.E. 90-871 (Que. Sup. Ct.); J.E. 95-1906 (Que. C.A.); rev'd by [1998] 2 S.C.R.
      3.
37.   The *Canadian Charter of Rights and Freedoms* came into force on 17 April
      1982. Part I of the *Constitution Act, 1982,* being Schedule B to the *Canada Act
      1982* (U.K.), 1982, c. 11 (hereinafter Canadian Charter).

The Court of Appeal increased the sentences to one and two years in prison.

102. *The Action for Civil Liability* – In March 1988—six years after the incident—the plaintiff brought an action for civil liability against his torturers and their employer, the Municipal Corporation of the Town of Brome Lake.

103. *At First Instance* – Before the Superior Court, the plaintiff attempted to justify his belated action by pleading that it was absolutely impossible for him to act due to the events in question, and that this impossibility prevented him from exercising his rights at an earlier time (art. 2232 C.C.L.C.). He also argued that a thirty-year prescription period applied to cases of interference with the fundamental rights protected under the Quebec *Charter of Human Rights and Freedoms*.[38] The Superior Court dismissed the action on the basis that it was prescribed. Indeed, section 586 of the *Cities and Towns Act*[39] required the plaintiff to institute proceedings within six months of the events. According to the judge, it had not been absolutely impossible for the plaintiff to act for a period of six years.

104. *The Criterion of Superior Force* – According to the experts for both parties, during this period of time the plaintiff experienced a situation in which it was practically impossible for him to institute proceedings. However, the judge distinguished between the ability to act, which includes the courage to institute proceedings, and the absolute impossibility to act. The fact that Gauthier was able to testify before the Police Commission convinced the judge that he was not in a condition in which it was absolutely impossible for him to act during the entire six-year period.[40] According to the judge, the impossibility to act must be equivalent to superior force.

The judge dismissed the argument that a thirty-year prescription period applied to an action based upon interference with rights protected under the Quebec *Charter of Human Rights and*

---

38. R.S.Q., c. C-12 (hereinafter Quebec Charter).
39. R.S.Q., c. C-19.
40. Therefore, we can deduce that the prescriptive period was suspended until the Police Commission inquiry, namely, from 1982 until 1985.

Freedoms;[41] instead, the judge applied the six-month prescription period provided for in the *Cities and Towns Act.*[42]

105. *In the Court of Appeal* – In a judgment written by Chief Justice Michaud, with which Justices Proulx and Trudel concurred, the Court of Appeal dismissed the appeal. It equated the absolute impossibility to act with superior force, just as the judge of first instance had done. While the court acknowledged that the appellant had been severely traumatized by the events and had experienced acute fear, the court considered that it was no longer absolutely impossible for him to institute legal proceedings against the police officers and the city as of 1985, the year in which he testified before the Police Commission, or in 1986, during the police officers' preliminary inquiry. The argument regarding the thirty-year prescription period was also dismissed.

106. *In the Supreme Court* – The Supreme Court allowed the appeal. Mr. Justice Gonthier wrote the majority opinion, with which Justices L'Heureux-Dubé and Bastarache concurred. Chief Justice Lamer, with whom Madam Justice McLachlin concurred, wrote the dissenting opinion.

107. *Rejection of Superior Force* – Mr. Justice Gonthier rejected superior force as the criterion for assessing the impossibility to act. He stated that the Quebec civil law recognizes that an impossibility to act may result from the debtor's fault—for example, when the plaintiff's psychological condition of fear is caused by the defendant's fault. Thus, in contractual matters, the prescription period is suspended in an action in rescission of a contract based on fraud or error, and it does not begin to run until the day the fraud or error is discovered (art. 2258, para. 2 C.C.L.C., art. 2927 C.C.Q.). Similarly, the prescription period is suspended in an action for rescission of a contract based on fear, and it does not begin to run until the day the fear ceases (art. 2258, para. 2 C.C.L.C., art. 2927 C.C.Q.).

108. *An Objective and Subjective Assessment* – Mr. Justice Gonthier applied this rule to extracontractual matters—a rule that reflects a principle of fundamental justice inspired by the basic moral precept that no one should profit from his or her bad faith or wrongdoing. He drew a link between fear as vitiating consent and fear as a cause

41.   Above, note 38.
42.   Above, note 39.

of an impossibility to act for the purposes of article 2232 C.C.L.C. (which has now been replaced by article 2904 C.C.Q.). He relied on article 995 C.C.L.C., which defines fear amounting to a lack of consent and sets forth the characteristics of such fear.[43] In order to protect the stability of legal relations—which are the objects of prescription periods—while at the same time accurately assessing a plaintiff's fear, Mr. Justice Gonthier adopted an assessment criterion that is both objective and subjective—one inspired by the criterion applied to fear vitiating consent. He stated that the court has to determine in an objective manner whether there was a present fear involving serious harm, but it also has to determine in a subjective manner whether the fear was determinative.

109. *Fear Leading to the Impossibility to Act* – After having defined the assessment criterion, Mr. Justice Gonthier applied it to the facts. He was of the opinion that the trial judge erred in law in making a distinction between the appellant's lack of courage to initiate legal proceedings and the absolute impossibility in fact to act. Just as the Court of Appeal, the Superior Court erred in applying the objective standard of the reasonable person. Mr. Justice Gonthier relied on the testimony of the expert witnesses to conclude that Gauthier was living with such fear that it was impossible for him to act until March 1988, at which time he instituted the proceedings. The fact that Gauthier testified before the Police Commission did not indicate that it was no longer psychologically impossible for him to act. Indeed, he was compelled to testify by way of subpoena and under police protection. After having settled the issue of prescription, Mr. Justice Gonthier held the police officers and their employer liable and set damages at $300,000.

110. *The Dissenting Opinion* – The Chief Justice, with whom Madam Justice McLachlin concurred, considered that Gauthier's action was prescribed, despite the odious nature of the events in question, and he would have dismissed the appeal.

---

43. Art. 995 C.C.L.C.: "The fear whether produced by violence or otherwise must be a reasonable and present fear of serious injury. The age, sex, character and condition of the party are to be taken into consideration." Art. 1402 C.C.Q.: "Fear of serious injury to the person or property of one of the parties vitiates consent given by that party where the fear is induced by violence or threats exerted or made by or known to the other party. Apprehended injury may also relate to another person or his property and is appraised according to the circumstances."

111. *Improved Access to Justice* – By rejecting the criterion of superior force and acknowledging the psychological impossibility to act, the highest court expanded the field of application of the impossibility to act. This decision will provide improved access to justice for victims of sexual and spousal abuse whose fear may, in certain cases, prevent them from instituting proceedings.

b)   The New Wording of Article 2904 C.C.Q.

112. *Disappearance of the Requirement of Absolute Impossibility* – The *Civil Code of Québec*, in article 2904 C.C.Q., drops the requirement for an absolute impossibility to act[44] and, instead, provides for the impossibility *in fact* to act. In its draft civil code, the Civil Code Revision Office had also abandoned "absolutely" as a qualifier for the impossibility to act.[45] As for the impossibility "in law" to act, found in article 2232 C.C.L.C., article 2904 C.C.Q. does not mention it, because this ground is set forth in other articles of the *Civil Code of Québec*.[46] What is the effect of removing this qualifier? Has this reduced the plaintiff's burden of proof?[47]

---

44.   Art. 2904 C.C.Q.: "Prescription does not run against persons if it is impossible *in fact* for them to act by themselves or to be represented by others" (emphasis added).

45.   Above, note 4, Book Seven, Title I, Chap. III, art. 11. The comments are silent as regards the reasons for, or scope of, this change. See above, note 4 at 925. See also Civil Code Revision Office, Committee on the Law of Prescription, *Report on the Law of Prescription* (Montreal: 1970) at 26.

46.   Art. 2905, 2906, 2907, 2908 and 2909 C.C.Q.

47.   This is the option chosen by the following authors: Daniel Gardner, *L'évaluation du préjudice corporel* (Cowansville, QC: Les Éditions Yvon Blais, 1994) No. 21 at 15; Maurice Tancelin and Daniel Gardner, *Jurisprudence commentée sur les obligations*, 6th ed. (Montreal: Wilson and Lafleur, 1996) at 806; Patrice Deslauriers, "Recent Civil Law Developments in Extinctive Prescription," in *Contemporary Law 1994, Canadian Reports to the 1994 International Congress of Comparative Law, Athens* (Cowansville, QC: Les Éditions Yvon Blais, 1994) 126 at 149; Patrice Deslauriers "L'action en justice et l'extinction du droit d'action," in *Responsabilité*, Collection de droit 1999–2000, vol. 4 (Cowansville, QC: Les Éditions Yvon Blais, 1999) at 186. *Contra*: Frenette, above, note 5, No. 25 at 574. It is interesting to note that the Barreau du Québec had proposed that the qualifier "absolute" be kept in the article in order to "avoid having our courts adopt the liberal interpretation found in the French jurisprudence." *Mémoire du Barreau du Québec sur l'avant-projet de loi portant réforme au Code civil du Québec du droit de la prescription* (Montreal, 1989) at 12 (our translation).

113. *Various Interpretations* – The *Commentaires du ministre de la Justice*[48] are silent as to the purpose of this change. We can argue that the legislature intended no longer to require an absolute impossibility, but rather only a *relative* impossibility, thereby making it easier to provide evidence and benefiting certain victims.[49] Two judgments have already adopted this approach.[50] However, this interpretation does not solve the problem of the meaning of *relative* impossibility. Can an impossibility be *relative*? What model should we chose to assess this impossibility—a subjective model or an objective one?

114. *Recognition of the Psychological Impossibility to Act* – The new wording of article 2904 C.C.Q. must be interpreted in light of the Supreme Court decision in *Gauthier* v. *Brome Lake (Town)*[51]: the impossibility in fact to act must not be equated with superior force. The courts must recognize that the impossibility to act in fact cannot be limited to a physical impossibility. A victim's psychological condition may also constitute an impossibility in fact to act.[52]

2. *Progressive Appearance of Damage*

Progressive appearance of damage, as provided for in article 2926 C.C.Q., is another mechanism that, like the impossibility to act, tempers the application of prescription periods. In the case of progressive appearance of damage, the legislature has proposed the

---

48. Above, note 13, art. 2904 C.C.Q.
49. The legislature's intention to ensure better compensation for victims is quite evident elsewhere in the Code. For example, as regards article 2930 C.C.Q., see *Doré* v. *City of Verdun*, [1997] 2 S.C.R. 862, as well as the *Commentaires du ministre de la Justice, Introduction*, above, note 13, at VI.
50. See *Beaudoin* v. *Indemnisation des victimes d'actes criminels (IVAC)*, J.E. 96-762 (Que. Sup. Ct.); *Droit de la famille – 2530*, [1996] R.J.Q. 2981 (Que. Sup. Ct.).
51. Above, note 12.
52. See the interesting case of *Beaudoin* v. *Indemnisation des victimes d'actes criminels (IVAC)*, above, note 50 at 7, in which the judge recognized that the plaintiff's post-traumatic stress had kept him in a state in which it was impossible for him to act and prevented him from instituting proceedings within the prescription period. However, it would seem that the judge adopted this liberal attitude based on what he qualified as the "new criterion" of article 2904 C.C.Q., which, according to him, is less demanding than that of article 2232 C.C.L.C. See the comments of Mr. Justice La Forest in the matter of *M. (K.)* v. *M. (H.)*, above, note 2 at 36ff, cited below note 99, in which he describes the post-traumatic stress disorder affecting the incest victim, which condition had prevented her from instituting proceedings against her aggressor.

criterion of appearance of the damage for the "first time" as the starting point for the prescription period. This criterion calls for several comments.

a)   Appearance of Damage for the First Time

115. *Codification of the Jurisprudence* – Article 2926 C.C.Q.[53] states a well-established jurisprudential rule: the starting point for prescription is not the date on which the fault was committed, but, rather, the date on which the damage manifested itself for the first time.[54] Indeed, as long as the damage does not appear, it is impossible for the person having suffered the damage to act.[55]

b)   Criticism of the Criterion of the First Time

116. *Two Criticisms* – The criterion of the "first time" raises two problems. First, what is the meaning of "first time"? Second, what point of view do we adopt in order to determine when the damage appeared?

117. *Significant Appearance* – The use of the expression "first time" is regrettable and seems to be a poor choice.[56] As Tancelin asks quite correctly, is it not the very essence of progressive or belated damage that it cannot be detected when it appears for the first time?[57] Gardner suggests, instead, the use of "significant" appearance.[58] Baudouin and Deslauriers suggest that prescription begins to run when the plaintiff notices the first appreciable or tangible sign of the occurrence of the damage.[59] Other areas of the law also have to

---

53.   Art. 2926 C.C.Q.: "Where the right of action arises from moral, corporal or material damage appearing progressively or tardily, the period runs from the day the damage appears for the first time."

54.   See *Creighton* v. *Les Immeubles Trans-Québec inc.*, [1988] R.J.Q. 27 (Que. C.A.); *Champagne* v. *Robitaille*, [1985] R.D.J. 271 (Que. C.A.). See Jean-Louis Baudouin and Patrice Deslauriers, *La responsabilité civile*, 5th ed. (Cowansville, QC: Les Éditions Yvon Blais, 1998) No. 1717 at 1028.

55.   See *Commentaires du ministre de la Justice*, above, note 13, art. 2926 C.C.Q.

56.   In its draft Civil Code, above, note 4, the CCRO proposed the same criterion, namely, the "first time," in Book Seven, Title III, art. 51, which reads as follows: "When the damage appears progressively, the period runs from the day when the damage appears for the first time."

57.   Maurice Tancelin, *Des obligations, actes et responsabilités*, 6th ed. (Montreal: Wilson and Lafleur, 1997) No. 1506 at 761.

58.   Gardner, above, note 47, No. 21 at 15, note 46. See also *Brodeur* v. *Côte*, J.E. 96-2086 (Que. Sup. Ct.).

59.   Baudouin and Deslauriers, above, note 54, No. 1717 at 1028.

deal with a gradual appearance of damage. Thus, as regards latent defects, the issue is the gradual appearance of the defect. Article 1739 C.C.Q. stipulates that when a defect appears gradually, the time period for giving the vendor a notice of the latent defect begins to run on the day the buyer could have suspected the seriousness and extent of the defect. The criterion set forth in this article is more relevant than the criterion of the first time, because the issue at hand is not that of suspecting the existence of the damage, but rather, that of suspecting the seriousness and extent of the damage. However, the verb "suspect" seems to be a poor choice: suspicions are rarely sufficient to cause a victim to worry and notify a vendor about a latent defect.

118. *The Extent of the Damage* – Given the foregoing, we propose that the criterion of the "first time" be defined as the moment when the plaintiff becomes aware of the significance and extent of the damage, even if the damage has not manifested itself fully.[60] In this regard, we agree with the comments made by Mr. Justice Bissonnette in *Gingras* v. *Cité de Québec*:

> "But, when the damage is prospective damage, that is, damage which starts, takes shape and develops in a sort of progression which derives all its destructiveness from the same cause and does not yet reveal all of its harmful effects, one certainly cannot impose as the starting point for prescription the very day on which the smallest manifestation of the damage occurred. To do so would be to confer a right of action, but deny its useful application."[61]

119. *The Assessment Model* – In determining the "first time," another criterion comes into play: do we assess the initial appearance of the damage from the point of view of the victim (the subjective model) or from the point of view of a reasonable person (the objective model)? The model of the reasonable person, who is theoretically placed in the same circumstances as the plaintiff, is open to debate. As previously suggested (see note 62), this model is meaningless, because it relies upon the judge's opinion, without taking into account the victim's point of view.[62] It is particularly problem-

---

60. On this topic, see *April* v. *Seltzer, succession*, [1997] A.Q. No. 3694 (Que. Sup. Ct.) (Q.L.); *Matte* v. *Lirette*, [1999] A.Q. No. 179 (Que. Sup. Ct.) (Q.L.).

61. [1948] B.R. 171 at 182 (Que. C.A.) (our translation).

62. On the issue of relying upon the objective model or the subjective model in civil law, see Louise Langevin, "Responsabilité extracontractuelle et harcèlement sexuel: le modèle d'évaluation peut-il àtre neutre?" (1995) 36 *Cahiers de Droit* 99.

atic in cases of sexual and spousal abuse, where it is difficult to determine how a "reasonable" victim would react. As we have seen, normal reactions to abuse vary depending on the victim, and these cannot fit neatly into one model of a reasonable victim. At the very least, the objective model must acknowledge and incorporate the victim's perspective.[63]

Thus, the starting point for prescription can be delayed through the use of these two mechanisms for easing the application of extinctive prescription: the impossibility to act and the progressive appearance of the damage.

II. EXTINCTIVE PRESCRIPTION AS REGARDS VICTIMS OF SEXUAL AND SPOUSAL ABUSE

120. *The Reality Experienced by the Victims* – In light of the general principles of extinctive prescription, and considering the situation of victims of post-traumatic stress, including victims of sexual and spousal abuse, we can apply the elements of impossibility to act and progressive appearance of the damage. In order to apply them, and failing legislative reform to meet the needs of these victims, we propose that the courts consider the reality experienced by the victims, by acknowledging a psychological impossibility to act. The Supreme Court has already applied this jurisprudential shift in *Gauthier* v. *Brome Lake (Town)*.[64] In doing so, it will be possible to counter the effects of short prescription periods by applying tempering mechanisms—namely, the impossibility to act and the progressive appearance of the damage. This interpretation introduces an element of equity, thereby satisfying the purpose served by the suspension of prescription.[65]

We will now re-examine the foundations of prescription periods, and the mechanisms for easing their application, in light of the situation of victims of sexual and spousal abuse.

---

63.   See *Matte* v. *Lirette*, above, note 60, in which the judge adopted a subjective model in order to determine the starting point of the prescription period. The plaintiff's mother, who had consulted the defendant in this case—a doctor—and who had been informed and reassured by her friends, did not have any expertise in this area and could not, before having consulted another doctor, have suspected a link between the damage suffered by her daughter and the defendant's fault.

64.   Above, note 12.

65.   See *Commentaires du ministre de la Justice*, above, note 13 at 1821.

A. The Foundations of Prescription in Light of the Situation of Victims of Sexual and Spousal Abuse

The arguments favouring short extinctive prescription periods are based upon the assumptions that the plaintiff has all the necessary information to institute proceedings and that the defendant must be protected against the plaintiff's belated actions.[66] However, these assumptions are inapplicable to plaintiffs who have been victims of sexual or spousal abuse.

121. *The Plaintiff's Failure to Act Diligently* – First, one cannot always blame the victim for a failure to act diligently, because her failure to institute proceedings can be explained by the defendant's behaviour. The victim is very often unable to establish a causal link between the damage she has suffered and the defendant's abuse. Moreover, the damage may remain hidden even after the victim has reached adulthood.

122. *The Defendant's Peace of Mind* – Second, the defendant's peace of mind is not threatened by the delay in instituting proceedings. The defendant is very well aware that he has caused damage to his victim. Therefore, there is no sword of Damocles hanging over his head. As Mr. Justice La Forest stated in this regard, in the matter of *M. (K.)* v. *M. (H.)*: "The patent inequity of allowing these individuals to go on with their life without liability, while the victim continues to suffer the consequences, clearly militates against any guarantee of repose."[67] It is clear that the public order would be shaken if prescription periods were used to protect defendants responsible for their victim's impossibility to act.

123. *Erosion of Evidence* – Third, there always exists a possibility that evidence will wither away, even when extinctive prescription is not an issue. For example, prescription does not run against minors with respect to remedies they may exercise against their representatives (art. 2095 C.C.Q.). Thus, one can presuppose a ten-year delay for the exercise of remedies in cases of sexual abuse perpetrated against children. If we can accept the possibility that evidence will perish in these types of cases, we should be able to do the same as regards proceedings instituted by adult victims of sexual abuse.

---

66. See Mosher, above, note 7 at 181ff.
67. Above, note 2 at 29.

124. *The Protection of Public Order* – Consequently, the arguments in support of short prescription periods are not justified as regards victims of sexual or spousal abuse. In fact, these arguments were rejected in the Supreme Court decision rendered in the matter of *M. (K.) v. M. (H.).*[68] Public order would not be jeopardized if the courts were to take into account the reality experienced by psychologically traumatized victims who institute civil proceedings several years after the occurrence of the events. On the contrary, public order would be offended if the prescription mechanism were actually to prevent a given class of victims from suing their abusers.

However, failing legislative intervention to set aside these rules, as has occurred in certain Canadian provinces,[69] these rules do apply to such victims. The courts must interpret them properly to ensure that these victims have more than an illusory remedy. It is in light of this analysis, that we will examine the means for neutralizing prescription periods.

B.   The Tempering Mechanisms in Light of the Situation of Victims of Sexual and Spousal Abuse

125. *The Input of the Supreme Court* – It would be shocking if victims of sexual and spousal abuse were refused any access to the civil courts due to the very nature of the fault, the behaviour of the defendant, and the social context that prevented them from instituting proceedings within the prescribed deadlines. Rather, the Supreme Court intervened in matters of extinctive prescription. First, it recognized, in article 2904 C.C.Q., the psychological impossibility to act resulting from a fear of the defendant—a concept that applies to the victims with whom we are concerned. Second, its conclusions in the common law case of *M. (K.) v. M. (H.)*[70] are entirely relevant to the law of prescription in Quebec. As a result of these

---

68.   Ibid., at 31.
69.   In British Columbia, the *Limitation Act* was amended: persons who were victims of sexual abuse during their childhood are not subject to the limitation periods. *Limitation Amendment Act, 1992*, S.B.C. 1992, c. 44. See also *Nova Scotia Limitations of Actions Act*, R.S., c. 258, s. 2, 1993, c. 27, s. 1, which amends subsection 2(5) in order to take into account the Supreme Court's ruling in *M. (K.) v. M. (H.)*, above note 2; in Saskatchewan, *The Limitation of Actions Act*, S.S., L-15, s. 3.1; in Alberta, Bill 341, *Limitation of Actions Amendment Act*, 1993; in Prince Edward Island, *An Act to Amend the Statute of Limitations*, P.E.I.A., c. 63, s. 1; and in Newfoundland, *Limitations Act*, S.N. 1995, c. L-16.1, s.8.
70.   Above, note 2.

two decisions, victims of sexual and spousal abuse will have a means to overcome the obstacle of extinctive prescription. We will first consider the relevance of the decision in *Gauthier* v. *Brome Lake (Town)* and then the relevance of the decision in *M. (K.)* v. *M. (H.)*.

1. The Relevance of the Decision in Gauthier v. Brome Lake (Town)

By recognizing that fear can cause a psychological impossibility to act, the Supreme Court's ruling in *Gauthier* v. *Brome Lake (Town)* will allow certain victims of sexual and spousal abuse to overcome the obstacle of prescription. It is therefore an important decision. However, the Supreme Court's conclusions in this matter will not settle all problems of extinctive prescription for the victims with whom we are concerned. We will now consider the limits of this decision.

a) Recognition of the Psychological Impossibility to Act

126. *Significance of the Decision* – By rejecting superior force as the criterion for assessing the impossibility to act, the Supreme Court's ruling in *Gauthier* v. *Brome Lake (Town)*[71] will allow victims of sexual and spousal abuse to have better access to justice. Since the Supreme Court's 1941 decision in the matter of *Semmelaack* v. *Ferguson*,[72] the concept of the impossibility to act had been crippled by equating it with superior force. Very few situations—those in which the plaintiff had been kidnapped, had gone off to war, or had been unconscious—could meet this criterion. In practice, this tempering mechanism was never able to play its proper role. By drawing a distinction between the concept of the impossibility in fact to act and that of superior force, and by recognizing the psychological impossibility to act, the Supreme Court's decision in *Gauthier* extended the scope of application of the concept and allowed it to evolve. Practically speaking, the plaintiff is no longer required to prove superior force—that is, that her failure to act was unforeseeable and irresistible (art. 1470 C.C.Q.), or beyond challenge—as the Superior Court had required.[73] The courts will have to be careful so as not to indirectly reintroduce the criterion of superior force.

---

71. Above, note 12.
72. Above, note 29.
73. See above, note 36 at 18.

It should be noted that although the *Gauthier* decision was handed down pursuant to the *Civil Code of Lower Canada*, it is nonetheless relevant to the interpretation of the *Civil Code of Québec*. Indeed, even if article 1402 C.C.Q. does not set forth the circumstances to be taken into account in assessing fear—contrary to article 995 C.C.L.C., which had set forth these circumstances—article 1402 C.C.Q. nevertheless stipulates that fear is to be appraised according to the circumstances.[74] This decision, then, marks a significant turning point for victims of spousal and sexual abuse.[75]

b) The Limits of Gauthier v. Brome Lake (Town)

127. *Two Limitations* – However, the *Gauthier* decision is not without shortcomings.[76] First, the subjective–objective criterion adopted by Mr. Justice Gonthier to assess fear will not benefit all victims of sexual abuse. Second, the decision will do nothing to help victims who have been unable to act for reasons other than fear.

i) The Mixed Criterion

128. *A Criterion with Two Components* – After having rejected superior force and a purely objective assessment, Mr. Justice Gonthier adopted a criterion with two components—one objective and the other subjective. He drew a link between fear as a defect of consent, which suspends prescription, and fear as a cause of an impossibility to act, which also suspends prescription within the meaning of article 2232 C.C.L.C. At first sight, this connection seems interesting. The *Civil Code of Lower Canada* already recognized that a psychological impossibility to act could suspend prescription in actions for rescission of a contract based on fraud, error, or fear. It would seem logical to apply the same situation to extracontractual matters.

One can understand why the highest court proposed a mixed criterion. A purely objective criterion would not allow the victim's situation to be taken into account and would lead to a distinction between the courage to institute proceedings and the impossibility

---

74. See Baudouin and Jobin, above, note 9, No. 239 at 226; *Commentaires du ministre de la Justice*, above, note 13, t. 1, art. 2925 C.C.Q. at 851.

75. To date, this Supreme Court ruling has been cited with approval in a case dealing with sexual abuse: see *G.B.* v. *A.B.* on appeal, above, note 8; and in a case dealing with spousal abuse: see *Marcoux* v. *Légaré*, above, note 8.

76. See Louise Langevin, "*Gauthier c. Beaumont*: la reconnaisance de l'impossibilité psychologique d'agir," (1998) 58 *Revue du Barreau du Québec* 167.

to act, as had occurred in the Superior Court.[77] However, a purely subjective criterion could result in abuses and could threaten the stability of legal relations. As Justice Gonthier stated, "not every fear constitutes a cause of impossibility to act as soon as it exists in the victim's mind."[78]

129. *The Objective Criterion* – The objective-subjective criterion proposed by the Supreme Court is not without reproach. There may be problems with the objective component of the assessment model, in that the plaintiff must prove two objective elements in order to suspend prescription. First, there must be present fear—the victim must perceive an imminent danger. Second, the fear must contemplate serious harm—it must have a degree of seriousness.[79] Both of these criteria are assessed objectively, by applying the model of the reasonable person.

130. *The Analogy with Self-Defence* – It is interesting to draw a connection with the refusal of the courts, until 1990, to recognize self-defence for abused women who kill their spouses. Traditionally, the courts had denied them the right to raise self-defence, because, from the abstract point of view of the reasonable person, the threat to their life was not considered imminent. By taking into account the context of economic, psychological, and social oppression in which these women live—a reality that specialists have termed the battered woman syndrome—and by accepting their testimony as evidence, the Supreme Court came to understand the reasonable nature of the fear experienced by these women, and it admitted self-defence.[80]

131. *The Model of the Reasonable Person* – The same problem can arise in assessing the fear of victims of severe trauma: a victim may perceive the danger to be imminent and may fear serious harm, but this would not be the case for the reasonable person. It may be a disadvantage for these victims to have their fear assessed on the basis of an objective criterion that does not take their reality into account. The model of the reasonable person who is theoretically placed in the same circumstances as the plaintiff is problematic. As we have

---

77.   Above, note 36.
78.   Above, note 12 at 50–1.
79.   Jean-Louis Baudouin, *Les obligations*, 3rd ed. (Cowansville, QC: Les éditions Yvon Blais, 1989) at 138 and 139, cited above, note 12 at 49–50.
80.   See *R.* v. *Lavallée*, [1990] 1 S.C.R. 852; see also above §§65ff.

previously suggested, it is a model devoid of content, because it is based upon the judge's opinion and fails to consider the victim's point of view.[81]

132. *A Problem of Concordance* – While the objective component of the assessment criterion is questionable, the mixed nature of the criterion can lead to practical problems. What would happen if the assessment of the objective criteria were not to match that of the subjective criterion, which examines the determinative nature of the fear? Although not all analysts agree,[82] we believe that a contradiction does in fact exist. The courts may find it easier to give precedence to the objective criteria as a means of corroborating the subjective evidence presented,[83] as the judges in the lower courts did in *Gauthier*. In matters of fear vitiating consent, the doctrine and jurisprudence have applied an *in concreto* criterion.[84]

133. *A Proposed Solution* – To make sense of the impossibility to act, the subjective criterion—the one that takes into account the effect of fear on the victim—should take precedence over the other two objective criteria.[85] As Mr. Justice Gonthier indicated, the courts will resort to the assessments of experts and to the victim's testimony in order to assess the effect of fear on the victim. To avoid these problems, it would have been preferable to propose a criterion for assessing the impossibility to act that considers only the victim's psychological condition on the basis of expert testimony and the victim's testimony. In such a case, an expert witness would serve solely

---

81.   See Langevin, above, note 62.

82.   See Baudouin and Jobin, above, note 9, No. 242 at 228.

83.   It should be noted that in matters of rescission of contracts based on a simple error, the courts have required evidence of corroboration. See, among others, *Rawleigh* v. *Dumoulin*, [1926] S.C.R. 551; *Faubert* v. *Poirier*, [1959] S.C.R. 459. There is no indication that this is otherwise under the *Civil Code of Québec*.

84.   See Jacques Flour and Jean-Luc Aubert, *Les obligations, 1. L'acte juridique*, 7th ed. by Jean-Luc Aubert (Paris: Armand Colin, 1996) No. 227 at 153; Mazeaud, above, note 10, No. 204 at 186; Jacques Ghestin, *Traité de droit civil, Le contrat: formation*, 2nd ed. (Paris: L.G.D.J., 1988) Nos. 450 and 452 at 497 and 498. See, among others, *Sous-ministre du revenu du Québec* v. *Caron*, [1992] R.J.Q. 1084 (Que. Sup. Ct.).

85.   See Jean Pineau, Danielle Burman, and Serge Gaudet, *Théorie des obligations*, 3rd ed. (Montreal: Les éditions Thémis, 1996) No. 95 at 154. *Contra*: Maurice Tancelin, *Sources des obligations, L'acte juridique légitime* (Montreal: Wilson and Lafleur, 1993) No. 140 at 81; he states that the criterion of reasonableness is replaced by the circumstances, which he considers to be an objective criterion.

to explain certain facts to a judge, who may not be familiar with the severe consequences of sexual or spousal abuse. The presence of the expert should not serve to transform the victim's experience into an illness.[86]

ii)   Situations Other Than Fear

134. *Situations Not Included* – The Supreme Court decision in *Gauthier* will not settle all problems of extinctive prescription. It has allowed the concept of impossibility to act to evolve for victims who are paralysed with fear caused by the defendant, as was the case with *Gauthier*. It will also apply to victims of sexual and spousal[87] abuse whose post-traumatic stress prevents them from instituting proceedings. However, it will be relevant only in situations in which the victim can show that her fear was caused by the aggressor. The decision does not contemplate situations in which the victim's failure to institute proceedings does not result from fear, but from the fact that she has not made the link between her injuries and the abuse suffered in the past[88] or from other causes that are not equivalent to a psychological impossibility to act. Thus, in *G.B.* v. *A.B.*,[89] in November 1997 the plaintiff instituted an action for extracontractual liability against the defendant, alleging sexual abuse that occurred over a period of thirteen years ending in 1985. The plaintiff stated that he had been unable to institute proceedings earlier because he was unable to accept the fact that the defendant had wronged him, and, due to his inability to hate the defendant, he hated himself.[90] At first instance, the court dismissed his action on the basis of prescription. According to the allegations set forth in the declaration, the plaintiff had begun therapy in 1990 and gradually began to understand the significance of the events in his life and to understand the fact that the defendant's behaviour constituted sexual abuse. In 1995, he filed a complaint with the police. The court concluded that the plaintiff had not been in a situation in which it was impossible for him to act until November 1997, the date on which the proceedings were instituted. The Court of Appeal overturned the trial judge's ruling on the ground that, as drafted,

---

86.   See Nathalie Des Rosiers, "Childhood Sexual Abuse and the Civil Courts," (1999) *Tort Law Review* 201.
87.   See *Marcoux* v. *Légaré*, above, note 8.
88.   As was the case in *M. (K.)* v. *M. (H.)*, above, note 2.
89.   Above, note 8.
90.   Ibid., at para. 6.

the procedure did not allow the court to determine exactly on which date the appellant had been able to overcome his impossibility to act.[91]

135. *Conclusion* – The decision in *Gauthier* is a step forward as regards the impossibility to act, in that it sets aside superior force as the assessment criterion. It is a judgment that should be interpreted liberally: judges should listen to the testimony of the victims rather than seek out superior force.

C.   The Common Law Solution: The Judgment in *M. (K.)* v. *M. (H.)*

The Supreme Court of Canada's judgment in *M. (K.)* v. *M. (H.)*[92] settled the issue of prescription periods applicable to incest victims who institute civil proceedings in a common law context. The spirit of this decision can certainly be applied to Quebec civil law: it provides for a better understanding of these victims' impossibility to act. Moreover, it offers a solution for those victims not helped by the decision in *Gauthier* v. *Brome Lake (Town)*.[93] We will summarize the facts and the judgments rendered in this matter and then analyse its relevance to Quebec law.

1.   The Judgment in *M. (K.)* v. *M. (H.)*

136. *A Solution to Injustice* – The trial judge and the Court of Appeal dismissed the plaintiff's action due to the prescription period. The Supreme Court of Canada, aware of the injustices caused to incest victims by short prescription periods, proposed a presumption of awareness as the trigger for prescription.

a)   The Rulings at First Instance and on Appeal

137. *The Prescription Periods* – In this Ontario case, the plaintiff, a twenty-eight-year-old woman who had been a victim of incest at the hands of her father, instituted proceedings against her parents in 1985—twelve years after the incest stopped. The events had taken place when the victim was between eight and sixteen years old. A

---

91.   Above, note 8.
92.   Above, note 2. For an application of this decision, see, among others, *John Doe* v. *Griggs*, [2000] M.J. No. 171 (Man. Q.B.) (Q.L.).
93.   Above, note 12.

jury dismissed the action against the mother, but held the father liable, and awarded the plaintiff $50,000 in damages. However, the judge refused the verdict because of the four-year extinctive prescription period in the Ontario statute of limitations.[94] Given that the plaintiff had been able to lead her life and retain the services of an attorney, the judge rejected the argument that she had been mentally unable to understand the events and institute proceedings at an earlier time. Moreover, at the age of sixteen, the plaintiff had confided in a school guidance counsellor. The judge ruled that the prescription period had begun to run as of that moment and that her right of action had been extinguished. The Ontario Court of Appeal dismissed the appeal on the same grounds.[95]

b) The Supreme Court Ruling

138. *A Major Obstacle* – In the Supreme Court, Mr. Justice La Forest, with whom Justices Gonthier, Cory, Iacobucci, and L'Heureux-Dubé concurred, allowed the appeal. He recognized the high incidence of incest in our society, the severe consequences for its victims, and the latent nature of the injuries. He also admitted that prescription is a problem for these victims, who are not always able to institute proceedings within the prescribed deadlines.[96]

139. *Dismissal of Rationales* – First, Mr. Justice La Forest dismissed the arguments put forth to justify extinctive prescription—namely, the defendant's peace of mind, the erosion of evidence, and the plaintiff's obligation to institute proceedings diligently: ". . . many, if not most, of the damages flowing from incestuous abuse remain latent until the victim is well into adulthood. Secondly, . . . when the damages begin to become apparent, the causal connection between the incestuous activity and present psychological injuries is often unknown to the victim."[97]

140. *The Presumption of Awareness* – In order to deal with the problem posed by the starting point for prescription, Mr. Justice La Forest proposed a presumption of awareness. The victim, who has been unable to institute proceedings due to "post-incest syndrome,"[98] is presumed to have become aware of the nexus between

---

94. Paragraph 45(1)(j) of the *Limitations Act*, R.S.O. 1980, c. 240.
95. (1989), 18 A.C.W.S. (3d) 490 (Ont. C.A.).
96. Above, note 2 at 17.
97. Ibid., at 31.
98. In order to describe this syndrome, the judge cites the following extract:

her injuries and the aggressor's fault when she undergoes therapy that allows her to make this discovery. Prescription begins to run as of that moment:

> The tort claim, although subject to limitations legislation, does not accrue until the plaintiff is reasonably capable of discovering the wrongful nature of the defendant's acts and the nexus between those acts and her injuries.[99]

> In my view the only sensible application of the discoverability rule in a case such as this is one that establishes a prerequisite that the plaintiff have a substantial awareness of the harm and its likely cause before the limitations period begins to toll. It is at the moment when the incest victim discovers the connection between the harm she has suffered and her childhood history that her cause of action crystallizes.[100]

The judge also considered the issue of fraudulent concealment as applied to incest cases.[101] Given the very nature of incestuous abuse, which tries to mask its reprehensible character in the victim's eyes, the victim's right of action is delayed.

As for Justices Sopinka and McLachlin, while they agreed with the conclusion reached by Mr. Justice La Forest, they rejected the concept of a presumption of awareness because of the uncertainty of the legal effects of presumptions and the difficulties that this presumption would create for trial judges and litigants.[102]

"Although the victim may know that she has psychological problems, the syndrome impedes recognition of the nature and extent of the injuries she has suffered, either because she has completely repressed her memory of the abuse, or because the memories, though not lost, are too painful to confront directly. Thus, until she can realize that her abuser's behavior caused her psychological harm, the syndrome prevents her from bringing suit. Often it is only through a triggering mechanism, such as psychotherapy, that the victim is able to overcome the psychological blocks and recognize the nexus between her abuser's incestuous conduct and her psychological pain." Jocelyn B. Lamm, "Easing Access to the Courts by Incest Victims: Toward an Equitable Application for the Delayed Discovery Rule," (1991) 100 *Yale L. J.* 2189 at 2194, 2195, cited in *M. (K.)* v. *M. (H.)*, above, note 2 at 37. See above §§30ff.

99.   Above, note 2 at 24.
100. Ibid., at 35.
101. The appellant was not entitled to raise this means of defence upon appeal, because she had not raised it previously. However, Mr. Justice La Forest touched upon this issue in order to clarify the law.
102. Above, note 2 at 83.

2. Criticism of the Presumption of Awareness

Clearly, the presumption of awareness is not perfect. As indicated by one author,[103] who favours the abolition of prescription periods for victims of incest, the presumption raises problems on three fronts: ignorance of the law or lack of financial resources; reasonableness of the presumption of awareness; and the imposition of a uniform model on individuals.

141. *Ignorance of the Law and Financial Resources* – The presumption of awareness does not help victims who are aware of the damage and its origins, but who are unable to institute proceedings because they are either ignorant of their rights or do not have the financial resources to take action. Indeed, the courts have refused ignorance of the law as a reason for the impossibility to act, unless the ignorance results from the debtor's fault.[104] As for the problem of financial resources, many plaintiffs in cases of sexual or spousal abuse have limited financial means. The presumption of awareness is of no help to them.

142. *Reasonableness* – How do we determine the reasonableness of the moment when the injury was discovered? As of when should the victim normally have discovered the injury, particularly if the victim has undergone several therapies?[105] In *M. (K.)* v. *M. (H.),*[106] the plaintiff had had several therapeutic relationships before becoming aware of the connection between the fault and her injuries. The same problem arose in *G.B.* v. *A.B.*[107] Given that the plaintiff in *G.B.*, a victim of sexual abuse that ended in 1985, had started therapy in 1990 and had gradually begun to understand the significance of the events in his life, as was alleged in the declaration, the judge concluded that it had not been impossible for him to act until November 1997, the date on which the proceedings were instituted. Therefore, she dismissed the action on the basis of prescription. In order for the presumption of awareness to serve a purpose, we must absolutely link the reasonableness of the moment of the discovery of the injury with the victim's point of view.

---

103. Mosher, above, note 7.
104. See *Oznaga* v. *Société d'exploitation des loteries et des courses du Québec*, above, note 26.
105. See the reasoning of Madam Justice McLachlin in *M. (K.)* v. *M. (H.)*, above, note 2 at 85.
106. Above, note 2.
107. Above, note 8.

143. *Imposing a Single Model* – How do we handle victims whose behaviour differs from behaviour usually observed in other victims of sexual abuse? Obviously, the courts must interpret "post-incest syndrome" correctly in order to ensure that the model does not work to the disadvantage of plaintiffs.

3.   The Presumption of Awareness Applied to Quebec Law

144. *Relevance to Quebec Law* – The presumption of awareness established by the Supreme Court in *M. (K.)* v. *M. (H.)*,[108] which presumption serves as the starting point for prescription in common law actions instituted by victims of sexual abuse, is entirely relevant to Quebec law.[109]

145. *The Impossibility to Act* – First, the presumption places the victim in a situation in which it is impossible for her to act. A victim of sexual abuse may be aware of her current problems, but she may not know their origins, either because she has forgotten the events or because she cannot make the connection between her personal problems and these events. This situation can be explained by the defendant's behaviour—and such behaviour has been recognized in the jurisprudence as a ground for the impossibility to act. Having recourse to the presumption of awareness confirms that the victim was in a situation in which it was impossible for her to institute proceedings until she had undergone therapy that allowed her to make a connection between her problems and the sexual abuse. Indeed, article 1607 C.C.Q. requires the victim to establish a causal link, because only damages that are an immediate and direct consequence of the fault will be compensated. In certain cases, it will not be necessary for the victim to have begun therapy in order for her to benefit from the presumption of awareness and in order for prescription to begin to run. In *A.A.* v. *B.*,[110] it wasn't until 1993, and a triggering event involving her daughter, that the plaintiff, a victim of incest, made the link between the problems she was then facing and the abuse she had suffered from 1976 to 1978. As of 1993, the plaintiff knew that she had not been responsible for the sexual abuse. She instituted proceedings against her father in 1994; the

---

108.   Above, note 2.
109.   Three relevant decisions reported in Quebec cite the Supreme Court ruling: *Sauveteurs et victimes d'actes criminels—1*, [1995] C.A.S. 1; *G.B.* v. *A.B.*, above, note 8; *A.A.* v. *B.*, above, note 8.
110.   Above, note 8.

action was not prescribed.[111] The crime victims compensation review board (*Bureau de révision de l'indemnisation des victimes d'actes criminels*) uses the criterion of the impossibility to act in order to explain why certain victims delay in filing an application for benefits pursuant to the *Crime Victims Compensation Act*.[112]

146. *Significant Appearance of the Damage* – The presumption of awareness established by the Supreme Court in *M. (K.)* v. *M. (H.)*[113] agrees with article 2926 C.C.Q. The victim became aware for the first time—that is, in a significant manner—of the damage she had suffered only after having begun the therapy; the therapy allowed her properly to understand the connection between the fault and the consequences, and to institute proceedings.

147. *Reducing the Burden of Proof* – The presumption facilitates the victim's task of presenting evidence: the impossibility ceases when the victim undergoes therapy that allows her to make a connection between the fault and her current problems. Clearly, it is up to the judge to decide at what moment the presumption of awareness applies. The defendant can then attempt to reverse the presumption.

148. *Other Presumptions of a Causal Link* – Reliance upon the presumption of a causal link—the presumption of awareness is of the same type—is not new to the civil law. The Supreme Court proposed such a presumption in *Morin* v. *Blais*.[114] When a provision of law seeks to avoid a situation, and the situation occurs, there is a presumption of a causal link between the breach of the safety standard and the resulting damage.

149. *A Legislative Amendment* – The Supreme Court, aware of the limits of its solution in *M. (K.)*, called for legislative reform in this

---

111. See also *L.J.* v. *G.T.*, [1998] O.J. No. 4777 (Ont. Gen. Div.) (Q.L.), in which the plaintiff realized the consequences of her father's abuse when she found her daughter, whom she had given up for adoption. The court concluded that prescription began to run as of that moment. See also *S.L.* v. *S.A.*, [1999] O.J. No. 1267 (Ont. Gen. Div.) (Q.L.).
112. R.S.Q., c. I-6. See *Sauveteurs et victimes d'actes criminels—1*, above, note 109; *Décision du Bureau de révision de la région de l'Outaouais*, File No. 0 0726 6745, 11 May 1995; *Décision du Bureau de révision de la région de Montréal*, File No. 0 0622 3457, 19 December 1994.
113. Above, note 2.
114. [1977] 1 S.C.R. 570.

area, and noted the proposals made by certain provinces to abolish prescription periods for victims of sexual abuse.[115] Should Quebec fall into step with the other Canadian provinces[116] and amend the Civil Code so that extinctive prescription periods will no longer apply to incest victims? An amendment would certainly be desirable, but this solution is not very practical. First, a solution is needed urgently; yet, given the slowness of the legislative process, particularly as regards the Civil Code, it would be wishful thinking to believe that the legislature will intervene quickly. Moreover, the possibility of legislative intervention provides an easy way out for a judge who is not inclined to intervene. We believe that the Civil Code already has the resources to adapt itself to the needs of these victims, as evidenced in the Supreme Court decision in *Gauthier* v. *Brome Lake (Town)*.[117]

III. CONCLUSION

150. *The Reality Experienced by the Victims* – Prescription periods, which constitute an obstacle to the compensation of victims of sexual and spousal abuse, must be adjusted to take into account the reality experienced by these plaintiffs. The arguments in support of prescription periods—arguments that generally seek to protect defendants—cannot be justified in such circumstances. A victim's right to compensation weighs more heavily than the defendant's right to speed and peace of mind. The starting point for prescription must be delayed either because the victim was in a state in which it was psychologically impossible for her to act or because, in the victim's eyes, the injuries had not appeared. In such matters, the Supreme Court is on the right track. It is now up to the courts of Quebec to show an open mind as regards these victims.

---

115. Above, note 2 at 49. The problem caused to victims by extinctive prescription does not seem to have been considered in the work of the CCRO, in the reform of the *Civil Code of Québec*, or in the doctrine. See Quebec, National Assembly, *Journal des débats (Hansard)*, Commissions parlementaires, sous-commission des institutions, 1st Session, 34th Legislature at SC1-1182ff. See Madeleine Cantin Cumyn, "Les principaux éléments de la révision des règles de la prescription," (1989) 30 *Cahiers de Droit* 611; Jean Pineau, "Les grandes lignes de la réforme portant sur le droit de la preuve et de prescription," (1989) 1 *Cours de perfectionnement du Notariat* 1; Barreau du Québec, *Mémoire du Barreau du Québec sur l'avant-projet de loi portant réforme au Code civil du Québec du droit de la prescription*, above, note 47 at 12.
116. For the provincial legislative reforms, see above, note 69.
117. Above, note 12.

Chapter 4
Remedies

151. *The Victim's Remedies* – Victims of sexual or spousal abuse may use several legal avenues. They may institute proceedings against several defendants for extracontractual civil liability pursuant to the *Civil Code of Québec* (C.C.Q.). They may also file a claim for compensation pursuant to the *Crime Victims Compensation Act* (C.V.C.A.)[1] or *An Act Respecting Industrial Accidents and Occupational Diseases* (A.I.A.O.D.).[2]

I. REMEDY IN EXTRACONTRACTUAL LIABILITY

152. *Overview* – By virtue of article 1457 C.C.Q., a victim who institutes proceedings for extracontractual liability must prove **three** essential elements: fault, causation, and injury.[3] Before analysing the conditions for the application of this remedy, we must first consider a preliminary matter: the remedy available pursuant to the Quebec *Charter of Human Rights and Freedoms*.[4]

A. Preliminary Question: Remedy under the Quebec *Charter of Human Rights and Freedoms*

Given the Supreme Court's position regarding the relationship between the Quebec Charter and article 1457 C.C.Q., with the exception of punitive damages, a plaintiff will not gain any addi-

---

1. R.S.Q., c. I-6 (hereinafter C.V.C.A.).
2. R.S.Q., c. A-3.001 (hereinafter A.I.A.O.D.). See also *S.T.* v. *Gaskell* (1997), 147 D.L.R. (4th) 730 (Ont. Gen. Div.).
3. Although a defendant's capacity to judge his actions also constitutes an essential element of extracontractual liability, we will not address this issue, because it does not pose a particular problem in the cases relevant to our discussion.
4. R.S.Q., c. C-12.

tional advantages from basing a remedy upon the Charter, regardless of whether she relies both on the Charter and the Civil Code or only upon the Charter.

153. *Interference with Fundamental Rights* – As we will see, sexual or spousal abuse constitutes a fault within the meaning of article 1457 C.C.Q. The abuse also constitutes interference with the victim's right to life, personal security, inviolability, freedom (section 1), dignity (section 4), and privacy (section 5), all of which are fundamental rights protected under the Quebec *Charter of Human Rights and Freedoms*. Therefore, as set forth in section 49 of the Charter, a victim can also exercise a remedy based upon the Charter. Does this mean that she can assert two separate grounds—fault pursuant to article 1457 C.C.Q. and unlawful interference pursuant to the Charter—and possibly be compensated twice?

154. *No Right to Combine Remedies* – A victim may rely upon the Civil Code and the Charter, but she will not be entitled to double compensation. In *Béliveau Saint-Jacques* v. *F.E.E.S.P.*,[5] the Supreme Court decided that an infringement of a right protected under the Charter also constitutes a civil fault and that the Charter does not create a compensation system that is parallel to the *jus commune*. Therefore, a victim cannot rely upon the Charter in order to obtain additional compensatory damages or even a symbolic amount on the basis that her fundamental rights have been infringed. However, recourse to the Charter is still useful: a plaintiff must rely upon the Charter to obtain punitive damages pursuant to the second paragraph of section 49, given that the Civil Code does not provide for such damages and they must be provided for by law (article 1621 C.C.Q.).[6]

155. *Trivialization of the Remedies* – In our opinion, by adopting the theory of an overlap between the infringement of a right protected under the Charter and a fault under article 1457 C.C.Q. in *Béliveau Saint-Jacques*,[7] the highest court opened the door to triviliazing remedies under the Charter, because plaintiffs will not be entitled to obtain other compensatory damages, such as a symbolic amount.[8]

---

5.   [1996] 2 S.C.R. 345, 405 (Gonthier, J.) (hereinafter *Béliveau Saint-Jacques*).
6.   The issue of punitive damages is discussed in greater detail below, §§317ff.
7.   Above, note 5.

Given this decision, we will focus on remedies based on article 1457 C.C.Q. However, nothing prevents a plaintiff from relying solely on the Charter or from relying upon the Charter in conjunction with the Civil Code. Indeed, the conditions for the remedy in extracontractual liability also apply to an action instituted under the Quebec Charter.

B. Fault

156. *The Various Defendants* – Actions for extracontractual liability for sexual or spousal abuse are often instituted against the aggressor. Other persons having been involved in the events may also be sued as a result of their wrongful conduct. These other persons include professionals who have failed to inform the appropriate authorities about the abuse and who have not abided by their duty to report. They may also include the other parent, who did not perpetrate the abuse, but who hid the aggression and failed in her duty to protect. Other elements in the social fabric, such as establishments working with children, child protection authorities, police and prison authorities, and hospitals, may also be sued for having failed to abide by their duty to protect. In addition to these defendants, who may be held liable for their own personal fault, there are defendants who are responsible for the faults of others; these may include the employers, parents, or educators of the aggressor. It is crucial that a victim be able to sue defendants for their own personal fault as well as for the fault of persons for whom they are responsible; this provides the victim with the assurance that she will be able to enforce her judgment if the aggressor is insolvent. Within the same vein of ensuring full compensation for victims, we will also examine the possibility of suing the insurers of the aforementioned defendants.

1. Responsibility for One's Personal Fault

Several people must answer for their own personal fault. In addition to the aggressor, who is responsible for the consequences of

---

8. As regards the trivialization of remedies under the Quebec Charter, see Louise Langevin, "Le harcèlement sexuel au travail: l'impact de la décision *Béliveau Saint-Jacques*," (1997) 9 *Revue Femmes et Droit* 17; Ghislain Otis, "Le spectre d'une marginalisation des voies de recours découlant de la Charte québécoise," (1991) 51 *Revue du Barreau du Québec* 561; Maurice Drapeau, "La responsabilité pour atteinte illicite aux droits et libertés de la personne," (1994) 28 *Revue juridiques thémis* 31.

the abuse, there are other people who may be held liable for having failed to abide by their duty to report and protect.

a)   The Abuse: The Aggressor's Fault

The plaintiff must prove the defendant's fault within the meaning of article 1457 C.C.Q. However, the aggressor, who may be the victim's biological or adoptive father, husband, uncle, or teacher, may try to raise certain defences.

i)   Determining Fault

157. *Fault Pursuant to Article 1457 C.C.Q.* – Sexual or spousal abuse is a fault pursuant to article 1457 C.C.Q., given that this type of behaviour constitutes an offence under the Criminal Code.[9] The wording of article 1457 provides that the rules of conduct applicable to everyone result from circumstances, usage, or the law—and the Criminal Code is a law.

158. *The Link between a Criminal Fault and a Civil Fault* – Although the breach of a legal obligation does not always constitute a fault,[10] the criminal nature of spousal or sexual abuse automatically makes it a civil fault. Nonetheless, in *Larocque* v. *Côté*,[11] where

---

9.   The following sections of the Criminal Code refer to offences of a sexual nature: ss. 151 (sexual interference), 152 (sexual exploitation of a child under fourteen years of age), s. 153 (sexual exploitation of a young person), s. 153.1 (sexual exploitation of person with disability), s. 155 (incest), s. 159 (anal intercourse), s. 160 (bestiality), s. 163.1 (child pornography), ss. 170 and 171 (aiding and abetting in sexual activities by young people), s. 172 (corrupting children), s. 173 (exposure), s. 173 (2) (exposure to a young child), s. 174 (nudity), s. 210 (bawdy house), s. 211 (transporting persons to bawdy houses), s. 212 (procuring), s. 212 (4) (juvenile prostitution), s. 213 (public prostitution), s. 265 (2) (assault—application of the section to sexual assault), s. 271 (sexual assault—included offence: s. 265 assault), s. 272 (sexual assault with a weapon, threats to a third party, or causing bodily harm), s. 273 (aggravated sexual assault), ss. 273.1, 273.2 (notion of consent with respect to sexual assault), s. 273.3 (removal of child from Canada), s. 810.1 (fear of offence of a sexual nature).

10.   See Maurice Tancelin, *Des obligations, actes et responsabilités*, 6th ed. (Montreal: Wilson and Lafleur, 1997), No. 634 at 318. *Contra*: Jean-Louis Baudouin and Patrice Deslauriers, *La responsabilité civile*, 5th ed. (Cowansville, QC: Les Éditions Yvon Blais, 1998), No. 149 at 109. See Pierre-Gabriel Jobin, "La violation d'une loi ou d'un règlement entraîne-t-elle la responsabilité civile?" (1984) 44 *Revue du Barreau du Québec* 222.

11.   *Larocque* v. *Côte*, [1996] R.J.Q. 1930 (Que. Sup. Ct.)

a soldier was sexually abused by his colleagues during boot camp, the judge attempted to assess the defendant's behaviour in light of the evolution of current standards. The judge had the following to say as regards the determination of fault: "In this case, the abuse constitutes a fault which results in liability because the defendants' conduct *is socially unacceptable in our day and age*, as we recently saw with respect to 'initiation rites' practised by certain Canadian Armed Forces battalions and the resulting outcry in the general public and the media."[12]

Is this to say that if the population and the media had not reacted negatively to the army's behaviour, such behaviour would not have resulted in liability? Certainly not, because the actions constituted a crime, and a reasonable person would not have acted in such a manner. Societal safety requires that a criminal fault must always constitute a civil fault within the meaning of article 1457 C.C.Q.

ii)   Grounds of Defence

In response to evidence of fault presented by a victim, the defendant may attempt to raise two grounds of defence: the victim's consent and the defence of spousal immunity.

(a)   The Victim's Consent

159. *The Relevance of Consent* – A victim's consent to the sexual act is not always relevant as a ground of defence. This defence cannot be raised under the criminal law when the victim's age does not allow one to conclude that there truly was consent. Similarly, a victim's consent will not exonerate a professional as regards determination of his fault. In other cases in which this ground of defence can be raised,[13] the defendant must show that the victim's consent was free and informed—that is, that it did not result from exploitation.

---

12.   Ibid. at 1933 (emphasis added; our translation).
13.   This defence was raised, and rejected, in *Pie* v. *Thibert*, [1976] C.S. 180 (Que. Sup. Ct.). In the Canadian common law provinces, the defence was accepted in *Lyth* v. *Dagg* (1988), 46 C.C.L.T. 25 (B.C. S.C.).

Consent in Children

160. *Consent in Criminal Law* – Pursuant to the Criminal Code, the absence of consent on the part of the victim is an essential element in matters of sexual assault.[14] Thus, evidence of the victim's consent is a means of defence for the accused. However, in certain cases, consent will not be admitted as a defence. It cannot be relied upon against a child who is less than twelve years old (s. 150.1 (1) Cr. C.). If the child is between twelve and fourteen years of age, the defence may be raised, but only when the defendant is of the same age and is not in a position of authority (s. 150.1 (2) Cr. C.). If the child is between fourteen and eighteen years of age, the defence of consent will be admitted, provided there is no relationship of authority between the parties (s. 153 Cr. C.). Consent is never admitted as a defence in cases of incest. The justification for this prohibition is our desire to avoid the exploitation of children and its adverse consequenses; as a result of the position of authority that aggressors have over these children, the children are not in a position to give a valid consent.[15]

161. *Consent in Matters of Extracontractual Liability* – The reasons why consent is not a valid defence with respect to certain offences of a sexual nature are entirely relevant in civil law matters. Indeed, one can certainly cast doubt on the free and voluntary nature of the consent given by a child or teenager in such a situation.[16] Moreover, to allow such a defence would be to shock the public order and frustrate the goals of protecting minors.

---

14.   Section 273.1 Cr. C. See William A. Schabas, *Les infractions d'ordre sexuel* (Cowansville, QC: Les Éditions Yvon Blais, 1995) at 125ff.
15.   See, among others, *R.* v. *Halleran* (1987), 39 C.C.C. (3d) 177 (Nfld. C.A.); *R.* v. *K.S.V.* (1994), 89 C.C.C. (3d) 477 (Nfld. C.A.); *R.* c. *Ferguson* (1987), 36 C.C.C. (3d) 507 (B.C. C.A.). See Phyllis Coleman,"Sex in Power Dependency Relationship: Taking Unfair Advantage of the 'Fair Sex'," (1988) 53 *Alberta Law Review* 95. See the testimony of Nathalie Schweighoffer in *J'avais douze ans . . .* (Paris: Fixot, 1990), where she explains how she submitted to her father because she had no other choice. Abusers obtain the cooperation of children in various ways. They often resort to physical abuse or authority, or they may achieve their purpose by using games or by presenting the sexual activity as punishment or affection, or as a means for perfecting the child's sexual education. See the testimony of victims in Women's Research Centre, *Recollecting our Lives: Women's Experiences of Childhood Sexual Abuse* (Vancouver: Press Gang Publishers, 1989), ch. 2.
16.   See *J.B.* v. *R.B.*, [1994] O.J. No. 324 (Ont. Gen. Div.) (Q.L.).

Consent in Matters of Disciplinary Law

162. *A Disciplinary Fault* – The *Code of Ethics of Physicians*[17] and the *Code of Ethics of Psychologists*[18] prohibit any physical contact between the psychologist, the psychiatrist, or the physician and his patient. Therefore, any such sexual relationship constitutes a breach of a legal obligation and, thereby, a fault within the meaning of article 1457 C.C.Q. Evidence that the patient consented or took the initiative,[19] or that the amorous relationship was not abusive,[20] is irrelevant. The prohibition is justified by the patient's vulnerability and her inability to give free and informed consent.[21] A judge of the Professions Tribunal stated the following in this regard:

"The objective fact of having had sexual relations with a client has a seriously prejudicial effect on the very essence of the profession which is based upon a relationship of assistance and trust between the client and her psychologist, regardless of the circumstances surrounding the actions which are reproached. It is the very basis of the client–therapist relationship which is affected."[22]

The Supreme Court of Canada also commented on this matter in *Norberg* v. *Wynrib*.[23] It recognized that consent given in a situation of dependency cannot be valid if the stronger party takes advantage of the situation, as is the case in a relationship between a parent and a child, a physician and a patient, a professor and a student, an attorney and a client, or an employer and an employee.

---

17. Section 2.03.08, *Code of Ethics of Physicians*, R.R.Q. 1981, c. M-9, r. 4.
18. Sections 13 and 58 (11), *Code of Ethics of Psychologists*, R.R.Q., c. C-26, r. 148.1.
19. See *Psychologues (Corp. professionnelle des)* v. *D'Souza*, [1993] D.D.C.P. 276 (Que. Prof. Trib.).
20. See *Psychologues (Ordre professionnel des)* v. *Choquette*, [1996] D.D.O.P. 142 (Committee on discipline of the Ordre professionnel des psychologues du Québec); *Psychologues (Ordre professionnel des)* v. *Trudel*, [1998] D.D.O.P. 183 (Committee on discipline of the Ordre professionnel des psychologues du Québec), AZ-98041086.
21. See *Médecins (Ordre professionnel des)* v. *Lapointe*, [1995] D.D.O.P. 104 (Committee on discipline of the Ordre professionnel des médecins du Québec); Kenneth S. Pope and Jacqueline C. Bouhoutsos, *Sexual Intimacy between Therapists and Patients* (New York: Praeger, 1986) at 37.
22. *Psychologues (Corp. professionnelle des)* v. *D'Souza*, above, note 19 at 279 (our translation).
23. [1992] 2 S.C.R. 224. See *L.T.* v. *McGillivray* (1993), 143 N.B.R. (2d) 24 (N.B. Q.B.) and *D.C.B.* v. *Boulianne*, [1996] B.C.J. No. 2183 (B.C. S.C.) (Q.L.), which applied *Norberg*. See P. Coleman, above, note 15.

In this case, the plaintiff, a drug addict, had been the victim of sexual abuse by her physician over a period of two years. She obtained drugs in exchange for sex. Under these circumstances, it was difficult to consider that she had consented to the sexual intercourse, as her physician had claimed.

Consent Pursuant to Article 1457 C.C.Q.

In some cases, a defendant may raise consent as a defence for his fault. However, the consent must be free and informed—that is, it must be free of any exploitation. We will now examine consent to sexual relations given by adolescents over fourteen years of age and by adults.

163. *Consent Given by an Adolescent* – In some situations, sexual relations between an adolescent and an adult aggressor may have begun when the child was younger and was not in a position to refuse. Such relations may have continued until the child became an adolescent. Some courts have had difficulty in determining whether or not consent was voluntary under such circumstances. In a tort action, the defendant, who was the plaintiff's foster father, raised the defence of consent against the victim, who was fifteen years old and had been in foster care with him for more than ten years. He had previously pleaded guilty to a sexual assault under section 153 Cr. C. The trial judge dismissed the action based, in part, upon the plaintiff's consent.[24] According to the judge, the victim had indicated her consent by means including discussions on the consequences of having sexual intercourse with the defendant and on the use of contraceptives.

On appeal, the court reversed the ruling and refused the argument based on consent, even if it accepted evidence that the victim had consented.[25] According to the court, the defendant's behaviour was equivalent to incest, and it would be unthinkable for the courts to allow such a defence in these types of cases. The court emphasized that consent is not a permissible defence against an accusation based upon section 153 Cr. C.

---

24.   *M.M.* v. *K.K.* (1987), 11 B.C.L.R. (2d) 90 (B.C. S.C.). See Nathalie Des Rosiers, "Limitation Periods and Civil Remedies for Childhood Sexual Abuse," (1992) 9 *Canadian Family Law Quarterly* 43.

25.   *M.M.* v. *K.K.* (1989), 38 B.C.L.R. (2d) 273 (B.C. C.A.).

The result of the court's reasoning is in keeping with the situation faced by these adolescents who are not in a position to give an unfettered consent. However, the grounds for its decision are debatable. What position would the Court of Appeal have adopted if no criminal indictment had been laid or if the indictment had resulted in an acquittal? The court would not have been able to establish a link between the criminal law and the civil law. In our opinion, the court should have focused on the victim's consent and analysed the relationship of authority between the parties.

This is the position the court adopted in the British Columbia case of *Harder* v. *Brown*.[26] As a defence to a civil action, the defendant argued that, over time and as the victim matured, she consented to the sexual activity. According to the facts, from the age of ten to the age of sixteen, the victim had gone to the home of the defendant, a friend of the family, in order to do some housework, at which time she would have sexual relations with the defendant. However, given the victim's psychological condition and her difficult family situation, the judge refused to consider her behaviour as an equivalent to consent, particularly when she was older. The judge stated the following:

> Deprived of love, and anything approaching a normal family life, the plaintiff was highly vulnerable to the very evil which the defendant visited upon her. Driven by his perverted lusts, he exploited his intimate knowledge of her family's weaknesses. He offered her the affection and attention which these weaknesses denied her and which she so desperately needed. As time went by, he gradually expanded the scope of his assaults and increased his influence over her self-respect to the point where there was no will left to resist that which others would too easily characterize as preventable. When she needed sympathy, understanding, an opportunity to unburden herself of her troubled thoughts and even money, he was always there. But there was a terrible price attached to his friendship and she paid that price so often that she gradually lost the ability to question it.[27]

In sum, the consent of an adolescent victim cannot always be deduced from her behaviour, because she is in a position of inferiority, whether psychologically, physically, or economically.[28]

---

26. (1989), 50 C.C.L.T. 85 (B.C. S.C.).
27. Ibid. at 94.
28. See also *G.B.R.* v. *Hollett* (1995), 143 N.S.R. (2d) 38, [1995] N.S.J. No. 328 (N.S. Sup. Ct.) (Q.L.) at para. 12: "Hollett abused his position of authority to seduce a naive and vulnerable young girl. Although not physically captive, the

164. *Consent Given by an Adult* – Similarly, consent given by an adult must be evaluated in the light of the relationship between the victim and her aggressor. In cases in which the victim is in a position of inferiority—whether physically, psychologically, or economically—her consent to the sexual relations may be vitiated if the stronger party exploits the situation.[29]

(b) The Defence of Spousal Immunity

165. *An Inapplicable Defence* – Certain defendants, faced with spousal abuse proceedings before the civil courts, have raised the defence of immunity between the spouses, which would prevent a wife from suing her husband for spousal abuse and which, in a way, would recognize a husband's right to discipline his wife. This argument has been rejected.[30] Thus, marriage cannot serve as an excuse for spousal abuse and will not prevent the institution of proceedings. Similarly, divorce proceedings will not settle such matters.[31]

The plaintiff can sue not only the aggressor, but also other defendants who committed a personal fault.

b)   Breach of a Duty to Report

166. *The Duty to Report* – Since its adoption in 1977,[32] the *Youth*

---

plaintiff was throughout the relationship, under Hollett's control psychologically. Any suggestion that the plaintiff consented to this activity is irrelevant in the circumstances. Hollett is liable for the abuse he inflicted upon the plaintiff."

29.   See *S.S.* v. *H.& D.P.M. Inc.*, [1999] O.J. No. 4802 (Ont. Sup. Ct.) (Q.L.).

30.   See *Beaumont-Butcher* v. *Butcher*, [1982] C.S. 893 (Que. Sup. Ct.). This is a common law argument that recognized immunity between spouses until the 1970s. See Wanda A. Weigers, "Compensation for Wife Abuse: Empowering Victims" (1994) 28 *University of British Columbia Law Review* 247 at 262ff.

31.   See *Droit de la famille – 2207*, [1995] R.J.Q. 1506 (Que. Sup. Ct.); *Droit de la famille – 1601*, [1992] R.D.F. 346 (Que. C.A.); *Lacombe* v. *D'Avril*, [1983] C.S. 592 (Que. Sup. Ct.); *Lakatos* v. *Sary*, J.E. 92-6 (Que. Sup. Ct.); *Bérubé* v. *Bilodeau*, J.E. 95-1244 (C.Q.). The following common law decisions have awarded damages for spousal abuse within the scope of divorce proceedings: *R.V.* v. *R.V.*, [1995] O.J. No. 3703 (Ont. Gen. Div.) (Q.L.); *Johal* v. *Johal*, [1996] O.J. No. 419 (Ont. Gen. Div.) (Q.L.), aff'd [1997] O.J. No. 4210 (Ont. C.A.) (Q.L.); *Valenti* v. *Valenti*, [1996] O.J. No. 522 (Ont. Gen. Div.) (Q.L.), aff'd [1998] O.J. No. 2242 (Ont. C.A.) (Q.L.); *Bellsmith* v. *Bellsmith*, [1996] B.C.J. No. 289 (B.C. S.C.) (Q.L.); *Surgeoner* v. *Surgeoner*, [1993] O.J. No. 2940 (Ont. Gen. Div.) (Q.L.).

32.   S.Q. 1977, c. 20, ss. 39ff.

Protection Act[33] has imposed the obligation on all persons to report suspected situations of sexual abuse against children.[34] Moreover, with the exception of attorneys, professionals also have the obligation to report all situations in which they suspect the child's well-being is in danger—that is, the existence of any of the grounds described in sections 38 and 38.1 of the *Youth Protection Act*.[35] In this regard, the approach in Quebec is similar to the approach adopted in the other Canadian provinces.[36]

167. *The Questions Raised* – These obligations to report raise a number of important questions. Does a breach of one's duty to report constitute a fault? Under what circumstances do the courts

---

33. R.S.Q., c. P-34.1.
34. Section 39 reads as follows: "Any person, other than a [professional], who has reasonable grounds to believe that the security or development of a child is considered to be in danger within the meaning of subparagraph g of the first paragraph of section 38 [sexual abuse or physical ill-treatment through violence or neglect] must bring the situation to the attention of the director without delay."
35. These grounds include the parents' failure to assume responsibility for the child's care or education (38(a)), the fact that the child's development is threatened by isolation or continuous emotional rejection (38(b)), the fact that the child's physical health is threatened by lack of appropriate care (38(c)), the fact that the child is deprived of the material conditions of life appropriate to his or her needs (38(d)), the fact that the child is in the custody of a person whose behaviour or way of life creates a risk of moral or physical danger for the child (38(e)), cases in which the child is forced or induced to beg or to perform for the public in a manner that is unacceptable (38(f)), cases in which the child has serious behavioural disturbances which his or her parents ignore (38(h)), cases in which the child leaves his or her own home or dwelling without authorization (38.1(a)), cases in which the child does not attend school, or is frequently absent without reason (38.1(b)), and cases in which the child's parents do not carry out their obligations to provide him or her with care and education, while he or she has been entrusted to the care of an institution or foster family for one year (38.1(c)).
36. See *Children's Services Act*, R.S.N.S. 1989, c. 68, s. 78; *Family Services Act*, S.N.B. 1980, c. C-2.1, s. 30; *Child and Family Services Act*, R.S.O. 1990, c. C-11, s. 72 ; *Child and Family Services Act*, C.C.S.M., c. C-80, s. 18(1); *The Family Services Act*, R.S.S. 1978, c. F-7, s. 16, as am. by R.S.S. 1989–90, c. C-7.2, s. 12; *Child Welfare Act*, S.A. 1984, c. C-8.1, s. 3; *Family and Child Services Act*, S.B.C. 1980, c. 11. It should be noted that pursuant to the *Children's Act*, R.S.Y. 1986, c. 22, s. 115, there is no obligation in the Yukon to report abuse against children. See also, to the same effect: *Child Welfare Act*, R.S.N.W.T. 1974, c. C-3, s. 15. See also Ronda Bessner, "The Duty to Report Child Abuse," (2000) 17 *Canadian Family Law Quarterly* 277, which provides a detailed analysis of the scope of the different provincial statutes. For a detailed analysis of the Alberta statute, see Wayne N. Renke, "The Mandatory Reporting of Child Abuse under the *Child Welfare Act*," (1999) 7 *Health Law Journal* 91.

impose consequences for such a fault? Should we distinguish between cases in which a child directly discloses the sexual abuse and those in which suspicions are aroused without direct knowledge of the abuse? These questions will be examined in the following sections.

i)   The Duty to Report a Child's Confidences

168. *Fault* – One might think that, for example, any person in whom a child has confided about incidents of abuse since 1977 has committed a fault if the person did not believe the child or failed to report the abuse. This would constitute a breach of a statutory obligation that is equivalent to any other breach of the law[37] and, therefore, constitutes a breach of a standard of conduct imposed by law (article 1457 C.C.Q.). Does such a fault always result in liability pursuant to article 1457 C.C.Q.?

169. *Difficulties Relating to Causation* – Given that a breach of an obligation imposed by law is a fault within the meaning of article 1457 C.C.Q., such a breach should result in liability if one can conclude that the failure to report "caused" an injury.[38] If the sexual

---

37.   See Baudouin and Deslauriers, above, note 10, at No. 149 at 109–10. See, however, *Coulonval* v. *M.L. et al.*, REJB 1998-08314 (C.Q.), where the court questions whether the wording of the *Youth Protection Act* obliges a professional to report when he or she considers that there is no imminent or real danger to a child. The court suggests that this amounts to granting to the psychologist and other professionals discretion to evaluate the reasonableness of grounds prior to reporting, as opposed to leaving such discretion up to the Youth Protection Services in their decision to act upon the complaint. A similar conclusion (i.e., that a discretion exists whether or not to report) was reached in the cases of criminal prosecutions. See below, note 42, for a full discussion and critique of these cases. Furthermore, there seems to be a growing backlash by plaintiffs claiming to have been falsely accused of sexually abusing a child against social workers or police who investigate sexual abuse allegations. The Youth Protection Services (*M.D.* v. *L.D. and J-R.S. and le Directeur de la Protection de la Jeunesse et al.*, REJB 1998-06122 (C.A.Q.) and the police (*Alain* v. *P.G. Québec et al.*, REJB 1999-14394 (Que. Sup. Ct.); *C.M.* v. *Procureur général du Québec et al.*, REJB 1998-08655 (Que. Sup. Ct.) have been sued by plaintiffs claiming to have been falsely accused of sexually abusing a child. Such liability may affect the conduct of agencies so that the "standard of care" in responding to allegations may change in the years to come. It may again become difficult to establish that failing to believe a child who discloses sexual abuse is, in and of itself, a fault.

38.   See the discussion of similar allegations made against a hospital employee: *Victoria General Hospital* v. *General Accident Assurance Co. of Canada*, [1995] 8 W.W.R. 106; (1995) 103 Man.R. (2d) 168; (1995) 32 C.C.L.I.(2d) 243; [1995]

abuse continued, the failure to report may have contributed to the severity of the injuries suffered. In our opinion, new instances of sexual abuse will not break the causal link, because they are a foreseeable consequence of the failure to report, particularly if the child is in continuous contact with the aggressor.[39] Although there can be no certainty that disclosure to the authorities will prevent further sexual abuse,[40] the breach of such an express statutory obligation must necessarily elicit a severe reaction on the part of the courts. At the very least, the child will have lost her chance to minimize the effects of prolonged sexual exploitation.[41] At this stage, there is little case law supporting extracontractual liability for the failure to act or to report sexual abuse.[42]

M.J. No. 276 (Man. Q.B.) (Q.L.), in which the plaintiff alleged that in 1973, while she was a patient at the hospital, she confided in a hospital employee that she had been sexually abused by a school counsellor. The hospital employee did nothing, and the abuse continued. In *A.J.* v. *Cairnie Estate* (1999), 136 Man.R. (2d) 84, the Manitoba Court of Queen's Bench concluded that a social worker and her employer were 25 per cent liable for the injuries suffered by a plaintiff who was abused by her stepfather.

39. For an application of this principle, see *Goodwin* v. *Commission scolaire Laurenval*, [1991] R.R.A. 673 (Que. Sup. Ct.), in which the court recognized the defendant's liability for the wounds that the young girl inflicted upon herself when she panicked while trying to flee her agressor. The judge considered the attempt to flee as a foreseeable consequence of the abuse. See also the analysis of the causal link, below, at §§259 ff.

40. Unfortunately, it would seem that, too often, the youth protection authorities are powerless to remedy situations of sexual abuse, either due to a lack of evidence or lack of personnel: see Lela B. Costin, Howard Jacob Karger, and David Stoesz, *The Politics of Child Abuse in America* (New York: Oxford University Press, 1996) at 157.

41. The Quebec courts will indemnify a victim for a loss of chance, if the act or omission did, in fact, cause a real injury: *Laferrière* v. *Lawson,* [1991] 1 S.C.R. 541; case comment: Claude Masse, "Une impasse conceptuelle: la perte de chance de survie – *Laferrière* c. *Lawson*," (1992), 3 *Sup. C. Law Rev.* (2d) 214. See also Baudouin and Deslauriers, above, note 10, No. 243 at 173. For an illustration of this principle within the context of the failure to abide by an obligation to report physical abuse against children, see: *Brown* v. *University of Alberta Hospital*, [1997] A.J. No. 298 (Alta. Q.B.) (Q.L.).

42. See *A.J.* v. *Cairnie Estate*, above, note 38, for an example of civil liability. As for criminal liability, the obligation to report has had a checkered history in the jurisprudence. A failure to abide by the obligation to report abuse will give rise to criminal sanctions. However, in the criminal law context, the obligation to report has been more or less minimized in the jurisprudence. See *R.* v. *Cook* (1983), 37 R.F.L. (2d) 93 (Ont. Prov. Ct.); appeal allowed (1984), 12 W.C.B. 248 (Ont. Dist. Ct.); acquittal at first instance re-established on appeal by the Ontario Court of Appeal (1985), 10 O.A.C. 101, 46 R.F.L. (2d) 174 (Ont. C.A.). In *Cook,* the court decided that the physician who had not reported the sexual abuse of the child was exonerated because she thought that the child was no

170. *Aggravation of the Injury Due to Rejection of the Secret* – Even if the sexual exploitation does not continue after the unsuccessful disclosure of the sexual abuse, the mere fact that someone refuses to believe the child is a factor that aggravates the injury suffered by the victim. Indeed, it seems quite clear that one of the determining elements in the rehabilitation of the survivor is the reaction of those to whom she discloses the abuse. If the victim is not believed, or if she is blamed for the abuse, her confusion and marginalization—as well as the other psychological effects of the sexual abuse—will be multiplied.[43] The issue regarding the legal system's response to the aggravation of the injury centres upon an appreciation of the causal link. In our opinion, the confidante's fault of omission—the failure to believe the victim—does not neutralize the aggressor's initial fault: there is no break in the causal link; in fact, the confidante has committed another fault, though less serious, that may give rise to the confidante's partial liability.[44]

---

longer in danger and that things had been "worked out." In our opinion, it is not appropriate to confer discretion upon physicians as to whether or not to comply with the law. If things are such that they can be "worked out," the Youth Protection Services (hereinafter the YPS) is just as capable of minimizing the participation of the authorities in order to ensure the interests of the family and the abused child. The YPS can also do a follow-up, while the family physician may not be able to do so. For a restrictive interpretation of the law, see also *R.* v. *Stachula* (1984), 40 R.F.L. (2d) 184 (Ont. Prov. Ct.), and for an application of the obligation to day care workers, see *R.* v. *Kates,* [1987] O.J. No. 2032 (Ont. Dist. Ct.) (Q.L.). See also the decision of the Quebec Court of Appeal in *Piquemal* v. *Cassivi-Lefebvre,* [1997] R.R.A. 300 (C.A.), in which the court dismissed the action of the day-care owners, who had instituted an action for defamation against the employees and the chairperson of the parents' committee, who had filed a complaint against the day care with respect to physical abuse inflicted upon the children. Mr. Justice Beauregard, writing for the Court of Appeal, recognized that the parent, the chairperson of the parents' committee, had an obligation to report the possible abuse and had acted reasonably in contacting the Office des services de garde à l'enfance. Further, Bessner, above, note 36, at 305ff. refers to two unreported cases of successful prosecution for breach of the duty to report: *R.* v. *Kates* and *R.* v. *Lee and Hipwell*. Both cases are discussed in Marvin M. Bernstein, L. Kerwin, and H. Bernstein, *Child Protection Law in Canada*, vol. 2 (Toronto: Carswell, 1996), chap. 10.

43.   See Louise Dezwirez Sas and Alison Hatch Cunningham, *Tipping the Balance to Tell the Secret: Public Discovery of Child Sexual Abuse* (London, Ont.: Family Court Clinic, 1995).

44.   This is the solution in *A.J.* v. *Cairnie Estate,* above, note 38. See also Baudouin and Deslauriers, above, note 10, No. 540 at 357. See also our analysis of the causal link, below, at §§259ff.

One can see how a teacher, the non-abusive parent, or a guidance counsellor in whom the child has confided about the sexual abuse will be liable if he or she does not report the abuse to the Youth Protection Services, particularly if the sexual abuse continues after the breach of the obligation to report. The law also imposes a specific duty to report situations in which there are suspicions of sexual abuse. Thus, the law encourages a duty to inquire or, at the very least, to be vigilant.

ii) The Duty to Report Suspected Sexual Abuse

It should be noted that the law imposes more than an obligation to report complaints made by children; it obliges people to report situations in which the sexual abuse is "suspected." Despite the fact that the child has not told her secret, will someone be liable if the circumstances should have raised some doubt in a reasonable person? The answer depends upon whether or not the person in question is a professional.

171. *Professionals* – The situation regarding professionals must be analysed differently from that of non-professionals. It is quite likely that a court will consider that a psychologist or a guidance counsellor should have recognized the symptoms of sexual abuse in a child. The standard of conduct applied is evidently one that reflects the ordinary knowledge of a professional at the time the fault was committed.[45] In this regard, it should be noted that sexual relations with children have always been prohibited.[46] The progress we have made in this area, as evidenced in psychological studies, relates to a better understanding of the effects of sexual abuse upon children, not to a change in the standard of conduct applicable to adults. It is also interesting to note that, since 1937, the psychological literature has identified the symptomatology of sexually abused children.[47] Any

45. See *Lapointe* v. *Hôpital Le Gardeur (No. 1)*, [1992] 1 S.C.R. 351. This explains our concern, above, note 37, regarding the implications of liability of agencies for investigating allegations of sexual abuse that are false or unable to be proved.
46. See Judith Herman, *Father–Daughter Incest* (Cambridge: Harvard University Press, 1981) at 50–1 and 60–1; Schabas, above note 14 at 50–67. For an analysis of the judicial records regarding incest in Quebec from 1858 to 1938, see Marie-Aimée Cliche, "Un secret bien gardé: l'inceste dans la société traditionnelle québécoise, 1858–1938," (1996) 50 *Revue d'histoire de l'Amérique française* 201.
47. Early articles relating to the adverse and dangerous effects of sexual relations between children and adults include: Lauretta Bender and Abram Blau, "The

assessment of the behaviour of persons entrusted with the education or support of children and adolescents in the 1970s, for example, should take into account the state of knowledge at that time.[48]

172. *Non-professionals* – The courts have been much more lenient
towards non-professionals who have been sued for their failure to
suspect sexual abuse. In such cases, the analysis focuses on the
behaviour of the reasonable person at that time and in the given circumstances.[49] Nevertheless, the fact is that the law does not impose
the requirement to "conclude" that there is sexual abuse, but rather

---

Reaction of Children to Sexual Relations with Adults," (1937) 7 *American Journal of Orthopsychiatry* 500. There are also several references found in the 1970s regarding the symptoms of sexual abuse in children: Ann Wolbert Burgess and Linda L. Holstrom, "Sexual Trauma of Children and Adolescents," (1975) 10 *Nursing Clinics—North America* 551; Norcyz Lukianowicz, "Incest," (1972) *British Journal of Psychiatry* 120 at 301–13; Reinhart Lempp, "Psychological Damage to Children as a Result of Sexual Offences," (1978) 2 *Child Abuse and Neglect* 243; Karin C. Meiselman, *Incest: A Psychological Study of Causes and Effects with Treatment Recommendations* (San Francisco: Jossey-Bass, 1978).

48.   For an application in a case of physical abuse against a child and the liability of physicians who could have alerted the authorities, see *Brown* v. *University of Alberta Hospital*, above, note 41. For an application of the principle of evolution in the prevailing standards of practice of professionals, see also the decisions regarding detection of potential AIDS infection: *ter Neuzen* v. *Korn*, [1995] 3 S.C.R. 674 and *Pittman Estate* v. *Bain* (1994), 112 D.L.R. (4th) 494 (Ont. Gen. Div.).

49.   On this topic, see *M.M.* v. *R.F.*, [1996] 22 B.C.L.R. (3d) 18 (B.C. S.C.), appeal allowed in part (1997) 52 B.C.L.R. (3d) 127 (B.C. C.A.), in which the court considered that the mother of a fifteen-year old aggressor was not liable for the injury caused to a young girl placed in foster care with the mother, on the ground that the mother could not have been aware of her son's activities. However, the mother had discovered a vibrator in the victim's room and photographs of the victim. The Court of Appeal concluded that there was no basis for interfering with the trial judge's finding that the foster mother was unaware of, not willfully blind to, the abuse. See also the decision of the Quebec Court of Appeal in *Piquemal* v. *Cassivi-Lefebvre*, above, note 42, in which the Court of Appeal recognized a parent's obligation to report possible abuse perpetrated against children. Finally, see *Lapointe* v. *Succession Jean-Pierre Lapointe et Louise Tassé*, REJB 1999-10712 (Que. Sup. Ct.), for an example of an unsuccessful case involving failure to denounce a perpetrator; in that case, the plaintiff alleged that she had talked with the defendant, Louise Tassé, in 1974 about sexual abuse that had taken place between 1958 and 1966. Twelve years later, the defendant married the perpetrator, father of the plaintiff, despite knowing about the abuse. The lawsuit was filed in 1998, after the perpetrator's death. The court dismissed the case on the ground that no case existed against Louise Tassé; her alleged failure to denounce the perpetrator occurred only after the abuse had ceased.

a duty to report, even when there is merely a suspicion of sexual abuse.

173. *Conclusion* – It seems to us that the failure to report a child's confidences should be judged more severely than the failure to report when there were only signs, actions, or behaviour. However, as regards professionals, such failures should be analysed as diagnostic errors. The state of knowledge at the relevant time should be used to determine the standard of conduct of the reasonable professional.

The jurisprudence has also imposed a specific duty upon certain persons not only to report the sexual abuse, but also to protect—one might even say "save"—the child victim.

c) *Breach of a Duty to Protect*

Is there a general duty to intervene when a person witnesses incidents of spousal or sexual abuse? This is the first question we will now address. We will then examine the issue of specific duties imposed by law upon certain persons, obliging them to provide assistance or protection.

i) *General Duty to Assist*

174. *The Relationship between Section 2 of the* Charter of Human Rights and Freedoms *and the* Civil Code of Québec – Section 2 of the *Charter of Human Rights and Freedoms*[50] imposes a duty to provide assistance to a person whose life is in danger. Moreover, pursuant to article 1457 C.C.Q., there is also a duty to protect others. Even in the absence of a duty defined by law or regulation, a person may have a duty to act because the reasonable person, in the circumstances, would have provided assistance. Under such circumstances, the failure to take the appropriate measures will result in

---

50. Above, note 4. See also Francine Drouin-Barakett and Pierre-Gabriel Jobin, "Une modeste loi du bon samaritain pour le Québec," (1976) 54 *Revue du Barreau canadien* 290; Sanda Rodgers-Magnet, "The Right to Emergency Medical Assistance in the Province of Quebec," (1980) 40 *Revue du Barreau du Québec* 373; Alain Klotz, "Le droit au secours dans la province de Québec," (1991) 21 *Revue de droit de l'Université de Sherbrooke* 479.

liability.[51] However, the obligation stipulated in the Civil Code is broader than that imposed by the Charter: it is not necessary that the person's life be in "danger"; in certain circumstances, if the person's physical well-being is threatened, this will be sufficient to give rise to the obligation to provide assistance. We will first examine the obligation set forth in the Charter.

(a)   The *Charter of Human Rights and Freedoms*

175. *A General Duty to Provide Assistance* – The Quebec Charter's obligation to provide assistance applies to everyone. Thus, it applies to each person who is a witness to abuse if, as stipulated in section 2 of the Charter, the victim's life is in danger.[52] Given the incidence of murders perpetrated as an outcome of the cycle of spousal abuse,[53] would it be appropriate to consider that the refusal to intervene in cases of spousal abuse can endanger the woman's life? Is there an infringement of the Charter when witnesses to spousal abuse refuse to act, unless to do so would involve danger to themselves or unless they have another valid reason (section 2, paragraph 2 of the Charter)?

176. *The Need for an Emergency or an Imminent Risk* – To date, the jurisprudence under section 2 seems to require a perceptible state of emergency in order to give rise to the obligation.[54] Many analysts

---

51.   See Baudouin and Deslauriers, above, note 10, No. 144 at 106. See also *Gélinas* v. *Wilfrid Poirier ltée*, [1995] R.R.A. 962 (Que. Sup. Ct.), in which the court concluded that the failure to intervene is equivalent to a fault when the circumstances seem to suggest a common adventure. In this case, two taxi drivers roughed up the plaintiff while two others blocked his way. The judge ruled that the four taxi drivers as well as the taxi company were liable.

52.   Section 2 of the Charter reads as follows: "Every human being *whose life is in peril* has a right to assistance." (emphasis added).

53.   Rosemary Gartner and Maria Crawford, *Women We Honor Action Committee* (Ontario, 1997) (research report obtained from the authors), note that 71 per cent of women killed in Ontario between 1991 and 1994 were killed at the hands of an "intimate partner." The mortality rate resulting from the actions of sexual partners is considerably higher than it was between 1974 and 1990. See, generally, Ann Jones, *Next Time, She'll Be Dead: Battering and How to Stop It* (Boston: Beacon Press, 1994); Murray A. Straus, "Physical Violence in American Families: Incidence Rates, Causes and Trends," in Dean D. Knudsen and JoAnn L. Miller, eds., *Abused and Battered: Social and Legal Responses to Family Violence* (New York: A. de Gruyler, 1991) at 17.

54.   See *Carignan* v. *Boudreau*, [1987] D.L.Q. 378 (Que. C.A.), in which the Court of Appeal refused to impose liability for the injury suffered by a neighbour who wanted to assist a child perched up on a roof. The Superior Court also ruled that the remedy provided for in section 2 of the Charter requires evidence of

share this opinion.[55] Klotz, among others, criticizes the decision in *Gaudreault* v. *Drapeau*,[56] in which the Superior Court imposed punitive damages of $300 on one of the defendants who had failed to act while his sister-in-law was punching and slapping the plaintiff. Klotz points out that there was no danger to the plaintiff's life, only to her physical well-being.

177. *Criticism* – We disagree with the restrictive approach that requires an emergency to give rise to an obligation. The decision of the Court of Appeal in *Carignan* v. *Boudreau*,[57] which required the existence of an emergency or an imminent risk, must be read within the context in which it was rendered, namely, where the Good Samaritan claimed damages for the injury suffered while fulfilling his duty to assist.[58] The courts have resisted the idea of imposing upon a person having received assistance the obligation to compensate the person having provided the assistance.[59] In our opinion, although the wording of the Charter seems to suggest a restrictive interpretation (only a threat to someone's life justifies the right to assistance), it is important to avoid overly limiting the scope of the duty to assist. Indeed, who can predict the effect of a punch to the head or the result of a slap that causes the victim to fall down the stairs? Should we rely on a witness who is passive and does nothing to decide that the abuse may be fatal? The proper approach is that adopted by Mr. Justice Philippon in *Gaudreault*.[60] This approach reinforces the perspective of the victim, who may subjectively have truly feared for her life. For example, in his article, Klotz[61] begins by referring to an American tragedy in which bar patrons let a young woman be raped on a pool table for hours without intervening. His

---

fault within the civilist meaning of the term in order for liability to be imposed: *Cloutier* v. *Centre hospitalier de l'Université Laval*, [1986] R.J.Q. 615 (Que. Sup. Ct.); appeal dismissed for other reasons [1990] R.J.Q. 717 (Que. C.A.). In this case, the hospital and the psychiatrist were not held liable for the suicide of one of their patients.

55.   See Klotz, Drouin-Barakett, and Jobin, and Rodgers-Magnet, all above, note 50.

56.   *Gaudreault v. Drapeau*, [1988] R.R.A. 61, J.E. 88-283 (Que. Sup. Ct.).

57.   Above, note 54.

58.   See *An Act to Promote Good Citizenship*, R.S.Q., c. C-20, s. 2, which allows an injured rescuer to obtain compensation from the Commission de la santé et de la sécurité au travail (Workmen's Compensation Board).

59.   See, among others, *Papin* v. *Éthier*, [1995] R.J.Q. 1795, [1995] R.R.A. 1140, J.E. 95-1384 (Que. Sup. Ct.) in which the court blamed the rescuer, who electrocuted himself while attempting to assist his neighbour.

60.   Above, note 56.

61.   Above, note 50.

proposed interpretation seems to indicate that, unless the Charter were amended, the courts should not impose an obligation to intervene upon people such as these who were indifferent to someone else's pain and suffering. We suggest that this approach is too restrictive: the young woman who is being abused may fear for her life.[62] In assessing whether there was an obligation to act, we should not ignore her perspective as to whether or not her life is in danger.[63]

178. *A Justification for Not Intervening* – We should also remember that, in order to excuse his or her failure to act, a witness can allege "any valid reason," including that intervention would have involved a personal risk. There is no jurisprudence to explain this type of justification. Would the fact that the witness is torn between an allegiance to the aggressor and an allegiance to the victim constitute sufficient justification? For example, the people who are most in a position to intervene to halt spousal or sexual abuse are those who are close to the abuser: his spouse, his children, or his friends. They may face an unbearable dilemma.[64] They may be psychologically or physically unable to react in a "reasonable" or "well-considered" manner. Nonetheless, the protection of human life must be favoured, and it seems unlikely that a court could decide that loyalty towards a friend justifies letting him endanger his spouse's life.

In conclusion, given that the courts have required an emergency situation or an imminent risk before invoking the application of the Quebec Charter, at this point in time it would seem that the Charter is restricted to imposing a duty upon bystanders who witness fatal or near-fatal accidents. The current state of jurisprudence and doctrine requires that a witness to spousal abuse, for example, be able to conclude that the battered woman's life was in imminent danger before the courts will impose upon the witness a duty to intervene.[65] Thus, it appears that a witness who "knows" that a

---

62.   See Judith Lewis Herman, *Trauma and Recovery* (New York: Basic Books, 1992) at 33, where the author mentions the fear of dying as one of the emotions felt during a rape.

63.   Consider, among other things, the fact that the Supreme Court recognized that a threat of rape is a serious threat: R. v. *McGraw,* [1991] 3 S.C.R. 72.

64.   See above, at §§9 and 10.

65.   For a similar change to the perspective of imminent danger, see also *R. v. Lavallée,* [1990] 1 S.C.R. 852, where the Supreme Court of Canada accepted that the victim's perspective regarding the risk involved must be taken into account.

woman is being battered would not have an obligation to report the abuse or help the woman leave the family home, at least not under the Quebec Charter, if that person considers that the woman's life is not in danger. In order to apply the Charter within the family context of spousal or sexual abuse, there would have to be a re-evaluation of the criterion of urgency or imminent risk. However, this is not the case for the obligation imposed pursuant to article 1457 C.C.Q.

(b) The *Civil Code of Québec*

179. *Is There a Duty to Protect under the Civil Code?* – Under what circumstances will the civil law impose a positive obligation on a person to prevent or react to abuse witnessed by that person? We will first consider whether the Civil Code provides a duty to assist based upon the vulnerability of the victim (child or protected adult). We will then examine the more general issue regarding the obligation to provide assistance even to an adult victim of abuse. For example, if a woman who has suffered spousal abuse goes to her neighbours, do they have the obligation to help her? Would the young woman who was raped in the presence of the bar patrons be entitled to institute proceedings against them because they did not intervene? Finally, we will examine the contents of this obligation: do people have the duty to do more than call the police?

180. *The Duty to Protect Children* – Pursuant to article 1457 C.C.Q., the failure to abide by an obligation prescribed by the legislature constitutes a fault; section 42 of the *Youth Protection Act* sets forth a duty for every person to assist a child who is attempting to reach the Youth Protection Services (hereinafter Y.P.S.). Therefore, a breach of this obligation might result in extracontractual liability for the injury suffered by the child after an unsuccessful attempt to reach the Y.P.S. It is possible, for example, that the parents of a friend of the child, to whom the child went to seek refuge after an incident of abuse, might be liable not only if they did not contact the Y.P.S. themselves,[66] but if they did not facilitate contact with the Y.P.S.

---

66. See above, at §§168ff. See *M.D.* v. *L.D. et al.*, above, note 37, where the Court of Appeal, per Baudouin J.A., discusses the scope of section 42 of the *Youth Protection Act.*

181. *A General Duty to Protect* – Several observers[67] have suggested that the adoption of section 2 of the *Charter of Human Rights and Freedoms* was not necessary, because the *Civil Code of Lower Canada* already included an obligation to provide assistance, which obligation was applicable, as all other obligations, in accordance with the criterion of the reasonable person. French law also recognizes the fault of omission to provide assistance. "He who omits, commits," stated Domat.[68] Notwithstanding this principle of altruism proposed by the Code, we cannot but notice that the courts have, on occasion, favoured a more individualistic approach to the duties of the reasonable person. In *Alliance Assurance Co. et al.* v. *Dominion Electric Protection Co.*,[69] the Supreme Court of Canada suggested that, absent a legal duty to protect others, there was no obligation to do so—in this case, calling the fire department. Other rulings have expressed a more generous appreciation of the duties of the reasonable person towards his or her fellow citizens.[70] The fault of failing to intervene in order to minimize the injury already caused to a person was recognized in *Osborne* v. *La Commission de transport de Montréal*,[71] in which the Supreme Court recognized that the failure of a bus driver to move his bus, which was crushing the hand of a small child, aggravated the injury. Thus, it may be that in certain circumstances in which a person, such as the bus driver, has the possibility of acting so as to minimize the pain of another person, if the person fails to do so, he or she will be liable. In the cases that interest us, a person who can reasonably offer refuge or protection to a woman fleeing her abusive spouse or to a child escaping a situation of sexual abuse may be held liable if that person fails to so act. The omission will be judged even more severely if the person had a specific duty to intervene.

---

67.   See André Nadeau, *Traité de droit civil du Québec*, t. 8 (Montreal: Wilson and Lafleur, 1971) at 36–7; Drouin-Barakett and Jobin, above, note 50; Klotz, above, note 50; Madeleine Caron, "Le Code civil québécois, instrument de protection des droits et libertés de la personne?" (1978) 56 *Revue du Barreau canadien* 196.

68.   See Geneviève Viney and Patrice Jourdain, *Les conditions de la responsabilité civile*, 2nd ed. (Paris: L.G.D.J., 1998), Nos. 452ff at 333ff (our translation).

69.   [1970] S.C.R. 1. This decision was criticized by Klotz, above, note 50 at 503.

70.   See also the decision of *Gaudreault* v. *Drapeau*, above, note 56, which ordered the indifferent witness to pay punitive damages pursuant to the *Charter of Human Rights and Freedoms*, without imposing liability pursuant to the Civil Code.

71.   [1958] S.C.R. 257. See also *Sherbrooke (City)* v. *Fortin*, [1960] B.R. 110.

ii) Specific Duties to Protect

When the law imposes an obligation to protect, the failure to abide by this obligation may constitute a fault. We will examine these duties as imposed upon various persons because of their relationship with the victim or because of their employment; these people include, among others, members of the aggressor's or the victim's family, establishments that work with children, and child protection services.

(a) Family Members

182. *The Problem Defined* – The members of the aggressor's and the victim's families are often witnesses to the sexual or spousal abuse. They may be torn between their loyalty to the aggressor and to the victim. How should the legal system respond when a mother, who knows that her spouse is abusing her child, does nothing and remains silent? What should happen when a son, who has become an adult, sees that his mother has been battered by his father and yet continues to pretend that the relationship is harmonious? How can the courts determine a reasonable response in such family tragedies?

The Non-Abusive Parent

183. *Quebec Civil Law* – The civil law considers the failure to fulfil a parental duty to protect a child from sexual abuse to be a fault within the meaning of article 1457 C.C.Q.[72] This duty is imposed not only under the *Youth Protection Act*,[73] but also under the Civil Code (article 32). Moreover, as we have seen above, the reaction of the confidante is one of the important factors contributing to the rehabilitation of a child victim of sexual abuse. Children who have not been believed will generally suffer more severe psychological conse-

---

72. The parents' duties of custody, supervision, and education of a child are set forth in article 599 C.C.Q.
73. Section 42 imposes a general duty to assist a child attempting to obtain youth protection services. See above, note 33. Moreover, the legislative scheme of the *Youth Protection Act* recognizes the primary role of the parents as regards their child's well-being. Since 1941, youth protection laws have imposed a duty upon parents or "any person in authority" to protect the child against "moral and physical dangers" (14 Geo. VI, c. 11, (s. 15)).

quences.[74] Can we find fault when a parent refuses to back up a child's story?

184. *The Criterion of the Reasonable Person* – The difficulty in assessing this issue lies in the uncertainty regarding the "reasonable" reaction of the non-abusive parent who learns that her spouse, brother, father, or friend has abused her child. The civil law imposes an objective examination of the behaviour of the person whose liability is alleged. The law attempts to determine what the reasonable person under the "same circumstances" would have done.[75] What must be done by the mother who learns that her spouse has abused her child? Should she contact the police? Should she immediately call the Y.P.S.? Should she consult a psychologist? Could she be hesitant to involve the authorities because she fears losing her child or because she fears that the child will be overly traumatized by the legal system?

We can also question whether an examination of the circumstances should include, for example, the parent's financial situation, her economic dependence upon the aggressor, or her past history. Parents who were sexually abused as children are often unable to accept that the same tragedy is befalling their children, and they tend to deny the occurrence of the events. Abuse perpetrated against their children may cause flashbacks and great emotional upheaval. There are few decisions to enlighten us on this subject.

185. *Canadian Common Law* – In 1993, in *J. (L.A.)* v. *J. (H.)*,[76] the General Division of the Ontario Court found a mother liable for having failed to prevent sexual abuse that she knew the father was committing. In this case, the judge recognized a duty to protect the child arising from the parent's position as a "fiduciary." The mother had advised her daughter not to mention an incident of sexual intercourse on an occasion when the Children's Aid Society had sought to intervene. The judge considered that she had breached her fiduciary obligations and that her actions constituted negligence. The ruling is ironic in that the mother was ordered to pay compensatory damages as well as punitive damages, but her husband, who was the aggressor, was ordered to pay only compensatory damages. Given that he had been found guilty under criminal law and had

---

74.   See above, at §10; Dezwirez Sas and Hatch Cunningham, above, note 43.
75.   See Baudouin and Deslauriers, above, note 10, Nos. 151–5 at 111–14.
76.   (1993), 13 O.R. (3d) 306 (Ont. Gen. Div.).

served his sentence, the trial judge ruled that he could not be subject to punitive damages.[77]

186. *Criticism* of J. (L.A.) v. J. (H.) – The decision has been criticized[78] because it is based upon a presumption of power on the part of mothers: it assumes that a mother always has a choice between her husband and her daughter, that she can always choose to leave her husband without causing injury to her child. Nonetheless, the decision established the liability of a parent who is not a party to the abuse, but actively participates in keeping the sexual abuse a secret.

187. *Taking a Position* – Determining the liability of the non-abusive parent is a delicate matter. The question that arises—and which we will now examine—is whether we should impose liability on a person, who has no special training, for having reacted poorly to an incident of sexual abuse. For example, if the non-abusive parent participates actively in keeping the secret by obliging the child to deny the accusations or by preventing the child from obtaining assistance, this should be considered a fault resulting in that parent's liability. However, when the fault is one of omission, the overall circumstances should be assessed in order to develop a realistic approach to the parent's situation: the courts should take into account psychological, economic, and physical handicaps.

An Adult Son or Daughter Who Is a Witness to Spousal Abuse

188. *Obligations towards Parents* – In the absence of protective supervision of a person of full age, the *Civil Code of Québec* does not provide an obligation for a child to "protect" his or her parents in the same manner as the obligation set forth in article 32 C.C.Q., which provides children with the right to protection and security and

---

77. See our analysis of punitive damages, below, at §§317ff.
78. See Elizabeth K.P. Grace and Susan M. Vella, "Vesting Mothers with Power They Do Not Have: The Non-Offending Parent in Civil Sexual Assault Cases—*J.(L.A.)* v. *J.(H.) and J.(J.),*" (1994) 7 *Canadian Journal of Women and the Law* 184. See also Linda J. Panko, "Legal Backlash: The Expanding Liability of Women Who Fail to Protect Their Children from Their Male Partner's Abuse," (1995) 6 *Hastings Women's L.J.*; *contra:* Amy L. Nilsen, "Speaking Out against Passive Parent Child Abuse: The Time Has Come to Hold Parents Liable for Failing to Protect Their Children," (2000) 37 *Houston Law Review* 253.

imposes a concurrent obligation upon the child's parents or the persons acting in their stead. The only obligation of adult children towards their parents is one of support (article 585 C.C.Q.).[79] Thus, the legislature has not imposed any specific obligation upon adult children to ensure the protection of their parents.

189. *The Duty to Protect Adults under Protective Supervision* – With regard to parents under protective supervision for whom a child is the tutor or curator, article 260 C.C.Q. stipulates that the tutor "is responsible for his custody and maintenance; he is also responsible for ensuring the moral and physical well-being of the protected person." In our opinion, this article imposes a special obligation to react when a protected person of full age is being abused. The obligation may include moving the protected adult to another place, having recourse to psychological support services, or resorting to the protective measures provided for in the Criminal Code. With regard to adults who are not "protected," the only applicable obligation is the general obligation of the reasonable person to come to their aid pursuant to article 1457 C.C.Q.

190. *Lack of Jurisprudence* – There are no jurisprudential decisions on this subject. It would be difficult to envisage a survivor of spousal abuse taking action against her children because they did not protect her against her spouse's blows.[80] It is more likely that she would institute proceedings against the aggressor. Nonetheless, we believe that the indirect victims of spousal abuse, such as the victim's children, might have a cause of action against adult witnesses to the abuse who refused to intervene or, even worse, encouraged the victim to remain in the family home.

191. *Conclusion* – In theory, the situation of the adult son or daughter is no different than that of any other witness to the spousal abuse, unless the child's parent is under protective supervision. However, the child's ability to intervene may be assessed from a dif-

---

79.   See *Droit de la famille–2626*, J.E. 97-691 (Que. Sup. Ct.), in which the court imposed upon a daughter who had won a lottery a duty to support her parents. For Ontario decisions to the same effect, see also *Whiteley* v. *Brodie*, [1994] O.J. No. 1038 (Ont. Prov. Div.) (Q.L.); *Godwin* v. *Bolcso*, [1993] O.J. No. 297 (Ont. Prov. Div.) (Q.L.).

80.   Many battered women feel guilt towards their children, particularly if the children were also the targets of the physical abuse. It should be noted that the abuse has a profound effect upon the children who witness it: see above, at §25.

REMEDIES   101

ferent point of view: the adult child is often in a better position to
intervene, because he or she knows the aggressor's violent nature
and is familiar with the characteristics of the cycle of abuse. It may
be that this particular knowledge imposes upon the child a greater
duty to intervene, because the "reasonable person" under similar
circumstances would probably have intervened.

(b) Establishments That Work with Children

Establishments that work with children assume a specific
responsibility to protect the children against abuse and even to prevent situations of abuse. This responsibility requires that the establishments pay particular attention when hiring personnel, as well
as throughout the employer–employee relationship.

192. *Responsibility at the Time of Hiring* – The courts consider that
establishments that work with children—whether schools, community or recreational centres, day-care centres, or summer camps—
have a certain responsibility to hire employees who do not present
any risks to the children; for example, the hiring of a pedophile who
has already been found guilty of sexual offences against children
would clearly constitute a fault.

193. *Responsibility after Hiring* – An establishment might also be
held liable as a result of the way it deals with its employees once
they have been hired. In *Gosselin* v. *Fournier*,[81] the Superior Court
was faced with sexual abuse perpetrated by a professor against a
student. The court dismissed the college's liability under former
article 1053 C.C.L.C. (now article 1457 C.C.Q.). The college administration had heard about two past incidents of questionable conduct on the part of the instructor; it had merely taken measures to
supervise his behaviour within the establishment's walls (not being
left alone with students), but it had not dismissed him. The court
explained that the first incident (in which the instructor had been
seen with a student on his lap) had occurred seven or eight years
earlier and was not sufficient to justify a dismissal. The second, and
more recent, indicent related to a complaint made by a parent, who
suggested ambiguous behaviour on the part of the instructor, without really suggesting it had been sexual touching. The parent had
asked that the instructor not be dismissed, for fear that a dismissal
might cause embarrassment to the son. The court concluded that

---

81.   *Gosselin* v. *Fournier*, [1985] C.S. 481 (Que. Sup. Ct.).

the college was not at fault "by not having dismissed an employee against whom it did not have sufficient evidence."[82]

It is possible that, at present, a court would assess the reaction of the college's administration differently: current expectations of a "reasonable college" would demand a more informed approach to allegations of sexual abuse. Dismissal is not the only solution available to a college, and a court might very well conclude that there were other appropriate measures for supervising the instructor. It is not so much the state of the law that has evolved since the *Gosselin* decision, but rather our appreciation of the facts: in particular, the conclusion might differ regarding the negligence of an establishment that "knows" that one of its instructors has a tendency towards pedophelia.

194. *The Common Law Solution* – More recent examples in Canadian common law indicate that the courts recognize the liability of establishments for the lack of training of their employees[83] or for having failed to follow up on complaints of abuse,[84] even when such establishments are administered by the government. However, governmental liability poses certain problems.

(c)   Child Protection Agencies

What happens when a report has been duly made, but the child protection authorities do nothing or carry out a sloppy investigation? Similarly, what happens when the Y.P.S. places the child in a foster family where she is further abused? Will the Y.P.S. be liable?

---

82.   Ibid. at 482 (our translation).
83.   See *G.B.R.* v. *Hollett*, above, note 28, which was confirmed on this point, upon appeal, in [1996] N.S.J. No. 345 (N.B. C.A.) (Q.L.); (1996) 139 D.L.R. (4th) 260 (N.B. C.A.), in *obiter*. Applications for leave to appeal and cross-appeal to the S.C.C. dismissed, 15 May 1997 (without reasons).
84.   See *G.B.R.* v. *Hollett*, above, note 28, in which the court found the employer personally liable for having failed to immediately dismiss an employee who had allegedly helped young girls run away from the reform school and had smoked drugs with them. At that time, there were no allegations of a sexual nature against the employee. Thereafter, the employee helped a young girl run away and hid her in his home. She was psychologically and sexually abused for over a year. In *W.K.* v. *Pornbacher*, [1997] 32 B.C.L.R. (3d) 360 (B.C. S.C.), the court blamed the bishop for having failed to implement a program to prevent the sexual abuse, given that he had knowledge of two cases of abuse among the priests in the diocese.

195. *Partial Immunity* – The Y.P.S. is protected under a provision that guarantees its immunity.[85] However, it may be held liable for its gross fault. In *Quenneville* v. *Directeur de la protection de la jeunesse*,[86] the Court of Appeal concluded that the plaintiff must prove bad faith in order to be successful. According to the Court of Appeal, it is not sufficient that the *Youth Protection Act* was poorly enforced; the Y.P.S. workers must "have intentionally violated the law, acted maliciously, in bad faith or acted in a gravely unjust manner."[87] In a more recent decision,[88] the Court of Appeal recognized that the Y.P.S. could rely on its confidential files to defend itself when sued.

196. *Liability of Public Bodies in the Civil Law* – In *Laurentide Motels Ltd.* v. *City of Beauport*,[89] the Supreme Court of Canada explained that public law determines when civil law applies to municipal corporations, and it ruled that "public" law in Quebec has two sources: the statutory law and the common law. According to "public" common law, a public body's policy decisions, but not its operational decisions, are immune from legal proceedings. Does this policy-implementation dichotomy[90] apply when determining the liability of the Y.P.S.? We believe so, because the Y.P.S. presents itself as a government agency that exercises powers of investigation and control. Article 1376 C.C.Q. subjects the state and its bodies, as well as all other legal persons established in the public interest, to the rules on obligations set forth in the Civil Code "subject to any other rules of law which may be applicable to them." In light of the doc-

---

85. See section 35 of the *Youth Protection Act*, above, note 33: "In no case may the director or any person acting under section 32 or 33 be prosecuted for acts done in good faith in the performance of his duties."
86. See *Quenneville* v. *Directeur de la protection de la jeunesse*, REJB 1997-04082 (C.A.) reversing [1996] R.J.Q. 115 (Que. Sup. Ct.), application for leave to appeal to S.C.C. denied on 4 June 1998. See also *Institut St-Georges* v. *La Laurentienne générale, cie d'assurances*, [1993] R.J.Q. 1676 (Que. C.A.).
87. *Quenneville* v. *Directeur de la protection de la jeunesse*, ibid., para. 5 (our translation).
88. *M.D.* v. *L.D. and J-R.S. and le Directeur de la Protection de la Jeunesse et al.*, above, note 37.
89. [1989] 1 S.C.R. 705.
90. This expression (our translation) originates from the article by Yves Ouellette, "Les recours en dommages contre le gouvernement et les fonctionnaires pour faute administrative," (1992) 26 *Revue juridique Thémis* 169 at 184.

trine and jurisprudence,[91] the applicable "other rules of law" include a distinction between policy decisions and operational decisions— that is, between making policies and implementing them.[92]

197. *Application of the Policy-Implementation Distinction to Matters of Sexual and Spousal Abuse* – There are some examples in the jurisprudence of operational decisions: the method and quality of an inspection system have been associated with the operational aspect.[93] The breach of a directive also fits into this category.[94] On the other hand, "policy" decisions are, among other things, associated with the establishment of budgetary allocations.[95] Thus, if a social worker fails to deal with a complaint when the government directive is to follow up on all calls, there might be fault. The question becomes more difficult when the government directive recom-

---

91.   See Baudouin and Deslauriers, above, note 10, No. 113 at 79–81. See also René Dussault and Louis Borgeat, *Traité de droit administratif*, t. 3, 2nd ed. (Quebec City: Presses de l'Université Laval, 1988) at 987; Jean-Denis Archambault, "Les sources de la responsabilité extracontractuelle de la Couronne du Québec: variations de droit public," (1992) 52 *Revue du Barreau du Québec* 513 at 516; *Commission hydro-électrique du Québec* v. *Cie internationale de papier du Canada*, [1987] R.J.Q. 2362 (Que. C.A.).
92.   It should be noted that the distinction between the two types of decisions has been criticized as being difficult to apply, if not impossible to determine: Baudouin and Deslauriers, above, note 10, No. 113 at 79–81. In fact, in the United Kingdom, it was abandoned and replaced by a return to fuller government immunity against proceedings: see *Murphy* v. *Brentwood District Council*, [1990] 2 All E.R. 908 (H.L.). See also Bruce Feldthusen, "Failure to Confer Discretionary Public Benefits: The Case for Complete Negligence Immunity," (1997) 5 *Tort Law Review* 17. Feldthusen recommends a return to a regime of full state immunity for all discretionary decisions. In our opinion, although the distinction is difficult to apply, the option of full immunity is not a satisfactory one. On this topic, see S.H. Bailey and M.J. Bowman, "The Policy/Operational Dichotomy: A Cuckoo in the Nest," (1986) *Cambridge L.J.* 430. Indeed, full immunity is incompatible with the history of law in Quebec, which long ago recognized the extracontractual liability of the state of Quebec: see *R.* v. *Cliche*, [1935] S.C.R. 561; *O'Brien* v. *Procureur général du Québec*, [1961] S.C.R. 184.
93.   See *Just* v. *British Columbia*, [1989] 2 S.C.R. 1228; Ouellette, above, note 90 at 189, who cites *2160-6892 Québec inc.* v. *Ville de Ste-Thérèse*, [1989] R.J.Q. 1991 (Que. Sup. Ct.).
94.   See *Michel Miller inc.* v. *P.G. Québec*, J.E. 90-457 (Que. Sup. Ct.); *Vézina* v. *Société d'assurances des Caisses populaires,* [1987] R.J.Q. 2335 (Que. C.A.).
95.   See *Just* v. *British Columbia*, above, note 93; *Brown* v. *British Columbia (Minister of Transportation and Highways)*, [1994] 1 S.C.R. 420; *Swinamer* v. *Nova Scotia (Attorney General)*, [1994] 1 S.C.R. 445; Peter Bowal and Lynn Boland, "Crowning Glory: Liability in Negligence of Public Authorities Revisited," (1994) 24 *Revue de droit de l'Université de Sherbrooke* 435.

mends that there be a follow up only on complaints made by professionals. Is this a policy decision, which is, therefore, immune from judicial intervention, or is it a method forming part of the inspection system, which might, therefore, result in a conclusion that there was fault if the evidence establishes that many cases of child sexual abuse are reported by the children themselves or by their parents or neighbours—in short, by people who are not professionals? Would this criterion of whether or not the report is made by a professional be considered so erroneous by the courts that it could not be justified and, consequently, constituted an operational fault?

What should be done if there are no directives, and if the social workers are overloaded and cannot physically follow up on all calls? In *City of Kamloops* v. *Nielsen*, Madam Justice Wilson suggested that "inaction for no reason or inaction for an improper reason cannot be a policy decision taken in the bona fide exercise of discretion."[96] Therefore, she would have imposed liability upon the public body under those circumstances. However, recent rulings by the Supreme Court seem to have narrowed the notion of an operational decision. In *Brown* v. *British Columbia (Minister of Transportation and Highways)*,[97] the decision to maintain a summer schedule, with all that it entailed in terms of reduced service, was ruled one of policy. This decision involved classic policy considerations of financial and human resources and significant negotiations with government unions. In *Swinamer* v. *Nova Scotia (Attorney General)*,[98] the department's decision to inspect and identify hazardous trees involved questions of expenditure and allocation of funds, clearly indicating that it was a general policy decision. Therefore, it would seem that although the method and quality of an inspection are operational elements, the courts are more and more willing to acknowledge the existence of immunity when the limits imposed upon the inspection system are motivated by budgetary reasons.

At present, there are only a few civil law decisions regarding the liability of the Y.P.S. It would be interesting to consider examples drawn from the common law in order to identify limits to the Y.P.S.'s extracontractual liability.

---

96. [1984] 2 S.C.R. 2 at 24.
97. Above, note 95.
98. Above, note 95.

198. *The Common Law Situation* – In common law jurisdictions, the wording of statutory immunity provisions for the youth protection authorities is often similar to that found in section 35 of the *Youth Protection Act*.[99] Application of this immunity has been set aside in cases of bad faith or gross fault. In this context, various faults have been alleged with more or less success. A total lack of supervision or the existence of gross negligence with respect to the supervision of children placed in foster homes constitutes a gross fault.[100] In particular, delays in carrying out an investigation, especially as regards children who are already under the care of the state, may constitute a fault.[101] A sloppy, poorly administered investigation, based upon a bias against the child's credibility, may also lead to a conclusion of gross fault.[102] However, faults committed in good faith,[103] or within the scope of budgetary restrictions or a restructuring,[104] will be exonerated.

199. *The Criterion of Taking Charge of the Child* – It would seem that, at common law, fault is assessed more severely if the state has

---

99. See section 8 of the Newfoundland *Child Welfare Act,* which was discussed in *C.D.* v. *Newfoundland*, [1996] N.J. No. 12 (Q.L.); 137 Nfld. & P.E.I.R. 206 (Nfld. S.C.), and section 23 of the British Columbia *Family and Child Services Act*, S.B.C. 1980, c. 11, which was discussed in *C.A.* v. *Critchley*, [1997] B.C.J. No. 1020 (B.C. S.C.) (Q.L.).

100. See *C.D.* v. *Newfoundland*, ibid.; *contra*: *M.M.* v. *K.K.*, above, note 25, in which the child protection authorities were not found liable, even where they had failed to follow the usual plan for supervising a child who had developed an incestuous relationship with her foster father, after he had separated from his wife.

101. See *C.D.* v. *Newfoundland*, above, note 99. See also *A.J.* v. *Cairnie Estate*, above note 38.

102. *C.D.* v. *Newfoundland*, above, note 99.

103. See *B.D.* v. *British Columbia (Superintendent of Family and Child Service)*, [1997] B.C.J. No. 674 (B.C. C.A.) (Q.L.), in which the Court of Appeal overturned the trial judge's ruling, [1995] B.C.J. No. 1921 (B.C. S.C.) (Q.L.). The trial judge had ruled that the social worker breached his duty to inform the foster mother that the foster child presented a risk for young children. The foster child eventually sexually abused the foster mother's three-year old child. The Court of Appeal considered that the foster child was a difficult child to place, and that if there had been a fault in failing to provide all the details in her file, this was a fault committed in good faith, without any resulting liability.

104. See *Brown* v. *British Columbia (Minister of Transportation and Highways)*, above, note 95; *Swinamer* v. *Nova Scotia (Attorney General)*, above, note 95; *Laurentide Motels ltd.* v. *City of Beauport*, above, note 89; M. Kevin Woodall, "Private Law Liability of Public Authorities for Negligent Inspection and Regulation," (1992) 37 *McGill L.J.* 83.

taken charge of the child—that is, if the state has "replaced" the parent. By taking charge of the child, the state is placed in a fiduciary position, which imposes a greater responsibility upon it and may even prevent any resort to the immunity provision.[105] In *K.L.B.* v. *British Columbia*,[106] the judge stated the following: "The conduct of the Crown in assuming to act for the benefit of children under its care is more than just an administrative or public action on the part of the Crown. It has its roots in the *parens patriae* power of the Crown to act in the best interests and for the benefit of those entrusted to its care due to inability to care for themselves."[107] With the *Protection of Children Act*, the legislature imposed upon the Crown the obligation to decide where the best interests of children committed to its care really lie. This meant that the obligation of the Crown was fiduciary in nature.

In this context, liability will arise if there is a failure to supervise foster families or reception centres, to follow up on complaints filed with the authorities, or to communicate with the child's parents when sexual abuse is revealed. Will the civil law, which does not recognize a fiduciary relationship within this context, impose broader responsibility in cases in which the Y.P.S. assumes tutorship of children who otherwise have no tutors (articles 180, 182, 186, 191, 199 C.C.Q.)?

200. *Tutorship as a Source of Extended Responsibility* – The argument of the British Columbia Supreme Court is interesting: it assumes that when a child protection service takes certain children under its tutorship, its obligation towards them becomes a parental obligation that cannot be set aside by statutory immunity. Given that there is no parental immunity, when the Y.P.S. becomes a parent, it, too, should not benefit from such immunity.

It is true that tutorship confers parental authority upon the Y.P.S. (article 186 C.C.Q.), and that it must be exercised in the interest of the minor so as to ensure his or her protection (article 177 C.C.Q.). However, due to the specific reference to tutorship in

---

105. This criterion of taking charge of the child will influence the finding of vicarious liability as well. See *Bazley* v. *Curry*, [1999] 2 S.C.R. 534, *Jacobi* v. *Griffiths*, [1999] 2 S.C.R. 570, and our discussion, below, at §215.
106. [1996] B.C.J. No. 3036 (B.C. S.C.) (Q.L.), confirmed at [1998] B.C.J. No. 470 (B.C. S.C.) (Q.L.).
107. For a history of the Crown's *parens patriae* power, the judge referred to *Re Eve*, (1986) 31 D.L.R. (4th) 1 at 13–22 (S.C.C.).

section 32 of the *Youth Protection Act*, we suggest that the Quebec courts cannot set aside the partial immunity conferred under section 35 of this act. At the very most, we might recommend that fault be assessed by taking reality into account: the fact the child has only the Y.P.S. as his or her tutor. In assessing the Y.P.S.'s fault, the court should consider the child's vulnerability. The "reasonable" Y.P.S. must take into account the specific needs of its various clients.

Imposing extracontractual liability on an overloaded agency that is already underfunded raises many problems about the role of judiciary power with respect to the allocation of government funds. A solution that rests in taking action against the Y.P.S. should be weighed carefully, as should a decision to institute proceedings against other agencies on which society traditionally relies for its protection: the police and prison authorities.

(d) Prison and Police Authorities

Prison and police authorities are responsible for protecting the public. Jurisprudence in Quebec has held police authorities liable for their faults. Most of these cases involve police aggression against suspects who had been arrested. What of their obligation to respond promptly to calls for help from citizens in danger? Where victims of spousal or sexual abuse were not protected by the police in a timely manner, or where the aggressor was known to police but was not apprehended, can there be extracontractual liability?

201. *The Problem* – The imposition of liability may have the effect of ending all efforts to rehabilitate offenders, or it may force police to arrest innocent persons in order to protect themselves against potential extracontractual liability. There is, therefore, considerable resistance to imposing this liability on prison and police authorities. Nonetheless, where the abuse was foreseeable, some courts may find that there was fault in the performance of the duty to protect or to safeguard, and that this fault contributed to the injury suffered.

202. *Common Law Examples of Fault in Instances of Spousal or Sexual Abuse* – In Canadian common law, the criterion of foreseeability[108] is used to determine police liability when a criminal abuses

---

108.   See Gerald H. L. Fridman, "Non-Vicarious Liability for the Acts of Others," (1997) 5 *Tort Law Review* 81, who suggests that Canadian and British com-

a victim. Where the prison or police authorities exercised negligence in guarding an incarcerated criminal, there may be liability: liability arises because it was foreseeable that the security of other people would be endangered by the fault.[109] Police and prison authorities may also be under a duty to protect prisoners from foreseeable abuse by other prisoners, or from themselves where they attempt self-mutilation.[110] Where the criminal has not yet been apprehended, it is much more difficult to establish fault on the part of police,[111] or even a causal link between the fault and the injury suffered.[112]

In our opinion, where the abuse has been perpetrated by someone other than the police, it is unlikely that either the police or the prison authorities will be held liable. Fault will be found to have occurred only in specific circumstances in which the risk was foreseeable. In similar situations where the plaintiff relies on security provided by another party—such as in a hospital, a hotel, or an apartment building—the same problem arises.

(e) Other People

The criterion of foreseeability of abuse may help in determining obligations owed by other establishments that, under certain circumstances, have assumed a duty to protect the plaintiff. We will

---

mon law differ on this point. The criterion of foreseeability is used in Canada, whereas the British use the criterion of control exercised by the police officer over the criminal, at 125.

109. See *S. et al.* v. *Clement et al.* (1995), 122 D.L.R. 4th 449 (Ont. Gen. Div.), where the federal penitentiary was ordered to pay damages to a woman who was terrorized and brutally raped shortly after the escape of a sexual delinquent. The court held that prison authorities did not search promptly enough once the prisoner was reported missing.

110. See *Funk* v. *Clapp* (1986), 68 D.L.R. (4th) 229 (B.C. C.A.), where the widow of a man who hanged himself with his belt in his cell after his arrest was awarded damages. The police had failed to remove his belt, contrary to existing policy.

111. See the decision of the House of Lords on this point in *Hill* v. *Chief Constable of West Yorkshire*, [1989] A.C. 53 (H.L.).

112. See, however, *Jane Doe* v. *Toronto (Metropolitan) Commission of Police* (1998), 39 O.R. (3d) 487 (Ont. Gen. Div.); where the court awarded the plaintiff damages of over $200,000. The police failed in their duty to protect the woman from a rapist. The police did not issue a warning because of stereotypical sexist biases, thereby violating the plaintiff's rights to equal protection and benefit under the law. The police were also found to have breached their private law duty of care.

discuss, in turn, the duty of hospitals, hotel owners, and landlords to prevent abuse against their "clients."

203. *Hospitals* – The *Act Respecting Health Services and Social Services*[113] imposes certain duties on hospitals, the nature and extent of which depends on their organization and the resources at their disposal.[114] The question is whether or not the establishment can be sued when a patient has been sexually abused by another patient.[115] Analysts suggest that a duty to supervise, as such,[116] does not exist under the *Act Respecting Health Services and Social Services.*[117] However, the establishment may be liable where violence by the patient was foreseeable and no steps were taken to isolate him.[118]

204. *Hotel Owners* – Similarly, a hotel that fails to take sufficient means to protect its guests from unauthorized entries into hotel rooms by strangers could be extracontractually liable.[119]

205. *Landlords* – The landlord of an apartment building could also be held liable if no steps were taken to protect tenants when the

113. R.S.Q., c. S-4.2.
114. See sections 5, 13, and 16 of the *Act Respecting Health Services and Social Services*, ibid.
115. Note that propensity for sexual deviancy of a patient is a diagnostic evaluation that must be carried out according to scientific methods accepted at the relevant time; see, above, at §171. See also *Kines Estate* v. *Lychuk Estate (Public Trustee of)*, [1996] M.J. No. 423 (Man. Q.B.) (Q.L.), where the court held that the treating psychiatrists were not liable where the patient, whom they had not hospitalized, committed a murder.
116. Andrée Lajoie, Patrick Molinari, and Jean-Marie Auby, *Traité de droit de la santé et des services sociaux* (Montreal: Presses de l'Université de Montréal, 1981) 82 at 631; see also Adrian Popovici, "La responsabilité médicale et hospitalière lors du suicide d'un malade mental," (1970) 30 *Revue du Barreau du Québec* 490.
117. Above, note 113; *Cloutier* v. *Centre hospitalier de l'Université Laval,* above, note 54.
118. See *Wellesley Hospital* v. *Lawson*, [1978] 1 S.C.R. 893, where the hospital was held responsible for an attack on a patient by a psychiatric patient known to have violent tendencies. See also *Wenden* v. *Trikha*, [1993] A.J. No. 121 (Alta. C.A.) (Q.L.), where the court rejected an action against the hospital and the psychiatrist for injuries caused by a psychiatric patient to a third party in an automobile accident. The patient had never previously harmed anyone and had been supervised at fifteen-minute intervals.
119. See, for example, *McGinty* v. *Cook* (1989), 68 O.R. (2d) 650, aff'd on appeal (1991) 2 O.R. (3d) 283 (Ont. C.A.), where the court held the owner of a camping ground liable for the attacks on a guest.

landlord permitted the aggressor to have access to the building (article 1854 C.C.Q.).[120]

If the abuse were committed by an employee[121] or by an agent of the establishment, the plaintiff is likely to invoke articles 1457 C.C.Q. and following, which impose liability for the fault of another.

2. Liability for the Fault of Another

In certain situations, the Civil Code imposes liability for the fault of another. Sexual abuse survivors may find it particularly advantageous to invoke these regimes of vicarious liability. In this section, we will examine the employer's vicarious liability for the acts of employees and the serious problems it presents. We will then examine the vicarious liability of educators and parents.

a) Vicarious Liability of the Abuser's Employer

206. *Vicarious Liability as an Additional Source of Liability* – Employers are not able to exonerate themselves from liability for the faults of their employees committed during the "performance of their duties" (article 1463 C.C.Q.). It is important to note that liability for the fault of another within the context of sexual abuse often accompanies an allegation of personal fault by the employer for failing to adequately protect the children by poorly selecting employees, by not providing training, by failing to investigate allegations of abuse, or by failing to dismiss an employee who has committed sexual abuse (1457 C.C.Q).[122] The following analysis attempts to demonstrate that the fault of sexual abuse may occur during the performance of an employee's duties, even though it has not been "authorized" by the employer.

207. *Conditions of Application* – In order for the principal to be liable, it is essential that the agent committed a fault, that a mas-

---

120. See *Q.* v. *Minto Management Ltd.* (1985), 49 O.R. (2d) 531, aff'd (1987) 57 O.R. (2d) 781 (Ont. C.A.), for an example of a common law action in damages where an employee of an apartment building committed sexual assault.
121. See *M. A. C.* v. *General Hospital (Grey Nuns) of Edmonton*, [1997] A.J. No. 48 (Alta. Q.B.) (Q.L.). See also *J. B.* v. *Jacob*, above, note 115.
122. See, among others, *G. B. R.* v. *Hollett*, above, note 28, where the government was held liable because, although it knew that a reform school guard disobeyed his superiors, smoked drugs with the young girls, and helped them to escape, it failed to dismiss him.

ter-and-servant relationship existed, and that the fault occurred during the performance of the employee's duties.[123] In the case of sexual abuse, the first condition is rarely difficult to establish.[124] Rather, the second and third conditions present difficulties for victims of sexual abuse.

To begin with, we will examine the issues pertinent to the existence of the master–servant relationship. We will then tackle the tricky question of the criteria applicable to the scope of vicarious liability. Under what circumstances can sexual abuse be perpetrated by the employee and engage the liability of his employer?

i)   The Master–Servant Relationship

The disclosure of abuse at Mount Cashel and in residential schools across Canada has attracted considerable interest in terms of the liability of religious communities and churches for the abuse committed by their representatives—priests, monks, nuns, or even lay employees working in an establishment managed by a religious community. The churches sought to deny the existence in common law of a "master-and-servant relationship" between the church and its public representatives.[125] What is the position in civil law?

---

123. See Baudouin and Deslauriers, above, note 10, Nos. 646-759 at 417–66; Claude Masse, "L'abus de fonctions dans la relation préposé-commettant en droit civil québécois," (1978) 18 Cahiers de Droit 595. In French jurisprudence, the principal appears to be liable for the faults of his agents committed "within the ambit of their duties" instead of "in the performance of their duties," as prescribed by the Civil Code of Québec. The French Civil Code refers to "injury caused . . . within the duties for which they were engaged" (art. 1384 C.N.) (our translation). See Henri, Léon and Jean Mazeaud, Leçons de droit civil, t. 2, vol. 1, 8th ed., by François Chabas (Paris: Mont chrestien, 1991) No. 479 at 498.

124. As noted earlier, above, at §157, the Criminal Code has always condemned sexual assaults against children; even though society's capacity to appreciate the general nature of these offences and their impact on victims has improved, the applicable standard of conduct relative to the commission of an assault has not evolved.

125. For an exhaustive discussion and findings on the subject, see Law Commission of Canada, Restoring Dignity: Responding to Child Abuse in Canadian Institutions (Ottawa: Law Commission of Canada, 2000), online: Law Commission of Canada <http://www.lcc.gc.ca/en/themes/mr/ica/2000/html/restore1.html> (date of access: 6 June 2001); Ronda Bessner, Institutional Child Abuse in Canada (Ottawa: Law Commission of Canada, October 1998), online: Law Commission of Canada <http://www.lcc.gc.ca/en/themes/mr/ica/besrep/index.html> (date of access: 6 June 2001); Goldie M. Shea, Institutional Child Abuse in Canada: Civil Cases (Ottawa: Law Commission of Canada, 1999), online: Law Commission of Canada <http://www.lcc.gc.ca/en/

208. *A Broad Definition of the Master–Servant Relationship* – In our opinion, the master–servant relationship is broadly interpreted in civil law. Baudouin and Deslauriers states that the only necessary requirement is that the agent "acts for another," whether or not a contract to this effect exists.[126] Nonetheless, it seems that an element of control and the authority to dismiss must also be present. Most religious organizations are characterized by a hierarchical structure that demands obedience from clergy or pastoral workers. Several religious organizations control the activities of their priests or preachers. They assign duties and parishes. In our opinion, the relationship between the church and its religious ministers satisfies these conditions. As regards other religious congregations and communities, we believe that the degree of control a community exercised over an individual should also be a factor in determining whether a master–servant relationship existed.

The real question in terms of abuse that occurs within the parameters of master–servant relationships concerns fault. Was the fault committed by the employee during the performance of his duties?

ii) Fault during the Performance of One's Duties

209. *The Problem* – Is the employer liable under article 1463 C.C.Q. when a teacher sexually abuses a student? School authorities will usually argue that the abuse by the teacher did not occur during the "performance of his duties" as an educator. This litigious issue has been the subject of considerable debate. Baudouin and Deslauriers, among others, have recommended criteria for determining what

---

themes/mr/ica/shea/civil/index.html> (date of access: 6 June 2001), Goldie M. Shea, *Institutional Child Abuse in Canada: Criminal Cases* (Ottawa: Law Commission of Canada, 1999), online: Law Commission of Canada <http://www.lcc.gc.ca/en/themes/mr/shea/crime/index.html> (date of access: 6 June 2001). See also *Renault* v. *Sheffield* (1988), 29 B.C.L.R. (2d) 171 (B.C.S.C.). This decision involves illegal appropriation of goods, not sexual assault. It was criticized by Judge Quijano in *W. K.* v. *Pornbacher*, above, note 84. See also Ian Stauffer and Christian Bourbonnais Hyde, "The Sins of the Fathers: Vicarious Liability of Churches," (1993) 25 *Ottawa L. R.* 561.

126. See Baudouin and Deslauriers, above, note 10, No. 675 at 427 See also on this point *Gélinas* v. *Wilfrid Poirier ltée,* above note 51, where the court imposed liability on a taxi company for attacks committed by its "mandataries." In fact, the right to use the name "Royal Taxi" was leased by the drivers, and the judge concluded that the principal was responsible for the fault of its mandatary in the performance of his mandate.

does and does not fall within the scope of the performance of one's duties.[127] We will examine those that are relevant to an action for sexual abuse: the perpetration of a crime; the time and place of work; the victim's knowledge that the abuser was acting outside the scope of the performance of his duties; whether the crime benefited the employee or occurred due to a defect in his personality.[128] Before we conclude our discussion on the vicarious liability of the employer, we will refer the reader to the equally unsatisfactory solutions to this question in Canadian common law.

(a) The Perpetration of a Crime

210. *An Irrelevant Criterion* – Principals will often try to argue that, because an employer could not have implicitly authorized the perpetration of a crime, it is impossible for the act to have occurred during the performance of the employee's duties.[129] Both the courts[130] and the doctrine have justifiably rejected this simplistic defence.[131]

(b) The Time and Place of Work

211. *A Promising Criterion* – It would seem reasonable for the employer to be liable vicariously for a fault committed by an employee at the workplace during work hours.[132] However, even this criterion does not seem to be applied systematically in sexual abuse cases. In *Goodwin* v. *Commission scolaire Laurenval*,[133] the Superior Court refused to impose liability on the employer for sexual abuse committed by a janitor after class hours, but in the school washrooms. This holding is somewhat surprising given that the facts showed that the janitor had followed the young girls into the washrooms in accordance with the employer's policy. This policy required the janitor to follow youths entering the school after class hours to ensure that no mischief was committed and that the youths did not wander the corridors alone. Applying the "personal benefit to the employee" criterion, discussed below, the judge decided that the

127. See Baudouin and Deslauriers, above, note 10, Nos. 727–59 at 451–65.
128. This expression is found in Masse, above, note 123.
129. See the opinion of Judge Mignault in *Curley* v. *Latreille*, [1920] S.C.R. 131, and also *Co. de transport provincial* v. *Fortin*, [1956] S.C.R. 258.
130. See *Hudson's Bay Co.* v. *Vaillancourt*, [1923] S.C.R. 414.
131. See Baudouin and Deslauriers, above, note 10, Nos. 727–9 at 451–2.
132. See *Trans Quebec Helicopters Ltd.* v. *Estate of David Lee*, [1980] A.C. 596; Baudouin and Deslauriers, above, note 10, No. 734 at 454.
133. Above, note 39.

aggressive gesture was not intended to satisfy the employer's interests.

Another Quebec case appears to indicate, in *obiter*, that the time and work hours criterion should be applied in instances of sexual touching by an employee. In *Gosselin* v. *Fournier*,[134] the Superior Court refused to hold a college liable for the sexual abuse of a student by an employee. The court held that under paragraph 7 of former article 1054 C.C.L.C., liability of the employer could not be imposed where the sexual touching "did not occur on the college premises nor during an activity organized by the college in any place whatsoever."[135] It seems, therefore, that the result could differ according to whether or not the abuse took place on the employer's premises or during an activity organized by the employer. Sexual abuse, in fact, is often committed after class hours, but in the school or during an outing organized by the school.

(c) The Victim's Knowledge That the Employee Was Acting outside the Scope of His Duties

212. *A Dangerous Criterion* – According to Baudouin and Deslauriers,[136] a victim cannot claim that an activity fell within the "scope of the employee's duties" if she knew that the employee was acting outside the scope of his duties.[137] It is important to properly analyse this potential defence of the employer, even though it has not yet been raised in a sexual abuse case. Can the courts exonerate an employer by relying upon the victim's presumed knowledge that sexual abuse does not fall within the scope of a teacher's normal duties? We feel that it is essential to restrict this defence to cases involving adults, who are not in a position of dependence. To impute such knowledge to students, and, along with it, the ability to reject advances and come out unharmed, does not correspond to the dynamic of power that exists between a teacher and his student.

---

134. Above, note 81.
135. Ibid. at 482 (our translation).
136. See Baudouin and Deslauriers, above, note 10, No. 733 at 454, where the authors draw support from *J.L. Lévesque & Beaubien ltée* v. *McMahon,* [1978] C.A. 561 and the comments of Viney and Jourdain, above note 68, Nos. 802ff at 881ff.
137. See, by analogy, *Norberg* v. *Wynrib*, above, note 23.

(d) The Employee's Personal Benefit or Personality Defect

213. *Proposed Standard* – According to Baudouin and Deslauriers[138] and to Masse,[139] the jurisprudence often invokes the criterion of personal benefit to the employee in response to the dilemma of determining whether the employee is in the performance of his duties.[140] The question is whether "the primary goal of the servant's act sought yes or no to satisfy a primary interest of the employer or to produce a direct benefit for the employer?"[141] Where the main purpose of the act is solely to benefit the employee's interests, it will not be considered to have occurred during the performance of his duties.

214. *A Controversial Application of This Standard in Cases Involving Sexual Abuse* – The Superior Court concluded in *Goodwin* that the school janitor who perpetrated sexual abuse was motivated primarily by his own benefit and, therefore, that the employer was not liable. The court suggested that sexual abuse, in contrast to physical violence, cannot be considered as a valid expression of the janitor's authority.[142]

We would like to make several critical observations at this point. Sexual abuse can be, and often is, a demonstration of one person's power, usually of a man over a woman or girl. Men often sexually abuse women to prove their power over them, whereas, if another man was involved, they might resort to physical violence. The distinction made in *Goodwin* supports the view that the use of sexual force was motivated by the employee's "lust" rather than by a desire to dominate his victim. We feel that this distinction reinforces the myth that sexual abuse is driven by love or sexual desire rather than by power.

---

138. Baudouin and Deslauriers, above, note 10, Nos. 754–8 at 460–5.
139. Above, note 123.
140. See *Goodwin* v. *Commission scolaire Laurenval*, above, note 39. See also *Dupras* v. *Canadian Acceptance Co. Ltd.*, [1968] Q.B. 228; *Samson* v. *Bergeron*, [1961] Q.B. 330.
141. *Goodwin* v. *Commission scolaire Laurenval*, above, note 39 (our translation).
142. He relies on the analysis in *Hudson's Bay Co.* v. *Vaillancourt*, above, note 130, where a foreman who fired a shot into the air in order to prove his authority was found to have physically assaulted an employee.

215. *A Suggested Application of the Criterion of the Employee's Personal Benefit* – Is the decision in *Goodwin* a correct application of the criterion elaborated in the doctrine? To conclude, as the court did, that the janitor's acts in no way served the employer's interests ignores an important element of the facts: the abuse was possible by virtue of the fact that the victim trusted the agent because he was employed by the school board. We should ask ourselves how to apply the criterion of personal benefit.[143] Through whose eyes do we analyse the primary goal of the agent's act? From the perspective of the employer? From the perspective of the employee? From the perspective of the victim?

The determinative criterion cannot be the perspective of the employer. In *Goodwin*, the employer obviously did not consider that its interests were satisfied by the sexual abuse, even though it could be argued that the employer's interests were being served when the janitor followed the young girls into the washrooms (the employer did not want the students wandering freely in the corridors outside of class hours). However, to opt for the employer's perspective ignores the jurisprudence, which recognizes that an employee's disobedience does not necessarily immunize an employer from liability.[144] The court seems to have preferred the perspective of the agent: the janitor who abused a young girl sought only his personal satisfaction, and the performance of his duties (accompanying the young girls to the washrooms) was but the "opportunity"[145] through which to satisfy his base urges. We should also consider the victim's perspective, for whom the "ultimate goal" of the janitor's act was to protect the employer's interests: the janitor followed her to ensure that she broke nothing.

Taking the victim's perspective into account is compatible with theories advanced in support of imposing vicarious liability on an employer, including the theories of representation and warranty.

---

143. The liability of the employer, a municipality that had employed the respondents, was discussed by Gonthier J., writing on behalf of the Supreme Court in *Gauthier* v. *Brome Lake (Town)* [1998], 2 S.C.R. 3, rev'g J.E. 95-1906 (Que. C.A.); J.E. 90-871 (Que. Sup. Ct.); see also *J.B.* v. *Jacob*, above note 115 (hospital found liable); *E.D.G.* v. *Hammer* (1998), 53 B.C.L.R. (3d) 89 (B.C. S.C.) (duty not breached by schoolboard); in civil law, see *Samson* v. *P.G. Québec* (Ministère de l'Emploi et de la Solidarité), REJB 2000-19410 (C.Q.), where the plaintiff's benefits were cut off by an agent of the Ministère de l'Emploi et de la Solidarité sociale.

144. See Baudouin and Deslauriers, above, note 10, Nos. 730-732 at 453–4.

145. This expression is found in ibid., No. 750 at 460–1.

216. *Compatibility between the Proposed Solution and the Theory of Representation* – The theory of representation holds that the employer is responsible because, in the eyes of third parties, the employee acts on behalf of the employer, and the employer acts through its agent, who is an extension of the employer. This theory is valuable because it properly situates the position of the victim.[146] The young girl may have been more wary of being followed into the washrooms by a stranger, whereas she acquiesced in the case of the janitor because he was a school employee. Similarly, as in *Gosselin*, the young adolescent who went to his teacher's residence and was abused, went to the residence because this formed part of the employer's educational project. The teacher invited the student over, using school work as a pretext. Moreover, the student went to his teacher's residence because children must obey their teachers' commands. This is the message communicated to the student by the employer—that is, the school board or the college.

217. *Compatibility between the Proposed Solution and the Theory of Warranty* – Another theory that has been advanced is that of warranty: the employer is liable because it is the warrantor of its employees' acts. The warranty theory is highly relevant in sexual abuse cases: the victims are in the presence of the faulty servant because the employer has explicitly or implicitly authorized these individuals to follow the students in the school or to give them private instruction. It is clear that, under these circumstances, there is a duty on the behalf of the employer to warrant the acts of employees and this duty should serve as the focal point from which to determine the ultimate purpose of an employee's duties.

218. *Compatibility between the Proposed Solution and the Jurisprudence* – Consideration of the victim's perspective when determining the ultimate objective of the agent's act does not contradict existing jurisprudence. In typical cases of this sort, such as *Curley* v. *Latreille*,[147] which rejected the employer's liability, the vic-

---

146.   Ibid., Nos. 667–8 at 425. Baudouin and Deslauriers criticize this theory as follows: "This explanation [the theory of representation] is criticized largely because it is indirectly based on the principle of fault. We are, in essence, relying on some vague concept of representation to impute the fault of the servant onto the master. Fault, however, remains personal and it is fictitious to maintain that the act of the servant becomes the act of the master. To maintain that the latter is at fault due to the act of the former by 'subrogation' describes, rather than explains, the phenomenon" (our translation).

147.   Above, note 129.

tim's perspective vis-à-vis the identity of the employee and his relationship to the employer was irrelevant. In *Curley,* the driver caused an accident after having borrowed his employer's car for his own pleasure, without authorization. The employer did not impose the relationship between the victim and the faulty employee in any way.[148] Given that the majority of cases involving vicarious liability of principals address the question of liability for automobile accidents, the circumstances of the victim–employee relationship are often ignored. The accident victim is determined by chance, and there is no pre-existing relationship between the victim and the employee or the employer.

219. *A Final Word on the Victim's Perspective* – In conclusion, we believe that good reasons exist for broadening the perspective when evaluating the ultimate goal of the agent's act. A more detailed contextual analysis should be undertaken. The victim's perspective should be considered, especially when her relationship with the faulty agent was due to the employer. The employer should be held liable where the abuse takes place under conditions that, for the victim, appear to have been organized by the employer, who, without a doubt, is often in the best position to minimize the risks of abuse.

220. *Common Law Solutions* – The common law provinces' approach to employer liability for the fault of another appears quite confusing. Several decisions have held the employer liable for the acts of the employee,[149] but the appeal courts have narrowed the criteria.[150] The current conservative standard developed by the author

---

148. We observed, however, that this aspect had been considered in certain cases in which the employer was found liable. See *Ouellet* v. *Léveillé,* [1945] K.B. 680, *Bourgeois* v. *Casino français inc.,* [1964] C.S. 537 (Que. Sup. Ct.), and *Clément* v. *Edgington,* [1953] C.S. 325 (Que. Sup. Ct.), where, in all three cases, it appears that the outcome of the case was influenced by the fact that the relationship between the servant and the victim was established by the employer or for his benefit.

149. See *Bazley* v. *Curry,* [1999] 2 S.C.R. 534, aff'g (1997) 146 D.L.R. (4th) 72 (B.C. C.A.); *W.K.* v. *Pornbacher,* above, note 84; *C.A.* v. *Critchley,* above, note 99; *G.B.R.* v. *Hollett,* above, note 28; *Gauthier* v. *Brome Lake (Town),* above, note 143.

150. See, for example, *Jacobi* v. *Griffiths,* [1999] 2 S.C.R. 570, rev'g [1997] B.C.J. No. 695 (B.C. C.A.), rev'g [1995] B.C.J. No. 2370 (B.C. S.C.) (Q.L.); *F.W.M.* v. *Mombourquette,* [1996] N.S.J. No. 260 (N.S. C.A.) (Q.L.), leave to appeal refused by the Supreme Court of Canada: [1996] S.C.C.A. No. 504 (Q.L.); *D.C.B.* v. *Boulianne,* above, note 23; *J.B.* v. *Jacob,* above, note 115.

Salmond has been applied and criticized:[151] "A master is not responsible for a wrongful act done by his servant unless it is done in the course of his employment. It is deemed to be so done if it is either (1) a wrongful act authorised by the master, or (2) a wrongful and unauthorised mode of doing some act authorised by the master."[152]

In sexual abuse cases, the first condition is rarely satisfied: no employer authorizes sexual contact with, or sexual abuse of, children. Whether or not the abuse or sexual contact was an erroneous—indeed, criminal[153]—execution of an employer's order is much more controversial.[154] For example, in *Bazley* v. *Curry*,[155] the employee's duties included tending to the children's intimate needs (he was to help them bathe and was to be affectionate and loving with them). When sexual abuse occurs in such circumstances, is the employer liable? The lower court found sufficient nexus between the tasks imposed by the employer and the inappropriate acts perpetrated. The British Columbia Court of Appeal concurred. However, the five judges were divided as to the reasons for holding the employer liable. According to Madam Justice Huddard, the determinative factors were the nature of the authority conferred by the employer and the risk this created of a fault being committed. She believed that the employer encouraged a certain degree of intimacy between his employees and the children and that the risk was foreseeable and to be assumed. Madam Justice Newbury relied more on the connection between the fault and the acts demanded by the employer from the employee. She also felt that Curry's abusive acts were sufficiently similar to the intimate care inherent in the job to justify the employer's liability. The following criterion was sug-

---

151. See *Bazley* v. *Curry*, above, note 149, for the Court's discussion on the standard in Salmond (paras. 10 to 15).

152. Sir John William Salmond, Robert Francis Vere Heuston, and Richard A. Buckley, *Salmond and Heuston on the Law of Torts*, 21st ed. (London: Sweet and Maxwell, 1996) at 437–8.

153. Note, however, that the employer may still be liable for the act of his or her employee under the principle of responsibility for the fault of another, regardless of the illegal character of the act. It is not enough, however, for the employment to have merely presented the "opportunity" for the commission of the crime.

154. Note that the courts have ruled that fraud and even theft (*R.* v. *Levy Bros. Co. Ltd. et al.*, [1961] S.C.R. 189) were capable of constituting "inappropriate" manners of performing the duties conferred by the employer, due to the link between the criminal gesture and the employment.

155. Above, note 149.

gested by Mr. Justice Hollinrake, with whom Justice Donald concurred:

> "In cases such as this [sexual assault] the general proposition for the imposition of vicarious liability is that there must be sufficient nexus between the duties of the employee as such and his misconduct. Whether or not there is that sufficient nexus will depend on the nature of the power conferred on the employee by his employment and the likelihood that that conferral of power will make probable the very wrong that occurred."[156]

Justice Finch refused to set forth a criterion and considered that the employer's liability should continue to be determined according to the facts of each case.

In *Jacobi* v. *Griffiths*, another vicarious liability case,[157] the British Columbia Court of Appeal exonerated the employer for the sexual abuse perpetrated by an employee because it considered that the employer was not responsible for the employee's fault. The employee was responsible for organizing recreational activities at a centre that the plaintiffs, a brother and sister, had frequented as children. One of the incidents took place on a school bus during an outing organized by the centre, while the others occurred at the employee's home. Madam Justice Newbury was the only one who felt that the incident on the school bus justified the employer's liability. The other judges held that "It is not reasonable to impose liability without fault on an employer for every act of groping by an employee, just because the employer provided the opportunity for that molestation."[158]

A similar restrictive trend is appearing in Nova Scotia. In *F.W.M.* v. *Mombourquette*,[159] the Nova Scotia Court of Appeal adopted an even more traditionalist attitude when it concluded that the diocese was not responsible for the abuse committed by the priest:

> The fact that the appellant employed him as a clergyman and authorized him to act in a privileged position is not sufficient to impose lia-

---

156. Ibid., at para. no. 115 of the decision of the Court of Appeal, [1997] B.C.J. No. 692 (Q.L.).
157. See *Jacobi* v. *Griffiths*, above, note 150.
158. Ibid., at para. no. 15 of the decision of the Court of Appeal.
159. Above, note 150 at para 47.

bility particularly where he acts criminally and totally contrary to the religious tenets which he has sworn to uphold. One may well ask how can it be said in such circumstances that he was acting in the course of employment? With respect, it is clear that he was not doing so when he approached and subsequently assaulted Mr. F.M.

Leave to appeal was rejected by the Supreme Court of Canada in *Mombourquette*, but granted in the cases of *Curry* and *Griffiths*.

The situation will no doubt continue to evolve. It is our opinion, however, that the common law jurisdictions should also adopt an approach that takes the victim's perspective into account. The court should consider the manner in which the victim views the authority conferred on the employee. In cases like *Curry*, where the employee is responsible for administering intimate care, it is natural for the victim to believe that the employer was responsible for the abuse; therefore, the employer should be held liable. The same result should occur, in our opinion, where the abuse is perpetrated on premises managed by the employer. In addition, we feel that it was essential in *Griffiths* to have considered the progression of events from the victim's point of view: would he have gone to Griffiths's had he not been an employee of the recreational centre? Would the parents have permitted such a visit had Griffiths not occupied this type of position?

Our analysis is not meant to impose liability on the employer in every instance of sexual abuse perpetrated by his employee. For instance, an employer is not liable for an employee who violently abuses a client who is no longer on the premises: the victim's presence at the scene of the abuse is unrelated to her relationship with the employer.

221. *Conclusion* – The principle of vicarious liability of an employer encounters difficult problems vis-à-vis sexual abuse by an employee. We feel that the courts should consider the victim's perspective when deciding whether or not the acts were committed during the "performance of the employee's duties." This is true especially when the victim's contact with her abuser is strictly a result of the employment contract between the abuser and the employer.

b)   Vicarious Liability of the Aggressor's Parent

In *Gagnon* v. *Béchard*, the first Quebec civil case involving sexual abuse against children, the parents of an adolescent were sued after he abused the young children he was babysitting. It is highly probable that other cases will also put parental liability at issue. However, parental liability under article 1459 C.C.Q. can be refuted with proof of adequate supervision and proof of a good education. These two means of exoneration merit further examination.[160]

222. *The Duty to Supervise* – The duty to supervise often depends on whether or not the parents were able to foresee the behaviour of the child or adolescent. A guardian parent will be expected to provide a greater degree of supervision in the case of a child who has a tendency to act recklessly or to perpetrate specific offences.[161] Note that in the case of adolescents, the intensity of the obligation to supervise is dependent on the greater degree of liberty enjoyed by the adolescent in contrast to the younger child.[162] It would appear that parents could be liable if they are aware of their child's aggressive tendencies towards the opposite sex, for example, and are able to exercise a certain element of control. Thus, a parent who has been informed by the school of his child's sexually deviant behaviour and who fails to have the child consult a psychologist, for example, could be held liable under the present state of the law. In such a case, the parents may also be liable for their own personal fault (article 1457 C.C.Q.).[163]

223. *The Duty to Provide a Good Education* – The courts will rarely impose liability on the parent where the only reproach is the failure to provide a good education.[164] There is a case, however, where phys-

---

160. *Gagnon* v. *Béchard*, J.E. 89-590 (Que. Sup. Ct.), rev'd by [1993] R.J.Q. 2019 (Que. C.A.). See Baudouin and Deslauriers, above, note 10, No. 600 at 394; Nathalie Des Rosiers, "La responsabilité de la mère pour le préjudice causé par son enfant," (1995) 36 *Cahiers de Droit* 61.
161. See *Boileau* v. *Lacroix*, [1983] C.S. 1200 (Que. Sup. Ct.), in which the parents were held liable for a fire lit by their son when they knew of his pyromania; *Laverdure* v. *Bélanger*, [1975] C.S. 612 (Que. Sup. Ct.), aff'd on appeal, C.A.M. No. 500-09-000116-856, in which the parents were held liable for the murder by their son of the young girl with whom he was obsessed. See the comments of Maurice Tancelin and Daniel Gardner, *Jurisprudence commentée sur les obligations*, 6th ed. (Montreal: Wilson and Lafleur, 1996), No. 127 at 378.
162. See *Kumps* v. *Côté*, [1988] R.R.A. 502 (Que. Sup. Ct.); *contra*: *Tremblay* v. *Pitre*, [1990] R.R.A. 101 (Que. Sup. Ct.).
163. To this effect, see *Gaudet* v. *Lagacé*, REJB 1998-05550 (C.A.Q.) on the parent's obligation to supervise; this is the case of the mother found liable in *Boileau* v. *Lacroix*, above, note 161, where she was personally at fault. See also *Laverdure* v. *Bélanger*, above, note 161.
164. See Des Rosiers, above, note 160 at 72; *contra*: *Denommé* v. *Pelland*, [1960] Q.B. 421.

ical abuse by an adolescent resulted in the parents' liability under article 1459 C.C.Q. on the grounds that they had provided a poor education.[165] In sexual abuse cases, it is acknowledged that children who abuse other children were often victims of abuse. A parent's inappropriate sexual conduct or physical or sexual abuse of a child should be considered a "breach of the duty to provide a good education." This breach may very possibly be sufficient to establish the parent's personal fault.

224. *Conclusion* – Unless the court is confronted with a parent who is either himself an abuser or is aware of his child's deviant sexual tendencies but fails to act, a suit against the abuser's parents is riddled with obstacles. The personal fault of the parent can often be established in these cases (article 1457 C.C.Q.), so an action founded on presumed fault under article 1459 C.C.Q. becomes superfluous. Finally, it should be noted that, to date, lawsuits in common law jurisdictions against the parents of adolescent abusers have not been very successful.[166]

c)   Vicarious Liability of the Aggressor's Educator

225. *The Duties of Supervision and Education* – Numerous incidents of sexual abuse occur on school grounds. What happens when the abuser is an adolescent and the abuse takes place on school grounds? As educators, school authorities are responsible for the acts of children and adolescents under their supervision (article 1460, para. 1 C.C.Q.). Their responsibility, analogous to that of parents, revolves around the duty to supervise, which is often difficult to exercise, and the duty to educate, which is even more difficult to accomplish.[167]

226. *Jurisprudence* – To date there has been no case in Quebec involving sexual abuse under these circumstances. The courts have addressed racial violence, however, and we can apply their reasoning to cases of sexual abuse. In *Roach* v. *Protestant School Board of Greater Montreal,* two students had engaged in a fight.[168] The Superior Court concluded that there were no grounds for imposing

---

165. See *Tremblay* v. *Pitre,* above, note 162. For a critical analysis of this decision, see Des Rosiers, above, note 160.
166. See *M.M.* v. *R.F.,* above, note 49.
167. In general, see Baudouin and Deslauriers, above, note 10, Nos. 613–37 at 400ff.
168. [1995] R.R.A. 698 (Que. Sup. Ct.).

liability on the school board, because it was felt that the board had provided appropriate supervision under the circumstances.[169] The court made no mention of the school authorities' awareness of the existence of racial violence or of their efforts to eliminate the problem. The passive attitude of a school aware of problems of racial violence will not always be tolerated. There are proactive ways in which a school may counter its students' racist attitudes, and we can assume that the courts will examine the systemic response of schools towards racism.

227. *Sexual Abuse and the Duty to Supervise.* – Similar problems will presumably emerge in the case of sexual abuse. Sexual abuse is not advertised, and abusers often commit these acts in secret. Victims stand little chance of success against educators and their employees if, upon further examination of a system of supervision considered to be appropriate, it is established that the abusers did everything possible to avoid detection by supervisors. We can assume, however, that a school that fails to educate children about sexual abuse can expect to be treated more severely by the courts.

228. *The Criterion of Foreseeability* – Besides proving that the supervision was generally appropriate, educators and their employees may exonerate themselves where the adolescent's act was judged to be "unforeseeable."[170] Where a child demonstrates sexually deviant tendencies or is known to be aggressive, the courts should be more demanding of educators.

3. *Liability of the Insurer*

Recourse to a regime of liability for the fault of another is explained by the need to ensure recovery where damages are awarded. The objective is to sue a solvent defendant, and in order to successfully achieve this objective, the possibility of suing the abuser's insurer must be examined.

229. *The Insurer as an Additional Defendant* – Liability insurance financially protects the insured against damages awarded for

---

169. See also, to the same effect, *Salova* v. *Commission scolaire du Sault St-Louis*, [1995] R.R.A. 555 (C.Q.).

170. See *Joly* v. *Commission scolaire de L'Ancienne-Lorette*, [1977] C.S. 603 (Que. Sup. Ct.), where the supervisor was not held vicariously liable because a fight between children was not foreseeable. See also Baudouin and Deslauriers, above, note 10, No. 631 at 406–7.

injuries to third parties (article 2396 C.C.Q.). A victim may now sue both the defendant and his insurer for damages (article 2501 C.C.Q.). The rewording of article 2501 C.C.Q. has eased the problems caused by the restrictive interpretation under the former code.[171] For many victims, access to indemnification guaranteed by the defendant's insurance policy remains the only hope of recovering damages awarded by the court.

We will examine the various defences the insurer may raise against an action instituted by a victim of spousal or sexual abuse. These defences differ depending on whether the action is launched against the insurer of the abuser or of the other defendants, and they address the intentional fault of the insured, the criminal nature of the act, exclusions pertaining to insured persons, the type of injury covered, or the timing of the event.

230. *The Importance of the Wording of the Contract* – Insurance contracts vary, and a policy may specifically exclude certain risks (article 2499 C.C.Q.); therefore, attempts to identify general principles must be undertaken cautiously. In some sectors, such as youth protection, liability insurance policies covering establishments now specifically exclude coverage for sexual abuse.[172] It is always imperative to carefully read the insurance policy in question.[173]

---

171. This possibility was not provided for by the jurisprudence under the *Civil Code of Lower Canada*: see *Cie d'assurance Traders Générale* v. *Laurentienne Générale Cie d'assurance inc.*, [1991] R.J.Q. 6 (Que. Sup. Ct.); *Union Québécoise Mutuelle d'assurance contre l'incendie* v. *Mutuelle des Bois-Francs*, [1984] C.A. 473. The plaintiff could not launch an action against both the insurer and the defendant who caused the injury. Since the *Civil Code of Québec* came into force on 1 January 1994, the combination of remedies is permitted, even where the action is based on a fault committed prior to 1994. See *Allstate du Canada* v. *Compagnie d'assurances Wawanesa*, [1995] R.R.A. 833 (Que. C.A.); *Champagne* v. *Collège d'enseignement général et professionnel de Jonquière,* [1996] R.J.Q. 2229, [1996] R.R.A. 991, J.E. 96-1795 (Que. C.A.); *contra: Félix* v. *Girouard,* [1995] R.R.A. 981 (Que. Sup. Ct.). However, where the action had been launched prior to 1 January 1994, the plaintiff could not invoke article 2501 C.C.Q. in order to cancel the effect of his or her choice and amend his or her action to include the insurer: *Wightman* v. *Richter & Associés inc.*, [1996] R.R.A. 67, J.E. 96-326 (Que. C.A.); *Certain Marine Underwriters at Lloyd's of London* v. *Royale Compagnie d'assurance du Canada,* [1996] R.J.Q. 40 (Que. C.A.).

172. See, for example, *Children's Aid Society of Halifax and Patrick Corkery* v. *Boreal Insurance Company* (1996), 155 N.S.R. (2d) 221, (1996) 39 C.C.L.I. (2d) 296 (N.S. S.C.), where the professional responsibility policy of a children's aid society excluded coverage for claims "resulting from, connected with, or alleging sexual behaviour or physical, mental or emotional abuse." The children's

231. *The Right to a Copy of the Insurance Policy* – Jurisprudence acknowledges the right of a plaintiff to obtain a copy of the defendant's insurance policy, as confirmed by the Quebec Court of Appeal in *Champagne* v. *Collège d'enseignement général et professionnel de Jonquière*.[174] In this case, in an action for defamation against Champagne and Radiomutuel, the plaintiff-college demanded the name of the insurer in addition to a copy of the policy. The defendants provided the insurer's name, stating that the circumstances alleged in the declaration were covered by the policy. However, they refused to provide a copy of the policy on the grounds that the information contained therein was confidential. The Appeal Court, confirming the Superior Court's decision, obliged the defendant to supply a copy of the policy. In the decision, Mr. Justice Forget explained that the right conferred under article 2501 C.C.Q. must be interpreted as recognizing the policy's relevance to the litigation between the plaintiff and the defendant. He also noted that the policy's relevance increases where punitive damages are claimed, because article 1621 C.C.Q. stipulates that the existence of an insurance indemnity may be determinative when deciding to award punitive damages and deciding their amount.[175] The court nonetheless agreed that the insurer may request that the court exclude certain sections of the policy that are irrelevant to the proceedings.

In a concurring opinion, Mr. Justice Brossard adopted a more cautious view of the policy's relevance. Although he agreed that the insurer was unable to prove that specific sections of the policy were irrelevant, Mr. Justice Brossard nonetheless believed that it was inappropriate to divulge the extent of financial coverage. It was his opinion that a plaintiff cannot claim "greater rights against the

---

aid society argued that this exclusion was applicable only if the assault was committed by its own employees and not where negligence for failing to divulge instances of sexual assault was alleged. The court interpreted the exclusionary clause to include all reference or allegation related to sexual abuse and held that the insurer was not obliged to defend the society.

173. See *Victoria General Hospital* v. *General Accident Assurance Co. of Canada*, above, note 38, where, in its decision that the insurer was under a duty to defend a hospital whose employee breached his duty to report confidential information pertaining to a sexual assault, the court relied specifically on the wording of insurance contract exclusionary clauses. The plaintiff alleged that while she was a patient in 1973, she confided in a hospital employee about sexual assaults committed against her by a school counsellor. The employee did nothing, and the assaults continued.

174. Above, note 171.

175. See below, at §§317ff.

insurer than against any other debtor."[176] Since a plaintiff cannot know the solvency of his defendant prior to judgment, "why should this same plaintiff be entitled to know the extent of financial protection offered under the liability insurance contract, which would, in my opinion, be the equivalent of revealing a debtor's solvency or the value of his property and assets?"[177]

The Court of Appeal's decision does not completely resolve the issue of the duty to divulge the financial protection offered under the policy: if punitive damages are not claimed, is it still relevant to divulge the extent of financial protection under the policy? Given that it is advisable to claim punitive damages in the types of cases with which we are concerned,[178] mentioning such a claim in the declaration should provide access not only to the limit of financial protection offered under the policy, but also to the wording of any exclusions. The wording of these exclusions will often be determinative of the outcome of these types of claims against insurers.

a)   Liability of the Abuser's Insurer

Although attractive, the possibility of suing the abuser and his insurer is problematic. For one thing, an insurer is never liable to compensate for injuries caused by the insured's intentional fault (article 2464 C.C.Q.). An overview of the existing Quebec jurisprudence on intentional fault in insurance law will assist us in understanding how this prohibition applies to sexual or spousal abuse victims who sue the abuser as well as his insurer. We will also examine the tricky issue of the relationship between intentional fault in insurance law and the illicit and intentional nature of acts required for the awarding of punitive damages, following which we will briefly discuss the approach in American common law. Finally, we will discuss general insurance policy exclusion clauses regarding injuries caused by the criminal acts of the insured.

i)   Exclusion of Injuries Caused by the Intentional Fault of the Insured

232. *The Problem* – Article 2464 C.C.Q. stipulates that the insurer is never obliged to indemnify injuries caused by the insured's inten-

176.   Above, note 171 at 2229 (our translation).
177.   Ibid. (our translation).
178.   See below, at §§317ff.

tional fault.[179] Therefore, when intentional fault is alleged, the insurer will be exonerated from the duty to defend the insured.[180] To what extent is this exclusion applicable to instances of sexual or spousal abuse? For example, does a father who abuses a child commit an intentional fault if he himself was a victim of sexual abuse? What about a violent spouse who strikes only when suffering from hallucinations or delusions of grandeur or when drunk?[181] In order to receive punitive damages, the plaintiff must show that the interference with her protected right to inviolability under the *Charter of Human Rights and Freedoms* was intentional.[182] Does this mean that a plaintiff who claims punitive damages under the Charter renounces her claim against the abuser's insurer? Does the expression "intentional fault" have the same meaning in both insurance and human rights law?

233. *Origin of the Statutory Provision* – Article 2464 C.C.Q. essentially reprises the second paragraph of article 2563 C.C.L.C.[183] Inspired by French law, reference to the insured's intentional fault dates back to the 1974 reform.[184] The provision's primary objective is to ensure that the abuser does not defraud the insurer by causing the loss himself. This prohibition applies, for instance, to the insured who burns down his or her own house in order to benefit financially. Article 2464 C.C.Q also fulfils a second objective: for reasons of public order, some acts should not be insurable.[185] Upon

179. The second paragraph protects only employers or parents vicariously liable for compensating the plaintiff's injuries. The insurer must indemnify even where the fault of the employee or the child is intentional. See art. 2464 C.C.Q.
180. See *Nichols* v. *American Home Assurance*, [1990] 1 S.C.R. 801. The allegations in the declaration define the duty to defend the insured, but the duty exists only if it is possible to conclude from the allegations that the insurance policy applies.
181. See *Ballard* v. *Cordeau*, [1990] R.J.Q. 1664 (Que. Sup. Ct.).
182. See below, at §§317ff.
183. Article 2563 C.C.L.C. stipulated: "However, the insurer is not liable, notwithstanding any agreement to the contrary, for prejudice arising from the insured's intentional fault."
184. See Claude Belleau, "Réflexions sur les origines et l'interprétation de certains articles du code civil en matière d'assurance," in *Le nouveau droit québécois des assurances: dix ans de contentieux* (Montreal: Les Éditions Thémis, 1988) at 12, who explains that the wording is borrowed directly from article 12 of the 1930 French law.
185. Ibid. According to Belleau, intentional acts "negate the uncertainty inherent in the notion of risk, on the one hand, and [contribute] to prohibiting the insurance of illicit risk, on the other," which explains why they are uninsurable (our translation).

further examination of these two objectives, we are able to conclude that it is possible, in certain circumstances, to claim against the abuser's insurer. The consideration of these two objectives also explains certain jurisprudential currents.

(a) Subjectivity of Intentional Fault

234. *Some Criteria* – The jurisprudence uses a variety of criteria when determining the absence or presence of intentional fault.[186] The insured must have "been conscious that the injury was inevitable."[187] It is necessary that the "injury itself was sought"[188] and "that the act was committed deliberately and willingly."[189] The intent to commit the act must be distinguished from the intent to inflict injury. The insured must not only want to commit the faulty act, he must also want to produce the consequences of such act. Jean-Pierre Lusignan comments that it is essential to distinguish correctly between the two types of intents—the intent to commit the act and the intent to cause the resulting injury.[190] According to Lusignan, this is the only interpretation compatible with the evolution of French law, the source of this reform.[191] He deplores certain

---

186.   See, among others, *Oppenheim* v. *Dionne*, [1996] R.R.A. 474 (Que. Sup. Ct.); *Royale du Canada, cie d'assurances* v. *Légaré*, [1991] R.J.Q. 91 (Que. Sup. Ct.); *Poirier* v. *Zurich, compagnie d'assurances*, [1993] R.R.A. 132 (Que. Sup. Ct.); *Pang* v. *Dilallo*, [1989] R.R.A. 205 (Que. Sup. Ct.); *Groupe Desjardins Assurances générales* v. *Dufort*, [1985] C.P. 174; *La Haye* v. *Assurances générales des Caisses Desjardins inc.*, [1994] R.R.A. 378 (C.Q.); *Groupe Desjardins Assurances générales* v. *Prévoyance, cie d'assurances*, [1988] R.R.A. 410 (Que. Sup. Ct.).

187.   The definition is drawn from the work of Didier Lluelles, *Droits des assurances: aspects contractuels*, 2nd ed. (Montreal: Les Éditions Thémis, 1986) at 135, cited in *Royale du Canada, cie d'assurances* v. *Légaré*, above, note 186 (our translation).

188.   Maurice Tancelin, *Des obligations: contrat et responsabilité* (Montreal: Wilson and Lafleur / SOREJ, 1984) No. 421 at 221, cited in *Royale du Canada, cie d'assurances* v. *Légaré*, above, note 186, and *La Haye* v. *Assurances générales des Caisses Desjardins inc.*, above, note 186; *contra: Ballard* v. *Cordeau*, above, note 181 (our translation).

189.   Jean-Louis Baudouin, *La responsabilité civile et délictuelle* (Cowansville, QC: Les Éditions Yvon Blais, 1985) No. 102 at 62 (see the 4th ed., 1994, No. 124 at 90), cited in *Royale du Canada, cie d'assurances* v. *Légaré*, above note 186, and *La Haye* v. *Assurances générales des Caisses Desjardins inc.*, above note 186, (our translation).

190.   Jean-Pierre Lusignan, "L'accident et la faute non intentionnelle en droit des assurances privées québécois," (1990) 31 *Cahiers de Droit* 155.

191.   See, however, the opinion of the Superior Court in *Ballard* v. *Cordeau*, above, note 181, where the court suggests that the Quebec legislature did not intend

aspects of the jurisprudence that occasionally bypass the subjective approach to intentional fault, substituting instead the average insured individual who should know and appreciate the foreseeable consequences of the conduct. We agree with this analysis and suggest that it also allows for the fields of insurance and human rights law to be distinguished.

235. *Distinguishing Intentional Fault from Intentional Interference under the Charter* – In *Québec (Curateur public)* v. *Syndicat national des employés de l'Hôpital Saint-Ferdinand,*[192] the Supreme Court of Canada, in an opinion written by Madam Justice L'Heureux-Dubé, declared that intentional interference with a protected right under the Charter must be analysed within a large and liberal interpretation of human rights legislation. This context differs totally from that of article 2464 C.C.Q., which is essentially intended to provide for an exclusionary protection rule and is therefore to be narrowly interpreted. In addition, in *Syndicat national des employés de l'Hôpital Saint-Ferdinand*, the judge explains:

> "there will be unlawful and intentional interference within the meaning of the second paragraph of s. 49 of the *Charter* when the person who commits the unlawful interference has a state of mind that implies a desire or intent to cause the consequences of his or her wrongful conduct, or when that person acts with full knowledge of the ... consequences. *This test is not as strict as specific intent, but it does go beyond simple negligence.*"[193]

We suggest that article 2464 C.C.Q. requires this "specific intent" in insurance law, which in our opinion is similar to the specific intent (*mens rea* or guilty intent) crucial to the commission of a criminal act. This intent must be subjectively evaluated.[194] The extent to which the consequences were foreseeable is merely one element that goes towards proving the true intent of the insured.[195]

---

to follow the evolution in French law. For a critique of this decision, see below, at §243.

192. [1996] 3 S.C.R. 211 (hereinafter *Syndicat national des employés de l'Hôpital Saint-Ferdinand*).

193. Ibid. at 262 (emphasis added).

194. In support of a "subjective" approach to intentional fault, see Jean-Guy Bergeron, *Les contrats d'assurance (terrestre): lignes et entre-lignes*, t. 2 (Sherbrooke: S.E.M., 1992) at 32.

195. Ibid., and Lusignan, above, note 190. On this note, see also *Bello* v. *Assurances générales des Caisses Desjardins inc.*, [1993] R.J.Q. 895 (C.Q.).

Our theory of specific intent is compatible with the majority of court decisions in insurance law. We will identify those decisions in particular that examine the insured's emotional state or his age.

236. *Psychological State of the Insured* – The Court of Appeal held in *Cie d'assurance Mutuelle contre le feu de Beauce* v. *Beaudoin*[196] that the fact that the insured burned down his own property in "a moment of mental incapacity" was not a ground for rejecting a claim under the insurance contract. The court thus recognized that the insured's capacity to form intent depended on his state of mind. In *Poirier* v. *Zurich, compagnie d'assurances,*[197] the Superior Court also ruled that the insured did not act voluntarily when he willingly swallowed a large dose of drugs and started a fire.[198] This decision is of particular interest to us because it emphasizes the unforeseeability of the insured Poirier's acts, the intentional nature of which was subjectively assessed by the Superior Court. The court focused on the fact that Poirier was not a habitual drug user and was in a seriously depressed state, and it rejected the argument that Poirier had consumed drugs in order to give himself the courage to kill his daughter and commit suicide by burning the apartment.

237. *The Insured's Age* – Many intentional fault decisions involve fires lit by young boys. In *La Royale du Canada, cie d'assurances* v. *Légaré,*[199] the Superior Court held that the fault committed by a group of adolescents, while reckless, if not stupid, was involuntary.[200] The Court of Quebec, however, decided otherwise in *La Haye* v. *Assurances générales des Caisses Desjardins inc.,*[201] a case involving physical abuse. Without going into much detail, it held that a young man who punched another boy did so intentionally where the act was unprovoked. This last decision appears to contradict jurisprudence established by the Cour de cassation, wherein proof of intentional fault is subjectively assessed.[202] According to the Cour

196. (1928), 45 B.R. 551 (Que. C.A.).
197. Above, note 186.
198. Indemnification for "intentional" acts by the insured was excluded under the policy. The exclusion for intentional acts may be broader than for unintentional acts. Once again, the wording of the contract is determinative.
199. Above, note 186.
200. *Contra: Oppenheim* v. *Dionne,* above, note 186, where a fourteen-year-old adolescent, acting alone, sprayed an accelerant into the air and lit it; see also *Groupe Desjardins, Assurances générales* v. *Dufort,* [1985] C.P. 174, where the fire was caused involuntarily, but during an illegal break-in.
201. Above, note 186.
202. See J.C.P. 1977.IV.168 (Cass., 10 May 1977), discussed in Lusignan, above,

de cassation, the evidence must show not only that the young boy intended to punch the other one, but that he meant to inflict the type of injury that resulted. We suggest that the courts should identify more clearly the subjective element in the insured's guilty intent. Given the position of the Cour de cassation, it is necessary, prior to rejecting a claim by a victim for indemnification from an insurer, to establish that the young boys appreciated and intended the consequences of their faulty acts.

Before applying the criterion of subjective intentional fault, it should be noted that this approach differs from the approach adopted under American law.

(b) Comparative Law Analysis

238. *Common Law Response* – Canadian common law jurisprudence has yet to resolve the issue of suing the abuser's insurer, whereas in the United States, there have been many instances of the insurer being sued. Courts of justice are generally hesitant to force the abuser's insurer to indemnify the victim, because most insurance policies contain exclusions similar to the exclusion regarding the insured's intentional fault.[203] The insurance contract often does not cover acts committed *with the intent to injure*. It is unclear whether the intent to injure must be subjectively or objectively assessed. The majority of courts have adopted an objective approach and presume the insured's malicious intent in cases of sexual abuse of children (this is the *inferred intent rule*[204]). In such cases, American courts

---

note 190 at 164. See Yvonne Lambert-Faivre, *Droit des assurances*, 7th ed. (Paris: Dalloz, 1990) Nos. 391ff at 220ff.

203. See David Florig, "Insurance Coverage for Sexual Abuse or Molestation," (1995) 30 *Tort & Ins. L.J.* 699; Ward S. Connolly, "Sexual Abuser Insurance in Alaska: A Note on *St. Paul Fire & Marine Insurance Co.* v. *F.H.*," (1996) 13 *Alaska L. Rev.* 265; Edward J. Walters, Jr., "Insurance Coverage for Sexual Molestation of Children: Is It Expected or Intended?" (1996) 56 *La. L. Rev.* 733; Linda Jorgenson, Steven B. Bisbing, and Pamela K. Sutherland, "Therapist–Patient Sexual Exploitation and Insurance Liability," (1992) 27 *Tort & Ins. L.J.* 595; Carolyn Mueller, "Ohio Homeowners Beware: Your Homeowner's Insurance Premium May Be Subsidizing Child Sexual Abuse," (1994) 20 *U. Dayton L. Rev.* 341.

204. Mueller, ibid., notes that since 1982, American courts in thirty-three states have been applying the inferred intent rule. See, for a sampling of decisions from different states that apply this rule: *Gearing* v. *Nationwide Insurance Co.*, 76 Ohio St.3d 34, 665 N.E.2d 1115 (Ohio, 1996); *State Farm Fire & Casualty Co.* v. *Smith*, 907 F.2d 900 (9th Cir.1990) (sexual abuse of an adopted child; insurance was excluded); *State Farm Fire & Casualty Co.* v. *Davis*, 612

refuse to accept the insured's allegations that he was unaware of the harmful effects of the sexual relationship on the child[205] or that he was incapable of forming the intent to harm.[206] Nonetheless, in cases involving sexual abuse between adults or committed by adolescents, courts of justice will accept that a duty to indemnify exists where the insured is unable to appreciate the consequences of his act due to his youth[207] or intoxicated state.[208]

So.2d 458 (Ala.1993); *J.C. Penney Casualty Ins. Co.* v. *M.K.*, 804 P.2d 689 (Cal.1991), case comment: Mary Sanchez, "Insurance Coverage for Child Sexual Abuse after *J.C. Penney Casualty Insurance Co.* v. *M.K.*," (1993) 22 *Sw. U. L. Rev.* 1229; *Landis* v. *Allstate Ins. Co.*, 546 So.2d 1051 (Fla.1989) (sexual abuse in a daycare); *Worcester Ins. Co.* v. *Fells Acres Day School, Inc.*, 558 N.E.2d 958 (Mass., 1990); *Estate of Lehmann* v. *Metzger*, 355 N.W.2d 425 (Minn., 1984); *State Farm Fire & Casualty Co.* v. *van Gorder*, 455 N.W.2d 543 (Neb., 1990); *Vermont Mut. Ins. Co.* v. *Malcolm*, 517 A.2d 800 (N.H., 1986); *Allstate Ins. Co.* v. *Mugavero*, 589 N.E.2d 365 (N.Y., 1992); *American Family Mut. Ins. Co.* v. *Purdy*, 483 N.W.2d 197 (S.D., 1992); *Rodriguez* v. *Williams*, 729 P.2d 627 (Wash., 1986); *Horace Mann Ins. Co.* v. *Leeber*, 376 S.E.2d 581 (W.Va., 1988). *Contra*: certain decisions do not apply the rule, or suggest that exceptions to the rule exist: *State Auto Mut. Ins. Co.* v. *McIntyre*, 652 F.Supp. 1177 (N.D.Ala., 1987) (sexual abuse by the grandfather: subjective intent to willingly harm another required), rev'd by *State Farm Fire & Casualty Co.* v. *Davis*, 612 So.2d 458 (Ala., 1993); *Zordan* v. *Page*, 500 So.2d 608 (Fla. Dist. Ct. App., 1986) (subjective intent required), rev'd by *Landis* v. *Allstate Ins. Co.*, 546 So.2d 1051 (Fla., 1989); *Roe* v. *State Farm Ins. & Casualty Co.*, 376 S.E.2d 876 (Ga., 1989) (suggested possible exceptions to the rule "only in the strongest of factual situations"); *MacKinnon* v. *Hanover Ins. Co.*, 471 A.2d 1166 (N.H., 1984) (required subjective intent, lacking in cases of intoxication).

205. *National Mutual Insurance Co.* v. *Abernethy*, 445 S.E. 2d 618 (N.C. Ct. App. 1994).

206. Wiley v. *State Farm Fire & Casualty Co.*, 995 F.2d 457 (3d Cir., 1993) (proof of alcoholism ruled irrelevant); *Pioneer State Mutual Insurance* v. *Weekley* (1997), 221 Mich.App. 34, 561 N.W.2d 408 (Mich. Ct. App.) (responsibility of insurer not greater where the insured's mental illness was proved); *Sara L.* v. *Broden*, 507 N.W.2d 24 (Minn. Ct. App., 1993) (allegation of pedophelia ruled irrelevant); *Public Employees Mut. Ins. Co.* v. *Rash*, 740 P.2d 370 (Wash. Ct. App., 1987) (did not consider inability to form proper intent); *N.N.* v. *Moraine Mut. Ins. Co.*, 450 N.W.2d 445 (Wis., 1990) (intoxication irrelevant); case comment: Joseph R. Long, "*N.N.* v. *Moraine Mutual Insurance Co.*: The Liability Insurance Intentional Injury Exclusion in Cases of Child Sexual Abuse," (1991) *Wis. L. Rev.* 139.

207. *Fire Insurance Exchange* v. *Diehl*, 450 Mich. 678, 64 USLW 2622; 545 N.W.2d 602 (S.C. of Mich., 1996).

208. *Aetna Life & Casualty Co.* v. *Barthelemy*, 33 F.3d 189 (3d Cir., 1994) (sexual assault committed by nineteen-year-old man; the victim was eighteen years old).

239. *Public Order in American Law* – It is particularly interesting to examine the manner in which public order arguments have been presented in the United States. In *Vigilant Insurance Co.* v. *Kambly,*[209] the court had to decide whether it was contrary to the public order to oblige the insurer to indemnify a victim who was abused by a psychiatrist insured against professional liability. The court asked three questions: Would others be incited to commit similar crimes if indemnification were allowed? Was the insurance policy contracted with the objective of breaking the law? Would the insured profit from his faulty conduct if indemnification were permitted? The court answered all three questions in the negative and concluded that it was not contrary to public order to indemnify a victim of sexual abuse where the abuser held professional liability insurance.[210] Thus, public order must be appreciated with respect to the goal of preventing the insurer from being defrauded. This approach to public order supports indemnification of victims of spousal and sexual abuse.

240. *Comparative Analysis* – Barring specific wording in the policy, it appears that indemnification of the victim by the abuser's insurer could be permitted under the Civil Code in certain circumstances, more easily so than under American common law. This conclusion stems from the narrow interpretation of intentional fault applied in French law requiring fault to be subjectively assessed and requiring specific intent of the insured not only to commit the faulty act, but also to produce the consequences flowing from that act. The insurer should indemnify where the insured can prove that he did not specifically intend to cause the type of irreparable damage for which he is responsible. These cases are rather rare, as we shall see.

(c) Application to Cases Involving Sexual or Spousal Abuse

241. *Incapacity to Form the Specific Intent* – Application of the specific intent criterion would justify indemnification of the victim by the abuser's insurer in two particular situations where capacity to

---

209.   114 Mich. App. 683, 319 N.W.2d 382 (C.A. Mich., 1982).
210.   In response to the third question, the court held that the victim benefits from the insurance indemnity, not the insured. However the insured does indeed benefit indirectly because he is exempt from paying himself, where he would be capable of paying the damages awarded.

form specific intent is lacking: mental illness causing sexually deviant behaviour and "voluntary intoxication."

242. *Precondition towards Sexual or Spousal Abuse* – The insurer should indemnify the victim where there is medical evidence supporting the incapacity to form specific intent, such as irresistible sexual impulse. Drawing on the examples cited above, we can then argue that an abuser who was himself sexually abused and is unaware of his condition does not commit an intentional fault as previously defined. The act must nonetheless be unforeseeable: for example, where the insured knows of his condition and refuses treatment, the fault becomes intentional. The element of unforeseeability is what distinguishes the two situations.[211] Pursuant to article 2464 C.C.Q., only the unforeseeable nature of an initial instance of sexual abuse or abuse caused by the insured's state of mind can justify indemnification.

243. *Voluntary Intoxication* – Family abuse and alcohol frequently accompany one another.[212] Abusive consumption of alcohol is often described as a "facilitator" of abuse:[213] the line between acceptable and unacceptable behaviour becomes blurred and awareness of acceptable behaviour may even be completely lost. Whether or not voluntary intoxication constitutes an intentional fault within the meaning of article 2464 C.C.Q. raises interesting issues. In *Ballard* v. *Cordeau*,[214] the Superior Court ruled that intoxication was an

---

211.   See *Poirier* v. *Zurich compagnie d'assurances*, above, note 186.
212.   Stephanie S. Covington, "Alcohol and Family Violence," in *L'alcool, les drogues et le tabac: perspectives internationales – le passé, le présent et l'avenir* (Proceedings of the 34th International Conference on Alcoholism and Drug Abuse, Vol. 1, 15) (Calgary: Alberta Alcohol and Drug Abuse Commission, 1985).
213.   This expression is found in *R.* v. *Daviault*, [1994] 3 S.C.R. 63, where Judge Cory cites the Saskatchewan Alcohol and Drug Abuse Commission, "Legal Offences in Saskatchewan," 1989.
214.   Above, note 181; see also *Moreau* v. *Prévoyants du Canada*, J.E. 83-156 (Que. Sup. Ct.). In *Ballard*, the decision of the Superior Court was based on *Co-operative Fire & Insurance* v. *Saindon*, [1976] 1 S.C.R. 735, which represents a trend discredited in Canadian common law. See Craig Brown and Julio Menezes, *Insurance Law in Canada*, 2nd ed. (Barrie, ON: Carswell, 1991) at 197–208; *Canadian Indemnity Co.* v. *Walkem Machinery & Equipment Ltd*, [1976] 1 S.C.R. 309; *Mutual of Omaha Insurance Co.* v. *Stats*, [1978] 2 S.C.R. 1153. For a good overview of the jurisprudence and the doctrine on defence of intentional fault of an intoxicated insured, see Mr. Justice Gagnon's analysis in *Frappier* v. *Bélair, compagnie d'assurances*, [1995] R.J.Q. 1930 (C.Q.). See *Général Accident, cie d'assurance du Canada* v. *Groupe Commerce, cie d'assurance*, REJB 2000-16651 (Que. C.A.), confirming the opinion of the great

intentional "voluntary" fault and the insurer was not responsible to indemnify for the resulting injury. Intoxication, however, even if voluntary, is an acceptable defence in criminal proceedings that require the accused to possess specific intent, even where it is a general intent crime. An accused may, in fact, succeed in exonerating himself where he introduces evidence of extreme intoxication, as demonstrated in the Supreme Court decision in *R. v. Daviault.*[215] If, as argued above, a parallel can be drawn between intentional fault in insurance law and guilty intent in criminal law, it is logical to conclude that proof of the insured's intoxication would negate a finding of "intentional fault." A drunken spouse, for example, could claim that although he possessed some type of nebulous intent to intimidate, he did not intend to cause the tragic consequences suffered by his wife when he pushed her down the stairs, such as paralysis or permanent total incapacity.[216]

In a dissenting opinion in *Daviault*, however, Mr. Justice Sopinka remarked that public order requires that the accused's intent to drink and his intent to commit the prohibited act be considered as one and the same. The majority of the Supreme Court opposed this view and felt it unjust that a pubic policy argument should impose criminal liability on an individual who was unaware of causing injury.[217] Could the public order argument also be raised to refute a finding that the necessary specific intent is absent in cases of intoxication and, thus, to deny indemnification by the insurer?

244. *Indemnification of Victims of Spousal or Sexual Abuse in Light of the Objectives of Article 2464 C.C.Q.* – Public order is one of two objectives underlying the intentional fault exclusion stipulated in article 2464 C.C.Q.; prevention of fraud is the other. It is only the

---

majority of the case law to the effect that damage caused by an inebriated person to himself or herself or to another is an accident, not gross negligence.

215. Above, note 213.

216. *Contra*: *Ballard* v. *Cordeau,* above, note 181.

217. In the area of insurance law, Quebec courts have been polarized by the debate surrounding the effect of the protection of public order on the legal consequences of intoxication: see *Duplessis* v. *Assurances générales des Caisses Desjardins inc.*, [1995] R.R.A. 1081 (Que. Sup. Ct.) where the judge made reference to public order in his decision to reject an action by an insured against his insurer for damages to his car following an accident caused by his drunken driving. For a contrary result, see *Frappier* v. *Bélair, compagnie d'assurances,* above, note 214. See also *Général Accident, cie d'assurance du Canada* v. *Groupe Commerce, cie d'assurance,* above, note 214.

objective of public order that warrants examination in cases of spousal or sexual abuse. In fact, where abuse has taken place, the insured does not profit financially from an action against the insurer. The "benefit"—that is to say the indemnity—will be paid to the victim. The second objective, which seeks to discourage fraud or prevent the insured from causing the event himself, is therefore inexistent. Only public order, the first objective, can justify a negative attitude towards suing the abuser's insurer. There are those who find it repugnant for a rapist or a pedophile to benefit from insurance, especially when the risk will eventually be split between all holders of a liability insurance policy. It is nonetheless important to avoid exaggerating this aspect of the public order.[218] Permitting indemnification by the insurer does not mean that society endorses the act committed or that the rapist "benefits" from the insurance. While professional negligence is certainly unacceptable, it is nonetheless insurable, and a victim of abuse deserves to be indemnified, however condemnable the abuse. Thus, in certain circumstances, the abuse should be deemed unintentional, such as when the insured is intoxicated.

245. *Conclusion* – Without a doubt, a victim who sues the abuser's insurer will have to overcome difficulties. Indemnification is possible if the insured's intent is subjectively assessed in situations where the insured was highly intoxicated or psychologically unstable. In our opinion, public order considerations inherent in article 2464 C.C.Q. should not prevent an indemnity from being awarded. We must nevertheless admit that in most cases it is not possible to prove the absence of specific intent. Sexual and spousal abuse is generally planned and repetitive, lending little credibility to the argument that the fault was unintentional. In addition, the policy normally contains a specific exclusion pertaining to the "criminal act" of the insured, which we will now examine.

ii) Exclusion of Injury Caused by the Insured's Criminal Act

246. *A Contractual Limitation Requiring a Narrow Interpretation* – All limitations on coverage must be expressly and restrictively stipulated in a policy (article 2464 C.C.Q.). The exclusion pertaining to the insured's criminal acts must be written into the policy in order to be applicable, in contrast to the exclusion pertaining to injury caused by intentional fault. The exclusion of an insured's criminal

---

218.   See *Frappier* v. *Bélair, compagnie d'assurances*, above, note 214.

act is a pure contractual limitation not dictated by the Civil Code[219] and, therefore, it must be narrowly interpreted.[220] Any ambiguous language must benefit the insured.

247. *Criminal Acts and Regulatory Infractions* – In this regard, following the example of French law, it is necessary to distinguish between a criminal act and a regulatory infraction.[221] The words in insurance policy exclusions are understood according to their ordinary meaning; therefore, "criminal act" should be understood in its most restrictive sense and should not encompass faults that constitute regulatory infractions, but are not criminal acts within the meaning of the Criminal Code. Thus, the existence of such a clause in the insurance policy should not be relied on in order to exclude the fault of failing to divulge confidences by a child victim of sexual abuse, in violation of the *Youth Protection Act*.[222] This violation is not a criminal act in the general sense and should not be excluded from insurance coverage.

However, since an abuser's acts are almost always prohibited by the Criminal Code, when the exclusion pertaining to criminal acts is written into the policy, an action launched against the abuser's insurer will be of little use. The victim should therefore seek relief from the other defendants' insurers, which involves another type of fault.

b)   Responsibility of Other Defendants' Insurers

248. *The Various Defendants* – We have shown that persons other than the abuser may be liable towards the victim. This includes individuals who should or could have protected the victim,[223] as well

---

219. Reference to criminal acts by the accused is permitted by the Code, but is deemed to be "unwritten"—that is, it is of no effect where the insurer relies on this clause to be released from any obligation in the event of a breach of the law (art. 2402 C.C.Q.).

220. This is due to the expression "restrictively stipulated" in article 2464 C.C.Q. See, among others, Lusignan, above, note 190. In addition, even in the absence of this statutory language, the *contra proferentem* rule is well established in Quebec insurance law: C. Belleau, above, note 184, and, among others, *Great-West Life Assurance Co.* v. *Paris*, [1959] B.R. 349; *Exportations Consolidated Bathurst ltée* v. *Mutual Boiler & Machinery Insurance Co.*, [1980] 1 S.C.R. 888.

221. See Lusignan, above, note 190.

222. See above, at §§168ff.

223. Ibid.

as the abuser's employer or parents.[224] We will examine the defences that can be raised by an insurer of these types of defendants against an action for sexual or spousal abuse: exclusion of the insured's family members, narrow definition of injuries covered, and time limitations under the insurance policy.

i)   Exclusion of the Insured's Family Members

249. *Multiple Insured Persons* – It is possible for the same policy to insure several persons. When one of the insured persons intentionally causes an injury, to what extent is the other insured covered when he or she did not commit the intentional fault but is nevertheless liable? For example, what of a mother who is liable for refusing to protect her child from sexual abuse by her spouse? The Code specifically provides for continued protection of the insured who did not commit an intentional fault (article 2464 C.C.Q.); hence, the mother's liability should be covered. Other clauses, however, may exclude coverage for the child under these circumstances.

250. *Permanently "Under the Roof"* – Policies often stipulate that coverage does not extend to injury caused by "persons living under your roof (specifically yourself) except if they are employed by the household."[225] This exclusion is meant to minimize the risk to the insurer of having to indemnify family members who suffer injuries due to accidents. As with any exclusion, Quebec jurisprudence has narrowly interpreted this clause. In *Bélair, Compagnie d'assurances* v. *Moquin,*[226] for example, the Court of Appeal ruled that a young girl staying temporarily at the home of her friend's father was not a person living "under the same roof." The young girl in this case had been seriously wounded when a gun was negligently fired by her

---

224. See above, at §§206ff.
225. This exclusion arises frequently, and its wording can be determinative. Consider the different results regarding insurer liability for indemnification of a parent sued in counterclaim by a defendant who injured a child. The counterclaim alleged that the child was poorly supervised by the parent, which in turn led to the accident caused by the defendant: *Re Sheppard and Co-operators General Insurance Company and Quick et al.* v. *MacKenzie et al.; Lumbermen's Mutual Casualty Company 1996* (1997), 33 O.R. (3d) 362 (Ont. C.A.). In one case, the clause "you are not insured for claims arising . . . between any persons insured by this policy" is interpreted as obliging the insurer to defend the counterclaim, but the clause "You are not insured for claims *arising out of bodily injury to you* or any person residing in your household," to the contrary, excludes insurer responsibility.
226. [1996] R.R.A. 941 (C.A.).

friend. In the court's opinion, a temporary sojourn does not qualify as "living under the roof" of the insured within the meaning of the policy.

251. *Application in Cases of Spousal and Sexual Abuse* – When sexual or spousal abuse occurs within the family, recovery from the abuser's insurer is unlikely due to exclusionary clauses that deny coverage to persons living under the same roof as the insured. The result will be the same whether a child sues her father for intentional sexual abuse or her mother for failing to protect her from the abuse:[227] the insurer will not be obliged to indemnify the victim.

Insurance policies typically contain clauses that result in denying indemnification for intrafamily abuse. However, other exclusionary clauses will be raised when the defendant is the abuser's employer or is a person who has breached a duty to report or protect.

ii)   Narrow Definition of Injury Covered

252. *Limits of the Protection* – The wording of the insurance contract is determinative of the coverage. We will examine two expressions that are frequently employed in insurance policies and that are capable of limiting coverage. Liability insurance contracts generally indemnify the insured for "compensatory damages and interest" paid as reparation for "personal injury" inflicted on another.

(a)   Compensatory Damages

253. *Exclusion of Punitive Damages* – The expression "compensatory damages and interest" in a typical liability insurance contract becomes meaningful only when understood in reference to "punitive damages." Compensatory damages are damages intended to return the victim to the state in which she was prior to the fault— that is, they are meant to indemnify the loss suffered and the profit of which she has been deprived (article 1611 C.C.Q.). Material, bodily, and moral damages are compensated, as are their pecuniary and non-pecuniary consequences (articles 1457 and 1608 C.C.Q.).[228] The insurer pays "interest" to the plaintiff as indemnification for

---

227. See above, at §§183ff.
228. See Hubert Reid, *Dictionnaire de droit québécois et canadien* (Montreal: Wilson and Lafleur, 1994) at 194, s.v. "dommages-intérêts."

the late payment (article 1617 C.C.Q.).[229] Only punitive damages, meant to deter rather than to compensate, are excluded (article 1621 C.C.Q.). This was the conclusion of the Manitoba Queen's Bench, albeit in *obiter,* in a Canadian common law case involving allegations of sexual assault and breach of the duty to protect.[230]

(b) "Personal Injury"

254. *Definition of Personal Injury* – Liability insurance contracts often protect against "pecuniary consequences arising out of civil liability of the insured due to 'personal injury' suffered by another 'caused by an incident that occurred during the present contract'."[231] The definition of "personal injury" includes "any bodily injury, that is, any interference with the physical integrity of a person, and includes disease." The question is whether a personal injury claim includes psychological loss, such as post-traumatic stress.

255. *Psychological Illness Included* – Psychological illness must be included in the definition of "illness" if we apply the insurance law general rules of interpretation.[232] Any other interpretation ignores medical science, which recognizes neuroses as illnesses.

256. *Common Law Jurisprudence* – The interpretation that illness includes psychological illness is now well established in Canadian common law. In *Wellington Guarantee* v. *Evangelical Lutheran Church in Canada,*[233] a divided British Columbia Court of Appeal concluded, after having reviewed the American jurisprudence, that the terms "bodily injury," "sickness," and "disease" included psycho-

---

229. This refers to moratory damages; see Gérard Cornu, *Vocabulaire juridique,* 8th ed. (Paris: Quadridge, P.U.F., 1990) at 561, s.v. "moratoire."
230. See *Victoria General Hospital* v. *General Accident Assurance Co. of Canada,* above, note 38. In this decision, the court noted that the insurer undertook to pay *"all sums,"* which includes punitive damages. The court also noted that in English Canada the law is not clear on whether public order prevents punitive damages from being insured.
231. The terms are drawn from the typical insurance contract, *Lloyd's Excellence-Assurance Habitation.* The wording of the contract is determinative. (our translation).
232. See above, at §246.
233. [1996] B.C.J. No. 872 (Q.L.). Note that in this decision, the Court of Appeal interpreted an exclusion in the coverage. For a favourable interpretation of the coverage, see also *Victoria General Hospital* v. *General Accident Assurance Co. of Canada,* above, note 38. *Contra: Dow* v. *Trumper,* [1995] O.J. No. 2261 (Ont. Gen. Div.) (Q.L.).

logical injury.[234] Survivors, however, may find it controversial to categorize the consequences of sexual assault as an "illness." This qualification could have symbolic negative impacts on their rehabilitation. Several victims argue that anger is a "normal" reaction and reject being labelled as "psychologically ill." Obviously this is an issue to be discussed with the client.[235]

iii) Time Limitations on Coverage

Given that spousal or sexual abuse can have taken place in the distant past, how does the passage of time affect the insurer's coverage? This is the question to which we now turn.

257. *Two Types of Policies* – In general, there are two types of policies: claim based and incident based. In the first case, the insurer is obliged to indemnify all claims filed during the period of coverage, regardless of the date of the original loss.[236] A claim-based policy, for example, would oblige the hospital insurer to indemnify a claim filed today based on a sexual assault committed by an employee five or ten years ago. Under this policy, the insured must divulge any incidents liable to engage his responsibility prior to entering into the policy (article 2408 C.C.Q.). Failure to do so may totally or partially exonerate the insurer from payment (articles 2410 and 2411 C.C.Q.). In contrast, coverage under the incident-based policy extends to the fault itself, regardless of whether or not the claim is launched within the time limit of the policy. It is possible in an incident-based policy, for example, for indemnification to occur today under a policy in effect during the 1960s, where the fault occurred during that period.[237] Two different policies could conceivably apply to the same claim.[238] Lawyers representing clients who are victims of abuse need to obtain copies of any pertinent policies.[239]

---

234. There is no reason for the French expression "préjudice personnel," however inelegant, not to be similarly interpreted.
235. See above, at §§69ff.
236. See *Reid Crowther & Partners Ltd* v. *Simcoe & Erie General Insurance Co.*, [1993] 1 S.C.R. 252 for a discussion on the two types of contracts. See also Robert Bell, "Sexual Abuse and Institutions: Insurance Issues," (1996) 6 *Canadian Insurance Law Reporter* 53.
237. Incidentally, prescription delays must also be respected. See above, at §§85ff.
238. For an example where the plaintiff alleged the overlapping of two policies, see *Victoria General Hospital* v. *General Accident Assurance Co. of Canada*, above, note 38.
239. See above, at §231.

258. *Conclusion* – Indemnification by the insurer raises interesting questions. Quebec law may distinguish itself from American common law in its interpretation of the insured's "intentional fault." Given that many insurers are multinational, they would no doubt resist any attempt to introduce a different interpretation, preferring instead the public policy argument in order to avoid indemnification.[240] In our opinion, these public policy arguments are appropriate where the insured is fully capable of understanding the consequences of his actions, thus excluding an insured suffering from mental illness. Voluntary intoxication of the insured is a more controversial issue. Logically speaking, intoxication, whose purpose is not to provide the insured with "courage," prevents intent from forming, and should therefore hinder a finding of intentional fault. The courts should be much more sensitive to the victim's need for indemnification when considering the insurer of other defendants who did not commit the specific fault of assault. In our opinion, in this situation the public policy argument carries much less weight and is unable to justify treating sexual assault or spousal abuse differently from other liability cases.

C. Causation

259. *Complexity of the Issue* – The plaintiff must prove causation in addition to fault (article 1457 C.C.Q.). The defendant is liable only for the direct and immediate consequences of his fault (article 1607 C.C.Q.). In the litigation under discussion, as with any action in civil liability, proof of causation can pose a problem and can result in the plaintiff's indemnity being denied or reduced. The issue is a delicate one, and both the doctrine and the jurisprudence attest to the hurdles to be overcome.[241] Yet, these difficulties must not serve as a pretext for avoiding the matter, given that plaintiffs are obliged to tackle this problem. We are aware that this subject is complex, and we hope that our examination will help resolve the debate.

260. *Different Manifestations* – Causation appears at various stages during an action for sexual and spousal assault, starting with prescription.[242] As we have demonstrated, if a victim of sexual assault

---

240. See Bell, above, note 236.
241. On the difficulties of applying causation, see Louise Langevin, "Réflexion sur le lien de causalité en matière de discrimination: une difficile intégration," (1996) 22 *Queen's L. J.* 51.
242. See "Extinctive Prescription," above, at §§85ff.

is incapable of proving the connection between her current problems and the defendant's abusive behaviour, she can argue that it was impossible for her to act or that the injury manifested itself gradually over the course of time, two mechanisms capable of suspending prescription.

Causation is also important when evaluating damages. A defendant will not deny causation in cases involving multiple sources of damage, where there was an interaction between various attackers and various faulty and faultless traumatic incidents. Instead, he will try to minimize its impact in order to reduce the amount of compensation. His defence will consist of evidence to show that the plaintiff's injuries were not caused exclusively by his acts, but were due to a pre-existing condition, to a previous attack or traumatic incident, or were aggravated by subsequent events or by the victim's own actions. The causation question is important, for once a court has determined fault, or it has been conceded by the defendant, apportioning causation and liability is the defendant's last chance for reducing compensation.

The various arguments of the defendant concerning the absence of a causal link are accepted in certain cases in Canadian common law, and the defendant's liability is reduced. The victim's indemnity may then be considerably decreased. In our opinion, the reduction of liability is questionable in some situations. There is no easy answer to the issue: an equitable solution must be found between the victim's right to full indemnification and that of the defendant to pay only for those injuries for which he was responsible. We will examine one by one the effect of previous and subsequent incidents on the defendant's liability.

1. *Previous Incidents*

261. *Allegation of Previous Incidents* – In order to reduce his share of liability, the defendant will often invoke incidents that occurred prior to the attack. For example, he may argue that the victim had already been abandoned by her parents,[243] that she had been abused in her foster home or had been sexually abused at an earlier time,[244]

---

243. See *J.L.M.* v. *P.H.*, [1997] B.C.J. No. 477 (B.C. S.C.) (Q.L.), overturned in part on appeal but on an unrelated point, [1998] B.C.J. No. 1546 (B.C. C.A.) (Q.L.).

244. For an illustration of this problem, see *A.D.C.* v. *J.H.P.*, [1996] B.C.J. No. 741 (B.C. S.C.) (Q.L.), in which the judge did not believe that the sexual assaults perpetrated by the grandfather had caused all the victim's problems. He took

or that she was suffering from attention deficit disorder[245] or anxiety.[246] According to the defendant, these incidents or conditions created within the victim a predisposition to her later problems—which would have manifested themselves regardless of the abuse—and they account for part of the victim's injuries. He will argue that he is not solely responsible for all the plaintiff's existing problems.

The reality is complex, making it difficult to ascertain the effects on causation of the victim's predispositions. First, it is the fate of every human being to be predisposed to something. Few people can boast of being in perfect health. Second, it is often impossible for medical science and psychology to apportion liability between the various causal factors. Legally the defendant is liable solely for those damages that he caused. We will now examine the question of predisposition from a legal perspective in light of judicial policy.

a)   Legal Analysis

262. *Civil Law Position* – Civil law distinguishes between predispositions that are asymptomatic and those that are symptomatic.[247] In the first case, the victim is more likely than other people to react to the injury.[248] The defendant is liable for the totality of the victim's

---

into account the fact that the plaintiff was also abused by her parents and that she had lost a child.
245.   See *W.K.* v. *Pornbacher*, above, note 84. Due to the victim's pre-existing condition, the defendant was held liable for 75 per cent of the damage.
246.   See *T.P.S.* v. *J.G.*, [1995] B.C.J. No. 1650 (B.C. S.C.) (Q.L.).
247.   See Baudouin and Deslauriers, above, note 10, No. 275 at 199; A.M. Honoré, *International Encyclopedia of Comparative Law*, Vol. 11, *Torts* (Tübingen: Association internationale des sciences juridiques, 1972), Ch. 7, No. 182; Bernard Cliche and Martine Gravel, *Les accidents du travail et les maladies professionnelles, indemnisation et financement* (Cowansville, QC: Les Éditions Yvon Blais, 1997) at 86ff. Note that French civil liability law does not use the expression "thin skull." The distinction is made, rather, between predispositions that aggravate the injury and predispositions that appear prior to the fault, in which case responsibility may be shared. See Jacques Flour and Jean-Luc Aubert, *Les obligations, Le fait juridique*, vol. 2, 7th ed., by Jean-Luc Aubert (Paris: Armand Colin, 1996), No. 178 at 172; Viney and Jourdain, above, note 68, No. 434 at 300; Jacqueline Nguyen Thanh Nha, "L'influence des prédispositions de la victime sur l'obligation à réparation du défendeur à l'action en responsabilité," (1976) 74 *Revue trimestrielle de droit civil* 1.
248.   See *Massé* v. *Bélanger*, [1990] R.R.A. 538 (Que. Sup. Ct.). In response to the defendant's argument that the plaintiff's reaction was disproportionate due to her personality disorders, the judge stated: "Whatever her personality, [the plaintiff] has suffered an emotional shock that has resulted in disturbances

injuries because his fault aggravated an asymptomatic predisposition. The defendant must take the victim as he found her. This principle reflects the common law "thin skull" doctrine. In the case of
symptomatic predispositions, the victim has already exhibited
health problems. The defendant is liable to the extent that his fault
exacerbated the victim's state of health.

263. *Three Situations* – In the cases we are examining, an overview
of Canadian jurisprudence indicates that there are three situations
in which the calculation of damages can be influenced by previous
incidents: the asymptomatic victim, the symptomatic victim without fault, and the symptomatic victim with fault. Unfortunately,
Canadian common law courts do not always make this distinction,
and they reduce the defendant's liability.[249] We believe this
approach to be erroneous. Let us examine these three situations
from a civil law perspective.

264. *The Asymptomatic Victim* – In this situation, the plaintiff
develops serious psychiatric problems following a sexual assault,
whereas previously she was asymptomatic. Other victims perhaps
would not have reacted similarly. The defendant attempts to prove
that the victim's reaction is abnormal, exaggerated, or unforeseeable. This is the classic "thin skull" situation: the defendant takes
his victim as he finds her and must compensate her injuries in their
entirety. His liability cannot be diminished in this instance.

265. *The Faultless Symptomatic Victim* – The sexual assault victim
in the second situation already exhibits physical or mental health
problems attributable to no one in particular. In such cases, the
defendant will plead that, for example, the plaintiff would not have
completed her studies in any event, given her previous condition.
The courts tend to reduce the defendant's liability where the victim
is symptomatic and her condition cannot be linked to the fault of the
defendant or any other individual.[250]

This method of proceeding is erroneous in civil law. The judge
allocates liability between the facts imputed to the defendant and
the facts without fault. This approach is not founded in law. First,

---

and has caused an injury with aftereffects" (at 540) (our translation). See also
Thomas v. *Publications Photo-Police inc.*, [1997] R.J.Q. 2321, 2334 (C.Q.).

249. See *W.K.* v. *Pornbacher*, above, note 84; *J.L.M.* v. *P.H.*, above, note 243; *A.D.C.*
v. *J.H.P.*, above, note 244.

250. See *W.K.* v. *Pornbacher*, above, note 84.

this is not a case of shared responsibility as provided in the Code. Article 1478 C.C.Q. states that the court may allocate responsibility between co-defendants according to the gravity of their respective faults, or between the defendant and the plaintiff where there has been contributory fault on the part of the plaintiff. Second, there cannot be shared liability because the victim's state does not qualify as superior force (1470 C.C.Q.), for it is neither unforeseeable nor irresistible. It was foreseeable that the fault would cause the victim to react negatively, and, in fact, a reasonable person would always be able to foresee the victim's weaknesses due to the defendant's assault. The court cannot invoke the defendant's faulty acts and the faultless acts of third parties or of the plaintiff in order to reduce the former's share of liability.[251] If causation is established between the defendant's fault and the injury suffered by the plaintiff, the judge must accept that but for the fault of the defendant, the injury would not have occurred. The fault does not have to be the sole cause of injury, but it must be determinative. Causation cannot be divisible. When evaluating damages, it is not possible to reduce the indemnity after the fact by considering non-faulty acts that could also have caused the injury. Thus, faced with the facts in the case of *Pornbacher*,[252] it would not be open to a Quebec judge to invoke the plaintiff's pre-existing attention deficit disorder in order to decrease the defendant's liability to 75 per cent.

The principle that causation is indivisible conflicts with the principle of complete restitution of the victim. Indeed, the defendant is obliged to restore the plaintiff to the state she was in prior to the assault. Accordingly, the defendant is not responsible for those problems that were present prior to the attack. But, in such cases, how is the judge to quantify the defendant's share of liability? Given this difficulty, we feel that the defendant's liability should not be reduced in the case of a symptomatic victim who is not at fault.

---

251. On this topic, see the common law decision in *Athey* v. *Leonati*, [1996] 3 S.C.R. 458 at 469. For an application of *Athey* in a case involving the sexual assault of a child, see *M.M.* v. *R.F.* in the Court of Appeal, above, note 49; *K.A.T.* v. *J.H.B.* (1998), 51 B.C.L.R. (3d) 259 (B.C. S.C.); *E.D.G.* v. *Hammer*, above, note 143.
252. Above, note 84. See also *D.W.* v. *Canada (Attorney General)*, [1999] S.J. No. 742 (Sask. Q.B.) (Q.L.), in which the judge reduced the amount awarded for past pecuniary loss by 50 per cent due to the plaintiff's particular family situation (alcoholism, family history of drug addiction, father's absence, no emotional security as a child, etc.), even though the defendant was found totally liable for the plaintiff's current situation.

266. *The Symptomatic Victim Due to Faulty Acts* – In the third situation, the victim has already suffered upsets in her life and has
experienced health problems prior to the defendant's attack. Some
of these problems can be attributed to faults committed by third
parties. To illustrate, in the British Columbia case, *J.L.M.* v.
P.H.,[253] the judge ruled that the plaintiff's personality disorders
would have manifested themselves irrespective of the sexual abuse
perpetrated by her adopted father. The judge discussed the victim's
troubled life. First, she was separated at birth from her biological
mother, then when she was finally adopted she was separated from
her foster mother, to whom she had become attached. She was psychologically abused by her adoptive mother. She was betrayed by a
cleaning woman, a mother-figure to her, when she was sexually
attacked by two baseball players introduced to the plaintiff by this
cleaning woman. In addition, she received no moral support from
her father. Following her adopted mother's death, she tried to commit suicide at the age of twelve. Given all these elements, which the
judge qualified as "predispositions," it was ruled that even in the
absence of the sexual abuse, the personality disorders would have
developed. The defendant was ordered to indemnify only those consequences arising from the sexual assault.[254] It is our view that a

253. Above, note 243. There are three other cases where the amount allocated to
the victim was reduced because of her past problems. In *M.M.* v. *R.F.*, above,
note 49, the judge found the defendant 60 per cent liable given that the plaintiff had been abandoned at birth, had been removed from her first foster home
at three years old, and had encountered subsequent problems in the many foster homes in which she had been placed. This part of the decision was overturned by the Court of Appeal based on *Athey* v. *Leonati*, above, note 251, and
the attacker was found 100 per cent liable for all the victim's problems. In
T.P.S. v. *J.G.*, above, note 246, the judge held the defendant 75 per cent liable.
Prior to meeting the defendant, the plaintiff already suffered from psychological problems because she had been abandoned by her mother. Finally, in
Colquhoun v. *Colquhoun*, (1994) 114 D.L.R. (4th) 151 (Ont. Gen. Div.), the
judge held the defendant, the victim's father, 60 per cent liable. The victim had
been previously assaulted by her stepfather, and her father, who was aware of
this, took advantage of her vulnerability.
254. See also *T.P.S.* v. *J.G.*, above, note 246 at No. 49: "I find that I am faced with
a pre-existing condition [anxiety disorder] which, but for the intervening sexual abuse, would have left the plaintiff disabled, although still able to lead a
functional life. The evidence also supports a finding that the plaintiff's pre-
existing condition amounts, in effect, to a pre-existing vulnerability, which
combined or intertwined with the subsequent abuse, has resulted in the dev-
astation of this young woman's life. By virtue of her pre-existing condition, the
sexual abuse has had a far more destructive effect on the plaintiff than might
have been the case for an emotionally healthy, emotionally supported young
woman." The defendant was held 75 per cent liable.

Quebec judge should not, even in the same fact situation, reduce the defendant's liability. First, as mentioned above, the judge may not take the faultless behaviour into account. Second, when faulty acts committed by third parties are considered, persons who are not defendants have been introduced into the proceedings.[255] It is the plaintiff's right to select the defendants, and she is not obliged to sue them all. It is the defendant who is liable solidarily with faulty third parties (article 1526 C.C.Q.) who must assume the entire obligation and call into warranty the other potential defendants (article 216 C.C.P.).

267. *The Vulnerable Victim* – There cannot be a reduction in responsibility if the defendant took advantage of the symptomatic victim's vulnerability, regardless of fault. This point was made by a British Columbia judge in a case where an employee of a youth centre sexually touched an adolescent on one single occasion. The defendant contested the extent of the damages inflicted upon the adolescent (now an adult) on the grounds that the incident was never repeated. The judge held that the fragile state of the victim at that time explained the subsequent negative impact of the sexual assault on his life as an adult, despite its one-time occurrence:

> "He was particularly vulnerable because of his general family background and especially because of the recent termination of the abusive G. marriage and the commencement of the S. relationship. He is not to be blamed or to bear the responsibility for those matters or their effect upon him. *A sexual predator will select such vulnerable victims and did so here.*"[256]

A defendant may also have been the source of the victim's vulnerability. In another British Columbia case, *L.T.* v. *R.W.T.*,[257] the father's liability was not reduced and he was held responsible for all the problems currently experienced by the plaintiff:

255. See Pierre Deschamps, "L'exonération et le partage de responsabilité," in *Responsabilité*, Collection de droit 1999–2000, Vol. 4 (Cowansville, QC: Les Éditions Yvon Blais, 1999) at 75.
256. *Jacobi* v. *Griffiths*, above, note 150, No. 54 (Q.L.) (emphasis added), reversed by the Court of Appeal and by the Supreme Court, with respect to the liability of the youth centre. The Supreme Court sent back the matter to trial for a determination as to whether the respondent club is directly liable under a fault-based cause of action.
257. [1997] B.C.J. No. 1232 (B.C. S.C.) (Q.L.).

"I have no doubt that the abandonment of the plaintiff and the infre-
quency of her father's visits throughout her life has adverse effects.
First, this treatment made her more vulnerable to her father's abuse
in the sense that she was a child who desperately wanted and needed
affection and attention from her father. When he abandoned the family and she discovered his betrayal of the whole family, it deepened
the negative effects of the abuse."[258]

It is easy to raise the victim's predispositions in cases involving children in foster homes abused by the owner or employees.
Children who are placed have often been rejected by their own families during periods of crisis, and they frequently manifest delinquent or behavioural problems, are vulnerable, and perform poorly
at school. The predispositions are obvious. It is precisely because of
these predispositions that the attack is possible.[259] The attacker cannot subsequently invoke them to reduce his liability.

b)   Judicial Policy Considerations

Causation must also be analysed in light of judicial policy considerations.

268. *Burden of Proof* – The burden of proving causation falls on the
plaintiff: she must prove that all of her injuries resulted from the
defendant's acts. The standard of proof is the balance of probabilities, and although the plaintiff need not satisfy scientific standards
of causation, the courts do rely on such studies. Scientific studies
proving that all of her injuries resulted from the defendant's acts
are not very developed. This shortcoming places an additional
financial burden on the plaintiff, even though it is the defendant
who has put her in this difficult situation.

Investigations and lengthy examinations delving into the victim's life and exposing weaknesses are foreseeable if a defendant
seeks to partially exonerate himself based on the victim's predispositions. The decision to allocate liability between the attacker and
other upsets endured by the victim during her life is an arbitrary
one. On what basis does the judge arrive at the decision that the
current injury suffered by the plaintiff is 60 or 75 per cent due to the
attacker, when medical science is unable to ascertain liability with
such certainty?

258.   Ibid. at para. No. 11 (Q.L.).
259.   See *C.A.* v. *Critchley*, above, note 99.

269. *Analogy to Article 1480 C.C.Q.* – The legislator has intervened in the past where the burden of proving causation was too heavy and unjust for the plaintiff. For example, article 1480 C.C.Q. establishes a presumption of causation where it was impossible to determine which distinct fault was effectively responsible where both were capable of causing the injury.[260] The defendants are then solidarily liable. As noted in *Commentaires du ministre de la Justice*, the solidarity rule was "introduced as a means of protecting the victim, who is unable in the circumstances to establish causation between the damages she suffered and the causal fault."[261] This solution is justified because it seeks to ensure that the victim receives the best possible indemnification. The equitable solution stipulated in article 1480 C.C.Q.—a lessening of the burden of proof—can be applied by analogy to victims of sexual and spousal abuse. Once the plaintiff has *prima facie* proven causation, the burden of proof should shift to the defendant, who must then prove that he is not entirely liable for the damage.

270. *Intentional Fault* – In addition, it is important to bear in mind that sexual aggressors or wife beaters generally intend to commit the faulty acts and they gauge the damages their acts cause.[262] Courts dispense with causation where there has been intentional fault. If the principles of civil responsibility can impose liability on a defendant who did not intend to commit the faulty act, they must *a fortiori* impose liability on the perpetrator of an intentional fault.[263] Where the fault was intentional, an attacker should be liable for all the direct and immediate damages resulting from that act, even if unforeseeable (article 1613 C.C.Q. *a contrario*).[264] In common law, according to Hart and Honoré, where there is deliberate intervention with the course of nature subsequent to which specific events occur, there is a presumption that these events were caused by this intentional intervention.[265] Therefore, because the acts in sexual or spousal abuse are often intentional, the issue of

260. See Baudouin and Deslauriers, above, note 10, No. 566 at 371.
261. Ministère de la Justice, *Commentaires du ministre de la Justice, Le Code civil du Québec*, t. 2 (Québec City: Publications du Québec, 1993), art. 1480 C.C.Q. (our translation).
262. See below, at §320.
263. See Baudouin and Deslauriers, above, note 10, No. 526 at 348.
264. See *Encyclopédie juridique Dalloz, Répertoire de droit civil*, t. VIII, s.v. "responsabilité du fait personnel," by Philippe Conte, No. 80.
265. Herbert L.A. Hart and A.M. Honoré, *Causation in the Law* (Oxford: Clarendon Press, 1959) at 30.

causation and its effects on the reduction of liability should not be raised in civil suits.

271. *Partial Compensation of the Victim* – In our opinion, too easily taking the victim's weaknesses into account—the proof of which is at the mercy of developments in medical science and insurance companies' financial resources—is tantamount to awarding the victim partial compensation[266] and imposing too heavy a burden of proof. Who can claim to be free of predispositions? If this notion were applied to its logical end, shared liability would become the rule. If the defendant must take his victim as he finds her, favourable economic situation included, it should be the same for the victim's psychological state. At the very least, when the victim's weaknesses are taken into account, she is reproved for aggravating her injury. French doctrine generally rejects the victim's predispositions as grounds for partially exonerating the defendant.[267] Once it is established that the defendant caused the plaintiff's injury, he must compensate all damages. French authors Flour and Aubert explain: "To pretend the contrary [to accept the pre-existing state of the victim as grounds for exonerating the defendant] is to deny that the victim is entitled to exist, a right enjoyed by every subject of law, or to be more exact, is to recognize only a reduced right to live."[268]

2. Subsequent Incidents

In addition to invoking pre-existing conditions as a means of reducing liability, the defendant may also raise subsequent incidents. This imposes a further obligation on the victim not to aggravate damages.

a) Subsequent Injuries Suffered by the Victim

272. Novus Actus Interveniens – The theory of *novus actus interveniens* may serve to interrupt the chain of causation, thereby reducing the defendant's liability. For example, the defendant may argue

266. The common law has adopted the same position on this subject, see *Athey* v. *Leonati*, above, note 251 at 468 and 469.
267. See *Encyclopédie juridique Dalloz, Répertoire de droit civil*, s.v. "Responsabilité du fait personnel," by Philippe Conte, No. 167; Yves Chartier, *La réparation du préjudice dans la responsabilité civile* (Paris: Dalloz, 1983) No. 42 at 60; Viney and Jourdain, above, note 68, No. 434 at 300; Mazeaud, above, note 123, No. 570 at 654, see the accompanying notes.
268. Flour and Aubert, above, note 247, No. 178 at 172.

that the victim aggravated her damages if she had successive violent spouses, became a prostitute, and developed a drug addiction.[269]

273. *Consequences of the Initial Injury* – It is accepted that victims
of sexual assault are at greater risk than other women of suffering
another attack, especially in cases of incest or if a young victim is
involved.[270] In fact, they are often drawn to violent men,[271] have little self-esteem, and submit easily to abuse. They frequently have
difficulty being mothers and may lose custody of their children.
There is thus a causal connection between the defendant's faulty act
and the plaintiff's current situation. It is essential that the courts be
made to appreciate the disastrous psychological impact of sexual
abuse on the victim. The judge in a British Columbia decision held
that the defendant was fully responsible for the victim's subsequent
problems:

> Further, I find that while there is no direct causal relationship, the
> sexual abuse was a significant factor in the causation of a variety of
> other problems i.e. her gravitating toward abusive men resulting
> from her low self-esteem and self-image, her pregnancies arising from
> emotional needfulness and inadequacy, and her difficulties achieving
> educational and vocational goals. I find that the majority of the
> "stressors" identified by defense counsel are either directly attribut-
> able to the sexual abuse or are the offshoot of her sexual or interper-
> sonal dysfunctions, which are in turn significantly related to the
> sexual abuse.[272]

274. *Non-Application of the Theory of* Novus Actus Interveniens –
The theory of *novus actus interveniens* is inapplicable where the victim's initial injury causes a chain reaction that leads to subsequent
injuries. The defendant has, through his acts, created a vulnerable
victim susceptible to subsequent injuries. He must therefore be
liable for all the injuries that are a direct and immediate result of
his fault (article 1607 C.C.Q.).

---

269. See *L.T.* v. *R.W.T.*, above, note 257. See Robert Pauzé and Jacques Mercier,
    Les agressions sexuelles à l'égard des enfants (Montreal: Les Éditions Saint-
    Martin, 1994) at 85.
270. See *D.M.M.* v. *Pilo*, [1996] O.J. No. 938 (Ont. Gen. Div.) (Q.L.), where the judge
    found the defendant, a doctor who had abused the plaintiff between the ages
    of nine and twenty-one, 50 per cent liable. According to the judge, the plain-
    tiff's current problems stemmed from the fact that she had subsequently been
    raped twice and that she suffered from alcoholism and drug addiction.
271. See Pauzé and Mercier, above, note 269 at 121, 133.
272. *T.P.S.* v. *J.G.*, above, note 246 at para. No. 45.

b) Plaintiff's Duty Not to Aggravate the Injury

275. *The Problem* – In examining causation, one must also consider the duty of the plaintiff not to aggravate her injuries. In *Gauthier* v. *Beaumont*,[273] where the plaintiff had been tortured by police officers, the trial judge rebuked the plaintiff for failing to consult with health professionals following the traumatic incident. According to the judge, this step may have reduced the gravity of the injury and allowed him to file suit within the prescribed time. The action was rejected for being prescribed.[274] In *Goodwin* v. *Commission scolaire Laurenval*, the victim was similarly rebuked: "Had the plaintiff commenced therapy immediately following the incidents, the effects would have been less serious and of shorter duration."[275] He therefore reduced the amount awarded for pain and suffering. This case involved a school janitor who touched the buttocks of the young plaintiff, who subsequently injured herself while trying to escape. She sued the janitor and his employer, the school board. In *A.A.* v. *B.*,[276] the judge did not award the plaintiff, an incest victim, any amount for future therapy expenses because the victim had made no effort to seek professional counselling, the costs of which were covered by the state.

Must the victim absolutely consult a therapist in order to avoid being reproached for aggravating her injury under article 1479 C.C.Q., and, if yes, at what point in time and for how long? Remember that this rule is not intended to deny the existence of an injury, but rather to curb its extent.[277]

276. *Consent to Treatment* – First, the victim is under no obligation to consult a therapist. She must consent to this treatment.[278] Article 10 C.C.Q. stipulates that: "Every person is inviolable and is entitled to the integrity of his person. . . . No one may interfere with his person without his free and enlightened consent." Article 11 C.C.Q.

---

273. Above, note 143 at 18. This case is examined in the chapter on prescription, above, at §§99ff.
274. The Court of Appeal dismissed the appeal for the same reason, above, note 143. The appeal was granted by the Supreme Court, which held that the prescription was not extinguished. See above, note 143.
275. Above, note 39 at 680.
276. [1998] R.J.Q. 3117 (Que. Sup. Ct.).
277. See Tancelin, above, note 10, No. 758 at 390.
278. See Édith Deleury and Dominique Goubau, *Le droit des personnes physiques*, 2nd ed. (Cowansville, QC: Les Éditions Yvon Blais, 1997) Nos. 93ff at 100ff.

stipulates that no one may be made to undergo care except with his or her consent. Therefore, neither the defendant nor the court may oblige the plaintiff to seek therapy.

277. *Reasonable Means* – An obligation of means exists under article 1479 C.C.Q. by which damages are to be "minimized."[279] It states: "A person who is liable to reparation for an injury is not liable in respect of any aggravation of the injury that the victim *could have avoided*" (emphasis added). The victim must therefore take reasonable steps to minimize her injury. Yet, on many occasions the victim fails to seek assistance because of the defendant's behaviour. Thus, in the British Columbia case of *C. A.* v. *Critchley*,[280] one of four plaintiffs abused by the owner of a foster home was incapable of speaking about the attacks he had suffered and was unable to consult a therapist, even though he had made appointments. The judge awarded $20,000 for therapy-related expenses in the future. The victim's inaction often depends on the defendant's behaviour and is, therefore, beyond reproach by the court.[281] In *Gauthier* v. *Brome Lake (Town of)*,[282] Mr. Justice Gonthier of the Supreme Court stated that it was not possible to reproach the appellant, a torture victim, for not having sought treatment diligently, because diligence is evaluated from the point of view of a reasonable person and ignores the psychological reality of a victim who has suffered severe post-traumatic stress. In other cases, the victim does not realize that she needs help.[283] In one case, the victim began therapy, which she felt to be useful, but stopped it when she discovered that the defendant could access her medical or psychiatric file during criminal or civil proceedings.[284] Moreover, therapy does not always produce the desired results.[285] Some victims must wait until they are ready for

---

279. See *Commentaires du ministre de la Justice*, above, note 261, art. 1479 C.C.Q.
280. Above, note 99.
281. See *B.I.Z.* v. *Sams*, [1997] B.C.J. No. 793 (B.C.S.C.) (Q.L.), where the judge did not oblige the victim of a road accident to undergo the treatment recommended by his doctors. He felt that the victim's refusal was a direct result of the accident, in which her brain had been affected and her judgment impaired.
282. Above, note 143, at 57.
283. See, for example, *D.W.* v. *Canada (Attorney General)*, above, note 252.
284. See *J.P.* v. *T.J.S.*, [1999] B.C.J. No. 1230 (B.C. S.C.) (Q.L.); see below, on the development of access to documents, at §§418ff.
285. For an unsuccessful therapy, see *S.T.* v. *Gaskell*, [1997] O.J. No. 2029 (Ont. Gen. Div.) (Q.L.). In this case, a social worker in training was sued by her patient for the unsuccessful therapy and the disastrous consequences. Her action was dismissed because she could not prove that the therapist had been professionally negligent. See also *Sauveteurs et victimes d'actes criminels – 1*, [1995] C.A.S. 1.

therapy,[286] and then must consult several therapists;[287] others are
not financially able to seek therapy, as pointed out by the judge in
the Ontario case of *S. (J.)* v. *Clement*: "Her failure to pursue treatment during the past two years cannot be held against her because
it is due to internalization of her pain, which is itself symptomatic
of her injury. In addition, Mrs. S., until recently, did not have the
financial means to seek treatment."[288] For these reasons, the court
cannot blame the victim for failing to consult a therapist, thereby
aggravating her damages.

278. *Conclusion* – Some analysts claimed that the evaluation of the
causal link depends on the judge's feelings.[289] It appears that causation, left largely to the discretion of the judge, is used to limit compensation of the victim and bears witness to the courts' inability to
comprehend the consequences of sexual assault. The courts must be
very vigilant with respect to the consequences of prior incidents. We
are dealing with complex situations where acts attributable to the
defendant or third parties and faultless acts are intermingled. The
theory of *novus actus interveniens* does not stand up to analysis,
because subsequent injuries suffered by the victim are a direct and
immediate consequence of the initial injury. The fact is that a defendant will seek any and all means by which to reduce his liability:
first he will raise the victim's weaknesses, then he will plead that
he is not responsible for subsequent incidents, or he will even take
advantage of the fact that the victim appears to have emerged relatively unscathed, all things considered.[290]

D. Injury

279. *Distinctiveness of Injury* – Regardless of the type of injury
involved, evaluating it is never an easy task, especially when calcu-

---

286. See *P.A.D.* v. *A.E.H.*, [1998] B.C.J. No. 930 at para. No. 83 (B.C. S.C.) (Q.L.).
287. In *M. (K.)* v. *M. (H.)*, [1992] 3 S.C.R. 6, the victim had consulted numerous
      therapists prior to realizing the connection between her current problems and
      the assaults she had suffered.
288. See *S. et al.* v. *Clement et al.*, above, note 109 at 522.
289. See Paul Esmein, "Le nez de Cléopâtre ou les affres de la causalité," D. 1964.
      Chron. 205, No. 1.
290. See *D.A.A.* v. *D.K.B.* (1995), 27 C.C.L.T. (2d) 256 (Ont. Gen. Div.), in which no
      amount was awarded by the court for future lost earnings. The plaintiff was
      not able to prove that the sexual assault resulted in loss of income. The judge
      concluded that, to the contrary, the plaintiff excelled at her work and had
      received several promotions, and that her income was greater than those of
      university graduates.

lating a lump sum. This difficulty is accentuated when victims of sexual or spousal abuse are involved, because the courts are unaccustomed to the particular manner in which the injury manifests itself. In a civil liability action for rape, an Ontario trial judge remarked as follows:

> As was pointed out by the expert evidence, the injuries of the sexual assault victim are compounded by the manner of their infliction. The deliberate, hateful imposition of power and force by one human being against another in violation of one's being is something that cannot be rationalized by the victim, nor by society. A sexual assault, then, is no mere accident with physical and psychological impact. By definition, a sexual assault deprives the victim of her dignity, her self-respect, her sense of self-confidence and leaves her fearful of places where she had previously found safety and solace. When that sexual assault is aggravated by acts of degradation, such as those inflicted upon Mrs. S., and where they are accompanied by a brutal beating inflicted in the sanctuary of one's home, the effect is devastating.[291]

280. *Discrimination against Women* – The distinctiveness of injury in sexual and spousal abuse cases is further compounded by another fact: the victims are primarily young girls and women.[292] Numerous studies have shown that the courts have some difficulty identifying the faults and injuries inflicted on young girls and women, and are therefore unable to fully compensate them.[293] This state of affairs is

291. *S. et al.* v. *Clement et al.*, above, note 109 at 520.
292. See Lise Julien and Isabelle Saint-Martin, *L'inceste envers les filles: état de la situation* (Quebec: Conseil du statut de la femme, 1995) at 32. An analysis of statistical studies on sexual assaults led these authors to conclude, among other things, that girls were assaulted more frequently than boys. See also the results of a study conducted by researchers at McMaster University, in Ontario, which concluded that girls were three times more likely to be sexually assaulted than boys (*Le Devoir*, 9 July 1997 at A-2). See also the tables summarizing all the available statistics on this subject in Pauzé and Mercier, above, note 269. These authors note that the studies summarized indicate that, by age eighteen eight girls will be sexually assaulted for every two boys.
293. See Louise Langevin, "Les difficultés d'indemnisation des femmes: l'indemnisation des frais d'entretien d'un enfant né à la suite d'une grossesse résultant d'une faute médicale," (1994) 19 *Queen's L. J.* 469; idem, "L'affaire *Cooke* v. *Suite*: la reconnaissance de la grossesse préjudice, mais à quel prix?" (1996) 56 *Revue du Barreau du Québec* 125. See the report of the Federal/Provincial/Territorial Working Group of Attorneys General Officials on Gender Equality in the Canadian Justice System, *Gender Equality in the Canadian Justice System: Substantive Law Bias against Women* (Saskatchewan / Prince Edward Island) (Ottawa: Department of Justice, 1992) at 29ff. See also Ken Cooper-Stephenson, "Past Inequities and Future Promise: Judicial Neutrality in Charter Constitutional Tort Claims," in

even clearer in sexual and spousal abuse, which violates a woman's physical and psychological integrity. This situation, described as systemic discrimination against these women, must be corrected.[294]

281. *Application of the Trilogy* – As with any other victim whose physical and psychological integrity has been violated, the court must apply the rules governing compensation of bodily injury established by the Supreme Court of Canada trilogy in order to provide a just, non-discriminatory indemnification.[295] These cases direct the court to classify injury as either pecuniary or non-pecuniary. Although these are common law cases, they have been applied by the Quebec courts.[296] The method of evaluation suggested in the trilogy reflects the same principle expressed in article 1611 C.C.Q., which holds that damages are meant to compensate the loss sus-

---

Sheilah L. Martin and Kathleen E. Mahoney, eds., *Equality and Judicial Neutrality* (Toronto: Carswell, 1987) at 226; Ellen Picard, "Women and Medical Malpractice," in Martin and Mahoney, eds., *Equality and Judicial Neutrality,* at 248; Jamie Cassels, "Damages for Lost Earnings Capacity: Women and Children Last!" (1992) 71 *Can. Bar Rev.* 445; idem, "(In)equality and the Law of Tort: Gender, Race and the Assessment of Damages," (1995) 17 *Advocates' Quarterly* 158; Elaine Gibson, "Identifying Gender Bias in Personal Injury Compensation," in Joan Brockman and Dorothy Chunn, eds., *Investigating Gender Bias, Law, Courts, and the Legal Profession* (Toronto: Thompson Educational Publishing, 1993) at 87. For an American critique on this subject, see: Leslie Bender, "An Overview of Feminist Torts Scholarship," (1993) 78 *Cornell L. Rev.* 575; idem, "A Lawyer's Primer on Feminist Theory and Tort," (1988) 38 *J. of Legal Educ.* 3; idem, "Changing the Values in Tort Law," (1990) 25 *Tulsa L. Rev.* 759; Lucinda M. Finley, "A Break in the Silence: Including Women's Issues in a Torts Course," (1989) 1 *Yale Journal of Law and Feminism* 41; Ann V. Scales, "Feminists in the Field of Time," (1990) 42 *Florida L. Rev.* 95; Martha Chamallas, "Questioning the Use of Race-specific and Gender-specific Economic Data in Tort Litigation: A Constitutional Argument," (1994) 63 *Fordham L. Rev.* 73.

294. Bruce Feldthusen, "Discriminatory Damage Quantification in Civil Actions for Sexual Battery," (1994) 44 *University of Toronto Law Journal* 133 at 133 and 134.

295. *Andrews* v. *Grand and Toy, Alberta Ltd.,* [1978] 2 S.C.R. 229; *Thornton* v. *Prince George School Board,* [1978] 2 S.C.R. 267; *Arnold* v. *Teno,* [1978] 2 S.C.R. 287.

296. See Judge Letarte's trilogy: *Bouliane* v. *Commission scolaire de Charlesbourg,* [1984] C.S. 323 (Que. Sup. Ct.); *Lebrun* v. *Québec Téléphone,* [1984] C.S. 605 (Que. Sup. Ct.); *Gravel* v. *Hôpital d'Amos,* [1984] C.S. 792 (Que. Sup. Ct.). The application of the trilogy in Quebec was confirmed in *Québec (Public Curator)* v. *Syndicat national des employés de l'Hôpital Saint-Ferdinand,* above, note 192. The Supreme Court, however, clarified that the functional approach used to evaluate non-pecuniary damages did not constitute a rule of law. See below, at §311.

tained and the profit of which the creditor is deprived. Damages
repair bodily, moral, or material injury (article 1607 C.C.Q.).

282. *Lump Sum or Annuity* – The first paragraph of article 1616
C.C.Q. applies the principle that the capital is payable in cash,
unless the parties have agreed otherwise. It is possible, however,
under the second paragraph of article 1616 C.C.Q., to receive an
annuity if the creditor is a minor who has suffered bodily injury.[297]
Given the long judicial delays and numerous obstacles that prevent
the victim from instituting an action sooner, very few plaintiffs are
able to take advantage of this provision. However, some observers
are uncertain that being eligible for an annuity is truly an advantage for minors.[298] In fact, the risk that the indemnity will be spent
unwisely is greatly reduced because the minor's tutor is bound to
respect the rules governing the administration of the property of
others (article 1299 *et seq.* C.C.Q.). In addition, because income generated from the capital is tax exempt, an annuity is not fiscally
advantageous for a victim under twenty-one years of age.[299]

283. *Possibility of Review* – The finality of a lump sum judgment[300]
can, in certain cases, adversely affect a victim of sexual abuse.
Despite judicial delays or the impossibility for the victim of suing at
an earlier date, it may be difficult to determine the evolution of the
victim's condition with sufficient precision at the time of judgment
and, consequently, the amounts to be awarded. These difficulties
arise mainly when the plaintiff is a child or an adolescent. It is difficult, for example, to determine the effect of the attack on the victim's psychological development, academic path, or future earning
capacity, nor can the importance or effectiveness of therapy be
gauged. In this case, article 1615 C.C.Q. permits the file to be
reopened within three years following judgment, upon the plaintiff's
express application; it is up to the discretion of the court whether or
not to grant the application.[301]

284. *Recourse to Precedents* – Generally speaking, when awarding
indemnities, courts rely on previous decisions rendered in the same

297. See Daniel Gardner, *L'évaluation du préjudice corporel* (Cowansville, QC: Les
      Éditions Yvon Blais, 1994), Nos. 55ff at 41ff.
298. See ibid., No. 77 at 57.
299. Section 81(1) g.1, *Income Tax Act*, R.S.C. 1985 (5th Supp.), c. 1, as amended.
300. Art. 165(1) C.C.P.
301. See Gardner, above, note 297, Nos. 103ff at 74ff.; *Commentaires du ministre
      de la Justice,* above, note 261, art. 1615 C.C.Q.

area. This approach is justified as preventing too large a disparity among victims' indemnities.[302] Moreover, in *Andrews*, Mr Justice Dickson mentioned the relevance of non-pecuniary damages awarded by other courts in similar cases.[303]

But this method is problematic. To begin with, the judge's evaluation is not personalized, as noted by Madam Justice L'Heureux-Dubé in *Syndicat national des employés de l'Hôpital Saint-Ferdinand*.[304] Hence, while the attack committed in one case may appear identical to that committed in another, some victims may react more severely than others and should not receive the same indemnity.[305] Some victims suffer less from the attack than others, due to their personal determination or the support of family and friends. These victims experience fewer problems and will receive smaller indemnities in a civil action.[306] In addition to ignoring the principle that damages are to be personalized, this method perpetuates those decisions whose sole accomplishment is that they were the first ones rendered, thereby preventing this area of the law from evolving. Recourse to precedents should serve only as a general orientation, especially in an area in full evolution.[307] It is not a question of granting identical amounts in similar cases, but of applying the same principles and evaluation criteria. The court should evaluate the plaintiff's injuries according to the facts of the case.

285. *Input of Experts* – The expert testimony of economists or psychiatrists is necessary, especially where large amounts are involved, for evaluating the costs of future therapy or the loss of

---

302. See *Y. (S.)* v. *C. (F.G.)* (1996), 30 *Canadian Cases on the Law of Torts* (2d) 82 at 99 (B.C. C.A.).
303. Above, note 295 at 265.
304. Above, note 192 at 248.
305. See our comments on causation, above, at §§259ff.
306. See *J.E.S.* v. *Estate of P.D.M. (Official Administrator of)*, [1998] B.C.J. No. 1461 (B.C. S.C.) (Q.L.), where the judge referred to the success of the victim, a fifty-nine-year-old woman who sued the estate of her stepfather, who had assaulted her: "In short, her own inner strengths overcame the abuse. She advised the court she simply decided not to become a victim. . . . To some extent her success has reduced the amount of damage to be awarded." Para. No. 21. See also *M.T.* v. *J.L.*, [1998] B.C.J. No. 1459 (B.C. S.C.) (Q.L.), where the judge did not award any amount for loss of future earning capacity because the victim, aged fifty-five, succeeded despite the assault.
307. See the judge's opinion in *Y. (S.)* v. *C. (F.G)*, above, note 302 at 99; see also *P.A.C.* v. *J.C.T.*, [1998] B.C.J. No. 1088, para. No. 18 (B.C. S.C.) (Q.L.).

past or future earning capacity, or even for explaining the psychological impact of sexual and spousal abuse to the judge. Although on occasion their testimony overshadows that of the victim, experts are there, above all, to inform the judge. Their absence can have adverse implications for the victim: faced with inadequate evidence, the judge is forced to award lower, thus inadequate, indemnities.[308] To soften the negative impact of expert testimony on the victim, the expert should be introduced as someone there to "interpret" the victim's economic or psychological situation for the judge, rather than as a specialist there to restructure the victim's story.[309]

286. *Objective* – Given the distinct nature of both the injury and the position of women within society and the justice system, our goal is to apply the rules governing compensation for bodily and moral injury to victims of sexual and spousal abuse, and to suggest solutions to the problems thus encountered. As there is little Quebec jurisprudence in this area, we will refer to Canadian case law for examples of evaluation of injury.[310] We will look first at the nature of the injury prior to examining its evaluation.

1.   *Nature of Injury Suffered*

287. *The Problem* – The question as to the nature of the injury sustained was examined in *Gagnon* v. *Béchard*.[311] The court had to decide whether this case, in which young boys were sexually touched by their babysitter, was prescribed. Governed by the *Civil Code of Lower Canada*, the action was instituted more than one but less than two years after the incidents. Since the victims were claiming moral, as opposed to bodily, injury, the Court of Appeal decided to apply the general prescription period of two years under article 2261(2) C.C.L.C., which was applicable to delictual and

---

308.   See *S.L.* v. *S.A.*, [1999] O.J. No. 1267, para. Nos. 40ff (Ont. Gen. Div.) (Q.L.), where the judge complained of the lack of experts able to explain the consequences of sexual and spousal abuse, and therefore awarded a lower, thus inadequate, indemnity. To the same effect, see *D.J.* v. *L.J.H.*, [1997] B.C.J. No. 2724 (B.C. S.C.) (Q.L.).

309.   See Nathalie Des Rosiers, Bruce Feldthusen, and Oleana Hankivsky, "Legal Compensation for Sexual Violence: Therapeutic Consequences and Consequences for the Judicial System," (1998) 4:1 *Psychology, Public Policy and Law* 433 at 444ff.

310.   See our comments in the introduction on the comparative law remedy, above. For a list of decisions, see above, chap. 3, note 8,.

311.   Above, note 160. See also *Michaud* v. *Québec (Procureur général)*, [1998] A.Q. No. 2399 (Que. Sup. Ct.) (Q.L.) (on appeal C.A.Q. 200-09-002136-981).

quasi-delictual acts, rather than the one-year period for bodily injury under article 2262(2) C.C.L.C.

This decision appears advantageous to the young victims, at least in the short term, because their right of action was not prescribed. Quebec courts no longer have to confront this type of problem because prescription periods have been standardized in the new Civil Code, which eliminates the distinctions described under articles 2261 and 2262 C.C.L.C. The prescription period for an extra-contractual civil liability action now stands at three years (article 2925 C.C.Q.).

However, the question is not yet settled as to the nature of the injury suffered subsequent to sexual and spousal abuse. Are the victims barred from receiving pecuniary damages if they claim moral injury? Does moral injury become bodily injury if the attack is violent or results in psychosomatic consequences?

288. *Distinction between the Nature and the Consequences of the Injury* – The Court of Appeal in *Gagnon* v. *Béchard*,[312] confuses the injury itself, regardless of its nature, with its consequences, both pecuniary and non-pecuniary.[313]

The *Civil Code of Québec* has adopted a new tripartite classification in this area,[314] recognizing material, bodily, and moral injury

---

312. Above, note 160.
313. See also *Michaud* v. *Québec (Procureur général)*, above, note 311, where the Superior Court was similarly confused, especially at paragraph No. 22: "Sometimes, moral injury may flow from a bodily injury or from an accident; it can be difficult to draw the line between what contributes to the reparation of bodily and moral injury" (our translation). In this case, the plaintiff was acquitted on twenty-four counts of incest regarding his two daughters. He sued the police investigator, the city employer, and several other defendants for abusive unjustified arrest, as well as for the abusive accusations and proceedings. The city invoked the six-month prescription period under section 586 of the *Cities and Towns Act*, R.S.Q., c. C-19. The judge decided that article 2930 C.C.Q., which circumvents the brief prescription delays in matters of bodily injury and imposes a three-year prescription delay, did not apply in the present case and that the action against the city and the police was therefore prescribed. In fact, the judge did not consider that the plaintiff was seeking reparation for a bodily injury.
314. Nathalie Vézina, "Préjudice matériel, corporel et moral: variations sur la classification tripartite du préjudice dans le nouveau droit de la responsabilité," (1993) 24 *Revue de droit de l'Université de Sherbrooke* 161.

(articles 1457, 1458, 1607 C.C.Q.).[315] But this classification addresses only the nature, not the consequences, of the injury. In fact, these three types of injury may have both pecuniary and non-pecuniary consequences. A bodily injury can cause pecuniary consequences, such as lost salary; non-pecuniary consequences, such as suffering, can also result. Pecuniary consequences caused by moral injury can occur even where there has been no interference with physical integrity. For example, sexual harassment can adversely affect both self-confidence and work performance. It is therefore essential to properly distinguish between the nature of the injury and its consequences.

289. *Danger of Confusion* – There is a real danger that the nature of the injury will be confused with its consequences. Moral injury, which can be more serious than bodily injury in cases of sexual and spousal abuse, is easily confused with non-pecuniary consequences. This confusion works against the plaintiffs because the courts, often uneasy with the task of evaluating a sum, rely on the small sums typically awarded under this heading and on the $260,000[316] cap on moral damages imposed under the Supreme Court trilogy.[317] The courts must recognize both the pecuniary and non-pecuniary consequences of the faults committed in sexual and spousal abuse.

---

315. It is interesting to note that the first paragraph of section 49 of the Quebec Charter refers to moral and material injury, but makes no mention of bodily injury. However, there is no difference with article 1457 C.C.Q., which recognizes moral, material, and bodily injury, and bodily injury is definitely indemnified under section 49 of the Quebec Charter. In fact, the Charter classification refers not to the nature of the injury, but to its consequences—that is, the pecuniary and non-pecuniary moral injury. On this point, see Tancelin, above, note 10, Nos. 763 and 764 at 392; Mazeaud, above, note 123, No. 409 at 396, who also adopt this bipartite classification.
316. This refers to the $100,000 cap that has been capitalized. However, certain courts have refused to apply this cap to victims of sexual abuse. See below, at §312.
317. Above, note 295. See *Thomas* v. *Publications Photo-Police inc.*, above, note 248. In this case, the photo of the plaintiff, whose husband had been accused of having distributed photos of his erect penis, was published in the newspaper *Photo-Police*. She sued the newspaper for invasion of privacy and the right to one's image. The plaintiff requested and the judge awarded $24,900 as compensation for psychological damages. The judge, however, did not take into account the pecuniary consequences: the victim was forced to quit her employment because she felt she was the object of discussion, she was living on social assistance, she had to move, and she was avoided by both her friends and her family. This decision constitutes a good example of the danger in confusing the nature of the injury with its consequences.

2. Evaluating Injury

290. *Framework* – The plaintiff can claim compensatory damages for both pecuniary and non-pecuniary consequences, regardless of whether the injury is bodily or moral. To these can be added punitive damages, claimed under the second paragraph of section 49 of the *Charter of Human Rights and Freedoms*, as well as moratory damages. Note that under subparagraph 178(1)(a.1)(i) of the *Bankruptcy and Insolvency Act*,[318] a bankrupt cannot be released from a judgment ordering payment of an indemnity for sexual assault.

a) Pecuniary Consequences

291. *Framework* – Pecuniary consequences resulting from sexual or spousal abuse comprise losses suffered prior to the trial as well as future losses.

i) Losses Suffered Prior to the Trial

292. *Amounts Not to be Underestimated* – Considering delays in instituting the action, as well as judicial delays, it is important not to underestimate losses suffered prior to trial.[319] The victim can claim expenses for experts,[320] therapy, transportation, medication, moving,[321] telephone,[322] and the like, incurred prior to the trial. She can also claim past lost salary.[323]

293. *Extrajudicial Costs* – In some cases, the victim will have incurred costs due to the criminal trial. For example, she will have had to hire a lawyer to ensure that the defendant did not have full access to her medical or psycho-social files.[324] Or she may have had to consult a therapist in order to cope with the defendant's cross-

---

318. R.S.C. (1985), c. B-3. See section 105(4) of the *Act Amending the Bankruptcy and Insolvency Act, the Companies' Creditors Arrangement Act and the Income Tax Act*, S.C. 1997, c. 12. This section came into force by decree on 30 September 1997.
319. See Gardner, above, note 297, Nos. 172ff at 123ff.
320. See *Hôpital Notre-Dame de l'Espérance* v. *Laurent*, [1978] 1 S.C.R. 605.
321. See *Beaumont-Butcher* v. *Butcher*, above, note 30.
322. See *S.C.* v. *R.L.L.* (1993), 133 N.B.R. (2d) 333 (N.B. Q.B.).
323. See on the loss of earning capacity, below, at §§300ff.
324. See below, at §§418ff.

examination. These expenses are reimbursable because they are a direct and immediate result of the defendant's fault.

Moreover, the pursuer can also request that extrajudicial costs occasioned by the civil suit be reimbursed. The general rule holds that the losing party must pay costs according to tariffs set by regulation.[325] Extrajudicial costs are not included. Nonetheless, certain exceptions have been introduced by the courts.[326] The judge can order the defendant to pay extrajudicial costs in the event of an unlawful, intentional interference with the victim's fundamental rights,[327] which clearly applies to the cases with which we are concerned.[328]

ii) Future Losses

294. *Detailed Itemization* – In accordance with the Supreme Court trilogy,[329] judges cannot grant a lump sum for future pecuniary injury without explanation. They must provide details regarding the amounts allocated, thereby avoiding approximate, often insufficient, sums, which can facilitate an appeal. The category of future losses is divided into two categories: extraordinary future expenses and loss of earning capacity.

295. *Definite Injury* – The second paragraph of article 1611 C.C.Q. indemnifies future injury that is certain and able to be assessed. The modifier "certain" must be tempered: no one can foretell the future. The injury need only be probable, not simply hypothetical.[330]

---

325. Art. 479 C.C.P., *Tariff of Court Costs in Civil Matters and Court Office Fees*, D. 256-95 (1995) 127 G.O. II, 1234.

326. See Baudouin and Deslauriers, above, note 10, No. 236 at 169-170; see *West Island Teachers Association* v. *Nantel*, [1998] R.J.Q. 1569 (C.A.).

327. See *M.M.* v. *S.V.*, J.E. 99-375 (Que. Sup. Ct.), where the victim was secretly filmed in her bathroom by her roommate; *Bélisle-Heurtel* v. *Tardif*, [2000] R.J.Q. 2391 (Que. Sup. Ct.).

328. *Contra: Lavallée* v. *Massé*, AZ-00036289 (C.Q.), where the judge in this sexual assault case refused to indemnify the victim for lawyer's fees. He did not feel that this was an expense occasioned by the attacker's acts. However, had the defendant not attacked the plaintiff, she would not have had to launch a civil action in order to be compensated.

329. See note 295.

330. See Tancelin, above, note 10, No. 748 at 385; Gardner, above, note 297, No. 11 at 8.

The victim, direct or indirect,[331] can thus claim an indemnity for future pecuniary injury.

296. *Capitalization* – As the plaintiff normally receives a lump sum payment,[332] the amount awarded by the court for future pecuniary loss caused by bodily injury must be capitalized—that is, the court must take into account the actual yield (considering interest rates, inflation, and taxation) that the sum granted can produce.[333] This task has been made easier for lawyers and judges alike since the Quebec government adopted a regulation fixing the capitalization rates (article 1614 C.C.Q.).[334] The regulation provides two rates: 2 per cent for amounts compensating future salary-related losses, and 3.25 per cent for future non-salary-related losses.[335] Article 1614 C.C.Q. works to the plaintiff's advantage because she is not obliged to enter expert evidence on this point.

(a) Future Extraordinary Expenses

297. *Costs for Future Therapy* – The category for future therapy costs includes expenses incurred for future care, mainly future therapy expenses and, where necessary, transportation and childcare costs occasioned by this treatment. In some cases, expenses related to detoxification and the purchase of antidepressants can be added.[336] Indemnification for these expenses must be specifically requested, as, given budget cuts, these treatments will not always be covered by the state health care plan.[337] In addition, certain alter-

---

331. See below, at §§337ff.
332. See above, at §282.
333. On this notion, see Gardner, above, note 297, Nos. 444ff at 323ff.
334. See the *Regulation under Article 1614 of the Civil Code Respecting the Discounting of Damages for Bodily Injury*, D. 271-97, 15 March 1997, G.O.Q.1997.II.1449 (came into force on 3 April 1997). See *Proulx* v. *Québec (Procureur général)*, [1997] A.Q. No. 2711 (Que. Sup. Ct.) (Q.L.), which applies this regulation; reversed on appeal, [1999] R.J.Q. 398 (Que. C.A.), but the Supreme Court of Canada affirmed the Superior Court decision, *R.* c. *Proulx*, [2001] S.C.J.No. 65 (Q.L.).
335. On the necessity for two rates of capitalization, see Gardner, above, note 297, Nos. 461ff at 334ff.
336. See *C.A.* v. *Critchley*, above, note 99.
337. *Contra*: see *D.W.* v. *Canada (Attorney General)*, above, note 252, where the judge refused to indemnify the plaintiff for future psychotherapy expenses or future medication expenses because the victim, who was sexually abused by an administrator at a residential school for young Aboriginals, could be reimbursed for these expenses by state programs. This decision raises three problems. The first is the question of whether this program will exist long enough

native therapies are not reimbursed under private insurance plans. The importance of these therapies must not be underestimated: the assistance of experts must be used to foresee the duration of treatment and the possibility of relapse. To illustrate, in a British Columbia case where the incest occurred for more than five years and the father's behaviour was considered particularly serious, the court awarded, among other things, $25,287 for therapy expenses over a four- to six-year period and $8,700 for transportation costs.[338]

298. *Recourse to Experts* – The calculation of future therapy expenses raises the question of the plaintiff's past recourse to experts. What is the impact of its absence? Does it mean the action will be dismissed? In *A.A.* v. *B.*,[339] the judge awarded no amount for future therapy costs because the victim had made no attempt to consult a professional whose services were paid for by the state.

We do not share this judge's opinion. Even if the victim has not consulted a therapist in the past, regardless of the reason,[340] the court must grant an indemnity for future treatments[341] if it feels they are necessary to redress an injury that is a direct and immediate result of the defendant's fault. Expert testimony can help quantify the cost of therapy.[342]

299. *Other Expenses* – A victim requested and received, in addition to therapy expenses, compensation for the installation of an alarm

---

to satisfy the plaintiff's needs. The second problem is that—unlike other defendants, who would have to pay such expenses—the defendant himself benefits from these programs because he does not pay for his fault. Third, Canadian citizens find themselves paying for the attacker's faults because their taxes finance these programs.

338. *P.* v. *F.* (1996), 26 B.C.L.R. (3d) 105 (B.C. S.C.). In *P.B.* v. *W.B.* (1993), 11 O.R. (3d) 161 (Ont. Gen. Div.), an amount of $50,000 was awarded for future therapy expenses. See also *E.D.G.* v. *Hammer*, above, note 143, where the court awarded $30,000 for future therapy expenses; *K.A.T.* v. *J.H.B.*, above, note 251, where the plaintiffs each received $30,000 for future therapy expenses.

339. Above, note 276; see also *J.C.* v. *R.K.* (1996), 133 Sask. R. 65 (Sask. Q.B.), where no amount was awarded for future therapy expenses.

340. See our comments on the duty to consult a therapist, above §§275ff.

341. See *G.* v. *R.*, [1991] B.C.J. No. 66 (B.C. S.C.) (Q.L.), where the judge awarded expenses for future therapy to the plaintiff, even though she stated that she wished to forget the incidents and that she did not want therapy; *C.A.* v. *Critchley*, above, note 99, where some of the defendants were incapable of consulting a therapist, but where the judge nonetheless awarded an amount covering all future therapy expenses.

342. See, for example, the costs presented in *J.L.M.* v. *P.H.*, above, note 243.

system in her house, the purchase of a guard dog, and housekeeping help.[343] Other sums that may be granted include costs for tutoring, especially in the case of young victims of sexual assault who experience difficulties with schoolwork,[344] or costs for guidance counselling and school fees so that the victim can complete her education.[345]

(b) Loss of Earning Capacity

In addition to future extraordinary expenses, the plaintiff can claim an indemnity for loss of earning capacity.

300. *Loss of Earning or Income Capacity* – In *Andrews*,[346] Mr. Justice Dickson indicated that it was the victim's loss of *earning* capacity, and not the loss of *income* capacity, that was indemnified. This position is easily understood: if we base indemnification on the loss of *income* capacity, people who have no income, such as housewives, will not be indemnified.[347] However, these people possess an earning capacity, even if they do not earn an income.[348] Despite Mr. Justice Dickson's point, the courts, for reasons of expediency and proof, have an unfortunate tendency to indemnify the loss of *income* capacity in light of the victim's previous salary.[349] This trend is disadvantageous for many women, in particular victims of sexual and spousal abuse who are without a salary or a stable income precisely because of the abuse that has been inflicted upon them.[350] The judge

---

343. See *S. et al.* v. *Clement et al.*, above, note 109. The victim received $72,074 for future therapy expenses, $22,691 for an alarm system and a dog, and $68,981 for housekeeping help.
344. See *B.D. v. British Columbia*, above, note 103.
345. See *D. (Guardian ad litem)* v. *F.*, [1995] B.C.J. No. 1478 (B.C. S.C.) (Q.L.).
346. Above, note 295 at 251.
347. On the difficulties of indemnifying this class of persons, see *Marchand* v. *Champagne*, J.E. 92-429 (Que. Sup. Ct.).
348. See *Tardif* v. *Ouellette*, [1996] A.Q. No. 3249 (Que. Sup. Ct.) (Q.L.), J.E. 96-2132, upheld on appeal, [2000] R.J.Q. 1386 (Que. C.A.), where the plaintiff, a member of a religious community, was seriously injured by a boat propeller shaft while swimming in a lake. He received no salary for his teaching work in Africa, therefore the judge evaluated his salary according to his level of education and the salary he would have been paid as a university professor in Canada.
349. Gardner, above, note 297, No. 268ff at 195ff; Denise Réaume, "Rethinking Personal Injury Damages: Compensation for Lost Capacities," (1988) 67 *Can. Bar Rev.* 82.
350. See, for example, *Québec (Commission de la santé et de la sécurité du travail)* v. *L.*, [1983] R.L. 503 (Que. Sup. Ct.).

must therefore assess these women's loss of earning capacity based on their foreseeable entry into the workforce up to their retirement.

301. *Difficulties in Assessing Damages* – One already measures the difficulty presented by the task of assessing damages. Asked to review the amount granted in a sexual assault case, the British Columbia Court of Appeal made the following comments on the pitfalls of assessing damages:

> What is fair and reasonable compensation for general damages, including aggravated damages, in this case is not easy to say. This is an evolving area of the law. We are just beginning to understand the horrendous impact of sexual abuse. To assess damages for the psychological impact of sexual abuse on a particular person is like trying to estimate the depth of the ocean by looking at the surface of the water. The possible consequences of such abuse presently are not capable of critical measurement.[351]

Recognition and Impact of Psychological Injury

Assessing damages gives rise to several problems: the recognition in and of itself of a psychological injury, its pecuniary impact, and its quantification.

302. *Recognition of Psychological Injury* – The court must first recognize the victim's psychological problems, which can prove difficult in the absence of a visible interference with physical integrity. It appears to be easier for a court to admit the pain and suffering of a physically handicapped person than of a psychologically traumatized victim. The judge in a Saskatchewan case, *J.M.T.* v. *A.F.D.*,[352] underlined this difficulty. He drew a comparison between whiplash, a condition that, twenty-five years ago, was not recognized by medical science because the source of pain could not be traced to a visible injury, and the impact of sexual abuse on the victims, where there is no apparent physical injury but significant psychological pain: "The plaintiff's pain and suffering and loss of amenities are not dissimilar to those experienced by a whiplash victim. The source of pain cannot be readily traced to an identifiable physical injury such as a fracture or damaged organ. Yet the pain is real."[353]

---

351. *Y.(S.)* v. *C.(F.G.)*, above, note 302 at 99.
352. (1995), 130 Sask. R. 270 (Sask. Q.B.).
353. Ibid. at 275.

303. *Pecuniary Consequences of Psychological Injury* – Once the existence of psychological problems has been admitted, the court must recognize their impact on the victim's earning capacity. The impact of psychological injury on earning capacity is readily recognized by Canadian courts.[354] Thus, the judge in the common law case *P.* v. *F.*,[355] after having heard the testimony of an economist, awarded $203,000 to the victim for loss of earning capacity, explaining

> " . . . there is no doubt that the plaintiff has been rendered less capable overall, from earning income as a result of the assaults upon her by her father; that she is less marketable to potential employers; that she has lost the ability to take advantage of employment opportunities; and that she is less valuable to herself as a person capable of earning income in a competitive market."[356]

Quantifying Loss of Earning Capacity

Once admitted, the impact of psychological injury on the victim's earning capacity must be assessed and a figure attributed to this loss. This task is easier when the victim has an income than when she does not.

304. *Victims with Income* – Where the victim was in the workforce prior to the attack, subsequent to which she is no longer able to perform the same tasks, the loss of income will be compensated by the judge.[357] This method is not without reproach, for the person's value is reduced to her value in the workforce, which is what Mr. Justice Dickson wished to avoid in *Andrews*[358] when he drew the distinction between loss of earning capacity and loss of income capacity. In

---

354. In the following decisions, the courts recognized an interference with the plaintiff's earning capacity: $314,750 was awarded in *J.D.B.* v. *F.M.*, [1998] O.J. No. 3786 (Ont. Gen. Div.) (Q.L.); $150,000 was awarded in *L.S.* v. *L.R.*, [1996] B.C.J. No. 898 (B.C. S.C.) (Q.L.); $93,750, or 75 per cent of $125,000, was awarded in *T.P.S.* v. *J.G.*, above, note 246; $100,000 was awarded in *D. (Guardian ad litem of)* v. *F.*, above, note 345; $125,000 was awarded in *A.D.Y.* v. *M.Y.Y.* (1994), 90 B.C.L.R. (2d) 145 (B.C. S.C.).
355. Above, note 338.
356. [1996] B.C.J. No. 951 (B.C. S.C.) (Q.L.), para. no. 32 at 22.
357. See, among others, *B.W.* v. *P.M.M.*, [1994] O.J. No. 2241 (Ont. Gen. Div.) (Q.L.). In this case, the rape victim earned an annual salary of $40,000 prior to the attack. She had to leave her employment and was earning no more than $13,500 per year. The judge felt that the rape figured significantly in her loss of income and that she had lost a competitive advantage (para. No. 11).
358. Above, note 295 at 270.

addition, it ignores possible career advancements or benefits (such as retirement plans) that the victim would have enjoyed had her future earning capacity not been reduced.

305. *Victims without Income* – How does one assess loss of earning capacity when, as is often the case, the victim has either not been, or has been only sporadically, present in the workforce? As with any other case involving loss of earning capacity, the plaintiff, supported by aptitude tests, must prove that she would have continued her studies and pursued a career in a given field if not for the incidents. The younger the victim at the time of the attack, the more dangerous this exercise and the more difficult this task for the judges: the victim's academic difficulties can arise at a very early stage, preventing her from developing her full potential. In order to determine the victim's likely profession, the courts in these cases have a tendency to take into account the levels of education and professions of the parents,[359] the victim's intellectual capacity, the courses she has studied, as well as past and present employment. They may also assess the injury's impact on boys differently than on girls. This approach is obviously open to criticism because it reinforces female stereotypes and denies the progress women have made. It is no longer justifiable to assess the injury differently between boys and girls.[360] The task of assessment is not an easy one, but the courts must attempt to return the victim to the state in which she would have been prior to the assault.

306. *Recourse to Statistics* – In certain instances, the courts will have recourse to statistics when assessing the victim's loss of earning capacity.[361] Use of these statistics is highly problematic: they distinguish between the average salaries of men and women, and thus reflect historical wage disparities between the sexes.[362]

---

359. See *Arnold* v. *Teno*, above, note 295, where the judge determined that the young victim would have been a teacher like her mother. See also *D.W.* v. *Canada (Attorney General)*, above, note 252, where the judge reduced the victim's past lost income by 50 per cent because of the family environment (alcoholism, drug addiction, absence of father, low level of education of brothers and sisters, etc.)
360. For example, in *Bouliane* v. *Commission scolaire de Charlesbourg*, above, note 296 at 344, the judge agreed with the experts and decided that the two victims, aged ten and eleven, would have become secretaries.
361. See, for example, *Marchand* v. *Champagne*, above, note 347, where the judge fixed the victim's salary according to the average salary of Quebec women in 1989, or $16,292.
362. See Cassels, "Damages for Lost Earnings Capacity," above, note 293; idem,

Although these statistics provide an exact picture of the average salary of a Canadian woman in a given period, using them to calculate loss of future earning capacity results in an inadequate, if not unjust, indemnity. In fact, the wage gap between men and women has been closing over the years.[363] This phenomenon can be explained by the fact that women are more educated,[364] have access to jobs traditionally occupied by men, and spend longer periods of time in the workforce.[365] Because the wage gap between men and women continues to close, it is erroneous today to award the current average salary of a Canadian woman to a girl or a young woman who has suffered a loss of earning capacity.[366] In fact, recourse to these statistics ignores both the future progress these women will make as well as the principle of full restitution.

"(In)equality and the Law of Tort," above, note 293; Susan A. Griffin, "The Value of Women: Avoiding the Prejudices of the Past," (1993) 51 *The Advocate* 545; Elaine Gibson, "Loss of Earning Capacity for the Female Tort Victim: Comment on *Toneguzzo-Norvell (Guardian ad litem of)* v. *Burnaby Hospital*," (1994) 17 *Canadian Cases on the Law of Torts* (2d) 78; idem, "The Gendered Wage Dilemma in Personal Injury Damages," in Ken Cooper-Stephenson and Elaine Gibson, eds., *Tort Theory* (Toronto: Captus University Publications, 1993) at 185.

363. In 1997, the wage gap between women and men ranged from 80.8 per cent for those 15 to 24 years to 64.6 per cent for those aged 45 to 54 years. See Statistics Canada, *Earnings of Men and Women 1997*, cat. No. 13-217-XIB at 14.

364. In 1997, a woman with eight years or less of education earned an average of $21,403, compared to $42,661 for a university graduate. In 1997, the wage gap between men and women stood at 64.6 per cent for employed individuals who had not completed high school and at 73.6 per cent for university graduates. See ibid., at 14. According to Statistics Canada, female university graduates had much greater earnings than less-educated women. See *Women in the Labour Force, 1994 Edition*, cat. No. 75-507XPE occasional at 43.

365. A study by the Conseil du Statut de la femme on the wage gap between men and women concluded that variables such as level of education, number of years worked, and type of experience had an effect on the level of income earned by women and men, as well as between members of the same sex. For example, as the level of education increases for women, the wage gap with men decreases, and the same applies to the number of years worked and experience. See Conseil du Statut de la femme, *Le salaire a-t-il un sexe? Les inégalités de revenus entre les femmes and les hommes* (Quebec: Les publications du Québec, 1987); idem, *L'équité en emploi pour les femmes* (Quebec: Les publications du Québec, 1993).

366. It is also erroneous to apply the average salary of Canadian women to an older worker. Gender-based statistics are age discriminatory, and the wage gap between men and women will decrease in the future.

In addition to poorly reflecting women's future progress, the use of such statistics is discriminatory. Section 16 of the Quebec Charter prohibits unlawful discrimination in working conditions, including salary.[367] It is difficult to imagine that a court would rely on statistics on the average salary of Aboriginal people in Canada, which is inferior to that of non-Aboriginals, when compensating an Aboriginal victim.[368] This would clearly be a case of racial discrimination.[369] What statistics would apply where the person's ethnic origin comprises a variety of backgrounds? In addition, these statistics represent a past average salary and do not respect the principle that holds that the assessment of the plaintiff's future loss of earning capacity be personalized. The victim may be more dynamic and determined than the average Canadian woman. For all these reasons, the court's habit of relying on statistics that indicate the average salary of Canadian women must be condemned.

Some analysts have suggested that this discrimination against women be rectified by applying the statistics on the average salary of Canadian men to women who have suffered an interference with their earning capacity.[370] Indeed, some courts have adopted this approach.[371] Thus, in a British Columbia Superior Court case, *B.I.Z.* v. *Sams*,[372] where the female plaintiff was seriously injured in an automobile accident, the judge calculated the loss of earning capacity based on statistics showing the average salary of Canadian men. He justified his rather innovative approach on the basis of the par-

---

367. Remember that the preliminary provision of the *Civil Code of Québec* stipulates that it must be interpreted in harmony with the Quebec Charter. The rules of indemnification must respect the principles of equality expressed in the Charter.

368. In 1990, the average salary of Canadians working in full-year, full-time jobs was $41,183 for men and $27,885 for women. See Statistics Canada, *Earnings of Men and Women 1995*, cat. No. 13-217-XIB at 17. For Aboriginals working in full-year, full-time jobs, it was $32,635 for men and $23,731 for women. See Statistics Canada, *Profile of Canada's Aboriginal Population*, cat. No. 94-325 at 26 and 27.

369. See the judge's comments in *Terracciano* v. *Etheridge* (1997), 33 B.C.L.R. (3rd) 328 (B.C. S.C.).

370. See Ken Cooper-Stephenson, *Personal Injury Damages in Canada*, 2nd ed. (Toronto: Carswell, 1996) at 296; Cassels, "Damages for Lost Earnings Capacity," above, note 293 at 488–91.

371. See *MacCabe* v. *Westlock Roman Catholic Separate School*, [1998] A.J. No. 1053 (Alta. Q.B.) (Q.L.) for a good summary of this question; *Terracciano* v. *Etheridge*, above, note 369; *J.P.* v. *T.J.S.*, above, note 284, para. No. 30; *D.A.A.* v. *D.K.B.*, above, note 290.

372. Above, note 281.

ticular facts at hand. The complainant worked in the business world, she occupied a position traditionally not held by women, and she would not quit working to stay at home if she had children. We agree with the judge's conclusion because the plaintiff's salary was greater than that of the average Canadian woman. However, would the court have applied the average salary of Canadian women if the plaintiff had worked in a traditional female occupation and if she had taken an unpaid leave of absence to raise her children—in brief, if she had not fit the profile of an ambitious worker? The fact that the judge imposed the profile of the traditional male worker on women worries us. The magistrate endorsed, rather than condemned, the discriminatory nature of these statistics.

We can also suggest that the statistics on the average salary of *all* Canadian workers be applied.[373] This is an interesting proposition because it avoids the trap of gender-based statistics. These statistics should be used for both men and women. We suggest that the courts avoid making reference to the stereotypical male ideal of success when assessing the victim's career potential.

b) Non-Pecuniary Consequences

307. *Framework* – Despite the economic indicators, the courts encounter numerous problems when assessing pecuniary impact on the plaintiff. The situation is even more complicated when assessing non-pecuniary injury. While civil law recognizes non-pecuniary injury, its assessment remains difficult and raises numerous questions.

We begin this section by examining the general approach used when evaluating this injury. The functional approach was suggested by Mr. Justice Dickson in *Andrews*.[374] The highest court in the land rejected this approach in a civil law context nearly two decades later, in *Syndicat national des employés de l'Hôpital Saint-Ferdinand*.[375] Then, we will examine the relevance of the $100,000 cap set in *Andrews* and questioned in *Hill* v. *Church of Scientology of Toronto*.[376] We discuss all these cases in turn and then conclude

---

373. See *Tu* v. *Cie de chemins de fer nationaux du Canada*, [2000] R.J.Q. 170 (Que. Sup. Ct.) at 192-193, on appeal, C.A.M. 500-09-009020-991.
374. Above, note 295.
375. Above, note 192.
376. [1995] 2 S.C.R. 1130 (hereinafter *Hill*).

this section by examining the elements to be considered when evaluating this category of injury.

308. *Recognition of Non-Pecuniary Damages in Civil Law* – Before beginning, it should be noted that non-pecuniary injury is compensated in civil law, despite the difficulties inherent in its assessment (articles 1457, 1607 C.C.Q.). Nonetheless, Quebec courts award lower indemnities than when compensating pecuniary injury for fear that the victim will be enriched or will exaggerate the claim, for fear that the indemnity will take on a punitive aspect, and for lack of any objective evaluation criteria.[377]

309. *Recognition of Non-Pecuniary Damages in Common Law* – For their part, Canadian common law courts have become more receptive to these types of claims and are awarding higher sums than in Quebec.[378] In a British Columbia case,[379] the Court of Appeal increased the indemnity for non-pecuniary injury granted by the trial court. Describing the indemnity as "inordinately low," the court raised it from $10,000 to $25,000 based on the indemnities awarded by the Supreme Court in *Norberg* v. *Wynrib*.[380] Similarly, in *M. (K.)* v. *M. (H.),* Mr. Justice La Forest affirmed that the jury award of $10,000 for general damages was rather low.[381]

310. *Functional Approach in Common Law* – The Supreme Court relied on the functional approach in *Andrews*[382] when fixing the amount of non-pecuniary damages. It holds that the victim will

---

377. See, however, the Supreme Court decision in *Gauthier* v. *Brome Lake (Town of)*, above, note 143, where the court awarded non-pecuniary damages of $200,000. Gauthier, a torture victim, received pecuniary damages of $50,000, including $15,000 for temporary total incapacity and $25,000 for permanent partial incapacity. See also *Quintal* v. *Godin*, [2000] R.J.Q. 851 (Que. Sup. Ct.), on appeal, C.A.M. 500-09-009438-003, where the plaintiff in a medical negligence action received $100,000 for non-pecuniary losses, but nothing for loss of future earning capacity.
378. See the amounts awarded as general damages in the following decisions: $250,000 was awarded in *S.Y.* v. *F.G.C.*, [1996] B.C.J. No. 1596 (B.C. C.A.) (Q.L.); $150,000 was awarded in *E.D.G.* v. *Hammer*, above, note 143; $150,000 was awarded in *K.A.T.* v. *J.H.B.*, above, note 251; $175,000 was awarded in *L.M.N.* v. *Munday*, [1998] B.C.J. No. 2591 (B.C. S.C.) (Q.L.); $175,000 was awarded in *P.A.C.* v. *J.C.T.*, [1998] B.C.J. No. 1088 (B.C. S.C.) (Q.L.).
379. *E.D.G.* v. *Drozdzik* (1993), B.C.L.R. (2d) 106 (B.C. C.A.).
380. Above, note 23.
381. Above, note 287 at 80. He nonetheless upheld this amount because he felt that the jury possessed all the elements required to evaluate the amount.
382. Above, note 295.

receive, as compensation for non-pecuniary injury, in contrast to pecuniary injury, a single lump sum without detailed explanation. The functional approach seeks to improve the victim's life, not to return the victim to his or her original state, which is impossible.[383] The highest court, by adopting this method, rejected both the conceptual approach, which sets an objective value for each injury, and the personal approach, whereby pain and suffering are assessed for each victim.[384] The court must take into account not only the seriousness of the injury, but also the particular circumstances of the victim in order to satisfy the objectives of the functional approach.[385]

311. *Functional Approach in Civil Law* – The legitimacy of the functional approach has raised many questions in civil law, especially where the victim is not able to profit from the sums awarded.[386] In fact, under this approach, the victim should not receive any amount for non-pecuniary damages because she is not conscious of her state and therefore the sums awarded cannot improve her life. This approach goes counter to civil law principles, whereby moral injury (non-pecuniary consequences of damages) is indemnified regardless of the victim's mental state.[387] In addition, where the victim does not die instantaneously, her right to damages is transmissible to the heirs (article 1610 C.C.Q.).

The question of the legitimacy of the functional approach was settled by the Supreme Court decision in *Syndicat national des employés de l'Hôpital Saint-Ferdinand.*[388] Under civil law, the mere existence of the non-pecuniary injury, and not the ability of the victim to benefit from it, justifies its indemnification; therefore, the functional approach cannot serve as a basis upon which to attribute this indemnity. Moreover, the functional approach was not generally applied by the majority of Quebec courts, as was noted by

---

383. See *J.M.T.* v. *A.F.D.*, above, note 352, where the judge referred to the functional approach used to evaluate general damages. He awarded $25,000, but did not explain in what way this amount would make the plaintiff's life happier.
384. See *Andrews,* above, note 295 at 261 and 262.
385. See *Lindal* v. *Lindal,* [1981] S.C.R. 629 at 637.
386. See, among others, Baudouin and Deslauriers, above, note 10, No. 363 at 242 and 243. *Contra*: Gardner, above, note 297, No. 227 at 162.
387. However, as Gardner notes, some courts have taken the plaintiff's reduced capacity into account when evaluating non-pecuniary damages, see above, note 297, No. 240 at 175.
388. Above, note 192.

Madam Justice L'Heureux-Dubé.[389] The three approaches—conceptual, personal, and functional—are applied in together. However, the functional approach continues to be relevant in civil law as a rule for calculating non-pecuniary injury. For the victims with which we are concerned, the task is that of evaluating the psychological impact of the violent acts rather than the cost of certain pleasures, such as the purchase of a stereo. We now turn to the question of the $100,000 cap, before examining the elements relevant to the assessment of non-pecuniary damages.

312. *Reconsidering the $100,000 Cap* – At the same time that it adopted the functional approach in *Andrews*,[390] the Supreme Court capped the amount for non-pecuniary damages at $100,000, the equivalent today of approximately $270,000. However, in the Canadian common law provinces this cap has not been applied to the indemnification of non-pecuniary injury in sexual assault civil proceedings.[391] This position is entirely justifiable because the cap envisaged victims of grave bodily injury who had already received large amounts of pecuniary damages.

In *Hill* v. *Church of Scientology of Toronto*,[392] the Supreme Court refused to apply the $100,000 cap to a damage award in an action for defamation. Mr. Justice Cory, writing for the majority, distinguished between injury in defamation cases and non-pecuniary injury suffered by a victim of bodily injuries. In his opinion, "defamation is the *intentional* publication of an injurious false statement. . . . Personal injury, on the other hand, results from negligence which does not usually arise from any desire to injure the plaintiff."[393] The judge went on to explain that the evaluation of injury in an action for defamation does not present the same difficulties as those in bodily injury cases prior to the introduction of the cap.[394]

---

389. Ibid. at 247.
390. Above, note 295.
391. See *Y. (S.)* v. *C. (F.G.)*, above, note 302; *E.D.G.* v. *Hammer*, above, note 143. *Contra*: see *D.A.A.* v. *D.K.B.*, above, note 290, where the judge applied the cap adopted in the trilogy.
392. Above, note 376 at 1197ff. See *Proulx* v. *Québec (Procureur général)*, above, note 334, which applies *Hill*.
393. *Hill*, above, note 376 at 1198.
394. Justice Cory summarized the problems as follows: "at the time the cap was placed on non-pecuniary damages, their assessment had become a very real problem for the courts and for society as a whole. The damages awarded were varying tremendously not only between provinces but also between different

If *Hill* proves to be well founded—we can question the wisdom of abandoning the $100,000 cap on non-pecuniary damages—an analogy can be drawn between actions for defamation and civil actions for sexual and spousal abuse. As with defamation, the injury sustained by a victim of sexual or spousal abuse differs fundamentally from that of a physically injured person in that the injury is more psychological than physiological. And, while it is difficult to assess the non-pecuniary injury suffered by these victims, it is definitely not as problematic as it was prior to the cap established in the trilogy. Consequently, there should be no maximum cap on the indemnification of this injury.[395]

313. *Factors to Be Considered* – Finally, let us look at the elements considered by Canadian courts when fixing the amount of non-pecuniary damages in cases of sexual or spousal abuse. The victim's suffering is intensified according to the length and frequency of the wrongful behaviour, as well as by its nature. The victim's age and vulnerability at the time of the incidents is also taken into account: the younger the victim, the more serious the consequences. She must live with her secret for many years. The relationship between the parties also weighs heavily in the balance. It is an aggravating factor if the attacker is the father, or someone filling a similar role: the victim was betrayed by someone she trusted. Other factors to consider are the use of force or violence. However, it is important not to underestimate the consequences of a passive relationship in which the child victim was convinced to participate.[396] The impact of this psychological tutorship has been well documented,[397] which is why damages should not be reduced due to the absence of violence. Finally, consequences such as suffering, angst, insomnia, nightmares, loss of self-confidence, fear, digestive problems, sexual prob-

---

districts of a province. Perhaps as a result of motor vehicle accidents, the problem arose in the courts every day of every week. The size and disparity of assessments was affecting insurance rates and, thus, the cost of operating motor vehicles and, indeed, businesses of all kinds throughout the land." (ibid. at 1197).

395. This analogy was drawn by the judge in *Y.* (S.) v. *C.* (F.G.), above, note 302 at 92 and 93.

396. See, among others, *M.M.* v. *R.F.*, above, note 49; *W.K.* v. *Pornbacher*, above, note 84; *E.D.G.* v. *Hammer*, above, note 143.

397. See Diana E.H. Russell, *The Secret Trauma: Incest in the Lives of Girls and Women* (New York: Basic Books, 1986). See the facts in *M. (K.)* v. *M. (H.)*, above, note 287.

lems, drug addiction, personal relationship problems, and psychological problems should be taken into account by the court.[398]

314. *Analysing the Victim's Condition* – In addition to the above factors, the case before the court will often be compared to other similar cases in order to determine its gravity, and an amount will be fixed accordingly. It therefore appears that—in much the same manner as sentencing—the gravity of the acts committed by the defendant, and not the victim's condition, will determine the amount of non-pecuniary damages.[399] Courts are therefore required to analyse the defendant's behaviour. This approach should be prohibited. While the defendant's behaviour is, to a certain extent, relevant when assessing the victim's injury, the trap of considering solely the gravity of the former's wrongful acts to the exclusion of the impact on the plaintiff must be avoided. The seriousness of the defendant's behaviour is relevant solely for the purposes of calculating punitive damages.[400]

315. *Moral Injury Caused by the Criminal Trial* – An additional consideration is that the plaintiff is forced to relive the events during the criminal trial.[401] For some victims, this can lead to a relapse or even to a suicide attempt. Can the traumatic experience of the criminal trial be claimed as a moral injury? On the one hand, the defendant is entitled to a just and equitable trial. He is not obliged to plead guilty and is entitled to cross-examine the plaintiff. By indemnifying the victim for the moral injury caused by the criminal trial, the defendant is being reproached for his right to defend himself, guaranteed under section 11 of the Canadian Charter. On the other hand, the criminal trial and the cross-examination both flow from the criminal act. The plaintiff can claim an indemnity for the moral

---

398.   See the following decisions that refer to these factors: *Y. (S.)* v. *C. (F.G.)*, above, note 302 at 100; *P.* v. *F.*, above, note 356, para. No. 20; *T.P.S.* v. *J.G.*, above, note 246, para. No. 46; *Jacobi* v. *Griffiths*, above, note 150, para. No. 53 (B.C. S.C.).

399.   See Nathalie Des Rosiers, "Childhood Sexual Assault: Will There Be a Meaningful Civil Remedy? *Gray* v. *Reeves*," (1992) 10 *Canadian Cases on the Law of Torts* 86; Kate Sutherland, "Measuring Pain: Quantifying Damages in Civil Suits for Sexual Assaults," in Cooper-Stephenson and Gibson, above, note 362 at 212, 218–22. See *D. (Guardian ad litem)* v. *F.*, above, note 345, para. No. 88, where the judge explains that it is not the analysis of the defendant's behaviour that influences the evaluation of damages, but rather the consequences to the victim.

400.   See below, at §§328ff.

401.   See *W.K.* v. *Pornbacher*, above, note 84; *L.M.N.* v. *Munday*, above, note 378.

injury occasioned by the trauma of the trial because it is a direct
and immediate consequence of the defendant's fault.

316. *Capitalization* – The wording of article 1614 C.C.Q., which
refers to the "future aspects of the injury," stipulates that non-pecuniary losses should be capitalized, at least as regards future losses.
The courts will have to distinguish between past and future non-
pecuniary losses if article 1614 C.C.Q. is to be respected.

c)   Punitive Damages

317. *Insufficient Amounts* – Under the second paragraph of section
49 of the Quebec Charter, the plaintiff can claim punitive damages
in addition to compensatory damages. Some Quebec decisions in the
area of sexual and spousal abuse have already granted such damages, although the amounts have been minimal.[402] The small sums
awarded thus far are no doubt due to the novelty of civil suits by victims of sexual and spousal abuse, the lack of evaluation criteria
prior to the adoption of article 1621 C.C.Q., the confusion with non-
pecuniary damages, the exceptional nature of punitive damages in
general,[403] and the fear of enriching the victim.[404] The situation calls

---

402.   In *Marcoux* v. *Légaré*, J.E. 2000-960 (C.Q.), AZ-00021467 (on appeal: C.A.Q.
       200-09-003076-004), the court awarded punitive damages of $10,000 to the
       plaintiff, a victim of twenty-five years of spousal abuse. In *Larocque* v. *Côté*,
       above, note 11, the plaintiff, who was sexually assaulted in a military training
       camp, received $10,000 in punitive damages. In *Pelletier* v. *Émery*, J.E. 97-
       1360 (Que. Sup. Ct.), the court awarded punitive damages of $10,000 to the
       plaintiff, who was harassed in various manners by her ex-husband. See also
       Bérubé v. *Bilodeau*, above, note 31, where in a case of spousal abuse, the court
       awarded punitive damages of $2,000 to the victim; *Lakatos* v. *Sary,* above,
       note 31, where, in a spousal abuse case, the victim received $5,000 in punitive
       damages; *Jacques* v. *Tremblay*, J.E. 89-734 (Que. Sup. Ct.), where the victim
       received punitive damages of $5,000 from the defendant, who was found crim-
       inally responsible; in *Gosselin* v. *Fournier*, above, note 81, where a student was
       sexually abused by a teacher, the student received $4,000 for moral, general,
       and punitive damages. For examples of punitive damages awarded by Quebec
       courts in extra-contractual civil liability actions, see Baudouin and
       Deslauriers, above, note 10, at 1195ff.
403.   See Mr. Justice Gonthier's opinion in *Béliveau Saint-Jacques*, above, note 5 at
       409.
404.   Article 1680 of the *Avant-projet de loi portant réforme au Code civil du Québec
       du droit des obligations,* 1st session, 33rd legislature, Quebec, 1987 (a draft
       bill to amend the law of obligations in Quebec), stipulated that punitive dam-
       ages would be granted to an association or public organization that was work-
       ing towards the prevention of the type of injurious act committed by the
       debtor, excepting for extrajudicial costs and costs expended by the creditor in

for change. We believe that this category of damages has a role to play, especially where sexual and spousal abuse is concerned. As noted by the judge in *Goodwin* v. *Commission scolaire Laurenval*: ". . . acts of aggression—particularly those of a sexual nature and those involving children—should be most severely denounced and are those most susceptible of incurring punitive damages."[405] Let us examine first the conditions of eligibility, then the evaluation criteria.

i)   Conditions of Eligibility

318. *Framework* – The victim, whether direct or indirect,[406] must first satisfy certain eligibility conditions. She must prove an unlawful, intentional interference with one of her rights guaranteed by the Quebec Charter. A certain jurisprudential trend, which we oppose, has also imposed an additional condition: absence of a previous criminal conviction by the defendant for the same assault.

(a)   Unlawful and Intentional Interference

319. *Unlawful Interference* – In order to receive punitive damages under the second paragraph of section 49 of the Quebec Charter, the victim must have suffered an unlawful interference with a right guaranteed by the Charter.[407] Sexual and spousal abuse violates the physical and moral integrity protected under section 1. In *Syndicat national des employés de l'Hôpital Saint-Ferdinand,* Madam Justice L'Heureux-Dubé defined inviolability thus: "The common meaning of the word 'inviolability' suggests that the interference with that right must leave some marks, some sequelae which, while not necessarily physical or permanent, exceed a certain threshold. The interference must affect the victim's physical, psychological or emotional equilibrium in something more than a fleeting manner."[408] Also violated are the right to honour and dignity, protected under section 4. Madam Justice L'Heureux-Dubé addressed the concept of dignity in this same Supreme Court case: "I believe that s. 4 of the Charter addresses interference with the fundamental attributes of

---

order to exercise his right. See Daniel Gardner, "Les dommages-intérêts: une réforme inachevée" (1988) 29 *Cahiers de Droit* 883, 904ff.

405.   Above, note 39 at 681.

406.   See our comments on the indirect victim, below, at §§337ff.

407.   In the case of the indirect victim, see below, at §§347ff.

408.   *Syndicat national des employés de l'Hôpital Saint-Ferdinand*, above, note 192 at 253.

a human being which violate the respect to which every person is entitled simply because he or she is a human being and the respect that a person owes to himself or herself."[409]

320. *Intentional Nature* – The unlawful interference must be intentional—that is, the defendant must have intended to cause the injury. In *Syndicat national des employés de l'Hôpital Saint-Ferdinand*, Madam Justice L'Heureux-Dubé defined intent:

> Consequently, there will be unlawful and intentional interference within the meaning of the second paragraph of s. 49 of the Charter when the person who commits the unlawful interference has a state of mind that implies a desire or intent to cause the consequences of his or her wrongful conduct, or when that person acts with full knowledge of the immediate and natural or at least extremely probable consequences that his or her conduct will cause. This test is not as strict as specific intent, but it does go beyond simple negligence. Thus, an individual's recklessness, however wild and foolhardy, as to the consequences of his or her wrongful acts will not in itself satisfy this test.[410]

This last condition is not problematic: attackers cannot ignore the seriousness of the impact on their victims. Moreover, any strategy employed by the defendants to silence the victim bears witness to their awareness that their acts have consequences for the victim. Anger can never justify violence where sexual abuse is concerned. When he strikes his spouse, a husband is certainly conscious that he is inflicting injury.[411]

(b) Prior Criminal Conviction

321. *The Addition of a Third Condition* – A third condition, in addition to unlawful and intentional interference, has been added by some courts. It appears that in *Papadatos* v. *Sutherland*,[412] the Court of Appeal decided that the plaintiff could receive punitive damages only where the defendant had not been previously crimi-

---

409. Ibid. at 256.
410. Ibid. at 262.
411. See *T.L.* v. *M.L.*, [1999] J.Q. No. 5783 (Que. Sup. Ct.) (Q.L.), where the judge awarded punitive damages of $2,000 to the victim of spousal abuse; *contra*: *Major* v. *Surette*, [1999] J.Q. No. 5060 (C.Q.) (Q.L.), where the judge refused to grant punitive damages to the victim of spousal abuse because he felt that the defendant had acted impulsively and without deliberate intent.
412. [1987] R.J.Q. 1020 (C.A.).

nally convicted for the same acts. This ruling is obviously disadvantageous for the victims with whom we are concerned in cases where the defendant has already been found criminally responsible. We will examine first the impact of this judgment, followed by the policy considerations that should govern the award of such damages.

322. *Papadatos v. Sutherland* – The essential reasons for judgment were drafted by Mr. Justice Rothman. After having conceded that punitive damages are a novelty in civil liability law,[413] he referred to their goals of punishment and deterrence. He then went on to explain that, in his opinion, section 49 of the Quebec Charter prevents civil courts from awarding punitive damages where the defendant has been found criminally responsible for the same acts. In his view, this would be equivalent to punishing the defendant twice. His position is based on the analysis by a common law author of two decisions to this effect.[414] Nonetheless, his position is qualified. Punitive damages can be awarded where the criminal conviction is not sufficient to punish or deter such acts. Since the defendant had been sentenced to ten years in prison, the punitive damages of $7,000 awarded by the Superior Court were overturned.

Mr. Justice Rothman's opinion was shared by Justices Kaufman and McCarthy. Mr. Justice Kaufman affirmed that section 49 of the Charter does not prohibit punitive damages where there has been a previous criminal conviction. Therefore, "we should not read such a limitation into this provision"[415] and, "as a matter of law," the trial judge could have considered the plaintiff's request for punitive damages. But the additional punishment represented by the punitive damages was unnecessary in the present case due to the previous criminal conviction. He also stated that, had the defendant not already been found criminally responsible, or had the sentence been insufficient, he would not have intervened. He added: "But this is a point which I need not now decide, and which should be left for another occasion."[416] Finally, Mr. Justice McCarthy refused to com-

---

413. In fact, punitive damages do not exist in Quebec civil law, in contrast to common law. They are now recognized under article 1621 C.C.Q., which sets out a list of criteria used in their evaluation, only where they are provided for by law, such as in the second paragraph of section 49 of the Quebec Charter.

414. Allen L. Linden, *Canadian Tort Law*, 3rd ed. (Toronto: Butterworths, 1982) at 53.

415. Above, note 412.

416. Ibid. at 1021.

ment on the effect of a previous criminal conviction, but he concurred with his colleagues that the amount for punitive damages be overturned. We are not given his reasons for doing so.

323. *Analysis of the Judgment* – How should we interpret these rulings? In our opinion, Justices Rothman and Kaufman admit that an earlier criminal conviction is not in and of itself a bar to punitive damages.[417] All the facts of the case are to be considered when determining whether the criminal conviction is adequate to fulfil the goals of punitive damages.[418]

324. *Policy Considerations* – It is our view that, for policy reasons, a criminal conviction should not be a bar to punitive damages. At most, it might serve to reduce the amount awarded.

First, it is not always certain that the criminal justice system functions well or satisfies the expectations of the community or the victim. It is possible that the defendant was not sufficiently punished by his criminal conviction. In fact, the prison sentence is frequently reduced by plea bargaining.[419] Moreover, certain incidents may not be held against the defendant for lack of proof, given that in criminal law the burden of proof is much heavier than in civil proceedings.[420] In addition, the rules governing conditional release[421] provide for the reduction of the sentence to be served.

Second, the attorney general's objectives in instituting criminal proceedings are different from those pursued by the victim who institutes civil proceedings.[422] The automatic application of the dou-

---

417. This is also the opinion of S.M. Waddams, *The Law of Damages*, 2nd ed. (Toronto: Canada Law Book, 1991) para. 11.470 at 11–29.
418. The Court of Appeal also took this position in *E.D.G.* v. *Drozdzik*, above, note 379, where the judge felt that it was sufficient for the defendant to be found criminally responsible and did not award punitive damages.
419. For an example of plea bargaining, see *P.B.* v. *W.B.*, above, note 338, where in exchange for a guilty plea by the accused to a charge of incest against the plaintiff, two charges (one for sexual assault and one for gross indecency) were not taken into account. The judge awarded punitive damages of $50,000.
420. See *J.D.G.* v. *Wutke*, [1996] B.C.J. No. 1491 (B.C. S.C.) (Q.L.); *M.M.* v. *R.F.*, above, note 49.
421. See the *Corrections and Conditional Release Act*, S.C. 1992, c. 20; Hélène Dumont, *Pénologie, Le droit canadien relatif aux peines et aux sentences* (Montreal: Les Éditions Thémis, 1993) at 296ff.
422. In the spousal abuse case, *Surgeoner* v. *Surgeoner*, above, note 31, the judge awarded punitive damages even though the defendant had been found criminally responsible. He had the following to say on double jeopardy: "I find it dif-

ble jeopardy rule means that a defendant, already held criminally responsible for the same acts, benefits from a reduction in the damages he owes to the plaintiff. Additionally, does a judge presiding over a civil action have to wait for the conclusion of the criminal trial before awarding punitive damages?[423] Are we to deduce, given the delays inherent in civil proceedings, that it is in the victim's best interest to first institute a civil action and obtain judgment prior to filing a complaint with the police?

There is another problem. What is meant by a criminal conviction? Does this include sanctions imposed by a disciplinary committee?[424] In a New Brunswick case involving a doctor who sexually assaulted an adolescent, the judge refused to award any punitive damages because the defendant had already paid a $5,000 fine to the College of Physicians and his licence to practise had been suspended for five years.[425] As with criminal convictions, we do not feel that disciplinary sanctions are a bar; at most, they may be taken into account when assessing whether the goals of punitive damages have been satisfied.

For these reasons, *Papadatos* v. *Sutherland*[426] should not be understood as requiring a third condition prior to awarding punitive

---

ficult to conclude that, simply because R.S. has been convicted of this assault, I cannot award punitive damages in this action, which is an action between husband and wife, where a special relationship exists. What does D.S. gain by that conviction? The answer is nothing. I am of the opinion that cases such as this, commonly referred to as domestic violence cases, arising because of the special relationship that is created by marriage and based upon trust, should be an exception to the general principle surrounding the award of punitive damages notwithstanding that such may result in "double jeopardy" (para. No. 40 at 46). See also *S.L.C.* v. *M.J.* (1996), 37 Alta. L.R. (3d) 90 at 106 (Alta. Q.B.); *H.R.* v. *F.M.* (1993), 129 N.B.R. (2d) 303 (N.B. Q.B.); *Bérubé* v. *Bilodeau*, above, note 31 at 13; *D.M.M.* v. *Pilo*, above, note 270; *Bellsmith* v. *Bellsmith*, above, note 31.

423. In *S.L.* v. *S.A.*, [1999] O.J. No. 1267 (Ont. Gen. Div.) (Q.L.), the judge refused to award the victim any punitive damages because the defendant's criminal proceedings were not yet settled.

424. While a disciplinary condemnation resembles a criminal conviction on certain aspects, it is not equivalent to such a conviction. See Gavin Mackenzie, *Lawyers and Ethics: Professional Responsibility and Discipline* (Toronto: Carswell, 1997) No. 26.2 at 26-2.

425. *L.T.* v. *McGillivray*, above, note 23; *contra*: *D.M.M.* v. *Pilo*, above, note 270.

426. Above, note 412.

damages.[427] We share the opinion of Judge Rousseau-Houle of the Court of Appeal on the interpretation of this case: "There is no statement of principle in this case to the effect that a Court seized of a civil action is prohibited from awarding exemplary damages if the defendant has already been convicted by a criminal court."[428]

325. *A Dissenting Trend* – Moreover, some authors[429] and judges[430] have veered away from the rule seemingly established in *Papadatos*. In a Quebec civil action for spousal abuse, an amount of $10,000 was granted even though the defendant had been criminally convicted.[431] In addition, although the rule against double jeop

---

427. See Baudouin and Deslauriers, above, note 10, No. 265 at 193; Gardner, above, note 297, No. 50 at 38; Louis Perret, "Les dommages punitifs en droit civil québécois," (1989–90) 16 *Can. Bus. L. J.* 285, 289. Article 1678 of the *Avant-projet de loi portant réforme au Code civil du Québec du droit des obligations,* above, note 404, stipulated that the court could not grant punitive damages if the debtor's injurious act had already been sanctioned by a provision of the penal code. This criterion was not present in the final draft of article 1621 C.C.Q.

428. *Noël* v. *Leblanc,* J.E. 96-218 (C.A.).

429. See Pauline Roy, "La difficile intégration du concept de dommages exemplaires en droit québécois," in *Responsabilité civile et les dommages, en constante évolution* (Toronto: Canadian Institute, 1990) text No. 8 at 78, which argues that a criminal conviction should not be a bar to an action, but rather a mitigating factor to be taken into account. Karl Delwaide is of the same opinion, "Les articles 49 et 52 de la Charte québécoise des droits et libertés: recours et sanctions à l'encontre d'une violation des droits et libertés garantis par la Charte des droits et libertés en matière civile," *Formation permanente du Barreau du Québec* (Cowansville, QC: Les Éditions Yvon Blais, 1988) at 95. See also Claude Dallaire, *Les dommages exemplaires sous le régime des Chartes* (Montreal: Wilson and Lafleur, 1995) at 79 and 80.

430. These cases refused to apply *Papadatos*: *Noël* v. *Leblanc,* above, note 428; *Monette* v. *Savoie,* J.E. 94-1174 (C.Q.); *Proulx* v. *Viens,* [1994] R.J.Q. 1130 (C.Q.); *Jeannotte* v. *Therrien,* [1992] R.R.A. 57 (C.Q.); *Viau* v. *Syndicat canadien de la fonction publique,* [1991] R.R.A. 740 (Que. Sup. Ct.). In *Augustus* v. *Gosset,* [1990] R.J.Q. 2641 at 2665 (Que. Sup. Ct.), Judge Guthrie narrowed the scope of *Papadatos*: the defendant's previous criminal conviction should not be an automatic bar to punitive damages, but should serve instead as a mitigating factor. The following cases applied *Papadatos*: *Belley* v. *Rougeau,* [1989] R.R.A. 325 (Que. Sup. Ct.); *Plante* v. *Frenette,* [1989] R.R.A. 53 (Que. Sup. Ct.); *Dumulon* v. *Morin,* [1991] R.R.A. 295 (Que. Sup. Ct.) (in these two last cases, the judge applied the principle in *Papadatos,* even if it was not cited); *Binette* v. *Di Caprio,* J.E. 94-318 (C.Q.); *Raiche* v. *Giard,* J.E. 94-1649 (C.A.).

431. See *Marcoux* v. *Légaré,* above, note 402; see also *Bérubé* v. *Bilodeau,* above, note 31; *Larocque* v. *Côté,* above, note 11; *T.L.* v. *M.L.,* above, note 411.

ardy applies to the common law,[432] some common law courts have refused to apply the rule in civil proceedings for sexual and spousal abuse.[433]

326. *The Position of the Supreme Court* – While it was in *obiter*, the Supreme Court made reference to this question in *Syndicat national des employés de l'Hôpital Saint-Ferdinand*.[434] Madam Justice L'Heureux-Dubé, speaking on behalf of the court, remarked that punitive damages were not automatically excluded or reduced where the author of an unlawful interference was otherwise punished. It was rather a question of whether or not the goals of punishment and dissuasion had already been satisfied by earlier punishments.[435]

327. *Solidarity between Defendants* – Finally, provided the conditions are met, the victim can request that other defendants[436] in

---

432. See *T.D.M.* v. *K.S.G.*, [1997] B.C.J. No. 2532 (B.C. S.C.) (Q.L.); *D.J.H.* v. *L.J.H.*, [1997] B.C.J. No. 2724 (B.C. S.C.) (Q.L.); *J.G.* v. *S.A.G.*, [1998] N.S.J. No. 234 (N.S. S.C.) (Q.L.); *E.D.G.* v. *Hammer*, above, note 143; *L.M.N.* v. *Munday*, above, note 378; *P.L.* v. *E.L.*, [1998] A.N.B. No. 49 (N.B. Q.B.) (Q.L.); *T.B.* v. *R.M.*, [1998] O.J. No. 2700 (Ont. Gen. Div.) (Q.L.); *D.M.* v. *A.R.S.*, [1999] O.J. No. 4409 (Ont. S.C.) (Q.L.); *N.C.* v. *W.R.B.*, [1999] O.J. No. 3635 (Ont. S.C.) (Q.L.); *J.L.H.* v. *D.H.H.*, [1999] N.B.J. No. 259 (N.B. Q.B.) (Q.L.); *J.P. (Litigation guardian of)* v. *L.L.*, [2000] O.J. No. 2833 (Ont. S.C.) (Q.L.); *R.L.* v. *A.V.*, [2000] O.J. No. 2661 (Ont. S.C.) (Q.L.); Waddams, above, note 417, para. 11.470 at 11-28; Allen M. Linden, *Canadian Tort Law*, 5th ed. (Toronto: Butterworths, 1993) at 57; Christopher P.M. Waters, "Multiple Punishment: The Effect of a Prior Criminal Conviction on an Award of Punitive Damages," (1996) 18 *Advocates' Quarterly* 35.

433. See *B. (A.)* v. *J. (I.)*, (1991) Alta. L.R. (2d) 84 (Alta. Q.B.); *Dhaliwal* v. *Dhaliwal*, [1997] O.J. No. 5964 (Ont. Gen. Div.) (Q.L.); *M.M.* v. *R.F.*, [1997] B.C.J. No. 2914 (B.C. C.A.) (Q.L.); *K.A.T.* v. *J.H.B.*, above, note 251; *P.A.C.* v. *J.C.T.*, [1998] B.C.J. No. 1088 (B.C. S.C.) (Q.L.); *J.P.* v. *T.J.S.*, [1999] B.C.J. No. 1230 (B.C. S.C.) (Q.L.); *P.B.* v. *W.B.*, above, note 338; *Queen* v. *Hodgins* (1992), 36 R.F.L. (3d) 159 (Ont. Gen. Div.); *Surgeoner* v. *Surgeoner*, above, note 31; *Bellsmith* v. *Bellsmith*, above, note 31.

434. Above, note 192 at 265.

435. See, along the same lines, *Gauthier* v. *Brome Lake (Town of)*, above, note 143, where the Supreme Court awarded punitive damages of $50,000 to the plaintiff, even though his attackers had been found criminally responsible. While Mr. Justice Gonthier makes no reference to the controversy surrounding the effect of the defendants' previous criminal convictions on the granting of such damages, it is possible to deduct from his silence that previous criminal convictions are not a bar to punitive damages and that the policemen's criminal convictions did not serve the punitive and deterrent objectives of these damages.

436. On the potential defendants, see above, at §§166ff.

addition to the attacker be ordered to pay punitive damages. In this case, all the defendants would be solidarily liable for the compensatory and punitive damages (article 1526 C.C.Q.).

The possibility of imposing punitive damages on defendants other than the attacker raises two difficulties. First, under the second paragraph of section 49 of the Quebec Charter, the court can condemn only the *guilty person* responsible for the unlawful interference. In the cases with which we are concerned, the other defendants did not commit the assault. In addition, the guilty person's interference must have been *intentional*. In order to satisfy these two conditions, the victim must prove that the other defendants' inaction made them parties to the unlawful interference and that they intended to cause the consequences.[437] In so doing, they themselves become guilty of an unlawful interference. Thus, in the Ontario case of *M.T.* v. *Poirier*,[438] the bishop was liable for punitive damages because he allowed the priest to continue spending time with the youths even though he was aware that the priest was sexually misbehaving with them.

The employer's vicarious liability for his employee's fault in the performance of his duties also raises the question of paying punitive damages (article 1463 C.C.Q.). When deciding whether the employer should pay punitive damages, the court must consider the orders issued by the employer, the knowledge of, or failure to prohibit, the unlawful acts, the failure to direct that the acts cease, as well as the position held by the faulty employee within the hierarchy of the employer's organization.[439] For example, the plaintiff/victim of sexual abuse must prove that the employer was aware of the employee/attacker's sexual misconduct, but did nothing to rectify the situation.[440] These two conditions must be satisfied if the other

---

437. On the intentional nature of the unlawful interference, see above, at §319. The position would be the same in common law. See *D.W.* v. *Canada (Attorney General)*, above, note 252, para. No. 57.
438. [1994] O.J. No. 1046 (Ont. Gen. Div.) (Q.L.).
439. See *Gauthier* v. *Brome Lake (Town of)*, above, note 143 at 67. The municipality, which had employed the policemen who tortured Gauthier, was held liable for punitive damages. Given that the chief of police, the principal torturer, held an important position within the municipality, Mr. Justice Gonthier felt that his desire to inflict the consequences of his acts was imputable to the municipality.
440. See the vicarious responsibility of the attacker's employer, above, at §§206ff. The United Church of Canada provides an example of the measures an employer may use to prevent sexual assaults by his employees and reduce his

defendants are to pay punitive damages. Strategically, however, if it is hoped that the insurers of the non-attacking defendants will compensate the victim, it is preferable to remain silent about the intentional aspect of their behaviour and forgo punitive damages.[441]

ii)   Evaluation Criteria

328. *Framework* – Once it has been decided that the victim satisfies the eligibility requirements for punitive damages, the court must then proceed to evaluate them. Article 1621 C.C.Q. mentions certain criteria that may assist the judges in their task.

329. *The Roles of Punitive Damages* – In addition to providing the evaluation criteria, article 1621 C.C.Q. refers to the deterrent role of punitive damages. The amount awarded cannot exceed what is needed to satisfy this role. Moreover, in *Béliveau Saint-Jacques*[442] the Supreme Court underlined that such damages were meant to punish and dissuade. We see no incompatibility between these roles: they constitute different facets of the same reality. Nonetheless, given the minimal amounts that have been awarded to date[443]—they can even be considered symbolic—deterrence, punishment, and dissuasion appear to come cheaply in the eyes of the courts!

330. *Criteria of Article 1621 C.C.Q.* – When assessing injury, the judge must, in conformity with the Supreme Court trilogy, clearly identify the amount awarded as punitive damages.[444] He or she can-

---

liability. The Church now conducts a criminal background check prior to engaging its ministers. See Richard Foot, "United Church to Run Police Checks on Clergy," *National Post*, 22 August, 2000 at A-1.

441.   On the remedy against the insurer, see above, at §§232ff.

442.   Above, note 5 at 408.

443.   See *Larocque* v. *Côté*, above, note 11, where the victim received $10,000 in punitive damages. In matters of loss of reputation, the punitive damages awarded are higher. See *Delfosse* v. *Paquette*, [1996] A.Q. No. 1026 (Q.L.), J.E. 97-879 (Que. Sup. Ct.), where an amount of $25,000 was awarded under this heading. Moral damages of $80,000 were awarded. Our research of Canadian law shows that the greatest amount of punitive damages awarded to a victim of sexual or spousal abuse was $55,000: see *G.K.* v. *D.K.*, [1997] O.J. No. 2863 (Ont. Gen. Div.) (Q.L.), upheld on appeal [1999] O.J. No. 1953 (Ont. C.A.) (Q.L.), see also *Y.(S.)* v. *C. (F.G.)*, above, note 302; *S.L.C.* v. *M.J.*, above, note 422; *P.B.* v. *W.B.*, above, note 338; *A.D.Y.* v. *M.Y.Y.*, above, note 354; *B.(A.)* v. *J. (I.)*, above, note 433.

444.   Above, note 295.

not award a single sum indemnifying both non-pecuniary and punitive damages. As with the assessment of non-pecuniary damages,
the accounting procedure is difficult and depends largely on judicial
discretion. Where possible, this exercise is aided by the criteria in
article 1621 C.C.Q.[445] that refer to the gravity of the debtor's fault,
his patrimonial situation, the extent of the reparation for which he
is already liable towards the creditor, and the fact that the payment
of damages is wholly or partially assumed by a third person.[446]

331. *Additional Criteria* – This list is obviously not exhaustive, and
the courts can base their assessment on other criteria. In *Augustus*
v. *Gosset*,[447] Judge Guthrie, the trial judge, listed nine evaluation
criteria: i) the preventive and deterrent role such damages play; ii)
the defendant's conduct prior and subsequent to the injurious act;
iii) the seriousness of the injury suffered; iv) the defendant's financial resources; v) the amount of compensatory damages awarded to
the victim; vi) the duration of the reprehensible conduct; vii) any
punishment already meted out to the defendant for the same act;
viii) the amount of any profit or benefit derived by the defendant
due to his wrongful behaviour; and ix) any provocation by, or contributory fault, of the victim.

332. *Application of These Criteria to the Cases under Study* –
Several comments can be made regarding these evaluation criteria
in relation to the complainants with which we are concerned.

First, in the majority of Canadian decisions analysed that held
the defendant responsible, punitive damages were awarded where
requested.[448] The judges specifically stated that these damages were
necessary in order to punish the defendant and to convey society's
disapproval. Second, these evaluation criteria resemble those used

---

445. See *Commentaires du ministre de la Justice*, above, note 261, article 1621
     C.C.Q.
446. According to Gardner, above, note 297, No. 51 at 39, these criteria come from
     a report published by the Ontario Law Reform Commission, *Report on
     Exemplary Damages*, Toronto, 1991.
447. Above, note 430 at 2664.
448. The only decisions that refuse to award these damages do so where there has
     been a previous criminal conviction. However, in *J.E.S.* v. *Estate of P.D.M.*,
     [1998] B.C.J. No. 1461 (B.C. S.C.) (Q.L.), the court refused to award punitive
     damages to the plaintiff, who waited until the attacker was dead before
     launching a civil action and who had never filed a complaint with the police.
     According to the judge, the issue of punitive damages would have been settled
     by the attacker's conviction had there been a criminal proceeding.

in the assessment of non-pecuniary damages. The main criterion retained is the severity of the fault and of the defendant's acts. The judges also consider the duration of the attack, the relationship between the defendant and the victim, the vulnerability of the victim, and the presence of violence. The defendant's patrimonial situation is never mentioned.

The courts have refused to award punitive damages in some cases where the severely injured victim receives substantial compensatory damages, alleging that the latter satisfies the punitive role of punitive damages.[449] This reasoning is problematic. First, the goal of punitive damages is confused with that of compensatory damages. The gravity of the defendant's fault is the reason why the compensatory damages are substantial. This reasoning implies that the criterion of the gravity of the defendant's fault could never be used to impose punitive damages. It also follows, according to this reasoning, that compensatory damages will fill a dissuasive role, while it was always clear that the role of these damages was strictly compensatory.[450] Thus, the significance of compensation already received by the victim should serve not as a ground for reducing or refusing punitive damages, but rather as grounds for increasing them in instances where the defendant is financially well-off.

The defendant's conduct may justify limiting punitive damages where, for example, he is repentant and admits his fault.[451] The possibility of falsely penitent defendants certainly exists. Leaving this possibility aside, the defendant's collaboration can be both psy-

---

449. In *Plante* v. *Frenette*, above, note 430, the court did not award any punitive damages because $56,800 had already been granted as compensatory damages and the defendant had been found criminally responsible for the same acts.

450. See *Augustus* v. *Gosset*, [1996] 3 S.C.R. 268, 286, where Madam Justice L'Heureux-Dubé referred to the compensatory nature of damages in civil responsibility. It is difficult, however, to believe that damages do not also have a punitive role. For example, shared liability in the event of the victim's contributory fault no doubt hides a punitive element (article 1478 C.C.Q.). By the same token, is there not a punitive element present when the judge takes into account the gravity of the defendant's behaviour when evaluating moral damages, as judges do in sexual abuse cases? See on this subject Suzanne Carval, *La responsabilité civile dans sa fonction de peine privée* (Paris: L.G.D.J., 1995). On the role of punitive damages as private punishment, see *C.* v. *M.* (1990), 74 D.L.R. (4th) 129 (Ont. Gen. Div.).

451. See *S.L.C.* v. *M.J.*, above, note 422, where the court considered the fact that the defendant was unrepentant. Punitive damages of $50,000 were awarded.

chologically and legally beneficial for the victim. Inversely, recidivism is possible where there is a refusal to collaborate in the civil proceedings, to admit fault in the face of overwhelming evidence,[452] or to appear repentant or remorseful. Such behaviour should be taken into account if the goal of these damages is to be satisfied. The courts in Quebec have considered the punitive role of punitive damages[453] and the defendant's refusal to admit fault in the few cases of spousal or sexual assault where such damages were awarded.[454]

333. *Extrajudicial Costs* – In a case of loss of reputation and harassment[455] the judge awarded punitive damages of $20,313.72, the amount spent in extrajudicial costs by the plaintiff to stop the defendant's harassment. This method of assessing punitive damages is disputable: such damages are meant to punish the defendant, not compensate the plaintiff. Moreover, article 1680 of the 1987 *Avant-projet de loi portant réforme au Code civil du Québec du droit des obligations*[456] (a draft bill to amend the law of obligations in Quebec) stipulated that punitive damages were to be paid to a charity, except the amount granted as compensation for extrajudicial costs and expenses incurred by the creditor in the exercise of her right. Extrajudicial costs should be compensated through pecuniary damages because they are a direct and immediate consequence of the fault.[457]

334. *Recipients of Punitive Damages* – The plaintiff in some cases may direct that punitive damages be paid to a third party, such as a shelter for battered women or a charity. This must be mentioned in the allegations. The courts have occasionally done so in defama-

---

452. See *W.K.* v. *Pornbacher*, above, note 84. When evaluating punitive damages, the judge noted that the defendant had subjected the plaintiff to cruel and abusive treatment by making him relive the traumatic events during both the criminal and civil trials because he denied the facts.
453. "It is time to put an end to the violence between spouses, such as the deliberate, savage attack inflicted on the plaintiff, an elderly woman" (our translation) (*Lakatos* v. *Sary*, above, note 31 at 21).
454. See *Bérubé* v. *Bilodeau*, above, note 31; *Jacques* v. *Tremblay*, above, note 402.
455. *Latreille* v. *Choptain*, [1997] A.Q. No. 2037 (Que. Sup. Ct.) (Q.L.).
456. See above, note 404.
457. See above, at §293.

tion cases;[458] other times it has been refused.[459] We know of no grounds for not agreeing to such a request, given that this has already been contemplated by the legislature in article 1680 of the *Avant-projet de loi portant réforme au Civil Code du Québec du droit des obligations.*[460]

d)   Moratory Damages

335. *Reduction of Judicial Delays* – The judge should grant moratory damages to encourage prompt performance of the defendant's obligation (article 1618 C.C.Q.).[461] The legal rate of 5 per cent can be supplemented by an indemnity (article 1619 C.C.Q.). Interest runs on all sums granted, including punitive damages.[462] Judges are entitled to determine the date on which these damages start, even if they have no discretion as to their application. Article 1618 C.C.Q. stipulates that moratory damages start " . . . from the date of default or from any other later date which the court considers appropriate, having regard to the nature of the injury and the circumstances." In *Larocque*,[463] the judge awarded interest as of the summons date. It is not to the plaintiff's advantage to have the interest run as of the judgment date, as this encourages the defendant to take advantage of every available dilatory measure. Gardner had the following opinion on this subject: "Aside from [those hypotheses where the victim is responsible for hearing delays], the victim should be enti-

---

458.   See *Groupe R.C.M. inc.* v. *Morin*, [1996] R.R.A. 1005 (Que. Sup. Ct.). This part of the judgment was upheld on appeal, see *Morin* v. *Groupe R.C.M. inc.*, C.A. Montreal 500-09-003006-962, AZ-00011154. See also the declaration in *Mulroney* v. *Canada (Procureur général)*, [1995] A.Q. No. 797 (Que. Sup. Ct.) (Q.L.), where the plaintiff indicated that he would donate the punitive damages to foundations and educational and medical research institutions in Montreal. This case was settled amicably, see [1997] A.Q. No. 45 (Que. Sup. Ct.) (Q.L.).

459.   See *Paquet* v. *Rousseau*, [1996] R.R.A. 1156 (Que. Sup. Ct.), *Dubé* v. *Cogéco Radio-Télévision*, [1998] A.Q. No. 668 (Que. Sup. Ct.) (Q.L.).

460.   Above, note 404.

461.   See Gardner, above, note 297, Nos. 544ff at 403ff; Jean-Louis Baudouin and Pierre-Gabriel Jobin, *Les obligations*, 5th ed. (Cowansville, QC: Les Éditions Yvon Blais, 1998), No. 815 at 649; Tancelin, above, note 10, Nos. 1108ff at 576ff.

462.   See *Larocque* v. *Côté*, above, note 11. In this case, interest started running on this amount as of the judgment date because the punitive damages were meant to punish, not to compensate. See, among others, *Association des professeurs de Lignery (A.P.L.), syndicat affilié à la C.E.Q.* v. *Alvetta-Comeau*, [1990] R.J.Q. 130 (C.A.).

463.   Above, note 11.

tled to damages caused by the defendant's fault in performing his obligation, as of the notice of default or the institution of legal proceedings."[464] Since judicial delays hinder access to justice, this problem is partially solved by having interest run as of the summons date.

336. *Conclusion* – When assessing injuries suffered by victims of sexual and spousal abuse, the courts must base themselves on the same criteria used in other cases of interference with physical and moral integrity. First, they must admit the pecuniary and non-pecuniary impact of these faults and apply the rules developed in the Supreme Court trilogy.[465] Then, when assessing pecuniary consequences, they must examine the interference with the victim's earning capacity. Despite the difficulty in assessing non-pecuniary consequences, the assessment must be personalized by the magistrate, who must consider, not the defendant's behaviour, but rather the impact on the victim. The amount of punitive damages should be sufficient to ensure that their role is fulfilled, which, given the low amounts awarded, is not the current situation.

E.   The "Indirect Victim"

337. *Disappearance of the Distinction* – Civil law recognizes the "indirect victim"—that is, the person who suffers an injury due to the injury suffered by the direct victim.[466] However, under article 1056 C.C.L.C. and a narrow interpretation in the jurisprudence, this principle received limited application if the direct victim died. This article has no equivalent in the *Civil Code of Québec*; thus, the

---

464.   Gardner, above, note 297, No. 578 at 423.
465.   Above, note 295.
466.   See Centre for Research in Private and Comparative Law, *Private Law Dictionary and Bilingual Lexicons*, 2nd ed. (Cowansville, QC: Les Éditions Yvon Blais, 1991), s.v. "indirect victim." For a critique on the reluctance of common law courts to indemnify indirect victims for non-pecuniary damages, see Louise Bélanger-Hardy, "Négligence, victimes indirectes et préjudice moral en common law: les limites à la réparation se justifient-elles?" (1998) 36 *Osgoode Hall L.J.* 399. In civil proceedings against residential schools for Aboriginals, see *Residential Schools (Re)*, [2000] A.J. No. 47 (Alta. Q.B.) (Q.L.), where the judge refused to recognize that claims by spouses and children of direct victims were legally founded in common law. He stated that this was an issue for the legislator. However, see *J.L.L.* v. *Ambrose*, [2000] B.C.J. No. 384 (B.C. S.C.) (Q.L.), where the judge awarded $7,000 to the spouse of a rape victim, who had quit work to take care of his wife. The judge held that the spouse's injury flowed directly from the sexual assault.

distinction between the direct and indirect victim has been eliminated. There is now just one class of victim under the *Civil Code of
Québec*—that is, the person who can prove fault, injury, and a
causal connection between the two.[467]

338. *The Need for Analysis* – Despite the disappearance of this distinction, we believe that the issue of the indirect victim merits
analysis for two reasons. First, we have noticed that claims by indirect victims are rare in the cases under study. We will therefore
examine several issues particular to these victims. Second, while
the term "another" is broadly interpreted in civil law, the same is
not true of public law, especially in the field of civil liberties. The
issue then becomes whether the Quebec Charter recognizes the
indirect victim. If, according to the theory of overlap developed in
Béliveau Saint-Jacques,[468] the fault in article 1457 C.C.Q also constitutes an interference under the Charter, does it not follow that
the indirect victim, recognized by the Civil Code, is also recognized
by the Charter? This question is relevant to compensatory damages,
but is even more so if punitive damages are sought, since the
Charter is the only legislation under which this class of damages
may be awarded. We will first examine the indirect victim's action
for civil liability, followed by the Charter remedy.

1.   *Remedy in Extracontractual Civil Liability*

The Civil Codes of Lower Canada as well as of Quebec recognize that the indirect victim is entitled to full compensation. We will
now examine the elements required for this remedy.

339. *Recognition of a Right to Indemnification* – The right to compensation under article 1457 C.C.Q. is not restricted to the direct
victim; the term "another"[469] encompasses any victim who can
demonstrate the elements required in order for this recourse to be
exercised. Therefore, the direct victim is joined by the indirect vic-

467.   See Tancelin, above, note 10, No. 766 at 393.
468.   Above, note 5. This expression appears in Madam Justice L'Heureux-Dubé's
       opinion at 362.
469.   See *Congrégation des petits frères de Marie* v. *Régent Taxi and Transport Co.
       Ltd.*, [1929] S.C.R. 650; *Hôpital Notre-Dame de l'Espérance* v. *Laurent*, above,
       note 320.

tim,[470] who may be a close relation, a parent, a spouse, or the direct victim's child.

340. *Limiting the Class of Plaintiffs* – Obviously the list of indirect victims can become quite long, and many people will wish to be included. Causation, however, serves to limit this class of plaintiffs:[471] they must prove that their injury flows from the injury to the direct victim caused by the defendant's faulty act—that is, that their injury is a direct and immediate consequence of the defendant's fault (article 1607 C.C.Q.).[472] The fear that there will be an avalanche of suits is not justified. While indirect victims are usually members of the direct victim's family, other persons may also seek indemnification under this class.[473]

341. *Rarity of Claims* – It is surprising that, despite recognition of the indirect victim under Quebec civil law, out of the few Quebec decisions involving sexual or spousal abuse of which we are aware,[474] there has been only one instance of an indirect victim requesting and receiving an indemnity.[475] Lack of injury cannot explain the rarity of claims by indirect victims. In a recent case, the victim's spouse testified about the negative impact the sexual assault had on their sex life.[476] But though she had suffered an

---

470. On this question, see Viney and Jourdain, above, note 68, Nos. 304ff at 128ff; *Encyclopédie juridique Dalloz, Répertoire de droit civil*, above, note 264, s.v. "Responsabilité du fait personnel"; Flour and Aubert, above, note 247, No. 97 at 59; Gardner, above, note 297, Nos. 344ff at 253ff; Baudouin and Deslauriers, above, note 10, Nos. 222ff at 158ff.

471. Baudouin and Deslauriers, above, note 10, No. 225 at 160–1.

472. As pointed out by Tancelin, above, note 10, No. 765 at 392, the indirect victim entitled to indemnification is not to be confused with indirect damage, which is not indemnified. Damages can be awarded only if they are a direct and immediate consequence of the fault.

473. Such as a business partner or an employer. In this case, it must be determined whether the damage is a direct and immediate result of the fault (art. 1607 C.C.Q.). See Baudouin and Deslauriers, above, note 10, No. 230 at 164; No. 439 at 280–1. Remember that in *Régent Taxi*, above, note 469, the religious community to which the deceased brother belonged claimed damages for his death. French law is hesitant to indemnify these types of victims. See Viney and Jourdain, above, note 68, No. 312 at 135.

474. See above, chap. 3, note 8.

475. See *Rousseau* v. *Quessy*, [1986] R.R.A. 222 (Que. Sup. Ct.), where the raped plaintiff's husband received an amount of $10,000 for loss of support, comfort, and affection, and an amount of $5,000 for mental anguish, depression, suffering, and various inconveniences.

476. See *Larocque* v. *Côté*, above, note 11.

injury as an indirect victim, she was not a plaintiff. In *Gagnon* v. *Béchard*,[477] discussed above regarding the nature of the injury, the parents of two children who had been sexually molested could have filed a personal claim as indirect victims, for these incidents surely inflicted an injury upon them.[478] The children of victims of sexual or spousal abuse may also suffer injury when the direct victim's ability to parent has been affected by the assault.[479] In other extracontractual liability actions, spouses will demand compensation for the loss of *consortium* and *servitium*, and children will demand compensation for disruption of the family life.[480] The virtual absence of this type of lawsuit can, perhaps, be explained by the novelty of such suits and by the difficulty in identifying and evaluating the consequences to the indirect victim of the attack on the direct victim.

342. *Conditions for Compensation* – Compensation requires that the indirect victim prove not only those elements required of the direct victim, but additional elements of proof as well. First, the indirect victim must prove: that the defendant was at fault in relation to the direct victim;[481] the injury suffered by the latter;[482] and the causal connection between the fault and the direct victim's injury.[483] The indirect victim must then prove his or her own injury as well as the causal connection between this injury and the injury caused to the direct victim by the defendant. Thus, a court could refuse to com-

---

477. Above, note 160.
478. See *J.D.B.* v. *F.M.*, [1998] O.J. No. 3786 (Ont. Gen. Div.) (Q.L.), where the parents of a sexual assault victim received $25,000 each under the *Family Law Act*, R.S.O. 1990, c. F-3, s. 61.
479. See *S. et al.* v. *Clement et al.*, above, note 109.
480. See, among others, *Cooke* v. *Suite*, [1995] R.J.Q. 2765 (C.A.), which confirmed [1993] R.J.Q. 514 (Que. Sup. Ct.), where the plaintiff's husband received an amount of $3,000 for loss of *consortium* and mental and psychological suffering when a medical error resulted in his wife's fourth pregnancy; see *St-Cyr* v. *Boucherville (Ville de)*, [1995] R.J.Q. 2445 (Que. Sup. Ct.), where the direct victim's sister received $1,000 for pain and suffering, inconvenience, loss of enjoyment of life, and disturbances to the daily rhythm of life after her brother was injured; see also *Tu* v. *Cie de chemins de fer nationaux du Canada*, above, note 373, where the parents of a train accident victim each received $60,000 for non-pecuniary loss. See also Baudouin and Deslauriers, above, note 10, No. 227 at 162 and the jurisprudence cited.
481. In fact in most cases, proof of fault is presented only one time by the direct victim, which is why a joint action is beneficial.
482. This eliminates the hypothetical situation wherein the direct victim would not suffer while the indirect victim would.
483. See above at §§156ff. for developments on these issues.

pensate a parent of a direct victim who died, if the parent had lost all contact with the child and could therefore not prove the injury resulting from the child's death.[484]

343. *Evaluating the Indemnity* – Once all the necessary elements have been proven, the indirect victim can claim the same damages as the direct victim, including bodily, moral, and material injuries resulting in pecuniary or non-pecuniary losses (articles 1457 and 1607 C.C.Q.). The same rules apply.[485]

Pecuniary damages include expenses for future therapy, transportation and childcare expenses related to therapy, past and future lost salary, and housekeeping expenses incurred following the direct victim's injury. Non-pecuniary damages include loss of affection and support.[486] Thus, a mother sued the British Columbia Superintendent of Family and Child Services after she personally suffered an injury when her three-year-old daughter was sexually abused by an adolescent placed in their foster care. The mother suffered from acute anxiety, guilt for failing to protect her daughter, and loss of self-confidence and self-esteem. The trial judge awarded her $30,000 for lost earning capacity, $25,000 for non-pecuniary damages, and $5,720 for therapy costs.[487] This decision was reversed on appeal because the court had failed to find the state-employed social workers at fault for placing the adolescent in the woman's home.[488] The decision of the lower court remains relevant nonetheless as an illustration of the types of damages that an indirect victim can claim.

---

484. See, among others, *Augustus* v. *Gosset*, above, note 450, where the indirect victim plaintiff, whose son Griffin was killed by police officer Gosset, was not awarded damages because he had not seen his son in several years.

485. See the discussion on injury, above, at §§279ff.

486. See *S. et al.* v. *Clement et al.*, above, note 109, where the husband received damages in the amount of $30,500, three children each received $4,500, one child received $7,500, and another $15,000 following the victim's rape by an escaped prisoner. The victim received $327,895. The attacker and Correctional Services Canada were held jointly responsible. The judge concluded: "In short, from a happy, close family functioning at a very high level of harmony, the S.s have become emotionally separate and the parents at least have become barely capable of functioning adequately" (at 512). See *Queen (Litigation Guardian of)* v. *Hodgins* (1991), 36 R.F.L. (3d) 159 (Ont. Gen. Div.).

487. *B.D.* v. *British Columbia (Superintendent of Family and Child Service)*, above, note 103. The direct victim of the sexual assault received $25,000 for non-pecuniary damages and $36,740 for pecuniary damages.

488. Ibid.

While the indirect victim must prove personal injury, the seriousness of the direct victim's state will influence the evaluation of indemnification.[489] It is likely that, the more serious the direct victim's injuries, the greater the pecuniary loss of the indirect victim. The amount of non-pecuniary loss is likewise dependant on the gravity of the direct victim's state. However, the court must also take into consideration the state of the indirect victim, who is entitled to full and personalized compensation.

344. *Independence and Interdependence of the Two Remedies* – Even where the actions are jointly filed in order to save on time and money,[490] substantially and procedurally[491] the claim by the indirect victim remains independent of the claim by the direct victim.[492] The indirect victim must prove his or her own injury, and each action must be judged on its own merits.

The principle of the independence of the two remedies, however, is limited. In fact, the result of an action by the indirect victim depends greatly on the direct victim's action. If the direct victim is unable to prove the elements essential to an extracontractual liability action—for example, where she is unable to convince the judge that the defendant was at fault—there is a good chance that the indirect victim's lawsuit will fail for the same reason.[493] Where the judge concludes that the attacker is not liable for all the direct victim's problems, and liability is shared, this will be reflected in the indirect victim's indemnity.[494] This position is justified because common sense dictates that the indirect victim should not receive greater compensation than the direct victim.

345. *Prescription* – As we have seen, prescription will be suspended where the direct victim can show that it was impossible for her to

---

489. Gardner, above, note 297, No. 359 at 261.
490. Art. 67 C.C.P. Denis Ferland and Benoît Émery, *Précis de procédure civile du Québec*, vol. 1, 2nd ed. (Cowansville, QC: Les Éditions Yvon Blais, 1994) at 94.
491. Hence, the indirect victim will not be affected by the transaction concluded by the direct victim.
492. Regarding the independence of this remedy, see Viney and Jourdain, above, note 68, No. 321ff at 143ff; Geneviève Viney, "L'autonomie du droit à la réparation de la victime par ricochet par rapport à celui de la victime initiale," D.1974. chr. at 3.
493. See *B.D.* v. *British Columbia (Superintendent of Family and Child Service)*, above, note 103.
494. See our discussion on causation and shared responsibility, above, at §§259ff.

act (article 2904 C.C.Q.), either because she did not make the connection between her injury and the defendant's faulty acts or because the latter's behaviour prevented her from launching an action within the prescribed delay. The indirect victim also benefits from this suspension.[495] In fact, the indirect victim may be incapable of launching her or his action because she or he may be unaware of the events causing the direct victim's problems or their source. Therefore, the indirect victim's cause of action arises at the same time as that of the direct victim (article 2880 C.C.Q.). It is worth noting that an indirect victim's cause of action can arise despite the fact that the direct victim's remedy is prescribed. For example, consider the direct victim who reveals to her spouse that she was sexually assaulted in the past. Even though she was aware of her injuries, she did not pursue the attacker within the prescribed time. Her spouse may nonetheless launch an action seeking compensation for his own injury, provided he respects the prescribed time limit. However, while prescription is interrupted for the direct victim when she files her action, this does not apply to the indirect victim, since the two plaintiffs are not solidary (article 2900 C.C.Q. *a contrario*).

346. *The C.V.C.A.* – As for the *Crime Victims Compensation Act*,[496] it compensates the indirect victim only if the direct victim has died (sections 1 (c) and 2 C.V.C.A.).[497] As a supplement to this indemnity, the indirect victim may file an action to gain additional sums (sections 8 and 10 C.V.C.A.). In the event the direct victim, also entitled to an indemnity under this plan, survives, nothing prevents the indirect victim from launching a civil action in court, given that she or he is not entitled to an indemnity under the C.V.C.A. Nothing in this act prohibits this type of remedy, in contrast to section 83.57 of the *Automobile Insurance Act*[498] and sections 438 and 442 of the *Act Respecting Industrial Accidents and Occupational Diseases*.[499] Note, however, that a child born following a sexual assault may be entitled to an allowance (section 5, para. 2 C.V.C.A.).

---

495. See prescription, above, at §§121ff.
496. Above, note 1.
497. See below, at §366.
498. R.S.Q., c. A-25.
499. Above, note 2. See below, at §§379ff.

2. Remedy under the Charter of Human Rights and Freedoms

347. *The Problem* – If civil law recognizes that the indirect victim is entitled to full compensation, what are the indirect victim's rights with respect to compensatory and punitive damages under section 49 of the Charter? Theoretically, it is possible that a direct victim will launch an action based solely on the Quebec Charter. The indirect victim's remedy based on the Charter then becomes an issue. Even if the direct victim invokes the Civil Code, it is possible that the indirect victim will invoke the Charter in order to obtain punitive damages. We will examine the indirect victim's remedy for compensatory damages under the first paragraph of section 49 of the Charter. Then we will examine the issue of punitive damages claimed under the second paragraph of section 49 of the Charter.

a) Compensatory Damages under the First Paragraph of Section 49 of the Charter

348. *Two Interpretations* – Two different interpretations will assist in determining whether the indirect victim is recognized under the Charter. The first interpretation requires the indirect victim to prove an unlawful interference with her fundamental rights. Under the second interpretation, this proof is unnecessary because it is sufficient for the direct victim's rights to have been infringed.

349. *Proof of Interference* – To start with, one could argue that, in order to receive compensatory damages under the first paragraph of section 49 of the Charter, the indirect victim must prove all the same elements as the direct victim. The indirect victim must, therefore, demonstrate an unlawful interference with her or his fundamental rights. This position is based on an individualistic approach to human rights: only the victim whose fundamental rights have been infringed may receive compensation. This approach is adopted under subsection 24 (1) of the *Canadian Charter of Rights and Freedoms*, the counterpart to the first paragraph of section 49 of the Quebec Charter.[500] It stipulates that "Anyone whose rights or free-

---

500.   See Ghislain Otis, "La responsabilité de l'administration en vertu de la Charte canadienne des droits et libertés," in *Développements récents en droit administratif*, Formation permanente du Barreau du Québec (Cowansville, QC: Les Éditions Yvon Blais, 1992) 65 at 85; Pierre Béliveau, *Les garanties juridiques dans les Chartes des droits*, 2nd ed. (Montreal: Les Éditions Thémis, 1995) at

doms, *as guaranteed* by this Charter, have been infringed or denied may apply to a court of competent jurisdiction to obtain such remedy as the court considers appropriate and just in the circumstances" (emphasis added).

Therefore, in each case the indirect victim must prove an infringement of his right to physical and psychological integrity guaranteed by section 1. According to the definition employed by Madam Justice L'Heureux-Dubé in *Syndicat national des employés de l'Hôpital Saint-Ferdinand*,[501] there has been an interference with bodily, psychological, moral, and social integrity once the after-effects exceed a certain threshold. An indirect victim of sexual or spousal abuse may demonstrate that following the injury inflicted on the direct victim, she suffered from after-effects or trauma.[502]

This interpretation transforms the victim from an indirect to a direct victim because the former is required to have suffered an infringement of her fundamental rights, thereby rejecting the civilian concept of indirect victim.

350. *Irrelevance of Personal Infringement* – Inversely, indirect victims do not have to prove that their fundamental rights were infringed. It is sufficient that the direct victim satisfies the conditions imposed by section 49 of the Quebec Charter and that indirect victims satisfy those imposed by the Civil Code. This position is based on the principle that the Charter recognizes indirect victims as such and their right to indemnification. The first paragraph of section 49 of the Charter stipulates that "any unlawful interference . . . entitles the *victim* to obtain the cessation of such interference." Contrary to subsection 24 (1) of the Canadian Charter, which stipulates that "anyone whose rights or freedoms, *as guaranteed* by this Charter, have been infringed or denied may apply to a court of competent jurisdiction," the Quebec Charter does not distinguish

---

G-64; Henri Brun and Guy Tremblay, *Droit constitutionnel*, 3rd ed. (Cowansville, QC: Les Éditions Yvon Blais, 1997) at 960.

501. Above, note 192 at 252 and 253.
502. See, for example, *Valenti* v. *Valenti*, above, note 31, in which the plaintiff's son was traumatized by the domestic violence to which his mother was subjected. He exhibited behavioural disorders as well as difficulties with his studies, and received $2,500. See also the injuries inflicted on a spouse and children in *S. et al.* v. *Clement et al.*, above, note 109; *B.D.* v. *British Columbia (Superintendent of Family and Child Service)*, above, note 103.

between the direct and the indirect victim: it guarantees the compensation of any victim, and this term is broadly interpreted.

351. *The Position of the Human Rights Tribunal* – This last interpretation is in keeping with the liberal trend exemplified by the decision of the Quebec Human Rights Tribunal in *C.D.P.Q.* v. *Thibodeau.*[503] This case involved a landlord who was sued for racial discrimination after refusing to allow the tenant to sublet to an Aboriginal couple. The judge rejected the defendant's argument that the plaintiff was not personally discriminated against and found in favour of the direct as well as the indirect victim. The tenant was awarded $192.42 in compensatory damages and $1,000 in punitive damages. The judge remarked:

> The Charter prohibits discrimination against anyone. It would serve no purpose if it was permissible to refuse to enter into a contract because: "I have nothing against you personally, but I don't like the 'Blacks', the 'Jews', the 'Frenchmen' or the 'Aboriginals' with whom you do business, therefore I will not enter into a contract with you." . . . It is of little significance that the discriminatory reason for refusing to sublet did not directly involve Mr. Lalancette. Mr. Thibodeau's refusal was targeted directly at Mr. Lalancette.[504]

This decision reflects the principle that the existence of discriminatory intent is irrelevant; only the negative impact of the discriminatory act counts.[505] A broad meaning of the term "victim" applies: as soon as a person experiences inconvenience or injury due to an unlawful act of discrimination, that person is a victim according to section 49 of the Charter and is entitled to reparation.

352. *Influence of* Béliveau Saint-Jacques – In addition, recognition of the indirect victim under the Charter is confirmed by the theory

503. [1993] R.J.Q. 2971 (Que. Human Rights Trib.). See also *C.D.P.Q.* v. *Zweigenberg* (1983), 4 C.H.R.R. D/1295 (C.P.); *Commission des droits de la personne et des droits de la jeunesse* v. *2655-5158 Québec inc.*, J.E. 2000-1871 (Que. Human Rights Trib.).
504. Ibid., at 2973. This situation, categorized as discrimination by association, resembles that of an employee who loses his job because he refuses to implement a discriminatory directive towards another employee. See Béatrice Vizkelety, *Proving Discrimination in Canada* (Toronto: Carswell, 1987) at 83ff; Daniel Proulx, *Discrimination dans l'emploi: les moyens de défense selon la Charte québécoise et la Loi canadienne sur les droits de la personne* (Cowansville, QC: Les Éditions Yvon Blais, 1993) at 23.
505. See *C.D.P.* v. *L'Homme* (1982), 3 C.H.R.R. 849 (C.A.Q.); *O'Malley* v. *Simpsons-Sears*, [1985] 2 S.C.R. 536.

of overlap developed in *Béliveau Saint-Jacques*.[506] In this case, the Supreme Court decided that section 49 of the Charter was based on the same legal principle of liability for wrongful behaviour expressed in article 1457 C.C.Q. Therefore, given that article 1457 C.C.Q. recognizes every victim, direct or otherwise, once all the conditions have been satisfied, this rule must also be respected by the Charter.

353. *Taking a Stand* – The broad and liberal interpretation is preferable to the narrow approach, in which only the direct victim is included. Both the Civil Code and state indemnification plans[507] recognize injuries suffered by the indirect victim, based on the injury inflicted on the direct victim. How then to justify that the Charter will award compensatory damages only upon proof of interference with the indirect victim's fundamental rights? This position ignores the Supreme Court decision in *Béliveau Saint-Jacques*.[508] No judicial policy argument prevents indemnification. The reluctance to recognize the indirect victim can be attributed to undue influence by the common law, which has been slow to accept this right of action.[509] We must be careful not to interpret section 49 of the Quebec Charter in light of subsection 24 (1) of the Canadian Charter, which has, in fact, been interpreted within the specific context of criminal law.[510] The fear that lawsuits may multiply is tem-

---

506. Above, note 5 at 404; above, at §§153ff.
507. The indirect victim is recognized only if the direct victim dies. See section 1 (c) of the *Crime Victims Compensation Act*, above note 1, and sections 6 and 60 *et seq.* of the *Automobile Insurance Act*, above, note 498. See Gardner, above, note 297, No. 355 at 258.
508. Above, note 5.
509. See Tancelin, above, note 10, No. 750 at 386; Gardner, above, note 297, No. 344 at 253; Bélanger-Hardy, above, note 466. Contrary to Quebec civil law, the common law recognizes the right of the indirect victim to compensation in specific legislation. For example, see the *Family Law Act*, R.S.O. 1990, c. F-3, s. 61, which compensates the indirect victim for the loss of services provided by the direct victim, as well as for the loss of guidance, care, and companionship. This act does not compensate the indirect victim's anguish or pain and suffering. See also *Fatal Accident Act*, R.S.A. 1980, c. F-5; *Fatal Accident Act*, R.S.B.C. 1979, c. 120; *Fatal Accidents Act*, R.S.M. 1987, c. F-50; *Fatal Accidents Act*, R.S.N.B. 1973, c. F-7; *Fatal Injuries Act*, R.S.N.S. 1989, c. 163; *Fatal Accident Act*, R.S.P.E.I. 1988, c. F-5; *Fatal Accident Act*, R.S.S. 1978, c. F-11.
510. See *R. v. Paolitto* (1994), 91 C.C.C. (3d) 75, 82 (Ont. C.A.); *R. v. Wijesinka*, [1995] 3 S.C.R. 422, 449; *R. v. Spinelli* (1996), 101 C.C.C. (3d) 385, 400 (B.C. C.A.) (leave to appeal to the Supreme Court denied, No. 24917).

pered by the causal connection requirement. For these reasons, we believe that the Quebec Charter recognizes the indirect victim.

b)   Punitive Damages under the Second Paragraph of Section 49

354. *Framework* – The Charter must be invoked where punitive damages are claimed, whether the direct or indirect victim claims compensatory damages based on the Charter or the Civil Code, or both.

355. *Two Interpretations* – The two arguments used in support of compensatory damages may also be used to found a claim for punitive damages. The first position does not recognize the indirect victim as such, since the latter must prove the conditions in the second paragraph of section 49,[511] whereas the second position accepts the principle of the indirect victim.

356. *Intentional Nature of the Interference with the Indirect Victim* – If we retain the first position, the indirect victim must prove not only unlawful interference but also that the interference was intentional—that is, that the consequences of the unlawful interference[512] were desired by the defendant. In the majority of cases involving incest or sexual assault perpetrated against children, the attacker will measure the impact of his acts not only on the direct victim, but on the indirect victim as well. The fact that he will silence the child by telling her that were she to denounce him, it would make her mother ill, break up the family, send her brothers and sisters to foster care, and possibly send him to prison, indicates awareness of the consequences. Alternatively, he will attempt to justify his acts by treating them as a form of punishment of the child, as a game, or as a method of contributing to her sexual education. In most cases, proving the intentional nature of the unlawful interference does not pose any problem.

357. *Intentional Nature of the Interference with the Direct Victim* – Under the second interpretation, the indirect victim is not obliged to prove the intentional nature of the unlawful interference of which

---

511.   See *Massé* v. *Bélanger*, above, note 248. The judge refused to award punitive damages to the indirect victim because "he is not entitled to them under the wording of the relevant sections of the charter" (our translation) (at 542).

512.   See the analysis of Madam Justice L'Heureux-Dubé in *Syndicat national des employés de l'Hôpital Saint-Ferdinand*, above, note 192 at 262.

he or she was a victim. It is sufficient that she prove the intentional nature of the unlawful interference with the direct victim. The arguments discussed above in favour of recognizing the indirect victim are relevant to the issue of punitive damages. Additionally, the dissuasive and punitive objectives of these damages are better satisfied. This appears to be the position adopted by the Supreme Court in *Augustus* v. *Gosset*.[513]

For the time being, regardless of the approach adopted, punitive damages will be granted where the indirect victim of sexual or spousal abuse can prove that there has been an intentional unlawful interference with one of her protected Charter rights.

358. *Evaluation Criteria* – When evaluating the amount of punitive damages to award to the indirect victim, the tribunal should apply the same criteria as those used for the direct victim. The issue is not to compensate the two victims, but rather to denounce publicly the defendant's behaviour.[514] It is therefore important to avoid the perverse effect of splitting in half the amount of punitive damages that would originally have been allocated to the direct victim.[515]

359. *Conclusion* – Quebec civil law has adopted a broad definition of the term "other" in article 1457 C.C.Q. and will indemnify any victim who can satisfy the conditions required by this remedy. In cases of sexual and spousal abuse, the victim of an attack is entitled to reparation, as is any victim whose injury stems from the injury to the original victim. The Charter should also adopt a broad interpretation of the term "victim" and indemnify not only the victim whose fundamental rights have been personally infringed, but all

---

513. Above, note 450 at 308. The court awarded punitive damages to the indirect victim, a mother whose son had died, under the second paragraph of section 49 of the Charter, without her having to prove an unlawful interference with her fundamental rights.
514. See above, at §§328ff for the criteria used in the evaluation of punitive damages.
515. In the Court of Appeal decision in *Syndicat national des employés de l'Hôpital Saint-Ferdinand* v. *Curateur public du Québec*, [1994] R.J.Q. 2761, Judge Nichols condemned the appellants globally and solidarily and ordered them to pay $200,000 in punitive damages to the 703 beneficiaries. This was because it was too difficult to retrace all the beneficiaries. Nonetheless, each beneficiary or the beneficiary's successors received $284.49 in punitive damages, a rather small amount. This demonstrates that it can be disadvantageous to award one global sum for this class of damages without regard to the individuals.

other individuals upon whom the repercussions of such an infringement befall.

II. STATE INDEMNIFICATION PLANS

360. *Framework* – In addition to launching a civil action, victims of
sexual or spousal abuse may seek compensation under the *Crime
Victims Compensation Act*.[516] In certain cases, compensation is also
available under the *Act Respecting Industrial Accidents and
Occupational Diseases*.[517] Let us take a closer look at the position of
victims of sexual and spousal abuse under these two state indemnification plans.

A. The *Crime Victims Compensation Act*

361. *Some Statistics* – Each year, only 5 per cent of the 40,000 victims of crimes against the person in Quebec file a claim under the
Crime Victims Compensation Act with the Direction de l'indemnisation des victimes d'actes criminels (hereinafter the C.V.C. Service,
which administers the law) of the Commission de la santé et de la
sécurité au travail (C.S.S.T., which is the equivalent of the
Workmen's Compensation Board).[518] According to the *Rapport
annuel d'activité 1999* of the organization administering the
C.V.C.A., women make up 54 per cent of the claims that are
accepted. In 1999, sexual assaults (including sexual assault perpetrated by a person in authority, incest, sexual assault, armed sexual
assault, and grievous sexual assault) represented 34 per cent of
claims filed by women.[519] Among these claimants, 71 incest victims,
335 sexual assault victims, and 20 armed sexual assault victims
were indemnified. Males were victims of armed assault in 44 per
cent of cases and victims of sexual assault in 11 per cent of cases. It
is worth noting that 46 per cent of women and 25 per cent of men
were attacked in their homes. These statistics confirm the hypothe-
sis that women are attacked more often by men they know.[520]

516.   Above, note 1.
517.   Above, note 2.
518.   See *Le Soleil*, 6 November 1993 at A-7. In 1999, the C.V.C. Service received
       3,397 new claims for benefits. See Direction de l'indemnisation des victimes
       d'actes criminels, *Rapport annuel d'activité 1999* at 17.
519.   Young female victims of sexual abuse are also included in these figures.
520.   See Canadian Centre for Justice Statistics, *Juristat, Service Bulletin* 12, No.
       21 (1992), Statistics Canada, cat. No. 85-002 at 8, 9 and 13; Louise Viau,
       "L'égalité des sexes en droit criminel: un parcours sans fin?" (1996) 1 *Can.*

362. *Number of Requests for Indemnification* – It appears that victims of sexual and spousal abuse file few claims for indemnification with the C.V.C. Service. According to the *Rapport du Groupe de travail sur les agressions à caractère sexuel*,[521] between 1990 and 1995, the Youth Protection Services received 4,000 complaints involving sexual assault and nearly as many involving sexual abuse. Few of these victims filed a claim for indemnification with the C.V.C. Service. As indicated in the C.V.C. *Rapport annuel d'activité 1999*,[522] 28 per cent of victims who were indemnified were younger than eighteen years of age, and sexual assault occurred in 63 per cent of these cases. The conclusion to be drawn is obvious: many victims of sexual abuse do not take advantage of the C.V.C.A. This situation can be explained by the fact that victims are unaware of the act, or that claims are filtered out prior to reaching the C.V.C. Service, as suggested by the *Rapport du Groupe de travail sur les aggressions à caractère sexuel*.[523] In its *Rapport annuel d'activité 1996*, the C.V.C. Service pointed out the presence of a new group of claimants, composed primarily of victims abused by therapists and survivors of incest. This is due to the increasingly broad interpretation adopted under the C.V.C.A.[524]

1. Conditions of Application

Let us first examine the conditions under which the C.V.C.A. applies before looking at specific problems that arise with respect to victims of sexual and spousal abuse.[525]

Crim. L. Rev. 89; idem, "Victimes des ambitions royales," (1996) 30 *Revue juridique Thémis* 115.

521. Quebec, *Les agressions sexuelles: stop, Le rapport du Groupe de travail sur les agressions à caractère sexuel* (Quebec City: Government of Quebec, 1995) at 111.
522. Above, note 518.
523. Above, note 521 at 111.
524. Above, note 518 at 8. See the Direction de l'indemnisation des victimes d'actes criminels, *Rapport annuel d'activité 1996* at 8.
525. For an analysis of this act, see Josée Coiteux et al., *Question d'équité: l'aide aux victimes d'actes criminels* (Montreal: Association québécoise Plaidoyer-victimes, 1996); Baudouin and Deslauriers, above, note 10, Nos. 986ff at 589ff; Katherine Lippel (under the dir. of), *L'indemnisation des victimes d'actes criminels: une analyse jurisprudentielle* (Cowansville, QC: Les Éditions Yvon Blais, 2000). See also Peter Burns, *Criminal Injuries Compensation*, 2nd ed. (Toronto: Butterworths, 1992).

363. *Commission of a Crime against the Person* – The claimant must have been a direct victim of a crime against the person listed in the schedule to the Act,[526] the crime must have been committed in Quebec, and it must have resulted in an injury. The victim need not be a citizen of Canada nor even a resident of Quebec, but must have been in Quebec at the time the crime was committed. Note that a victim of an attempted sexual assault is not always compensated, as inchoate infractions do not appear in the schedule to the act, attempted murder being the exception.[527] However, attempted sexual offences are considered to be assaults by the C.V.C. Service (section 266 Cr.C.), if the attempt included touching. Alternatively, the C.V.C. Service relies on the wording of section 3 of the C.V.C.A. to include any after-effects of such an attempt. In these cases, the victim is in fact injured "by reason of the act . . . occurring in or resulting directly from. . . ." Similarly, a victim of harassment cannot be indemnified because this crime does not appear in the list of infractions, unless it involves intimidation using violence (section 423 C.C.).

364. *Commission of Crime after 1 March 1972* – In theory, the crime must have been committed after 1 March 1972, the date on which the C.V.C.A. entered into force.[528] Despite the principle of non-retroactivity of legislation, and the elimination of the transitory provision stipulated in the 1971 Act,[529] the C.V.C. Service has adopted a liberal attitude and will compensate victims of crimes against the person that were committed prior to 1972,[530] provided that the

---

526. Section 3 (a) C.V.C.A., crimes against the person: assault, murder, sexual assault, etc. See *Sauveteurs et victimes d'actes criminels—10*, [1989] C.A.S. 34; *Sauveteurs et victimes d'actes criminels—2*, [1994] C.A.S. 4.

527. See *Sauveteurs et victimes d'actes criminels—11*, [1996] C.A.S. 449.

528. By analogy, see *Assurance-automobile—31*, [1991] C.A.S. 870, where the court refused to compensate a road accident victim prior to the entry into force of the *Automobile Insurance Act* on 1 March 1978.

529. Section 25(2) of the *Crime Victims Compensation Act*, S.Q. 1971, chap. 18, stipulated: "However, the Commission may consider the application of any person injured between the 1st of November 1966 and the date of the coming into force of this act in the circumstances contemplated in section 3 if such person is totally or partially disabled as a result of the injury he then sustained and if compensation has not been granted by the Legislature to him for such injury." Our research shows that this section of the act has not been officially repealed, or omitted. Perhaps it is simply an oversight of the legislature.

530. However, the *Guide sur l'indemnisation des victimes d'actes criminels*, prepared by the C.V.C. Service (1993), confirms the contrary: "You must remember that any incident occurring prior to March 1, 1972, the date on which the

injury is still present and that the claim was filed within the proper time period.[531] In a case before the Review Board,[532] the claimant had been sexually assaulted in 1967, but these incidents resurfaced only in 1992 after she began therapy due to personal problems. The Review Board overturned the original decision on the grounds that the injury caused by the criminal act manifested itself only after therapy had commenced, which was after the act had come into force. Also, the claimant had filed her claim within the prescribed time period.

365. *Proof of a Crime* – The burden of proof the victim must satisfy is the civil standard of the balance of probabilities. This burden of proof is much less demanding than the criminal standard of beyond a reasonable doubt.[533] Where the accused has been convicted, the conviction is sufficient proof of the crime (section 19 C.V.C.A.).[534] However, the claimant can enter into evidence the police and medical reports if the attacker is unknown or if there has not been a conviction because no formal charge has been filed, because the trial is on-going, or because there has been an acquittal (section 13 C.V.C.A.).[535] The C.V.C. Service may conduct its own inquiry or hear witnesses if additional evidence is required. The attacker is generally not present at these hearings.[536]

366. *Categories of Compensation* – Once the eligibility conditions have been satisfied, bodily and moral injuries will be compensated (section 1 (b) C.V.C.A.) according to the conditions and rates set forth under the former *Workmen's Compensation Act* (W.C.A.)[537]

C.V.C. Act entered into force, does not give rise to the application of the Act" (our translation) (at 3).

531. See below, at §371.
532. See *Décision du Bureau de révision IVAC/civisme, région de Montreal*, File No. 0 0622 345 7, 19 December 1994; *Décision du Bureau de révision IVAC/civisme, région hors Québec*, File No. 0 0682 6697, 27 February 1997.
533. See *Sauveteurs et victimes d'actes criminels*—22, [1992] C.A.S. 376.
534. See *La Commission de la santé et de la sécurité du travail au Québec* v. *L.*, [1983] R.L. 503 (Que. Sup. Ct.).
535. See *Décision du Bureau de révision de la région de l'Outaouais*, File No. 0 0622 1642, 12 April 1995.
536. However, the presence of the defendant is always possible. Because the C.S.S.T. is subrogated in the rights of the victim, the defendant remains an interested party who is entitled to intervene and to be heard. See Lippel, above, note 525 at 129.
537. Sections III, IV, and V of the *Workmen's Compensation Act*, R.S.Q., c. A-3 [hereinafter *W.C.A.*], remain in force for the purposes of the C.V.C.A.

(section 5 C.V.C.A.). The victim may be indemnified for total temporary disability, representing 90 per cent of her net income up to a maximum annual amount of $50,500 (amount indexed yearly), during the period in which she is unable to work or fulfil her usual tasks. She is entitled to expenses for physical rehabilitation (such as medication, medical and hospital services, etc.), social rehabilitation (psychotherapy costs, for example, which in 1999 represented about 25 per cent of medical help, moving costs, the costs of installation of a security alarm, etc.) as well as occupational rehabilitation (such as training, help in finding work, etc.). If after-effects continue following the total temporary disability, the partial permanent disability (physical and mental impairment) will be evaluated, and the victim will receive a proportionate monthly allowance.[538] If the victim is unemployed, the C.S.S.T. will look at the victim's capacity to fulfil her regular tasks or duties and will award 90 per cent of the minimum wage during the period of disability.[539] Temporary benefits may also be granted to help defray therapy costs, for example (section 16 C.V.C.A.). These amounts are not recoverable should the victim later be judged ineligible. Pregnancy due to a sexual assault or incest qualifies as an injury, and the mother may receive an allowance for the child (section 5 C.V.C.A.).

The original decision may be appealed to the CVC/CIVISME Administrative Review Board, and thereafter to the Tribunal administratif du Québec (which replaced the Social Affairs Commission on 1 April 1998). The delays for such action are rather short. The claimant has thirty days to file a request for revision with the Board, except as regards the degree of partial permanent disability, where the delay is ninety days. The delay is sixty days for the Tribunal administratif du Québec.[540]

---

538. *Regulation respecting the impairment scale*, R.R.Q. 1981, c. A-3, r. 3.1. This regulation lists a number of injury after-effects and establishes an impairment percentage corresponding to the level of interference with physical or mental integrity.

539. Section 18 of the C.V.C.A. See the *Politique relative à l'indemnisation des victimes d'actes criminels ou de civisme ayant pour objet les calculs des indemnités*; Rolande Couture and Marielle Hétu, "L'IVAC au service de la personne", in Josée Coiteux et al., *Question d'équité: l'aide aux victimes d'actes criminels* (Montreal: Association québécoise Plaidoyer-victimes, 1996) 135 at 143. Note that the majority of Canadian provinces, with the exception of Manitoba, do not grant an indemnity for financial loss where the victim is unemployed. Ibid. at 141; Burns, above, note 525 at 203.

540. Sections 64 and 65 of the *W.C.A.*, above, note 537. Sections 7, 8, and 9 of the

367. *The Indirect Victim* – This plan indemnifies the indirect victim, such as the spouse or the dependants, only where the direct victim dies (section 1 (c), 2 C.V.C.A.).[541] Civil proceedings may be instituted in order to obtain additional monies (sections 8 and 10 C.V.C.A.). Where the direct victim has survived, the indirect victim may institute an action in civil liability against the defendant in order to claim damages for her or his personal injuries.[542]

368. *No Right to Combine Remedies* – Victims may not combine a remedy under the C.V.C.A. with other state compensation plans. In general, when the offence gives rise to claims under the A.I.A.O.D.[543] or the *Automobile Insurance Act*,[544] these acts have priority (section 20 (a) C.V.C.A.).

369. *Civil Proceedings in Court* – In addition to indemnification under this plan, the victim may also institute an action in civil liability, for the balance of the damages, against any individual responsible for the injury (sections 8 and 10 C.V.C.A.).[545] Aside from the attacker, the action may include the attacker's employer, among others.[546] The victim has the option to pursue such civil action, but she must inform the C.S.S.T. of her decision within a year after the injury occurred (section 11 C.V.C.A.).

Act Respecting Administrative Justice, S.Q. 1997, c. 43, amended sections 64, 65 and 65.1 of the *W.C.A.*, and replaced the Commission des affaires sociales with the Tribunal administratif du Québec. Section 184 of the *Act Respecting Administrative Justice* (came into force on 1 April 1998 by decree D. 1524-97, 26 November 1997, G.O.Q. 1997, II at 7361) repealed the *Act Respecting the Commission des affaires sociales* and amended section 12 of the C.V.C.A. (section 303 of the *Act Respecting Administrative Justice*, also entered into force 1 April 1998 by the same decree); see *Rapport annuel d'activité 1999*, above, note 518 at 6.

541. An amount of $500 is thus awarded. An amount of $2,000 is awarded to the parents of a minor child who died following a criminal act.
542. On the remedy available to the indirect victim, see above, at §§337ff.
543. The victim must be a worker as defined under the A.I.A.O.D. See below, at §§379ff, *Québec (Procureur général)* v. *Commission scolaire C . . . et Madame P.*, [1993] C.A.L.P. 648.
544. Above, note 498.
545. See *Perreault-Globensky* v. *Chine*, J.E. 87-864 (Que. Sup. Ct.); *Grenier* v. *Morin-Booth*, [1991] R.R.A. 807 (Que. Sup. Ct.); *Dubé* v. *Carnaval de Québec inc.*, [2000] J.Q. No. 484 (Que. Sup. Ct.) (Q.L.); *Major* v. *Surette*, above, note 411.
546. For possible defendants, see above, at §§166ff.

370. *Impact of the Election* – Two different options are available to the victim. She may institute civil proceedings immediately and, in the year following judgment, file a claim with the C.S.S.T. for the difference between the amount she was awarded and the amount stipulated according to the W.C.A. scale. If the defendant is insolvent, the C.S.S.T. will indemnify the victim without regard to the amount awarded under the judgment. Or, she may opt to claim the benefits offered under the act first and, at the same time, sue the attacker for the difference—that is, for damages that are not indemnified or that are only partially indemnified under the W.C.A.,[547] such as loss of future earning capacity.[548] A claim for benefits interrupts prescription under the Civil Code (section 12 C.V.C.A.). In the event the attacker is subsequently found liable, the court will deduct the amount of indemnities received from the damages awarded.[549] Remember that the C.S.S.T. is subrogated in the rights of the victim (section 9 C.V.C.A.).[550] It is more advantageous for the victim to first claim the benefits under the act, because therapeutic services and indemnification are available immediately.

371. *Delays for Filing an Application* – As previously discussed, prescription constitutes a major obstacle to victims of sexual abuse.[551] However, both the C.A.S. and the C.V.C. Review Boards have adopted an open policy towards this class of victim[552] and apply the principles developed by the Supreme Court in *M. (K.)* v. *M. (H.)*.[553] We hope that the CVC/CIVISME administrative review boards and

---

547.   Above, note 537.
548.   See above, at §§300ff.
549.   See *Comeau* v. *Anctil*, [1989] R.R.A. 882 (Que. C.A.); *Kouroumalis* v. *Papiernik*, [1997] R.J.Q. 1061 (Que. Sup. Ct.).
550.   See *La Commission de la santé et de la sécurité du travail au Québec* v. *L.*, above, note 534. But, in this case, the right of subrogation was never exercised given the lack of resources.
551.   See above, at §§85ff.
552.   Note that it was not always this way. In 1994, out of 202 requests that were rejected on grounds of prescription, 155 concerned sexual assault of minors. See Direction de l'indemnisation des victimes d'actes criminels, *Rapport annuel d'activité 1994* at 17. See also Direction de l'indemnisation des victimes d'actes criminels, *Rapport annuel d'activité 1991* at 2, which discusses the rejection of a claim by a victim of incest because it fell outside the prescribed period. The C.V.C. Service does not take into account the victim's fear of the attacker or that she may fear tearing apart the family. In 1999, 82 applications were rejected because they were prescribed. See the *Rapport annuel d'activité 1999*, above, note 518 at 18.
553.   Above, note 287.

the Tribunal administratif du Québec, which replaced the former boards in April 1998, will maintain this approach.

Although the victim must claim an indemnity within a year of the *occurrence* of the injury (section 11 C.V.C.A.), this delay has been interpreted by the jurisprudence to be not simply a prescription delay or deadline, but rather "a simple lapse of time at the expiration of which it may be presumed that there has been a renunciation [of the benefits under the act]."[554] Once this delay has passed, it is presumed that the right to benefits under the act has been renounced. This presumption, however, is rebuttable. The victim can prove that she did not renounce her benefits but that she was unable to apply for indemnification due to a state of shock, or to disturbing or traumatic incidents she experienced, or because she did not make the connection between her current problems and the past aggressive acts.[555] She is not, however, obligated to prove that it was impossible for her to act,[556] because in each case the court will evaluate the reasonableness of the circumstances. Note that ignorance of the existence of the act is insufficient to reverse the presumption of renunciation.[557]

372. *The New Act* – The current C.V.C.A. was to be replaced by *An Act Respecting Assistance and Compensation for Victims of Crime*,[558] amalgamating the C.V.C.A. and the *Act Respecting Assistance for Victims of Crime*.[559] The new act appears, however, to

---

554. See *Sauveteurs et victimes d'actes criminels—1,* above, note 109 at 4; *Sauveteurs et victimes d'actes criminels—2,* [1995] C.A.S. 5; *Sauveteurs et victimes d'actes criminels—5,* [1996] C.A.S. 19.

555. See *Sauveteurs et victimes d'actes criminels—9,* [1990] C.A.S. 46; *Sauveteurs et victimes d'actes criminels—9,* [1994] C.A.S. 354; *Sauveteurs et victimes d'actes criminels—1,* [1996] C.A.S. 1; *Décision du Bureau de révision I.C.A.V.—civisme,* File No. 9980 645, 8 December 1989; *Décision du Bureau de révision de la région de l'Outaouais,* File No. 0 0726 674 5, 11 May 1995; *Décision du Bureau de révision de la région de Montréal,* File No. 0 0622 345 7, 19 December 1994; *Décision du Bureau de révision IVAC/civisme, région hors Québec,* File No. 0 0682 6697, 27 February 1997.

556. See *Sauveteurs et victimes d'actes criminels—2,* above, note 554.

557. See *Décision du Bureau de révision IVAC/civisme de la région de Montréal,* File No. 0 0729 1529, 8 November 1996; *Sauveteurs et victimes d'actes criminels—24,* (1998) C.A.S. 5 (C.A.S.); *Sauveteurs et victimes d'actes criminels—22,* (1997) C.A.S. 422 (C.A.S.). The C.V.C.A. is the only Canadian legislation in this area that does not recognize this as a reason for extending the delays. See Couture and Hétu, above, note 539 at 140.

558. S.Q. 1993, c. 54 (Bill 106), not yet in force.

559. R.S.Q., c. A-13.2.

have been relegated to the back burner, and the chances of it coming into force are rather slim. However, in the hopes of avoiding during the next reform the errors in the proposed new act, we will examine the major changes that are relevant to our purposes. The victim's close relatives are entitled to an indemnity, to reimbursement of expenses, and to rehabilitation services, even where the direct victim has not died (section 9). The act imposes both the duty to cooperate as far as possible with the authorities responsible for applying the act (section 7) and the duty to file a complaint with the police within a reasonable delay (section 12 (4)). The act also sets out the different categories of compensable injuries and eliminates all reference to the W.C.A. (section 111 *et seq.*).

The delay for filing an application for benefits is increased to three years, in conformity with articles 2925 and 2930 C.C.Q. The delay starts to run at the moment the injury manifests itself (section 113). This delay may be extended, with the permission of the minister, where it was impossible for the victim to act either by herself or through a representative (second paragraph of section 113). This section parallels article 2904 C.C.Q.[560] Extending the delay from one to three years does not affect the jurisprudential trend to the effect that this is not a prescriptive delay. It is still possible for exceptional circumstances to justify a delayed application for benefits. In spite of the substantially longer delay for filing a claim, it may still be impossible, for exceptional reasons, for certain victims to respect it.[561] As regards manifestation of the injury as the starting point for the delay, we propose that it be the moment when the manifestation becomes significant for the claimant.[562]

2.   *Specific Problems*

373. *Disadvantage to the Victims* – Certain aspects of both the current act and the new act disadvantage victims of sexual or spousal abuse, specifically the denial of indemnification in instances of gross negligence and the requirement to make a statement to and cooperate with the police.

---

560.   See above, at §§121ff.
561.   See above, at §§121ff.
562.   See above, at §118.

a) Refusal to Indemnify Where Gross Negligence

374. *The Concept of Gross Negligence* – Section 20 (b) C.V.C.A. (section 12 (2) new act) denies benefits to a claimant who has been grossly negligent. Indeed, the claimant's behaviour must not have contributed to her injury. Developed by the C.A.S. as well as the doctrine, this concept has been described by one observer as: "A rash and gross recklessness or negligence equivalent to a prior acceptance of the probable and foreseeable risks, the presence of an intentional factor approaching voluntary injuries and the desire to harm oneself, almost self-mutilation, bordering on and indistinguishable from fraud."[563] Gross negligence arises when claims are filed by prostitutes and female victims of spousal abuse. In 1999, slightly more than one quarter of claims filed with the C.V.C. Service were rejected on grounds of gross negligence.[564]

375. *Women Victims of Spousal Abuse* – The Criminal Injuries Compensation Board in Saskatchewan refused to indemnify a victim of spousal abuse on the grounds of contributory fault because she continued to live with her spouse, whom she knew to be violent.[565] This decision was upheld on appeal, despite evidence introduced by the victim's lawyer in support of battered wife syndrome.[566] These two decisions were overturned on the grounds of a lack of impartiality. The Board granted the victim an indemnity after a new hearing, but it was reduced because the victim continued to live with her violent spouse and had provoked him by packing his bags. This decision was upheld by the Court of Queen's Bench.[567]

---

563. Diane Girard, "La faute dans le 'sans faute': L'article 20 (b) de la *Loi sur l'indemnisation des victimes d'actes criminels*," in *Congrès annuel du Barreau du Québec (1992)*, Formation permanente du Barreau du Québec (Cowansville, QC: Les Éditions Yvon Blais, 1992) 815 at 819 (our translation). See, among others, *Sauveteurs et victimes d'actes criminels—42*, [1986] C.A.S. 357; *Sauveteurs et victimes d'actes criminels—53*, [1988] C.A.S. 425; *Sauveteurs et victimes d'actes criminels—50*, [1989] C.A.S. 659; *Sauveteurs et victimes d'actes criminels—50*, [1992] C.A.S. 55; *Sauveteurs et victimes d'actes criminels—9*, [1996] C.A.S. 33.
564. According to the *Rapport annuel d'activité 1999* of the C.V.C. Service, 214 applications out of 729 were rejected for gross negligence, above, note 518 at 20.
565. *L.(A.)* v. *Saskatchewan Criminal Injuries Compensation Board*, 2 June 1988, decision No. 1901/88.
566. 15 March 1990, decision No. 2511/90.
567. [1991] 5 W.W.R. 315 (Sask. Q.B.).

None of the decisions rendered in the various versions of *L. (A.)* took account of the reality of battered women. The claimant's passivity was reproached and treated as gross negligence: she should have left her violent spouse. For many reasons, however, battered women are not always in a position to leave the family residence: they are afraid of the violent spouse's reaction, they do not want to see their children harmed, they have nowhere else to go, or they have no money. In this case, the victim was also chastised for being too aggressive and having provoked her spouse by packing his bags. The inference is that she should have submitted to the latter's authority, sending a rather ambiguous message to battered victims of spousal abuse.[568]

In Quebec, the Tribunal administratif recognizes that it is not gross negligence to live with a violent spouse, or even to participate in drinking binges: for the female victim of spousal abuse, it is neither foreseeable nor probable that she will be subjected to other violent acts.[569] In accordance with the Supreme Court of Canada decision in *R. v. Lavallée*,[570] both the Tribunal administratif du Québec and the C.V.C. Service recognize the existence of the battered wife syndrome, which prevents such women from leaving the family residence.

376. *Assaulted Prostitutes* – Both the C.A.S. and the Review Board use the grounds of gross negligence to refuse to compensate prostitutes who are victims of criminal acts, where they were able to appreciate the risks inherent in their trade.[571] Thus, in *Sauveteurs et victimes d'actes criminel—3*,[572] a young woman who was prostituting herself for the first time, and who was therefore not in a position to evaluate the risks of the trade, received an indemnity. Nonetheless, in a decision before the Review Board in the District of Montreal, the reviewer refused to indemnify the victim's dependants.[573] He applied the theory of gross negligence and maintained

568. See above, at §§44ff; Weigers, above, note 30 at 278–90; Kathleen Mahoney, "The Legal Treatment of Spousal Abuse: A Case of Sex Discrimination," (1992) 41 *New Brunswick Law Journal* 21; Patricia Hughes, "How Many Times a Victim?" (1993) 6 *Canadian Journal of Women and the Law* 502; Burns, above, note 525 at 311.
569. *Affaires sociales—63*, (1998) T.A.Q. 387, AZ-980991130.
570. Above, note 65.
571. See Burns, above, note 525 at 306.
572. [1990] C.A.S. 14.
573. Decision No. 0 0229 713 3, 22 June 1992.

that the victim, a prostitute murdered while at work, knew the risks of her trade. Her behaviour was the equivalent of gross negligence within the meaning of the C.V.C.A.

In our opinion, this application of gross negligence and assumption of risk is open to criticism. It is not compatible with a realistic appraisal of the situation faced by women as recognized by the Supreme Court in *R. v. Lavallée*.[574] It is, in fact, far from clear that prostitutes choose their lifestyle or that they are able to change trades easily.[575] Every aspect of the victim's reality must be considered in order to truly appreciate gross negligence in an egalitarian manner. Many occupations that are legal, such as prostitution, involve risk.[576] Taxi drivers or small grocery store owners, for example, are often victims of violence during work. When seeking indemnification under the C.V.C.A., they do not find themselves reproached for working in trades prone to violence.[577] Evaluating prostitutes differently is equivalent to applying the law in a discriminatory fashion. In fact, these workers, the majority of whom are women and historically form part of a disadvantaged group, are treated differently because of their sex and because of the stigma associated with their occupation.

Note that, in civil law, assumption of risk requires a clear understanding of the foreseeable danger.[578] In addition, article 1477 C.C.Q. stipulates that the assumption of risk by the victim does not mean that she renounces her remedy; it may be used to share liability between the victim and the perpetrator of the fault (second paragraph of article 1478 C.C.Q.). The reviewer in the decision cited earlier (see note 573) erroneously interpreted the doctrine of assumption of risk. His position appears rife with stereotypes and may set a dangerous precedent.

---

574. Above, note 65.
575. See Canada, Special Committee on Pornography and Prostitution, *Pornography and Prostitution in Canada: Report of the Special Committee on Pornography and Prostitution* (Fraser Report), vol. 2 (Ottawa: Minister of Supply and Services Canada, 1985) c. 28, section 4 at 406–8.
576. The C.A.S. refers to this in *Sauveteurs et victimes d'actes criminels—3*, above, note 572 at 20. See also Schabas, above, note 14 at 106; *Reference Re ss. 193 and 195.1(1)(c) of the Criminal Code (Man.)*, [1990] 1 S.C.R. 1123; *R. v. Corbeil*, [1991] 1 S.C.R. 830 at 835.
577. If it involves workers who satisfy the conditions of application under the A.I.A.O.D., this act has precedence over the C.V.C.A. See below, at §381.
578. See Baudouin and Deslauriers, above, note 10, No. 553 at 362.

*b)   The Requirement of Filing a Complaint and Collaborating
with the Police*

377. *New Requirements* – Under the new act, the claimant must
report the offence to the police within a reasonable delay (section 12
(4)) and must collaborate with them (sections 7 and 12 (5)), otherwise she will not be indemnified.[579] These two obligations help to
facilitate the identification of the attackers and permit the subrogation of the Commission in the rights of the victim.[580] Under section 13, these requirements may be bypassed where the physical or
mental state of the victim presents an obstacle, or if her participation in criminal proceedings risks compromising her physical or
mental state.[581]

378. *A Dissuasive Effect* – Without commenting on the wisdom of
denying indemnities to claimants who refuse to cooperate with the
police,[582] we may nonetheless inquire as to the heavy burden that
obtaining authorization from the minister places on the claimant.
This could further dissuade women, many of whom have various
reasons for not reporting the attacks to police.[583] Conferring decision-making authority on the C.V.C. Service would have been less
damaging. Let us point out that no citizen is under a duty to cooperate with the police. These two duties are not mentioned in the current act,[584] but the courts have nevertheless refused to compensate
criminals who did not want to cooperate with the police.[585]

---

579.   See Burns, above, note 525 at 296.

580.   See *Sauveteurs et victimes d'actes criminels—4*, [1996] C.A.S. 14, 18.

581.   This is a duty imposed on the minister. Section 13(2) stipulates: "The Minister
must exempt the claimant from the requirement" (emphasis added).

582.   See *Sauveteurs et victimes d'actes criminels—4*, [1994] C.A.S. 13.

583.   See Quebec, *Les agressions sexuelles: stop,* above, note 521 at 111; Julian V.
Roberts, "Sexual Assault in Canada: Recent Statistical Trends," (1996) 21
Queen's L. J. 395, 401. On the reluctance of immigrant women to report inci-
dents of domestic violence to the police, see Dianne L. Martin and Janet E.
Mosher, "Unkept Promises: Experience of Immigrant Women with the Neo-
Criminalization of Wife Abuse," (1995) 8 *Canadian Journal of Women and the
Law* 3.

584.   See *Sauveteurs et victimes d'actes criminels—7*, [1996] C.A.S. 27. *Contra*:
Sauveteurs et victimes d'actes criminels—4, above, note 582. See Lippel, above,
note 525 at 128.

585.   See *Sauveteurs et victimes d'actes criminels—4*, above, note 582; *Sauveteurs et
victimes d'actes criminels—4*, above, note 580.

B. An *Act Respecting Industrial Accidents and Occupational Diseases*

379. *Arising out of or in the Course of Work* – If the attack arose out of or in the course of work,[586] and the victim falls within the definition of "worker" under the A.I.A.O.D.,[587] the attack is defined as an industrial accident in the A.I.A.O.D. and the victim is entitled to be indemnified by the C.S.S.T. The claim must be filed within six months of the assault. However, sexual assault committed by the employer, by an employee, or by a third party against a worker does present certain problems. If the attack took place at the workplace while the worker was at work, it is presumed to be an employment injury under section 28 of the A.I.A.O.D., and the victim's burden of proof is eased somewhat. The employer may attempt to rebut this presumption by proving that there was no connection between the event and the work. The jurisprudence has established that any violent act, such as a sexual assault, committed at work must be work-related—that is, it has an indirect or accessory link to work.[588] In *Québec (Procureur général)* v. *Commission scolaire C . . . et Madame P . . . ,*[589] the plaintiff, a secondary school teacher, was a victim of attempted murder by a student as she was leaving the police station where she had gone to meet the student in question and his parents. The student had previously threatened to kill her. The employer contested the ruling that this was an industrial accident. The C.A.L.P. held that an industrial accident had occurred even though the events had taken place after work hours, far from the workplace, and without the consent of the employer. The death threats were uttered against the teacher after she tried to impose a disciplinary measure during her work. The murder attempt occurred after the teacher had lodged a complaint and the school administration had disciplined the student.

---

586. Section 2 of the A.I.A.O.D. ("industrial accident").
587. Section 2 of the A.I.A.O.D. ("worker").
588. See Marie-Christine Dufour, "Les victimes de la violence en milieu de travail ont-elles droit à l'indemnisation prévue à la *L.A.T.M.P.*?" in *Les récents développements en droit de la santé et sécurité au travail*, Formation permanente du Barreau du Québec (Cowansville, QC: Les Éditions Yvon Blais, 1997) 65 at 70; Reine Lafond, "L'indemnisation des lésions psychologiques liées au travail: dernières tendances," in ibid. at 245. See *Québec (Procureur général)* v. *Commission scolaire C . . . et Madame P . . .* , above, note 543.
589. Above, note 543.

In *Rousseau* v. *Quessy*,[590] however, the judge ruled that the injuries were not caused by an industrial accident. In this case, a waitress in a bar was sexually assaulted by a customer in the work-place as the establishment was closing. She had just telephoned her husband to come pick her up when the events took place. The attacker was convicted of attempted rape. The evidence showed that the attacker had returned to the bar at the end of the evening and that he had planned the entire attack. The victim sued both the attacker and the bar owner for failing to protect her adequately. The latter argued that this was an industrial accident covered under the *Workmen's Compensation Act*, which was in force at the time of the assault.[591] He pointed out that the plaintiff had filed a claim with the C.V.C.A., but that her claim had been transferred to the C.S.S.T. because she was considered to have suffered an industrial accident under the act. The judge did not believe that this was an industrial accident: "There is therefore no relationship of cause and effect between the work performed by the plaintiff and the brutal assault she suffered. In other words, the incident was not the result of an occupational hazard, neither on the part of the assailant nor on the part of the assaulted."[592]

We believe that this decision is not well-founded. The judge applied an excessively narrow interpretation of the cause-and-effect relationship that must exist between the work and the injury. Even though the decision was rendered under the aegis of the former *Workmen's Compensation Act*,[593] the causal connection requirement had been liberally interpreted by both the doctrine and the jurisprudence.[594] Remember that the old act, like the current act, did not insist upon the traditional causal link. There only had to exist a certain link between the work and the injury. In this case, evidence was introduced to the effect that this bar had often been subject to armed robberies and burglaries. It is obvious that had the plaintiff not worked that evening, she would not have been attacked. If the same events were to occur today, the worker would benefit from the presumption under section 28 of the A.I.A.O.D. and the burden of

---

590.   Above, note 475.
591.   R.S.Q. 1964, c. 159.
592.   Above, note 475 at 229.
593.   Above, note 591.
594.   Baudouin and Deslauriers, above, note 10, No. 911 at 549; Cliche and Gravel, above, note 247 at 167ff.

proving the lack of any connection between the work and the injury would fall on the employer.

380. *Indemnification* – The C.S.S.T. indemnifies the victim for loss of earning capacity (sections 44 and 45 A.I.A.O.D.) at a rate of 90 per cent of net income to a maximum of $50,500 (amount indexed yearly). If the victim has suffered any permanent physical or mental impairment (section 83 A.I.A.O.D.), she is entitled to an indemnity fixed by regulation based on a percentage of the disability. The victim is also entitled to medical and rehabilitation services. When the A.I.A.O.D. applies, the victim forfeits all civil law remedies against the employer (section 438 A.I.A.O.D.) and the co-worker (section 442 A.I.A.O.D.).[595] Indemnification of a sexual assault victim, however, poses certain problems.[596] While sexual assault can have physical consequences, the impact is primarily psychological. The particular circumstances must therefore be taken into account by the C.S.S.T.[597]

381. *Precedence of the A.I.A.O.D.* – The A.I.A.O.D. has precedence in the event of a work-related accident, and claims cannot be cumulated with the C.V.C.A. (section 20 (a) C.V.C.A.). A claim that has been filed under the A.I.A.O.D. and is rejected because it should have been filed under the C.V.C.A. is considered to have been validly filed under the latter (section 22 C.V.C.A.). There is no equivalent section in the A.I.A.O.D. protecting a victim who has erroneously filed an application for indemnification with the C.V.C. Service and whose claim is thus prescribed under the A.I.A.O.D. It is therefore preferable to first file a claim under the A.I.A.O.D., because if the incident does not involve an industrial accident, the victim's rights are nonetheless protected.[598]

382. *Action against a Third Party* – In addition to an indemnity under the A.I.A.O.D., it is possible to institute civil proceedings

---

595. See *Béliveau St-Jacques*, above, note 5.
596. See above, at §§279ff.
597. For a discussion of the difficulties faced by injured women workers seeking indemnification from the C.S.S.T., see Katherine Lippel and Claudyne Bienvenu, "Les dommages fantômes: l'indemnisation des victimes de lésions professionnelles pour l'incapacité d'effectuer le travail domestique," (1995) 36 *Cahiers de Droit* 161; Katherine Lippel and Diane L. Demers, "L'invisibilité, facteur d'exclusion: les femmes victimes de lésions professionnelles," (1996) 11 *Can. J. Law and Society* 87.
598. See Lippel, above, note 525 at 57.

against a third party other than the employer or another employee—for example, against a customer who assaults a waitress in a bar. In this case, the victim must inform the C.S.S.T. of her decision to sue the third party in court, or to first receive an indemnity and then institute civil proceedings (section 443 A.I.A.O.D.). Where she receives an award in the civil proceedings that is less than the amount to which she would have been entitled under the act, she may receive a benefit to cover the difference (sections 444 and 445 A.I.A.O.D.).

C.   Advantages and Disadvantages of State Compensation Plans

383. *Advantages of a Compensation Plan* – Although these plans are not perfect, indemnification under these plans has its advantages for victims of sexual or spousal abuse. In contrast to civil law court proceedings, indemnification is fairly rapid, irrespective of the defendant's solvency, does not incur lawyers' fees,[599] attracts little publicity, does not require cross-examination, and does not require that the victim identify or confront the attacker. Note that the Quebec crime victims compensation plan is certainly the most generous in Canada: it has no cap on the amount of compensation.[600] A crime victim may receive a lifelong pension if she is absolutely incapable of working. Additionally, once the claim is accepted, the crime victim has access to, among others, the services of a therapist. Reports on the victim's psychological state, prepared by state-employed therapists, may be used in the civil proceedings. The victim thus avoids incurring additional costs. Moreover, amounts granted by the C.V.C.A. may be used to finance the civil suit. In contrast to a judgment, which is definitive, the C.S.S.T. may adjust the benefits in the event of a relapse.[601] In order to improve the system, studies should be conducted into the level of satisfaction experienced by women who have filed compensation claims under the C.V.C.A.[602]

---

599. Representation by a lawyer is still possible, however.

600. In Ontario, for example, the maximum amount that a crime victim can receive is $25,000. See the *Compensation for Victims of Crime Act,* R.S.O. 1990, c. C-24, s. 8. In *N.C.* v. *W.R.B.,* [1999] O.J. No. 3633 (Ont. Gen. Div.) (Q.L.), the plaintiff, a victim of sexual and spousal abuse, received $6,000 under the Ontario Act and $91,017 from the civil action.

601. With the exception of article 1616 (2) C.C.Q. See above, at §282.

602. See Des Rosiers, Feldthusen, and Hankivsky, above, note 309; Bruce Feldthusen, Olena Hankivsky, and Lorraine Greaves, "Therapeutic Consequences of Civil Actions for Damages and Compensation Claims by

384. *Advantages to a Civil Action* – Despite the advantages of state indemnification, a civil suit enables the victim to obtain a larger sum, including punitive damages, where the attacker and the other defendants are financially solvent. The court will deduct any indemnities received under the C.V.C.A. from damages awarded. In contrast to compensation under the C.V.C.A., a civil suit, if successful, publicly recognizes that a wrong has been committed by the attacker, who must personally compensate the victim.

385. *Conclusion* – State plans indemnifying victims of sexual or spousal abuse, particularly the C.V.C.A., should not be ignored. They enable victims to obtain therapeutic services rather quickly. We must underline the liberal approach that the C.V.C. Service has adopted. This approach permits a greater understanding of the realities experienced by these complainants. It is deplorable that so many victims are unaware of the existence of the C.V.C.A.

Victims of Sexual Abuse," (2000) 12 *Canadian Journal of Women and the Law* 66.

Part III
Instituting Proceedings

386. *Framework* – This part examines the issues encountered once civil proceedings have been instituted. Our goal is to minimize those obstacles a victim may face prior to and during the trial. We will also examine the possibility of an action in defamation filed by the defendant in reply to the allegations.

Chapter 5
Preparation for Trial

.

387. *Introduction.* – We will now examine the rules of procedure applicable to filing an action for sexual and spousal abuse. Of particular interest are those issues problematic for the victims of such abuse. Initially, the preliminary steps taken prior to a proceeding will be examined. These raise many questions: When is the best time to sue? How should one draft pleadings so that they are able to defeat a motion for particulars but at the same time are sufficiently flexible to adapt to changes in the law? How should one prepare and protect the client during the discovery process? Finally, how does one best represent the client in an out-of-court settlement?

I. WHEN TO FILE SUIT

388. *Need for Speed* – Prescription delays demand a certain rapidity when instituting civil actions. What is one to do when concurrent remedies can or must be initiated? Prior to serving notice of a civil action, is it wiser to wait until a claim filed under the *Crime Victim's Compensation Act* (C.V.C.A.) has been processed, or until the criminal trial is completed? What are the possibilities of a class action suit? What would be the potential effect of such a suit on individual actions?

389. *Cumulating an Application under the C.V.C.A. and a Civil Suit* – The C.V.C.A. imposes a one-year delay as of the date on which the injury manifests itself.[1] It is thus important to quickly set the administrative procedure in motion. It is no doubt preferable to sus-

---

1.   Section 11 *Crime Victims Compensation Act*, R.S.Q., c. I-6 (hereinafter C.V.C.A.). This delay is extended to three years in the new *Act Respecting Assistance and Compensation for Victims of Crime*, S.Q. 1993, c. 54, which is still not yet in force. For a discussion of the proposed amendments, as well as the measures the plaintiff may invoke in order to extend the prescription period, see above, at §372.

pend prescription (section 12 C.V.C.A.) by first filing a claim with the Commission de la santé et de la sécurité au travail (C.S.S.T.), which is responsible for administering the C.V.C.A. Indeed, the victim may use any monetary support received from the C.S.S.T. to help finance her civil action and especially any therapy being pursued. While the legislative scheme of the C.V.C.A. appears to indicate that the victim must opt for either a civil action or the statutory remedy, nothing in the law obliges her to wait for the conclusion of the application filed with the C.S.S.T. It would therefore be advantageous to start civil proceedings as well.[2] The commission evidently enjoys a right of subrogation[3] in the event the civil action succeeds,[4] and the damages awarded will be used to reimburse any indemnities received.

390. *Cumulating Criminal and Civil Proceedings* – It is much more difficult to manage the interaction between the criminal and civil proceedings. The civil action frequently takes place once the criminal proceedings have concluded. In fact, a guilty conviction may encourage the victim to file suit before the civil courts.[5] However, because the burden of proof is different, a finding of not guilty does not rule out a civil action.[6] The true complications arise with concomitant proceedings. Thus, the question arises, should a civil action be delayed because of a criminal trial?

391. *The Common Law Solution* – There is no automatic right to suspend civil proceedings in Canadian common law due to pending criminal charges based on the same incidents.[7] Such a suspension is

---

2.   Section 10 C.V.C.A.
3.   Section 9 C.V.C.A.
4.   Subsection 8 (2) C.V.C.A. states that "If the sum awarded and collected under civil proceedings is less than the amount of the compensation the claimant would have obtained under this act, he may invoke this act to claim the difference by notifying the Commission and filing his application within one year from the date of the judgment."
5.   See below, at §§536ff.
6.   See the discussion on the degree of proof required, below, at §§470ff. Under section 13 C.V.C.A., above, note 1, it is possible to file an application "whether or not any person is prosecuted for or convicted of the offence giving rise to material damage, injury or death"; the Commission can, of its own initiative, or upon application of the attorney general, adjourn the proceedings pending the termination of prosecution.
7.   See *Stickney* v. *Trusz* (1974), 2 O.R. (2d) 469, upheld by the Divisional Court, (1974) 3 O.R. (2d) 538 and the Ontario Court of Appeal, (1974) 3 O.R. (2d) 539 (leave to appeal to the Supreme Court of Canada denied: [1974] S.C.R. xii); see also the decision by the British Columbia Court of Appeal in *Haywood*

permitted only under exceptional circumstances where the accused's rights may be prejudiced.[8] Courts in the common law provinces have applied this principle to proceedings instituted by sexual abuse victims.[9] To date, the argument that the duty to testify in civil proceedings violates section 7 of the *Canadian Charter of Rights and Freedoms* has been rejected.[10] In *Belanger* v. *Caughell*, the Ontario Court General Division explained the following:

"Assuming for the purpose of this motion that the compulsion to attend upon discovery imposed on the defendant by the Rules of Civil Procedure constitutes an infringement of the defendant's right to liberty, the circumstances of the deprivation of liberty are not, in my view, contrary to the principles of fundamental justice. I believe that the protection given to the defendant by the provisions of s. 11(c) and s. 13 of the Charter . . . provide to the defendant sufficient protection."[11]

Securities Inc. v. *Inter-Tech Resource Group inc.* (1985), 68 B.C.L.R. 145 (B.C. C.A.) (appeal rejected 14 December 1990, S.C.C. Bulletin, 1990, p. 2872). See also John Sopinka, Sidney N. Lederman, and Alan W. Bryant, *The Law of Evidence in Canada* (Toronto: Butterworths, 1992) at 611.

8.   Note, on this subject, the possibility of obtaining an order banning the publication of the civil proceeding record until the conclusion of the criminal proceedings. See *J.L.D.* v. *Vallée*, [1996] R.J.Q. 2480 (Que. C.A.). See also *L.H.* v. *Caughell*, [1996] O.J. No. 3331 (Ont. Gen. Div.) (Q.L.), where the Ontario court adopted the principle that evidence obtained during discovery should be used only for the purposes of the civil proceedings. The court did not allow the plaintiff to transmit certain documents to the disciplinary committee, which had also instituted proceedings against the defendant, a doctor accused of sexually assaulting the plaintiff. The court applied the new regulation 61/96, adopted under the *Courts of Justice Act*, R.S.O. 1990, c. C.43, adding Rule 30.1 to the rules of practice. This rule presumes that there is an undertaking not to use evidence obtained during the discovery other than in the civil proceedings.

9.   See, for example, *S.A.G.* v. *Kenneth Norman Numella*, [1996] B.C.J. No. 527 (B.C. S.C.) (Q.L.), (1996) 21 B.C.L.R. (3d) 42, (1996) 48 C.P.C. (3d) 236, where the defendant wanted access to the transcript of the examination on discovery on the grounds his answers to the questions could be used against him in the criminal proceedings. The judge denied the defendant's motion for suspension of proceedings. See also *Belanger* v. *Caughell* (1995), 22 O.R. (3d) 741 (Ont. Ct. Gen. Div.), that dismissed a motion by a doctor, sued for sexual assault, who sought the suspension of civil proceedings while the criminal proceedings were taking place. The interest of the child in youth protection proceedings demands that such proceedings not be suspended while awaiting the outcome of criminal proceedings: See *Catholic Children's Aid Society of Metropolitan Toronto* v. *L.M.O.* (1996), 139 D.L.R. (4th) 534 (Ont. Gen. Div.), aff'd (1997), 149 D.L.R. (4th) 464 (Ont. C. A.).

10. Part I of the *Constitution Act 1982*, being Schedule B of the *Canada Act 1982* (1982, U.K., c. 11).

11. Above, note 9 at 748.

392. *Quebec Law* – In civil law, the Superior Court recognized in *Turcotte* v. *Gagnon*[12] that there was no *lis pendens* justifying a suspension of criminal proceedings for compensation even though an action based on the same fraudulent act was before the civil courts. The same principle was reiterated by the Quebec Court of Appeal in *R.* v. *Vallée*.[13] It stated: "Evidently, nothing prevents the victim from filing a criminal complaint as well as instituting civil proceedings, and the appellant has failed to prove that this is an abusive case wherein the creditor filed criminal charges as a means of forcing his creditor to pay him."[14]

It therefore appears possible to proceed before both the civil and criminal courts at the same time. Neither of the two proceedings should be suspended due to the other, except in exceptional circumstances.[15] Therefore, for our purposes, nothing prevents a civil action from being instituted even though the criminal proceedings are not yet terminated.

393. *Possibility of a Class Action* – Institutionalized abuse[16] may lend itself to a class action. A victim may sue on behalf of all those who have been abused in a given establishment (article 1002 *et seq. Code of Civil Procedure* (C.C.P.)).[17] A victim who has filed an individual action based on the same facts as those on which the class action is based is deemed to be excluded from the class action (article 1008 C.C.P.). In those cases where the class action precedes the individual action, it is appropriate for the victim to take the proper steps to exclude herself from the group, if she so desires.

II. DRAFTING THE DECLARATION

In this section we will examine how to draft the pleadings, specifically those elements pertaining to the plaintiff—in particular

---

12. [1974] R.P. 309 (Que. Sup. Ct.).
13. *R.* v. *Vallée*, [1996] A.Q. No. 3549 (Que. C.A.) (Q.L.), J.E. 96-2067.
14. Ibid., para. No. 38 (Q.L.) (our translation).
15. It would be unusual, if not inappropriate, to suspend the criminal proceedings due to the civil proceedings, because there is too great an interest in public protection in criminal proceedings: *Thames Launches* v. *Trinity House* (1961), 1 All E.R. 26 (Ch. D.), cited by Judge Hugessen in *Turcotte* v. *Gagnon*, above, note 12 at 315.
16. See above, at §14.
17. See *Kelly* v. *Communauté des Soeurs de la charité de Québec*, J.E. 95-1875 (Que. Sup. Ct.), appeal abandoned on 8 February 1996, where such procedures were dismissed because they were prescribed. See our discussion, above, at §§85ff.

the identification of the defendants and the wording of the allegations and the conclusions. Note that compensation for indirect victims must also be mentioned in the declaration if the proceedings are to be joined.[18]

394. *Identification of Defendants* – It is obvious that the correct identification of the defendants is crucial.[19] The victim can decide to sue some or all of the defendants. The advantage of suing the abuser and the other defendants is a financial one: liability towards the plaintiff is joint and several (article 1526 C.C.Q.) and an institutional defendant is more often capable of executing judgment.[20]

395. *The Insurer* – Under the *Civil Code of Québec,* it is possible to sue the insurer directly (article 2501 C.C.Q.). In this case, the insurer becomes a defendant that must also be identified in the originating process. It is possible to access the insurance policy to determine the insurer's name and perhaps the amount of the coverage.[21]

396. *Legal Description of Facts* – In fields where the law is evolving, such as in the area of civil suits brought by victims of sexual or spousal abuse, specific attention must be paid to drafting the declaration. The law may change radically between the date of drafting or service and the date of the trial or the appeal. It may be particularly important to describe the impact of the abuse in such a manner as to circumvent any potential prescription issues.[22] According to the jurisprudence, the insurer's obligation to defend or compensate depends on the wording of the pleadings.[23]

397. *Need for Detailed Allegations* – When drafting allegations of sexual abuse, a balance must be found between allegations of a general nature and details meant to establish their credibility. The description of facts the party intends to prove must be "precise" (article 76 C.C.P.). It is true that precise details render the allegations more credible: why would she remember the colour of her panties or the arrangement of the chairs unless these details were

---

18. See above, at §§337ff.
19. For example, execution of the judgment can be prevented if the defendant's name is incorrect.
20. See above, at §§166ff.
21. See above, at §231.
22. See above, at §§85ff.
23. See *Nichols* v. *American Home Assurance*, [1990] 1 S.C.R. 801.

associated with a traumatic incident? The number of details surrounding an incident is often interpreted as an indication that the
memory is reliable. For example, in the British Columbia case
A.D.C. v. *J.H.P.*,[24] the reliability criteria expounded by the defendant's expert was adopted by the court and included, among others,
the detailed description of the context in which the incident
occurred and the relationship between the victim and the abuser.

398. *Need for Flexibility* – Yet, victims do not always clearly remember the sequence of events, their frequency, or the dates on which
specific incidents occurred. The mention of precise details that subsequent testimony may prove erroneous or uncertain should be
avoided. A balance must be established between a description that
is just detailed enough to be credible and one that is overly detailed
and allows a thorough cross-examination on such questions as the
victim's age at the time of the first incident of abuse (e.g., was she
six or seven years?).[25]

399. *Impossibility to Act* – While the plaintiff is not obliged to use
the words "impossible to act" in her declaration, this impossibility
must nonetheless be indicated with sufficient precision[26] to defeat a
motion to dismiss for prescription, or at least to enable an easy
defence. Thus, in *G.B.* v. *A.B.*,[27] the trial judge granted the motion
to dismiss based on prescription because she felt that the male
plaintiff, a victim of sexual abuse over a period of several years, was
in a position to institute proceedings as of 1993 or 1994, but had
waited until 1997. Her decision that the action was prescribed was
based on the allegations, and in particular on the fact that the
plaintiff had begun psychotherapy in 1990 and had gradually over

---

24.   [1996] B.C.J. No. 741 (B.C. S.C.) (Q.L.); J.L.M. v. *P.H.* (1997), 40 B.C.L.R. (3rd)
       73 (B.C. C.A.); *J.L.M.* v. *P.H.* (1998), 109 B.C.A.C. 165; appeal granted in part
       on the assessment of damages awarded.
25.   See, on this subject, *Québec (Commission de la santé et de la sécurité du tra-
       vail)* v. *L*, [1983] R.L. 503 (Que. Sup. Ct.), where the court attached great
       importance to the fact that the victim contradicted her testimony as to the
       date of a sexual assault that had occurred more than six years earlier. To the
       contrary, see the decisions rendered by the British Columbia Court of Appeal
       in *J.L.M.* v. *P.H.* (1997), 40 B.C.L.R. (3d) 73 (B.C. C.A.); see *Dans la situation
       de: B.(L.)*, REJB 2000-16406 (C.Q.).
26.   See *O'Hearn* v. *Roy*, [1997] R.R.A. 64 (Que. C.A.); *Mailhot* v. *Bolduc*, [1996]
       J.T.D.P.Q. No. 10 (T.D.P.Q.) (Q.L.).
27.   [1998] Q.J. No. 1588 (Que. Sup. Ct.) (Q.L.), motion rejected for dismissal on
       grounds of prescription, rev'd by the Court of Appeal [1999] Q.J. No. 5129
       (Q.L.).

a period of seven years begun to understand the significance of the events in his life. This decision was overturned by the Court of Appeal because the conclusion that prescription was extinguished could not be drawn from the allegations as drafted in the victim's declaration.[28] Out of caution, a plaintiff must be clear as to when the impossibility to act began and when it ceased.

400. *Extrajudicial Admission* – Extrajudicial admissions must also be alleged in the declaration because they are juridical facts.[29] Given that defendants will have often admitted to the sexual relation,[30] it is important to relate the circumstances surrounding this admission in the declaration.

401. *Amount of Damages* – It is essential to request the appropriate amount of damages.[31] Not infrequently, the courts have overturned decisions in which damages greater than the amount requested were awarded.[32]

402. *The C.S.S.T.* – Where the plaintiff received benefits under the C.V.C.A.,[33] the declaration must include conclusions as to the C.S.S.T.'s right of subrogation for these amounts.

Service of the declaration sets in motion the discovery process, which may also present certain challenges for the plaintiff.

III. DISCLOSURE OF EVIDENCE

403. *The Problem* – Proceedings such as the examination on discovery (articles 397 to 398.2 C.C.P.), the medical examination (articles 399 and 400 C.C.P.), and the production of documents (article 402 C.C.P.) are intended to provide the parties with access to the infor-

---

28. Ibid.
29. See Jean-Claude Royer, *La preuve civile,* 2nd ed. (Cowansville, QC: Les Édi-tions Yvon Blais, 1995) No. 862 at 527, No. 942 at 572.
30. See *D. (Guardian ad litem of)* v. *F.*, [1995] B.C.J. No. 1478 (B.C. S.C.) (Q.L.).
31. See above, at §§279ff. In *Roberge* v. *Carrier,* REJB 1997-03743 (C.Q.), the judge pointed out that he "arbitrarily" awarded damages to the victims for psy-chological and moral damages given that no expert was called to testify on this subject.
32. See *Téléson Électronique inc.* v. *Développements Iberville ltée,* [1996] R.R.A. 995 (Que. C.A.), where the plaintiff omitted to ask for damages under the *Charter of Human Rights and Freedoms,* R.S.Q., c. C-12.
33. See above, at §§360ff.

mation on which the adverse party will rely so that they may better evaluate their chances of success.[34] An examination on discovery essentially consists of an exchange of information relevant to the litigation.[35] Moreover, if the physical or mental state of a given party is put into issue during the litigation, the adverse party can demand that the other party undergo a medical examination. Certain aspects of this preliminary proceeding can be particularly troubling for the victim. Should she impose upon herself the duty to reveal her entire life? Will the defendant have access to her entire medical and psychiatric record, as well as her personal diary? How many psychiatrists must she meet? These are some of the concerns the plaintiff must deal with when instituting proceedings.

We will begin by studying the examinations of the victim and other persons. We will then look at the plaintiff's obligation, under certain circumstances, to undergo a medical examination. Finally, problems related to access to documents will be analysed.

A.   Examination on Discovery

404. *Types of Examinations on Discovery* – The *Code of Civil Procedure* provides for examinations both prior to filing a defence (article 397) and once the defence has been filed (article 398). The former essentially involves the examination of the plaintiff, while the latter is applicable to any party. In both cases it is possible, with the court's permission, to examine "any other person" (paragraph 4 of article 397 and paragraph 3 of article 398 C.C.P.).

405. *Questions Raised* – Two issues arise in actions for sexual or spousal abuse. Quebec courts must decide, first, who may be summoned for examination and, second, the extent of the examination. For example, must the victim supply the names of everyone who is participating or has participated in her therapy group?

---

34.   See *Poulin* v. *Vaillancourt*, J.E. 88-1362 (Que. Sup. Ct.), where Judge Rousseau-Houle, then of the Superior Court, relied on this principle when allowing questions to be answered that would provide greater detail about the allegations in the declaration. The plaintiff alleged that he was forced to explain to third parties that the defendant's false accusations were not founded. The judge ordered the plaintiff to reveal the names of the third parties to whom he had made reference.

35.   See *Royer* v. *J.E.C. Giroux ltée*, [1967] C.S. 123 (Que. Sup. Ct.).

1. Persons Summoned

406. *Plaintiff* – The examination on discovery constitutes an important part of the preliminary proceedings. During this examination the plaintiff must answer questions asked by the defendant's representative. These questions generally concern the description of events giving rise to the action. Other critical aspects of this examination involve disclosure of the abuse, which determines whether the action is prescribed,[36] and the impact of the attack on the victim's life.[37] It is important for the plaintiff to be well prepared for this examination because the defendant will exploit any discrepancies in the description of events.[38]

407. *Children* – The *Code of Civil Procedure* seems to allow minor victims to undergo preliminary examination: the wording of paragraph 3 of article 397 refers to the "person for whom the plaintiff claims as tutor." In spite of this, the jurisprudence is hesitant to impose the trauma of such an examination on child victims unless a judge is present to protect their interests. The courts have prohibited the examination of child victims younger than seven: the child's capacity to testify had to be assessed by the trial judge.[39] Children whose capacity to swear an oath is not in issue can be examined.[40] It is not certain that the sole presence of a judge is sufficient to minimize any trauma the child may suffer during the examination.[41] At the very least, the child should be accompanied and assisted by a person other than her lawyer.[42]

---

36. See above, at §§85ff.
37. See above, at §§279ff.
38. Coherence and consistency in the plaintiff's description of events are among the criteria most often used to evaluate her credibility. See below, at §503.
39. See *King Ruel* v. *Centre de ski Le Relais (1988) inc.*, [1994] R.D.J. 618 (Que. C.A.); *Yamaha Motors Canada ltée* v. *Corbeil*, [1993] R.D.J. 419 (Que. C.A.); *Whitty* v. *Zellers inc.*, J.E. 94-335 (Que. Sup. Ct.), where it was decided that children aged three and five at the time of the incident, and aged five and seven at the time of the motion, could be examined only in the presence of the judge. The judge cited *Ouellette* v. *Remy*, [1954] R.P. 57 (Que. Sup. Ct.) (a child of seven years could not be examined); *Corbeil* v. *Desjardins Ste-Adèle Marine inc.*, J.E. 93-217 (Que. Sup. Ct.).
40. See *Guénette* v. *Lapierre et Bédard*, [1976] C.S. 1786 (Que. Sup. Ct.), where it was decided that children aged ten years at the time of the discovery could be examined.
41. See our discussion on the credibility of testimony given by children, below, at §481.
42. See the measures that can be taken to protect the child, below, at §487.

408. *Presence of the Defendant or the Therapist* – It may be important for the victim to have her therapist present during the examination. In addition, the victim might prefer not to have to confront the defendant at this preliminary stage of the proceedings. The rules concerning the presence or exclusion of persons during the trial also apply during the examination on discovery.[43] The therapist, if present, should not intervene during the examination. Her role should be limited to providing the plaintiff with psychological support.

409. *Examination of the Defendant* – The abuser/defendant can also be examined once the defence has been filed. It is, once again, important to be well prepared for this examination: the defendant's version of the various events giving rise to the action must be known. The defendant's credibility is undermined at trial if the version of the events differs from those presented at examination.[44]

410. *Institutional Defendants* – It is possible to examine a representative of an institutional defendant, such as the school board or the Youth Protection Service (Y.P.S.) (paragraph 1 of article 397 and paragraph 1 of article 398 C.C.P.).[45] This examination is an opportunity both to obtain documents and to ascertain the official position of the institutional defendant. Any written or verbal policy regarding the treatment of children must be obtained. Any disciplinary procedure involving the abuser is also relevant.[46] The repre-

---

43. See *Farnell* v. *Canadian Tire-D.Bossy inc.*, J.E. 88-411 (C.Q.); see also the common law decision *G.K.* v. *D.K.*, [1994] O.J. No.1680 (Ont. Gen. Div.) (Q.L.), where the judge decided that there was no reason to refuse the defendant the right to be present during the plaintiff's examination on discovery.

44. See, among others, *Ballard* v. *Cordeau*, [1990] R.J.Q. 1664 (Que. Sup. Ct.) where, in a case of spousal abuse, the judge adopted the plaintiff's version after noting that the defendant's version given during the discovery differed from the trial version; see also *A.D.C.* v. *J.H.P.*, above, note 24, where the contradictions of the abuser (the grandfather by relation) regarding his possession of pornographic magazines was used by the judge to undermine his credibility and discredit his complete denial of sexual touching.

45. On the choice of representative, see, among others, *Boiler Inspection and Insurance Company of Canada* v. *Saint-Louis-de-France (corporation municipale de la paroisse de)*, [1994] R.D.J. 95 (Que. C.A.).

46. See *G.B.R.* v. *Hollett*, [1996] N.S.J. No. 345 (N.S. C.A.) (Q.L.), motion for leave to appeal to the Supreme Court dismissed, [1996] S.C.C.A. No. 541 (Q.L.), where the Court of Appeal dismissed the appeal of a judgment finding the employer liable for failing to dismiss an employee guilty of supplying reform school girls with cigarettes. The employee later sexually assaulted one of the students at the school and established an abusive sexual relationship with her that lasted over a period of several years. The Court of Appeal felt that the

sentative can undertake to obtain information from other persons if he is not in a position to answer adequately.

411. *Third Parties* – The C.P.C. also permits the examination of "any other person" (paragraph 4 of article 397 and paragraph 3 of article 398 C.C.P.). This right is an exception.[47] It cannot be used to dig into the private life of a person who is not a party to the litigation[48] or to obtain the names of the plaintiff's witnesses in order to have them served.[49] Contrary to what is done in the Canadian common law jurisdictions, the plaintiff should refuse to reveal the names of her witnesses, or, for example, the members of her support group.[50]

2. *Scope of the Questions*

The true obstacle for the plaintiff will be the scope of the questions asked of her. Must every question pertaining to her past be answered?

---

continued employment contributed to the sexual assault suffered by the victim. See also *D.E.P.* v. *N.J.P.*, [1997] B.C.J. No. 1634 (B.C. S.C.) (Q.L.), where the court had to assess at what point to limit the right to obtain names of individuals who had previously lodged complaints against the defendant and who were also entitled to their privacy.

47. See *Allstate Insurance Co. of Canada* v. *Sarrieu*, [1986] R.D.J. 457 (Que. C.A.); for permission to examine a third party in exceptional circumstances where the life of the witness was in danger: *Hôtel de la Grande Allée inc.* v. *Canada Permanent Trust Company*, [1985] R.D.J. 608 (Que. C.A.).

48. See *R.J.R. MacDonald inc.* v. *Procureur général du Canada*, J.E. 89-1136 (Que. Sup. Ct.), commented on by Denis Ferland and Benoît Émery, *Précis de procédure civile du Québec*, vol. 1, 2nd ed. (Cowansville, QC: Les Éditions Yvon Blais, 1994) at 372.

49. See *McCallum Transport Québec ltée* v. *Commission des accidents de travail du Québec*, [1987] R.D.J. 190 (Que. C.A.); *Mulroney* v. *Canada (Procureur général)*, [1996] R.J.Q. 1271 (Que. Sup. Ct.); *Fortier-Bolduc* v. *Centre hospitalier de la région de l'Amiante*, J.E. 95-1424 (Que. Sup. Ct.). See also *Atelier d'usinage G.D. inc.* v. *Produits d'énergie du Canada inc.*, [1994] R.D.J. 172 (Que. C.A.); *Paquin* v. *Daigneault*, J.E. 94-1417 (Que. Sup. Ct.).

50. See, for example, *V.P.* v. *Linde*, [1996] B.C.J. No. 454 (B.C. C.A.) (Q.L.); [1996] 7 W.W.R. 19; (1996) 19 B.C.L.R. (3d) 338; (1996) 47 C.P.C. (3d) 6, where the Court of Appeal reviewed the procedure for evidentiary disclosure when faced with requests to examine the plaintiff's private diaries and for access to the names and addresses of her sisters and other women who participated in her group therapy or Alcoholics Anonymous meetings, as well as the victim's writings, possessed by a sexual assault prevention centre. Only this last point was raised on appeal. All the other requests appear to have been considered legitimate.

412. *General Principle* – Every question relevant to the litigation
must be answered, subject to the right to confidentiality. Questions
on relevancy and the right to confidentiality, which results from the
right to professional secrecy and the plaintiff's right to privacy, usually arise respecting access to documents and are therefore
analysed in that section.[51] We nonetheless feel that it is important
to point out that relevancy also applies to the scope of questions
asked during the examination on discovery. We must not presume
that the victim has completely waived her right to privacy because
she is exercising her right to obtain damages from her abuser.[52]

413. *Abusive Questions* – Questions that do no more than intimidate
the victim, that are unrelated to the allegations in the declaration,
or that are part of a fishing expedition are not allowed.[53] It is thus
important to closely monitor the defendant's right to question the
plaintiff regarding allegations contained in his defence. For example, a defendant who alleges in a sexual abuse case that the plaintiff had always been a nymphomaniac, and is thereby attempting to
justify a presumed consent to sexual relations, should not be
allowed to ask details regarding the number of sexual partners the
plaintiff has had. This information is irrelevant to "the litigation,"
and is meant only to support an allegation made by the defendant.

414. *Names of Witnesses* – It is not necessary during an examination on discovery to provide the names of actual or potential witnesses.[54] Therefore, in our opinion, it is inappropriate for the
defendant to try to obtain the list of participants in a support group
to whom the plaintiff has turned for assistance. While it may be relevant for the plaintiff to answer questions regarding the precise

51.   Below, at §§418ff.
52.   See, for an example of this principle in common law, *A.M.* v. *Ryan*, [1997] 1
      S.C.R. 157, where Madam Justice McLachlin stated: "I accept that a litigant
      must accept such intrusions upon her privacy as are necessary to enable the
      judge or jury to get to the truth and render a just verdict. But I do not accept
      that by claiming such damages as the law allows, a litigant grants her oppo-
      nent a licence to delve into private aspects of her life which need not be probed
      for the proper disposition of the litigation" (at 180).
53.   See *Westinghouse Canada inc.* v. *Arkwright Boston Manufacturers Mutual
      Insurance Company*, [1993] R.J.Q. 2735 (Que. C.A.).
54.   See *Laroche* v. *Roy Marchand inc.*, [1991] R.D.J. 491 (Que. C.A.); *Poulin* v.
      Vaillancourt, above, note 34; *Aluminium du Canada* v. *Domaine de la Rivière
      inc.*, [1982] C.A. 239 (Que. C.A.).

moment at which she was in a position to denounce the abuse,[55] it is unnecessary to name the people to whom this information was confided. The scope of questions asked often brings into play the plaintiff's right to privacy, as does the order to undergo a medical examination. We will now consider to what extent medical examinations can be used as a mechanism for evidentiary disclosure.

B. The Medical Examination

415. *Relevance of the Examination* – Under article 399 of the *Code of Civil Procedure*, the adverse party can request that the person whose physical or mental condition is in issue undergo a medical examination. The plaintiff's physical or mental condition can be relevant to the amount of damages eventually awarded. It is within this context that a medical or psychiatric examination can be ordered.[56] Access to this provision has been narrowly interpreted by the courts because medical examinations intrude on a person's privacy.[57] Thus, the plaintiff is not obliged to undergo difficult or

55. It may be that the first manifestation of injury is the moment when the attack is disclosed or when the victim first makes the connection between the attack and the injury. It is at this point that prescription starts to run. See above, at §§115ff.

56. See *Commission des droits de la personne et des droits de la jeunesse du Québec et M.B.* v. *Virage Santé Mentale inc.*, [1997] J.T.D.P.Q. No. 25 (Quebec Human Rights Tribunal) (Q.L.), where the defendant asked that the plaintiff undergo a psychiatric examination in order to establish that she was motivated by vengeance. The plaintiff was suing him for damages arising out of sexual harassment. The court rejected the request for a psychiatric examination because it did not feel that proof of fault required medical evidence. The court also rejected the argument that the claim for moral damages put into issue the plaintiff's physical or mental condition. For the final decision on the matter of sexual harassment, see [1998] R.J.Q. 2199 (Quebec Human Rights Tribunal). See also *T.(L.)* v. *Commission des droits de la personne et des droits de la jeunesse*, REJB 1997-05505 (Que. C.A.), where the court dismissed the appeal and confirmed that the psychiatric evaluation was not relevant. Yet the common law courts in Canada are more willing to agree to this examination. See *C.* v. *A.*, [1997] B.C.J. No. 447 (B.C. S.C.) (Q.L.), where the judge, without much discussion, ordered that the child-victim and the mother, who was also claiming psychological damages, be examined by a doctor of the defendant's choosing.

57. See *Beaumont* v. *Beaumont*, [1968] B.R. 522 (Que. K.B.); *Kasowicz* v. *Barzik*, [1990] R.J.Q. 2800 (Que. C.A.); *Union des employés du transport local et industries diverses, local 931* v. *Delécolle*, [1990] R.D.J. 227 (C.A.); *Syndicat des travailleurs(euses) de l'enseignement Chauveau-Charlesbourg* v. *Robitaille-Rousseau*, [1988] R.D.J. 259 (Que. C.A.); *Audet* v. *Hôtel-Dieu de Salaberry de Valleyfield*, [1974] R.P. 236 (Que. C.A.).

painful medical examinations,[58] or procedures whose sole purpose is to annoy.[59] Moreover, the necessity of such an examination must be justified.

416. *Assessing the Examination's Relevance* – The relevance of the examination must have been explicitly raised in the allegations made in the declaration. The Human Rights Tribunal held, in an interesting decision rendered in a sexual harassment case, that simply mentioning a claim for moral damages was insufficient justification for ordering a medical examination.[60] The tribunal relied on the restrictive interpretation adopted by the jurisprudence regarding the need for medical examinations under article 399 C.C.P. It is our opinion that this decision should be applauded for its refusal to order the medical examination so that the defendant could find out "why" he was being sued by the plaintiff. Parties to a civil action do not have to explain why they are suing if they are able to prove an interference with their rights.[61] The tribunal, therefore, refused to consider as "sick" those women who were exercising their rights of action.

417. *Examination of the Defendant* – Note, however, an Ontario family law case where the trial judge ordered the defendant to

---

58.   See *Suite* v. *Cooke*, [1993] R.J.Q. 514 (S.C.), where the plaintiff was not obliged to undergo difficult medical examinations that the defendant requested as part of his defence against a claim of professional negligence. Note that the plaintiff claimed damages for the birth of her child after she believed herself to have been sterilized by the defendant. See the decision by the Court of Appeal, [1995] R.J.Q. 2765 (C.A.). For a commentary on damages in these situations, see, Louise Langevin, "Les difficultés d'indemnisation des femmes: l'indemnisation des frais d'entretien d'un enfant né à la suite d'une grossesse résultant d'une faute médicale," (1994) 19 *Queen's L. J.* 469; idem, "L'affaire *Cooke* c. *Suite*: la reconnaissance de la grossesse-préjudice, mais à quel prix?" (1996) 56 *Revue du Barreau du Québec* 125.

59.   See *Kasowicz* v. *Barzik*, above, note 57 at 2807 (C.A.), where the Court of Appeal identified the risk of frivolous procedures in this context.

60.   See *Commission des droits de la personne et des droits de la jeunesse du Québec et M.B.* v. *Virage Santé Mentale inc.*, above, note 56, confirmed on appeal; *T.(L.)* v. *Commission des droits de la personne et des droits de la jeunesse,* above, note 56.

61.   The court also refused to order a medical examination to establish causation between damages claimed and the harassment. This decision appears to us to be more controversial. In the case, the result is perfectly justified given the lack of detail provided by the defendant in his alleged reasons for requesting the medical examination. However, proof of injury and the connection between this injury and the fault could justify such an examination in other cases.

undergo a psychiatric examination to prove that he possessed personality traits compatible with the psychological abuse alleged by the plaintiff.[62] It is highly unlikely that this approach will be condoned by Quebec courts. To date, Quebec judges have shown themselves to be more cautious than their Canadian common law colleagues, and rightly so. The *Civil Code of Québec* expressly recognizes the right to inviolability and integrity of the person (articles 3 and 10), as does the *Charter of Human Rights and Freedoms* (section 1).[63] A restrictive approach to ordering medical examinations is appropriate.[64] However, if the courts start routinely ordering plaintiffs to undergo medical examinations to prove that they exhibit personality traits compatible with post-traumatic stress disorder, for example, it would perhaps be appropriate to order that the defendants also be subjected to medical examinations.

C. Access to Documents

A summons to produce the plaintiff's medical and psychiatric records often accompanies the medical examination.[65] To what extent does the defendant have access to these documents?

418. *The Problem* – Access to documents in the possession of third parties is provided for under article 402 of the *Code of Civil Procedure*.[66] The defendant is also entitled to copies of any relevant

---

62. See *Robinson* v. *Kilby* (1996), 45 C.P.C. (3d) 11; (1996), 20 R.F.L. (4th) 413; [1996] O.J. No. 423 (Ont. Div. Ct.) (Q.L.). The case was appealed and the appeal allowed by the judge of the Divisional Court. He felt that the need for this type of examination required preliminary proof in the form of an expert's affidavit.
63. Above, note 32.
64. Note that the expertise on personality traits of abusers is far from definitive. See above, at §6. Conclusions respecting the psychological make-up of the victim are also rather superficial. The utility of an expert report on this topic appears minimal, and it may be justifiable to refuse such examinations given their breach of privacy and integrity of the person. See *Dans la situation de: B.(L.)*, REJB 2000-16406 (C.Q.), where the judge relied on common law jurisprudence when rendering judgment.
65. See *Commission des droits de la personne et des droits de la jeunesse du Québec et M.B.* v. *Virage Santé Mentale inc.*, above note 56.
66. "If, after defence filed, it appears from the record that a document relating to the issues between the parties is in the possession of a third party, he may, upon summons authorized by the court, be ordered to give communication of it to the parties, *unless he shows cause why he should not do so*" (emphasis added). Article 400 C.C.P. specifically concerns documents in the possession of an establishment covered by the *Act Respecting Health Services and Social*

document the plaintiff has in her possession (article 397 C.C.P.). We will examine certain problematic aspects of the procedure for the production of documents. To begin with, victims often resent intrusive demands for documents: their entire lives can suddenly come under the defendant's scrutiny. Therefore, we will evaluate first the "relevance" criterion applicable to orders to produce, which often proves to be problematic in sexual and spousal abuse cases. Victims are also opposed to the introduction of their medical or psychiatric records, their personal diaries, or the notes taken by their therapists. These documents can be exempt from production for reasons of professional secrecy, the right to privacy, or common law privilege. This will be the subject of the second half of our review.

1.   *Irrelevant Documents*

419. *General Approach* – Only "relevant" documentation must be produced.[67] The courts have adopted a very liberal approach towards the determination of relevance during preliminary proceedings.[68] According to the Court of Appeal, "objections made to questions on the grounds that they are irrelevant to the proceedings should be overruled unless their irrelevance is obvious to the judge; where doubt exists, it is better to let final judgment determine the objection's fate."[69] In sexual abuse proceedings, an overly liberal

---

Services, R.S.Q., c. S-42, required for the medical examination stipulated in article 399 C.C.P.

67.   The jurisprudence uses the term "relevant" to designate the type of document that must be disclosed. The document must reveal facts in relation to the litigation that can serve as evidence as between the parties, as explained by Judge Baudouin in *Frenette* v. *Métropolitaine (La), compagnie d'assurance-vie*, [1992] 1 S.C.R. 647; [1992] R.R.A. 466, (sub nom. *Frenette* v. *Metropolitan Life Insurance Co.)* 89 D.L.R. (4th) 653, (sub nom. *Métropolitaine, compagnie d'assurance-vie* v. *Frenette)* 4 C.C.L.I. (2d) 1, 134 N.R. 169 (appeal allowed by the Supreme Court, below, note 77, on the issue of waiver of professional secrecy). See also, among others, *Coffey* v. *Tran*, [1991] R.D.J. 107, 51 Q.A.C. 225 (Que. C.A.); see also *Jagura-Parent* v. *Dvorkin, ès qualités "Médecin"*, REJB 1997-09462 (C.Q.); see also *D. (M.)* v. *D. (L.)*, REJB 1998-06122 (Que. C.A.) for a review by Baudouin J. of the case law on this subject.

68.   See *Kruger inc.* v. *Kruger*, [1987] R.D.J. 11 (Que. C.A.); *Croteau v. Perreault Mathieu Cie ltée*, [1990] R.D.J. 217 (Que. C.A.); *Parizeau* v. *Société Radio-Canada*, [1995] R.D.J. 132 (Que. Sup. Ct.), where the liberal position of the courts with respect to allegations of relevance was confirmed by the Superior Court.

69.   See *Les Restaurants Mikes* v. *Les Restos Van-Mil inc. et Yvan Milot*, J.E. 93-1746 at 2 (Que. C.A.) (our translation).

approach to the relevance of documents concerning the plaintiff's psychological history can be traumatic, if not re-victimizing. The approach to questions of relevance therefore merits discussion.

420. *Evaluation of Relevance in Proceedings for Sexual and Spousal Abuse* – Particularly difficult issues arise when assessing a document's relevance in a claim for spousal and sexual abuse. Relevance is not to be evaluated based on "mere speculation as to the contents of the records or biased hypotheses about such plaintiffs."[70] The traditionally sexist attitude prevalent in the rules of evidence held that such claims were presumed to be frivolous;[71] therefore, when evaluating relevance, particular attention should be paid to whether the alleged relevance reflects a sexist stereotype or whether it actually exists. A person is not obliged to reveal her entire psychological history to strangers just because she is claiming moral damages. For example, barring exceptional circumstances, disclosure of the plaintiff's psychiatric record prior to the abuse is inappropriate. This motion is too often meant to label a plaintiff who has alleged sexual abuse: she is "unstable" or "hysterical" and thus should not be believed in her attempt to implicate the defendant.[72] Where the plaintiff alleges that she cannot work because of a back injury suffered when hit by her spouse, the court may consider the plaintiff's previous medical condition relevant when determining whether or not her pre-existing back condition was aggravated by the physical abuse. If, however, a plaintiff in a sexual abuse proceeding alleges that following the abuse she has been incapable of sexual relations, does this mean the defendant is entitled to examine her entire gynecological record to see whether she may have mentioned experiencing sexual difficulties prior to the abuse? Or is this a fishing

---

70. Madam Justice L'Heureux-Dubé in *A.M.* v. *Ryan*, above, note 52 at 180. While she dissented in this case, her opinion on relevance is restated by Madam Justice McLachlin on behalf of the majority, as well as by Justices Lamer and Sopinka in *R.* v. *O'Connor*, [1995] 4 S.C.R. 411. For a commentary on *O'Connor*, see Bruce Feldthusen, "Access to the Private Therapeutic Records of Sexual Assault Complainants," (1996) 75 *Can. Bar Rev.* 538.
71. See the *obiter* by Lord Diplock in *D.P.P.* v. *Hester* (1973), 57 Cr. App. R. 212 (H.L.).
72. One of the prevailing myths is that women with personal psychological problems imagine sexual assaults. See, for example, the defendant's motion in a sexual harassment case requesting that the plaintiff undergo a psychiatric examination: *Commission des droits de la personne et des droits de la jeunesse du Québec et M.B.* v. *Virage Santé Mentale inc.*, above, note 56. While false allegations do occur, the presumption of good faith should also apply to female victims of sexual assault.

expedition? As noted by Madam Justice McLachlin in *A.M.* v. *Ryan*: "Fishing expeditions are not appropriate where there is a compelling privacy interest at stake."[73]

421. *Time Limit on Access to Documents* – Within this framework, time limitations on access to documents may be relevant. The plaintiff's medical or psychiatric records dating back to birth need not be produced to the defendant. In fact, in 1977 the Quebec Court of Appeal decided in *Société centrale d'hypothèque et de logement* v. *Pagé*[74] that the right of access to medical records was not an open door to the plaintiff's entire medical history. The court relied on the wording in the *Code of Civil Procedure*, referring to the record "whose examination has been authorized." According to the court, access to the medical file was limited to the file authorized pursuant to the medical examination prescribed by the C.C.P.—that is, the medical examination relative to the victim's condition *subsequent* to the wrongful behaviour.

However, in 1992 the *Code of Civil Procedure* was amended and the rules on evidentiary discovery were liberalized.[75] It would appear that the Court of Appeal decision to permit access only to medical records created subsequent to the wrongful conduct must be re-evaluated.[76] In fact, the Supreme Court decision in *Frenette* v. *Metropolitan Life Insurance Company*[77] conflicts with this position. Even if the decision in *Société centrale d'hypothèque et de logement* v. *Pagé* is to be discarded, time limitations are often necessary and are justified by the need for a relevant connection between the

73.   Above, note 52 at 179.
74.   [1977] C.A. 560.
75.   See the wording of the new article: above, note 66.
76.   See the decision by the Court of Appeal in *Les héritiers de feu Léon Rousseau* v. *Le Groupe Desjardins*, [1989] R.J.Q. 785, which recognized that article 402 C.C.P. applies to the disclosure of medical records. Article 402 is not limited in time. See, for a discussion on this case, Hélène Langlois, "La Cour d'appel et la confidentialité des dossiers médicaux et hospitaliers," in *Développements récents en droit de la santé* (Cowansville, QC: Continuing Education Department of the Barreau du Québec, Les Éditions Yvon Blais, 1991) at 101, 103.
77.   [1992] 1 S.C.R. 647. The Supreme Court in *Frenette*, at 677, challenged the liberal trend identified in *Société centrale d'hypothèque et de logement* v. *Pagé*, above, note 74. However, the entire discussion is *obiter* because the issue was resolved by the Court based on the insured's express waiver of privilege. See Royer, above note 29, No. 1177 at 724 and 725.

demand for production and the allegations in the declaration.[78] Motions for access to documents that pre-date the faulty act should be examined carefully. In our opinion, the contents of pre-abuse medical records are irrelevant, unless there is a serious indication that the abuse aggravated a previously existing medical condition.[79] In the post-abuse medical or psychiatric record, only those aspects relating to the injury suffered and alleged are relevant.

To avoid having the plaintiff's privacy invaded by the defendant, careful attention must be paid to the determination of a document's relevance. As we have seen, exemption of the disclosure of documents as offered under the *Charter of Human Rights and Freedoms*[80] and pursuant to other privileges has, to date, been narrowly interpreted.

2. *Documents Exempt from Disclosure*

There are several reasons for claiming that certain documents, even where relevant, are exempt from disclosure in the cases under study. The plaintiff can invoke her right to professional secrecy, her right to privacy, or her right to certain privileges drawn from common law.

a) *Right to Professional Secrecy*

422. *General Principle* – Section 9 of the *Charter of Human Rights and Freedoms*[81] guarantees the right to professional secrecy.[82] Confidentiality of these documents must be protected except where authorized by "an express provision of law." Does this mean that the plaintiff's medical or psychiatric records are protected against the

---

78. Note that even in *Frenette*, ibid., the Supreme Court allowed access to medical records covering only the last two years of the insured's life.
79. See, on this subject, the section on causation, above §§259ff., where we describe the subtle difference between taking the victim as you find her and compensating her solely for the aggravation of a previously existing condition.
80. Above note 32.
81. Ibid.
82. See also sections 7 and 8 of the *Act Respecting Health Services and Social Services*, above, note 66, and section 42 of the *Medical Act*, R.S.Q., c. M-9. Also to be considered is the effect of article 2858 C.C.Q., which stipulates that any evidence obtained in violation of professional secrecy is automatically inadmissible. See *Gobeil, ès qualités "Personne autorisée par le Directeur de la protection de la jeunesse"* v. *D.(C.)*, REJB 1998-12645 (C.Q.), where the social worker was not compelled to appear.

defendant's attempts to gain access? In *Frenette* v. *Métropolitaine (La), cie d'assurance-vie,*[83] the Supreme Court of Canada favoured a two-tiered approach in response to this question. The judge must order the health care institution to produce the record if the plaintiff has explicitly or tacitly waived confidentiality or if the law provides for access to the medical record. In all other cases, the recommended approach is to leave it up to the discretion of the judge, who must balance the defendant's right to evidentiary disclosure against the plaintiff's right to professional secrecy.

423. *A Tacit Waiver?* – For some, the fact of putting one's physical or psychological condition in issue before the courts is tantamount to a tacit waiver of professional secrecy.[84] Without having clearly resolved this issue, the Supreme Court appears to have endorsed this view in *Frenette*. The Court identified two instances where, in its view, the right to professional secrecy is definitely tacitly waived: an action in civil liability against a doctor or a hospital, and an action for performance of a disability or life insurance policy where the insured's state of health is relevant. The Supreme Court relied on certain common law decisions[85] and also cited the decision of the Court of Appeal in *Laprise* v. *Bonneau,*[86] written by Judge Jacques, whereby "the fact of mentioning his physical condition in a court is, *in the absence of indications to the contrary which are not present here*, implicit authorization to disclose the appellant's medical records provided that the contents of the record are only admitted in evidence in accordance with the usual rules of relevance and cau-

---

83.   Above, note 77.
84.   See Langlois, above note 76, which cites in support of this position Judge Gendreau's opinion in *Goulet* v. *Lussier*, [1989] R.J.Q. 2085 (Que. C.A.): "He who seeks compensation for a violation of physical or psychological integrity waives his right to confidentiality of records as against the defendant" (at 2087) (our translation).
85.   See, among others, the decision of the Ontario Court of Appeal in *Cook* v. *Ip* (1985), 52 O.R. 289, where Judge Cory, at the time a member of this court, explained: "There can be no doubt that it is in the public interest to ensure that all relevant evidence is available to the court. This is essential if justice is to be done between the parties. . . . No doubt medical records are private and confidential in nature. Nevertheless, when damages are sought for personal injuries, the medical condition of the plaintiff both before and after the accident is relevant. . . . The plaintiff himself has raised the issue and placed it before the court. In these circumstances there can no longer be any privacy or confidentiality attaching to the plaintiff's medical records" (at 292 and 293, cited in *Frenette*, above, note 77 at 689).
86.   [1985] C.A. 9.

sation."[87] Therefore, according to the Supreme Court, where there is a tacit waiver to professional secrecy the relevant documents must be produced, and the judge has no discretion to protect the plaintiff's right to professional secrecy.

424. *Critique of the Presumption of Tacit Waiver* – The presumption that a party who institutes civil proceedings waives the right to professional secrecy is subject to criticism. First, it is surprising that the exercise of one fundamental right—the right to compensation for infringement of one's physical integrity—would give rise to a presumption of waiver of another fundamental right. Recourse to the courts is a legitimate means of protecting one's rights and should not be associated with a complete waiver of all one's other fundamental rights. As stated by Madam Justice L'Heureux-Dubé in *A.M.* v. *Ryan*,[88] "her privacy is not waived by the mere fact that an action was instituted. Rather, the appellant has engaged a process where the reasonable expectation of privacy must be balanced against society's need to ensure that such litigation be conducted fairly and effectively."[89]

In addition, it is not appropriate to define the substance of an article in the *Code of Civil Procedure* in reference to common law.[90] In fact, in *2747-3174 Québec inc.* v. *Québec (Régie des permis d'alcools)*,[91] Madam Justice L'Heureux-Dubé suggested that the *Code of Civil Procedure* draws its inspiration from civil, not common, law.[92] Upon what sources should the resolution of this issue depend, given that the law on examination on discovery is founded in common law?[93] Even if the examination on discovery is inspired by common law, it is a procedural mechanism that has had to adapt to the particularities of Quebec laws of evidence, including the fundamental protection of the rights to professional secrecy and privacy.[94] In this respect, the common law solution is poorly attuned to the substance

---

87. Ibid. at 12 (emphasis added).
88. Above, note 52 at 200.
89. Madam Justice McLachlin, on behalf of the majority, agreed on this point.
90. See *Frenette*, above, note 77 at 685, where it is mentioned that the position in Quebec is very similar to common law.
91. [1996] 3 S.C.R. 919. See Royer, above, note 29, No. 1171 at 719; François Aquin, "Le secret professionnel du notaire," (1970–1) 73 *Revue du Notariat* 207, 218–19.
92. Ibid. at 974. This is stated in *obiter*.
93. See Royer, above note 29, Nos. 597–9 at 349 and 350.
94. Royer explains that these provisions in the *Code of Civil Procedure* do not permit the admission of evidence that is otherwise inadmissible under the rules

of section 9 of the *Charter of Human Rights and Freedoms* and article 2858 C.C.Q., which accord primacy to professional secrecy.[95] Finally, it is perhaps unwise to adopt a common law solution that has not only been criticized for uselessly expanding the discovery procedure,[96] but that has recently been rejected in common law in sexual abuse civil proceedings.

425. *Recent Developments in Common Law –* In *A.M.* v. *Ryan,*[97] the Supreme Court examined a case concerning access to the psychiatric record of a patient who was suing a psychiatrist for damages arising out of a sexual abuse committed when she was just seventeen years old. The British Columbia Court of Appeal ordered the disclosure of the new treating psychiatrist's notes and reports detailing discussions between herself and the victim. However, certain conditions were imposed by the Court of Appeal regarding disclosure of these documents. Examination of the documents was reserved only for the defendant's lawyers and expert witnesses, not the defendant himself. Any person having access to the documents was not to divulge their contents to a person unauthorized to examine them. The documents were to be used only during the litigation, and the defendant's lawyers were to make only one copy of the notes. The Supreme Court dismissed the appeal and endorsed the approach taken by the British Columbia Court of Appeal.[98]

On behalf of the majority, Madam Justice McLachlin rejected the idea that judicial proceedings were tantamount to a waiver of privilege.[99] She also confirmed that the British Columbia rules of

---

of evidence in the *Civil Code of Québec* or the Quebec Charter. See Royer, above, note 29, No. 1230, at 770.

95. See, for the same critique, ibid., No. 1230 at 769.

96. Note also that the extent of common law examinations on discovery is often associated with the staggering delays in civil proceedings. See, among others, the Ontario *Civil Justice Review: First Report* which suggests that the procedure for examination on discovery is "out of control," Ontario, Civil Justice Review Project, *Civil Justice Review: First Report* (Toronto: Ontario Civil Justice Review, 1995), chap. 13.7. There is no harm in rejecting solutions that have proven harmful.

97. Above, note 52.

98. Madam Justice L'Heureux-Dubé dissented. She would have preferred that the judge in chambers have access to the documents beforehand in order to determine their relevance, thus balancing the plaintiff's right to privacy with the defendant's right to the truth. She suggested adopting a pre-authorization procedure similar to that recommended in *R.* v. *O'Connor*, above, note 70.

99. In this case, the only one objecting to disclosure was the psychiatrist. The plaintiff had not directly alleged her right to privacy or professional secrecy.

practice applicable to access to documents during the preliminary stages of the trial force a judge in chambers to determine whether a privilege exists exempting the documents from disclosure. If a privilege or even a partial privilege[100] is established, the court must refuse or limit the disclosure. However, where there is no privilege, the court must allow disclosure. There is no additional discretion to prevent or limit disclosure of a non-privileged document.[101] In conclusion, the Supreme Court considered that the psychiatrist–patient relationship benefited from only a "partial" privilege,[102] thereby authorizing a controlled disclosure of documents. The Court endorsed the limits developed by the Court of Appeal on the right to reproduce the documents and the list of persons entitled to access.

426. *Current Approach in Quebec* – In *Frenette,*[103] the Supreme Court of Canada suggested that tacit waiver of the right to professional secrecy occurred within the context of a civil action in which the plaintiff's physical or mental condition was in issue. The Supreme Court relied on Quebec and common law cases in arriving at this conclusion. However, the common law has since evolved. In addition, the Quebec decisions cited allowed for exceptions to this waiver.[104]

---

100. A "partial" privilege justifies limiting the individuals who have access to the documents and the availability and reproduction of "partially" privileged documents. The Supreme Court held that a partial privilege applied to the disclosure of the psychiatric record in the civil trial between A.M. and her psychiatrist/abuser.

101. This is the main point on which the dissent was based. Madam Justice L'Heureux-Dubé suggested that the court should always have discretion to prevent the disclosure of documents that violate the right to privacy.

102. She rejected the solution suggested by the United States Supreme Court, which, in *Jaffee* v. *Redmond*, 116 S. Ct. 1923 (1996), aff'd 51 F.3d 1346 (1995), sanctioned the existence of an absolute privilege as regards psychotherapy records.

103. Above, note 77.

104. See above, at §423, where we cite part of Judge Jacques's opinion in *Laprise* v. *Bonneau*, above, note 86. He is not clear as to what are the "indications to the contrary" (our translation) susceptible of justifying a finding that the plaintiff had not waived the right to professional secrecy. We suggest that a motion to proceed using a pseudonym, below, at §§453ff., or a simple statement to this effect should suffice. See, for an explicit waiver respecting communication of a psychological report, *Pouliot* v. *Biochem Pharma inc.*, [1996] A.Q. No. 3827 (Que. C.A.) (Q.L.).

427. *Proposed Solution* – In our view, it is not judicious to presume a tacit waiver that removes all discretion from the judge. First, it is far from true that the plaintiff's actions are always indicative of an indifference to the protection of professional secrecy. To the contrary, the plaintiff can try to protect her privacy while pursuing a civil action.[105] Second, it is unthinkable that civil law, which, like French law,[106] places professional secrecy in a position of primacy, would endorse an approach that maximizes, more than the common law, access to documents protected by professional secrecy.[107] We therefore propose that the civilian system recognize that a plaintiff who institutes legal proceedings does not totally waive the right to professional secrecy and that the court must balance the protection of this right against the defendant's interests.

428. *Exercising the Court's Discretion* – In *Frenette*, Madam Justice L'Heureux-Dubé suggested a discretionary approach that would balance the defendant's right to a full defence and the plaintiff's right to professional secrecy. Some would suggest that the defendant has no constitutionally protected right to answer the allegations in the declaration, because non-constitutional rights can never, or can only very rarely, defeat the right to professional secrecy guaranteed by section 9 of the *Charter of Human Rights and Freedoms*.[108] However, the nature of the allegations made against the defendant—pedophilia or sexual deviance, for example—may constitutionalize his right to answer the plaintiff. It has been considered by several courts that the impact of allegations of sexual abuse on a defendant's reputation significantly interfered with his right to security.[109] Irrespective of whether what is recognized is the

---

105. See on the use of pseudonyms for example, below, at §§453ff.
106. See Royer, above, note 29, Nos. 1160–1 at 708–10.
107. Logically, we must believe that Madam Justice L'Heureux-Dubé is in favour of discretion, because this is the point of her dissent in *A.M.* v. *Ryan*, above, note 52. She seems to prefer an approach that attempts to protect the victim from invasions of her privacy. See also her position in *R.* v. *O'Connor*, above, note 70, and *R.* v. *Carosella*, [1997] 1 S.C.R. 80.
108. See above, note 32.
109. See *Labre* v. *Dr. Marcil*, unreported judgment (C.S.M. No. 500-05-003988-860), rendered 22 October 1986, cited by Langlois, above, note 76; see also *Protection de la jeunesse—95*, J.E. 83-630 (T.J.), where the Youth Court considered that in a proceeding for protection from a father accused of having abused his child, he was entitled to protection under section 35 and to the services of a lawyer. See also *Hill* v. *Church of Scientology of Toronto*, [1995] 2 S.C.R. 1130 and *Kodellas* v. *Saskatchewan (Human Rights Commission)* (1989), 60 D.L.R. (4th) 143 (Sask. C.A.).

predominant interest of the defendant to defend himself, or of the court to gather all the information necessary to judge the parties' position,[110] these interests must be balanced against the therapeutic effect on the plaintiff as well as the consequences of disclosure on access of other plaintiffs to therapy and their right to equality before the courts.[111] On this subject, Madam Justice McLachlin notes: "A rule of privilege which fails to protect confidential doctor/patient communications in the context of an action arising out of sexual assault perpetuates the disadvantage felt by victims of sexual assault, often women. The intimate nature of sexual assault heightens the privacy concerns of the victim and may increase, if automatic disclosure is the rule, the difficulty of obtaining redress for the wrong."[112]

Thus, guided by certain evaluation criteria, the court should exercise its discretion, keeping in mind the objective of protecting the plaintiff's right to professional secrecy as well as her right to equality in the exercise of her civil rights.

429. *Evaluation Criteria* – Madam Justice L'Heureux-Dubé, in her dissent in *A.M.* v. *Ryan,*[113] proposed the following criteria for granting access to the plaintiff's records:

- the necessity of the record to ensure a fair trial;

- the probative value of the record;

- the nature and extent of the reasonable expectation of privacy in the record;

- whether the production of the record would be premised on any discriminatory belief;

- the potential prejudice created by disclosure to the plaintiff's dignity, privacy, and security of the person;

---

110. This is the position taken by Madam Justice L'Heureux-Dubé in *Frenette,* above, note 77, and in *A.M.* v. *Ryan,* above, note 52.
111. See, on this subject, the comments made by Madam Justice L'Heureux-Dubé in *A.M.* v. *Ryan,* above, note 52 at 189: "If the result is that all records, and thus all of the information they contain, are released to the defence, albeit subject to restrictions, many plaintiffs will be deterred from undertaking civil suits and/or therapy to address the assault's effects on them."
112. Ibid. at 175.
113. Ibid.

- the potential benefit both parties would gain from a fair discovery process;

- the control the plaintiff has over whether she undertakes civil litigation; and

- the potential deterrent effect of this process on plaintiffs in civil litigation cases for sexual abuse.

These criteria closely resemble the weighting that occurs during criminal trials for sexual assault.[114] It may be necessary to modify the ordinary procedure for disclosure of evidence when considering these different criteria.

430. *Need for Changes to the Procedure* – In her dissent in *A.M.* v. *Ryan*, Madam Justice L'Heureux-Dubé suggested that the judge in chambers before whom the motion is argued should examine and determine the relevance of a document and whether or not it is absolutely necessary to disclose it in light of the professional secrecy and equality considerations mentioned above.[115] She favoured a preliminary authorization approach whereby the party who seeks production and those who oppose it on grounds of confidentiality argue their respective positions by affidavit presented before the judge in chambers. The party seeking disclosure must present the arguments in favour of production. The court must then order that the

---

114. In criminal law, the Supreme Court, in *R.* v. *O'Connor*, above, note 70, sets out safeguards that can be used to balance the conflict between the right to information and the right to professional secrecy and privacy. *O'Connor* addressed the accused's right to full answer and defence guaranteed under section 7 of the *Canadian Charter of Rights and Freedoms*. The Supreme Court, in this instance, was of the view that it was the trial judge's responsibility to evaluate the probable relevance of the victim's socio-psychological records. According to the Court, this step must be undertaken for every other document, including academic records, personal diaries, or activity reports written up by social workers. Proof of the probable relevance should be free of the stereotyping that currently imbues numerous motions for access to therapeutic records. Once relevance has been established, the judge must decide whether the benefit gained from access to the documents outweighs the prejudice to the victim. In May 1997, the Canadian Parliament adopted amendments to the Criminal Code limiting access to the victim's therapy records (Bill C-46). These amendments were ruled unconstitutional because they violated sections 7 and 11 of the *Canadian Charter of Rights and Freedoms*: See *R.* v. *Mills*, [1997] 56 Alta. L.R. (3d) 301 (Alta. Q.B.), [1999] 3 S.C.R. 668. *Contra*: *R.* v. *Curti*, [1997] B.C.J. No. 2367 (B.C. S.C.) (Q.L.).
115. See *Frenette*, above, note 77; *A.M.* v. *Ryan*, above, note 52 at 203.

relevant document be remitted to it so that the court may examine the document and may suppress any information that is probably irrelevant or protected from production due to the balance of interests at stake.

In a 1989 decision,[116] Judge Mailhot suggested another solution whereby this issue would be resolved by the trial judge. She stated:

> Thus, in my opinion, the court's decision to set aside the principle of confidentiality of hospital medical records should not be taken *in abstracto*.
>
> . . . I am of the opinion that when exercising discretion in the matter, a request of this nature should only be examined and decided at last instance, (*in fine litis*), that is to say by the trial judge once all the other evidence has been heard.

Judge Mailhot's solution offers more advantages than Madam Justice L'Heureux-Dubé's because the right to professional secrecy will be overlooked only if the evidence contained in the medical record is truly necessary. The trial judge is often in a better position to determine whether the defendant's evidence can be made without violating the right to professional secrecy. However, the utility of pretrial evidentiary disclosure as a time-saving tool and as a motivation for out-of-court settlements is minimized by this approach.[117] In this regard, the defendant may demand an adjournment in order to study the medical record if access is allowed. This is perhaps a lesser evil than systematic violation of the right to professional secrecy.

431. *Limiting Persons Who Have Access to the Documents* – In *A.M.* v. *Ryan*,[118] a majority of the Supreme Court endorsed the possibility of limiting the number of people entitled to access documents protected by partial privilege. In this case, only the defendant's lawyer and expert witnesses, not the defendant himself, were given access to the documents. This solution did not satisfy Madam Justice L'Heureux-Dubé, who indicated that the right to privacy had been

---

116. *Les héritiers de feu Léon Rousseau* v. *Le Groupe Desjardins*, above, note 76 at 789 (our translation).
117. See Langlois, above, note 76 at 106, citing Judge Gendreau in *Goulet* v. *Lussier*, above, note 84, where the defendant was allowed to introduce preliminary evidence during the motion proving the plaintiff's mental or physical condition.
118. Above, note 52.

violated in this case, regardless of whether the document was read by one person or ten people.[119] This solution, while imperfect and not highly recommended, is still part of the range of options before a court. It is possible that the plaintiff will be particularly traumatized by the abuser's access to the document, and, in this respect, it is acceptable to prohibit such access.

432. *Narrowing the Concept of Relevance* – The courts may in the long run uphold the presumption of tacit waiver. They would, however, be required to pay specific attention when evaluating the relevance of documents protected by professional secrecy. As Judge Tourigny so aptly stated in *Coffey* v. *Tran*: "In my view, it would be a violation of professional secrecy if, for example, disclosure of abortions or psychiatric treatments undergone by the plaintiff were permitted in the context of an action in damages arising out of poor treatment of a fractured ankle."[120]

433. *Documents Not Protected by Professional Secrecy* – In conclusion, it should be noted that the right to professional secrecy under the Quebec Charter covers only documents created by members of a professional corporation during the performance of their occupation. It does not protect documents created by other types of therapists who are not recognized under the *Professional Code*[121] or who have not adopted a regulation to that effect.[122] Does this mean that documents generated by these therapists must automatically be produced for the defendant? In our opinion, there is still room to distinguish between the Quebec and common law positions and to further study the impact of disclosure on the right to privacy.

b)   Right to Privacy

434. *Current Situation* – In Quebec law, protection of privacy within the context of evidentiary disclosure is currently commingled with professional secrecy.[123] This is also, in some respects, the common

---

119. The judge was nonetheless ready to accept that the court may and should read these documents prior to balancing the opposing interests.
120. Above, note 67 at 7 (our translation).
121. R.S.Q., c. C-26.
122. See Royer, above, note 29, Nos. 1181–6 at 726–9.
123. *Frenette*, above, note 77, appears to assimilate breach of the right to privacy with breach of the right to professional secrecy. See, however, the provisions in the *Act Respecting the Protection of Personal Information in the Private Sector*, R.S.Q., c. P-39.1.

law position, given that the Supreme Court, in *A.M.* v. *Ryan*,[124] refused to extend protection beyond the Wigmore criteria regarding privilege.[125] It is our view that protection of privacy in Quebec law should be recognized independently from professional secrecy. Otherwise, section 5 of the *Charter of Human Rights and Freedoms* serves no purpose.

435. *Concrete Application of the Right to Privacy* – Protection of privacy above and beyond protection of professional secrecy is important in sexual and spousal abuse cases. The victim's therapy sometimes consists of alternative therapy that is not regulated by the *Professional Code*,[126] participation in a support group, or keeping a personal diary that allows her to freely express intense emotions in an uncensored way. The victim's dreams, psychosomatic reactions, or post-traumatic stress may be recorded in her personal diary, or communicated to her fellow support group members or her therapist.[127] She may discuss the emergence of new memories. This last aspect can be of particular interest to the defendant, especially if he is arguing that these new memories are fictitious and were suggested by the therapist.[128] Does the possibility of uncovering such revelations in a personal diary, or in the notes of support group participants or of the therapist, justify access by the defendant to these documents, which are, after all, secret?

436. *Uncertainty in Quebec Law* – The trend appears to be leaning in favour of respecting the right to privacy, even though no case directly on point exists in Quebec. In fact, the Court of Appeal indicated in *Compagnie d'assurance-vie Crown* v. *Allaire*[129] that documents of a private nature, such as personal notes and the like, need not be disclosed to the other party.[130] We suggest that this trend should continue and that a procedure similar to that used in the protection of professional secrecy be applied.[131] In this regard, it is

---

124. Above, note 52.
125. This is the criticism in Madam Justice L'Heureux-Dubé's dissent. See below, at §438.
126. Above, note 121.
127. See above, at §52.
128. See our analysis on false memory syndrome, above, at §§36ff.
129. [1986] R.D.J. 484 (Que. C.A.).
130. See the comments by La Forest J. to this effect in *Godbout* v. *Ville de Longueuil*, [1997] 3 S.C.R. 844 at para. 97; *Aubry* v. *Éditions Vice-Versa inc.*, [1998] 1 S.C.R. 531.
131. See above, at §430.

important to avoid the common law excesses present in evidentiary disclosure procedures.[132]

In our opinion, if the presumption of tacit waiver to these rights is dismissed, protection offered under the *Charter of Human Rights and Freedoms* to privacy and professional secrecy should be more effective than in common law. Where such presumption is not dismissed, reference should be made to other privileges capable of offering exemption from evidentiary disclosure.

c)   Other Privileges

437. *Privilege as to Documents Created in Preparation for Trial* – Some common law privileges are recognized in civil law. They are either stated in a specific statute[133] or derived from the jurisprudence.[134] A privilege can be used to protect from disclosure a medical or psychiatric record created following the abuse. In fact, information gathered in preparation for trial is privileged.[135] In order to benefit from this privilege, the document must have been created primarily as part of the evidence to be entered at trial.[136] For example, a psychiatrist's report specifically drawn up to evaluate the plaintiff's injury is privileged. If, however, the preparation of a report detailing the psychological impact of the abuse and the prognosis for recovery is incidental to the psychologist's treatment of the plaintiff, the document is not protected by the privilege in preparation for trial.[137]

438. *The New Privileges* – In *A.M.* v. *Ryan*,[138] among others, the Supreme Court indicated that it was possible to develop "new" privileges, including a "class" privilege, a privilege specific to the facts

132. See *V.P.* v. *Linde*, above, note 50. *Contra: K.L.V.* v. *D.G.R.*, [1994] B.C.J. No. 1978 (B.C. C.A.) (Q.L.), (1994) 118 D.L.R. (4th) 699 (B.C. C.A.).
133. For example, articles 307, 308, 309, and 815.3 C.C.P. See also Royer, above, note 29, No. 1042 at 644.
134. Royer, above, note 29, No. 1043 at 645.
135. See ibid., note 29, No. 1138 at 690.
136. See *Ciments Canada Lafarge ltée* v. *Société d'énergie de la Baie James*, [1989] R.J.Q. 2559 (Que. Sup. Ct.), on appeal, [1991] R.J.Q. 637 (C.A.); *Federal Insurance Co.* v. *Cité de Lasalle*, [1985] R.D.J. 230, 233 (Que. C.A.).
137. It may, however, be protected by professional secrecy; see above, at §422.
138. Above, note 52.

of the case,[139] or even a partial privilege. These privileges protect certain otherwise relevant documents from being disclosed. The court must apply Wigmore's four criteria when determining the existence of a privilege or a partial privilege:[140]

1. the communication must originate in a confidence;

2. the confidence must be essential to the relationship in which the communication arises;

3. the relationship must be one that should be "sedulously fostered" in the public good; and

4. the interests served by protecting the communications from disclosure outweigh the interest in getting at the truth and disposing correctly of the litigation.

The application of Wigmore's criteria has led to the recognition of a partial privilege[141] on communications between a psychiatrist and a patient who is the victim of sexual abuse.[142] Analysis of these criteria has also resulted in the recognition of a privilege on details regarding services and treatments received by the plaintiff following the abuse.[143]

439. *Application of These New Privileges in Quebec Law* – To determine the existence of a privilege in *Société d'énergie de la Baie James* v. *Lafarge Canada inc.*, the Quebec Court of Appeal adopted

---

139. See *R.* v. *Gruenke*, [1991] 3 S.C.R. 263, where the Supreme Court recognized the existence of two categories of privilege in common law, a "class" privilege and a "case-by-case" privilege.
140. J.H. Wigmore, *Evidence in Trials at Common Law*, vol. 8 (Boston: Little Brown, 1961), revised by John T. McNaughton.
141. Partial privilege allows disclosure of a limited number of documents, their review by the court so that those that are unnecessary may be eliminated, and the imposition of conditions as to who may have access to these documents or make copies thereof.
142. See *A.M.* v. *Ryan*, above, note 52.
143. See A.A. *(L.L.)* v. *B. (A.)*, [1995] 4 S.C.R. 536, where the Court unanimously concluded that a complainant in a sexual assault criminal proceeding can, by virtue of a privilege based on the particular circumstances of each case, prevent private documents from being communicated to the defence. In this case, various establishments, with whom the complainant had consulted following the alleged assault, were ordered by the trial judge and the Court of Appeal to disclose to the defence records regarding treatment.

the criteria established by Wigmore.[144] However, there are those[145] who maintain that since the disappearance of provisions formerly contained in articles 1206 and 2712 C.C.L.C., it is not possible to rely on these new privileges, because recourse to French suppletive law or common law in Quebec has been eliminated. Does this mean that plaintiffs in Quebec civil law will not be as well protected? As was suggested above, the Wigmore criteria are not required under Quebec civil law,[146] provided the rights to professional secrecy and privacy under the Charter are properly applied.

440. *Conclusion* – We feel that the law in Quebec protecting privacy and professional secrecy should guarantee better protection than the common law to the victim during disclosure. Accordingly, the courts should abandon the presumption of tacit waiver to professional secrecy that is now raised once a party has instituted legal proceedings claiming damages for bodily or moral injury. Judicial discretion should be permitted that aims to balance the defendant's right to prepare his defence, the court's need for all the relevant information required to decide the litigation, and the plaintiff's rights to professional secrecy and privacy. The evaluation criteria should include, among others, the impact of disclosure on the therapeutic and legal choices of other plaintiffs. The possibility that intensely personal information about the plaintiff will be exposed during evidentiary disclosure is particularly traumatic in cases involving sexual and spousal abuse. We also believe that there is cause to consider introducing a special procedure that eliminates the defendant's full and immediate access to documents.

IV. OUT-OF-COURT SETTLEMENT

The goal of evidentiary disclosure is not only to prepare for trial, but to allow the parties to evaluate their respective chances for success and, consequently, to negotiate with a view to arriving

---

144. Above, note 136 (C.A.). See also *Lab Chrysotile inc. et autres* v. *Société Asbestos limitée*, [1995] R.J.Q. 757 (Que. C.A.), leave to appeal to the Supreme Court of Canada denied, [1995] S.C.C.A. No. 237 (Q.L.).

145. See Léo Ducharme, "Le nouveau droit de la preuve en matières civiles selon le Code civil du Québec," (1992) 23 *Revue général du droit* 5, 10.

146. A document protected by professional secrecy in Quebec satisfies the three first conditions of Wigmore. The fourth criterion also fulfils the weighting recommended in *Frenette,* above, note 77, in the absence of a tacit or express waiver of professional secrecy.

at an out-of-court settlement. This process presents its own problems when one is representing a victim of spousal or sexual abuse.

441. *Objectives* – The savings in costs is an obvious advantage to out-of-court settlements, but many other advantages are available to parties who opt for this course of action. Compensation can be made in several ways, thus allowing greater consideration to the plaintiff's needs. This section briefly explores the options available in an out-of-court settlement. Given the broader range of possibilities, the lawyer's creativity will often be put to the test. The options described in this section are classified into three categories: first, deferred payment of amounts claimed before the courts; second, non-pecuniary conclusions; and third, the development of an alternate dispute resolution mechanism applicable primarily in cases of institutionalized sexual abuse and class actions.

A. Deferred Payment of Amounts Claimed before the Courts

442. *Actual Compensation for Therapy Expenses* – Payment of sums, such as therapy expenses and loss of earning capacity,[147] that would have been awarded in court are traditionally spread out in out-of-court settlements. Reimbursement of therapy-related expenses for the victim and her family can be staggered over several years. Child-care expenses incurred to attend therapy, or relocation expenses in the event the victim wants to physically and psychologically distance herself from her abuser, may also be included. Compensation should also be stipulated for therapies not covered by the public health insurance plan. Specialized treatment offered in the United States for multiple personality disorders have been negotiated. Esthetic treatment is often required: the victim who has attempted suicide might wish to remove the scars on her arms. One should also consider the costs of detoxification treatments, AIDS medication, or even life insurance premiums.

443. *Compensation for Economic Loss* – Concrete compensation for economic loss suffered as a result of the abuse is also feasible. An agreement regarding payment of school fees or guidance counselling fees accompanied by a temporary alimentary pension or child-care

---

147. See above, at §§297, 300ff. On this subject, see Yvonne Lambert-Faivre, "L'indemnisation des victimes de préjudices non-économiques," (1998) 39 *Cahiers de Droit* 537.

expenses facilitating a return to studies may also be possible. Investment counselling respecting monies received or the lump sum paid for loss of earning capacity may also be considered.

444. *Payment to Third Parties* – Payment can sometimes be made to persons other than the victim: to the victim's children, to other victims of whom the plaintiff has knowledge, or even to a support group for women in difficulty. Payment to third parties is often the case where the plaintiff is an alcoholic or drug addict and wants to protect her family.

All these deferred payment options are obviously in addition to the more traditional payment options such as payment deferred over several years and payment for all legal and expert costs and other disbursements. The out-of-court settlement may also be used to compensate non-pecuniary injury.

B.   Non-Pecuniary Injury

445. *Admission of Guilt* – In reaching an out-of-court settlement, the victim's reality needs to be validated or affirmed: several settlements require personal or written apologies to the victim or her family. It is often essential for the victim that the defendant recognize his guilt; in such cases, provision should be made for a written signed confession by the defendant.[148] Also to be considered are the defendant's undertakings regarding his own rehabilitation or practical changes to be implemented by institutional defendants.

446. *Clauses Respecting the Victim's "Silence"* – Much more controversial are clauses guaranteeing the plaintiff's silence, which the defendant may try to impose during negotiations. Although the parties often agree not to publish the terms of settlement, can a victim be made to promise during civil litigation settlement negotiations

---

148.   See *D. (Guardian ad litem of)* v. *F.*, above, note 30, where the plaintiff was particularly distressed by the testimony of the defendant abuser, who minimized the number of assaults. Acceptance of guilt must be total if it is to have any meaning. See also *M.M.* v. *S.V.*, J.E. 99-375 (Qué. Sup. Ct.), where the defendant gave the plaintiff a letter of apology after the plaintiff had requested such a letter. See also Susan Alter, *Apologising for Serious Wrongdoing: Social, Psychological and Legal Considerations*, Final Report for the Law Commission of Canada (Ottawa: Law Commission of Canada, 1999), online: Law Commission of Canada <http:// www.lcc.gc.ca/en/themes/mr/ica/2000/html/ apology.html> (date of access: 13 June 2001).

that she will not contact the police?[149] First, it is doubtful that this undertaking can be faithfully respected. The victim's contractual undertaking of silence will obviously be ignored if she is summoned as a witness in court. In addition, it would be contrary to the duty to report suspicions of sexual abuse—and, thus, contrary to public order—for the plaintiff to enter an undertaking of silence where the defendant continues to pose a threat to children.[150] On the other hand, where the plaintiff is reasonably assured that the defendant will not attack other people, can she undertake to conceal a crime of which she was the victim? There is no duty in Canadian law to cooperate with the police or to denounce criminals; thus, no legal duty owed by the citizen is contravened by such an agreement. Such a provision, therefore, is legally possible, barring instances where the defendant remains a danger to the life or security of others. It would, however, be prudent to stipulate a condition whereby the plaintiff is relieved from this obligation where she suspects that the defendant is a recidivist. Otherwise, her silence could contribute to injury suffered by third parties, thereby rendering her extracontractually liable.

C. Alternate Dispute Resolution

447. *Response to Institutionalized Abuse* – Class actions instituted on behalf of victims of institutional abuse often resort to arbitration mechanisms that distribute monies among the victims.[151] The advantages are numerous: minimized costs, the decreased role of the courts, and the informal nature of the proceedings. When formulating the chosen mechanism, consideration must be given to the particular nature of institutional abuse.

---

149. See the facts in *R.* v. *Vallée*, above, note 13, where the victim contacted the defendant in an attempt to obtain an extrajudicial admission. Within this context, the young man had promised not to contact the police if his family was satisfied with the settlement of the civil action against the defendant. The criminal court viewed this as blackmail, but nonetheless accepted the victim's explanation and did not suspend the criminal proceedings against the accused-defendant.

150. See above, at §§166ff.

151. For an exhaustive analysis of this question, see Law Commission of Canada, *Institutional Child Abuse, Restoring Dignity: Responding to Child Abuse in Canadian Institutions,* Final Report to the Minister of Justice (Ottawa: Law Commission of Canada, 2000), online: Law Commission of Canada <http://www.lcc.gc.ca/en/themes/mr/ica/2000/html/restore1.html> (date of access: 13 June 2001).

448. *Group Needs* – Victims often exhibit a lack of confidence in institutions or bureaucracies, such as the judicial system. An informal procedure is possibly better suited to the needs of the group if the abuse occurred in a government institution such as a prison or an institution for the protection of youth or the mentally handicapped. Efforts must be made to retrace all the victims. Certain measures can be foreseen with this goal in mind: setting up a telephone crisis hotline or financing a project publicizing the abuses committed—a television documentary, for example.

Where an out-of-court settlement is not possible, the plaintiff must face a trial. Specific attention must be paid to certain aspects of this final stage of the proceedings, including the public nature of the trial.

Chapter 6
The Trial

This chapter, which examines the problems encountered by a plaintiff during a civil trial, is divided into two main sections. The first part examines the extent to which the trial is public; the second looks at the different methods of proof available to the plaintiff.

I.   PROTECTING THE PLAINTIFF'S IDENTITY

449. *The Problem* – Once the decision is made to sue the presumed abuser for damages, the public nature of the proceedings becomes an issue. Article 13 of the *Code of Civil Procedure* (C.C.P.)[1] and section 23 of the *Quebec Charter of Human Rights and Freedoms*[2] express the principle that hearings are public, except in the interests of good morals or public order. Yet, in certain instances, public legal proceedings can harm a victim of sexual abuse. The victim's therapy risks being undermined by the possible public revelation of intimate details of her life.[3] Publicity can have consequences for her career, given the taboos that exist against these victims,[4] and the

---

1.   Article 13 C.C.P.: "The sittings of the courts are public wherever they may be held, but the court may order that they be held *in camera* in the interests of good morals or public order. However, in family matters, sittings in first instance are held *in camera*, unless the court, upon application, orders that, in the interests of justice a sitting be public."

2.   Section 23, *Quebec Charter of Human Rights and Freedoms*, R.S.Q., c. C-12: "Every person has a right to a full and equal, public and fair hearing by an independent and impartial tribunal, for the determination of his rights and obligations or of the merits of any charge brought against him. The tribunal may decide to sit *in camera*, however, in the interest of morality or public order."

3.   On the role of the media in respecting the crime victim's privacy, see Arlène Gaudreault, "Un regard sur la situation des victimes d'actes criminels," in Pierre Trudel, ed., *Droit du public à l'information et vie privée: deux droits irréconciliables?* (Montreal: Les Éditions Thémis, 1991) at 83.

4.   See *J. Doe* v. *T.B.H.*, [1996] O.J. No. 839 (Ont. Gen. Div.) (Q.L.); *R.K.* v. *McBride*, [1994] B.C.J. No. 2791 (B.C. Prov. Ct.) (Q.L.); *Re Hirt and College of*

publicity can make the plaintiff even more nervous. All of these factors can prevent her from testifying clearly, thereby impugning her credibility. The victim may also fear the impact of publicity on family[5] or friends who are unaware of the abuse. Revelation of the parties' identities may harm the defendant's ability to sell his property in the event of a judgment against the defendant and execution of the judgment.[6] A public hearing can infringe the plaintiff's rights to security and integrity of her person (section 1 of the Quebec Charter), to safeguards on her dignity and reputation (section 4 of the Quebec Charter), and to respect for her private life (section 5 of the Quebec Charter). Such effects can, in turn, create yet another obstacle that compromises the victim's ability to institute such an action and receive compensation.[7]

450. *Safeguards* – In response to these potentially harmful effects, the victim can, prior to the commencement of proceedings, make a motion for authorization to use a pseudonym or her initials, to have the record sealed, to have a temporary publication ban to protect her identity, or for an order that the proceedings be held *in camera*. The various defendants may make the same motions. These motions obviously conflict with the citizen's right to a public hearing and restrict the freedom of the press. It is up to the courts to arbitrate between these conflicting fundamental rights.

We will examine the criteria retained by the jurisprudence in order to justify *in camera* hearings, publication bans on the parties' identities, or sealed records in actions for damages in cases of sexual or spousal abuse. Having analysed the basis for making legal disputes public, we will examine the exceptions to this rule in criminal and civil trials. We propose that the special measures used in criminal law to protect the privacy of victims of sexual abuse during the trial should also apply during a civil action, given that the aims are the same.

Physicians and Surgeons of British Columbia (1985), 17 D.L.R. (4th) 472 (B.C. S.C.).

5.   See *S.M.* v. *J.R.C.* (1993), 13 O.R. (3d) 148 (Ont. Gen. Div.).

6.   See *D. (Guardian ad litem of)* v. *F.*, [1995] B.C.J. No. 1478 (B.C. S.C.) (Q.L.).

7.   See *D.H.* v. *L.J.H.*, [1997] B.C.J. No. 2724 (B.C. S.C.) (Q.L.), where the victim of several years of sexual and physical abuse testified by affidavit to protect her privacy. Because of the limited evidence, the amounts awarded did not adequately compensate the plaintiff.

A. The Principle: The Public Trial

451. *A Strong Public Policy* – The public nature of legal proceedings, criminal as well as civil, constitutes one of the fundamental principles of our legal system.[8] This principle is now entrenched in section 11 (d) of the Canadian Charter. It is also recognized by section 23 of the Quebec Charter, as well as article 13 of the *Code of Civil Procedure*.[9] Mr. Justice Dickson noted in *A.G. (Nova Scotia)* v. *MacIntyre* that in legal proceedings, "covertness is the exception and openness the rule."[10] The public nature of trials is justified for several reasons. Madam Justice Wilson summarized these grounds in *Edmonton Journal* v. *Alberta (Attorney General)*:

> . . . the public interest in open trials and in the ability of the press to provide complete reports of what takes place in the courtroom is rooted in the need (1) to maintain an effective evidentiary process; (2) to ensure a judiciary and juries that behave fairly and that are sensitive to the values espoused by the society; (3) to promote a shared sense that our courts operate with integrity and dispense justice; and (4) to provide an ongoing opportunity for the community to learn how the justice system operates and how the law being applied daily in the courts affects them.[11]

Mr. Justice Dickson referred in *MacIntyre* to the transparency of legal proceedings as constituting "a strong public policy."[12] Given that the majority of the public is not in a position to observe the

---

8.   See *Scott* v. *Scott*, [1913] A.C. 417. On this subject, see Pierre Trudel, "Liberté de presse ou procès public et équitable? À la recherche du fondement au droit d'accéder aux audiences et de diffuser des informations judiciaires," (1989) 49 *Revue du Barreau du Québec* 251; M. David Lepofsky, *Open Justice: The Constitutional Right to Attend and Speak about Criminal Proceedings* (Toronto: Butterworths, 1985).

9.   It is the same in disciplinary law. See also section 142, *Professional Code*, R.S.Q., c. C-26: "Every hearing shall be public. Notwithstanding the first paragraph, the committee on discipline may, of its own initiative or upon request, order that a hearing be held *in camera* or ban access to or the publication or release of any information or document it indicates, in the interest of morality or public order, in particular to preserve professional secrecy or to protect a person's privacy or reputation. Every person who, by performing or omitting to perform an act, infringes an order to hold a hearing *in camera* or an order banning access, publication or release is guilty of contempt of court."

10. [1982] 1 S.C.R. 175 at 185; see also *Canadian Broadcasting Corp.* v. *New Brunswick (A.G.)*, [1996] 3 S.C.R. 480 at 495.

11. [1989] 2 S.C.R. 1326 at 1361.

12. Above, note 10 at 183.

workings of the courts, the media obviously play a pivotal role in the diffusion of information. They must therefore have access to the courts.[13] Any measure that restricts their access to legal disputes or documents is an infringement of freedom of the press guaranteed under section 2 (b) of the Canadian Charter.[14] Section 1 of the Charter then comes into play, and the determination must be made as to whether this infringement constitutes a reasonable limit demonstrably justified in a free and democratic society.

B.   The Exception: Secret Proceedings

452. *Protecting the Innocent* – The principle of public trials is, however, not absolute. Exceptions do exist in both criminal and civil proceedings to ensure that all parties benefit from an equitable trial. Mr. Justice Dickson established the following basic rule in *MacIntyre*: "In my view, curtailment of public accessibility can only be justified where there is present the need to protect social values of superordinate importance. One of these is the protection of the innocent."[15] First the safeguards for protecting privacy in the criminal trial, followed by the civil trial, will be examined.

1.   Safeguarding Privacy during the Criminal Trial

453. *Protecting the Complainant's Identity* – The public nature of criminal trials created problems for victims of sexual abuse. Fear of having their private lives published in the newspapers is one reason many victims did not file a complaint. Offences of a sexual nature are not often reported.[16] The government has adopted specific provisions in an effort to redress this situation.[17] A judge, where requested to do so by a complainant, must issue an order under section 486 (4) (b) Cr.C. prohibiting the publication or broadcast in any way of the identity of the complainant or a witness, or information

---

13.   See *Canadian Broadcasting Corp.* v. *New Brunswick (A.G.)*, above, note 10 at 493–9; *Edmonton Journal* v. *Alberta (A.G.)*, above, note 11 at 1340, per Justice Cory.

14.   See *Canadian Broadcasting Corp.* v. *New Brunswick (A.G.)*, above, note 10 at 500, per Mr. Justice La Forest.

15.   *A.G. (Nova Scotia)* v. *MacIntyre*, above, note 10 at 187.

16.   See Julian V. Roberts, "Sexual Assault in Canada: Recent Statistical Trends," (1995) 21 *Queen's L. J.* 393 at 401.

17.   See William A. Schabas, *Les infractions d'ordre sexuel* (Cowansville, QC: Les Éditions Yvon Blais, 1995) at 241ff.

that could disclose their identity (section 486 (3) Cr.C.).[18] At the first reasonable opportunity, the judge must advise the complainant of the right to request this order (section 486 (4) (a) Cr.C.). As noted by Mr. Justice Lamer in *Canadian Newspapers Co.* v. *Canada (Attorney General)*, this provision is intended to "foster complaints by victims of sexual assault by protecting them from the trauma of wide-spread publication resulting in embarrassment and humiliation. Encouraging victims to come forward and complain facilitates the prosecution and conviction of those guilty of sexual offences."[19]

In the *Canadian Newspapers* case, the Supreme Court recognized that, although section 442 (3) Cr.C., now section 486 (3) Cr.C.,[20] infringed on the right to freedom of the press guaranteed under section 2 (b) of the Canadian Charter, this violation was justified under section 1 of the Charter. The first requirement was satisfied, that of the importance of the legislative objective that the limitation was designed to achieve. This measure was one of several adopted by the government in an attempt to redress the low rate at which sexual crimes were reported due to fear of publicity surrounding the legal proceedings. The second criterion, proportionality, was also satisfied. There was a rational connection between section 442 (3) Cr.C. and the objective it was designed to serve, and the impact on the media's rights was minimal.

454. *In Camera* – The judge can also order that the public be excluded during the preliminary inquiry (section 537 (1) (h) Cr.C.) and during the criminal trial (section 486 (1) Cr.C.). The constitutionality of section 486 (1) Cr.C. has been attacked because it violated the right to freedom of the press guaranteed by section 2 (b) of the Canadian Charter. Mr. Justice La Forest held in *Canadian Broadcasting Corp.* v. *New Brunswick (A.G.)*[21] that freedom of the press was infringed by section 486 (1) Cr.C. Restricting the media's

---

18. Section 486 (3) (order restricting publication): "Subject to subsection (4), where an accused is charged with an offence under section 151, 152, 155, 159, 160, 170, 171, 172, 173, 271, 272, 273, 346 or 347, the presiding judge or justice may make an order directing that the identity of the complainant or of a witness and any information that could disclose the identity of the complainant or witness shall not be published in any document or broadcast in any way."
19. [1988] 2 S.C.R. 122 at 130. To the same effect, see Madam Justice L'Heureux-Dubé's opinion in *R.* v. *O'Connor*, [1995] 4 S.C.R. 411 at 504.
20. Note that an order under section 486(4)(b) Cr.C. is now obligatory if requested by the complainant.
21. Above, note 10.

freedom to gather and broadcast information pertaining to the workings of the courts infringes on the public's right to access legal proceedings. However, he believed that section 486 (1) constituted a reasonable limitation under section 1 of the Canadian Charter. It was designed to protect the innocent, to safeguard privacy and to increase the number of complaints filed regarding sexual offences.

2.   Safeguarding Privacy during the Civil Trial

455. *Discretionary Powers of the Court* – The plaintiff can also request that her identity be protected during the civil trial, either by making a motion for an *in camera* hearing under article 13 C.C.P., or by a motion to place a publication ban on the parties' names, to seal the records, or for the right to use a pseudonym under article 46 C.C.P.[22] The court's discretionary power to grant these orders is not unlimited. It is not to be exercised arbitrarily but rather within the limits prescribed by the principles expressed in the charters of human rights and freedoms.[23] The court must weigh the public's right to access proceedings against the complainant's right to privacy and to physical and psychological integrity as well as against respect for her reputation. Note that, like the plaintiff, the defendant is also entitled to present motions aimed at protecting his identity.

a)   The Plaintiff's Anonymity

456. *Recourse to Criminal Decisions* – As we have seen, the adoption of section 486 (3) Cr.C. by the legislature was designed to eliminate one of the barriers preventing victims of sexual offences from reporting the offence. We believe that the same rationale justifies the granting of an order for anonymity during the civil trial. Such an order will spare the plaintiff the trauma of having her private life revealed in the newspapers during her action for damages. Without re-victimizing the plaintiff, the court will attempt to facilitate the pursuit of abusers and the compensation of victims, as in the criminal trial.[24] This is the reason why we are relying on decisions rendered during criminal trials that have arbitrated the con-

---

22.   See *B.A.* v. *B.* (20 August 1990), Montreal 500-09-001495-894 (C.A.) at 8, where Judge Rothman clarifies this point.
23.   See *J.L.D.* v. *Vallée*, [1996] R.J.Q. 2480 (Que. C.A.); *Dagenais* v. *Canadian Broadcasting Corp.*, [1994] 3 S.C.R. 835 at 875.
24.   See *DC* v. *371158 Ontario Ltd.* (1994), 113 D.L.R. (4th) 150 at 154 (Ont. Ct. Gen. Div.); *Symons* v. *United Church of Canada* (1993), 16 O.R. (3d) 379 (Ont.

flict between the right to freedom of expression and the plaintiff's right to privacy.

Some observers distinguish between the victim who must testify in a criminal proceeding and the victim who chooses to launch civil proceedings.[25] In the former instance, the victim might not have had a choice as to whether or not to testify; in the latter, she decided to use the legal system and therefore, it is argued, should accept the public hearing rule. Thus, treating motions for anonymity differently is justified because, in civil cases, the plaintiff herself made the decision to go before the courts. This argument should be rejected. The fact that the plaintiff has chosen to go before the courts does not mean that she accepts total disclosure and waives her Charter rights.[26] All rights and interests at stake should be weighed.

457. *The Rule in* Dagenais – The four respondents in *Dagenais* v. *Canadian Broadcasting Corp.*,[27] members or former members of a religious order, were accused of having physically and sexually abused young boys under their care during the time they taught at various Catholic correctional education institutions. Just prior to the judge's charge to the jury during the trial of one of the respondents, the Canadian Broadcasting Corporation scheduled a broadcast of a mini-series entitled *The Boys of St.Vincent*, a fictional story depicting sexual and physical abuse committed against children in a Catholic institution. The respondents, arguing their right to a fair and equitable trial under section 11 (d) of the Canadian Charter, obtained an injunction prohibiting the broadcast of the mini-series anywhere in Canada. On appeal, the ban was restricted to Ontario and Station CBMT-TV in Montreal.

Application was made to the Supreme Court for a ruling on the validity of the publication ban. Chief Justice Lamer proposed using a rule in which the essential criteria stated in *R.* v. *Oakes*[28] were summarized. At the same time, he noted that there is no hierarchy

---

Gen. Div.); *Re Hirt and College of Physicians and Surgeons of British Columbia*, above, note 4 at 479.

25. See *R.K.* v. *McBride*, above, note 4, in which this argument is raised and subsequently rejected by the judge.

26. See *J.L.D.* v. *Vallée*, above, note 23 at 2482; *A.M.* v. *Ryan*, [1997] 1 S.C.R. 157 at 180, per Madam Justice McLachlin.

27. Above, note 23.

28. [1986] 1 S.C.R. 103.

of fundamental rights under which one right would take precedence over another.[29] Hence, a court asked to grant a publication or broadcast ban must examine: 1) if the publication ban is necessary in order to prevent a real and substantial risk to the fairness of the trial, and 2) if the salutary effects of the publication ban outweigh the deleterious effects to the free expression of those affected by the ban. He stated: "it is necessary to consider the objective of the order, to examine the availability of reasonable alternative measures that could achieve this objective, and to consider whether the salutary effects of the publication ban outweigh the deleterious impact the ban has on freedom of expression."[30]

Mr. Justice Lamer suggested guidelines to be followed when determining whether or not to order publication bans during a criminal trial, some of which apply to civil trials. Among others, he noted that publication bans maximize the chances that people will testify given that they feel protected from publicity. They may also serve to protect vulnerable witnesses and the privacy of those involved. The applicant bears the burden of proof.[31]

458. *The Situation of the Victim of Sexual or Spousal Abuse* – How does this rule apply to victims of sexual or spousal abuse?[32] First, a publication ban issued within the context of a civil liability action is meant to spare the complainant and, in certain instances, her family any trauma and, where applicable, any harmful economic consequences. The complainant can decide not to sue based on these reasons alone. Where such a ban is refused, the victim's accessibility to the justice system could therefore be limited. Because both the public and the media can attend proceedings, orders protecting the complainant's anonymity—such as the use of a pseudonym during the proceedings, the protection of information leading to her identity, or the sealing of records for a specific period—are reasonable. No other meaningful measure is capable of achieving the same objective. Expert testimony regarding the potential trauma of a public trial serves no purpose, given that the Supreme Court has on several occasions discussed the harmful effects of publicity surrounding a trial.[33] It is sufficient for the complainant to explain to

---

29.   Above, note 23 at 877.

30.   Ibid. at 878.

31.   *A.G. (Nova Scotia)* v. *MacIntyre*, above, note 10 at 405, per Dickson, J.

32.   This criterion is applied in *J.L.D.* v. *Vallée*, above, note 23. See *A.A.* v. *B.*, [1998] R.J.Q. 3117 (Que. Sup. Ct.).

33.   See *Canadian Newspaper Co.*, above, note 10 at 130.

the judge the traumatic effects she is seeking to avoid in her situation.

Second, the advantages of a publication ban are more significant than the deleterious effects to freedom of expression. On the one side, a refusal to grant the ban would have serious implications for the victim and her family. On the other, the public nature of the hearing is not affected by concealing the victim's identity because the media retain access to the courtroom and can report the events. The public need not know the victim's identity. In most Canadian civil actions for sexual or spousal abuse, the parties remain anonymous.

459. *Public Order* – While decided prior to *Dagenais*, the criteria invoked by the judge in *Re Hirt and College of Physicians and Surgeons of British Columbia* resembled those suggested in *Dagenais*. A doctor appealed the decision by the British Columbia College of Physicians to revoke his licence to practise for having sexually abused one of his patients. Both the college and the complainant made a motion to protect the latter's identity. The motion was dismissed at trial, but the Court of Appeal ordered that the plaintiff's identity be protected by a publication ban. The decision was based on the fact that the principle of public hearings would not be violated because no purpose would be served by revealing the plaintiff's identity.[34] To the contrary, public order would be infringed by the refusal to allow the motion. Victims would, in fact, fail to denounce abusers who could possibly commit other crimes:

> To secure that public interest [preventing doctors who abuse their patients to continue], victims must be encouraged to come forward. If the price of attaining that objective be the non-disclosure to the general public of the identity of the victim, that is not too high a price to pay. It is also in the public interest, as it is in the case of victims of sexual offences, that persons who do come forward to advance a worthy public objective be protected from the adverse personal and economic consequences which, as in this case, may inevitably follow disclosure of their identities.[35]

460. *Irrelevant Motives* – According to the jurisprudence, embarrassment,[36] unease, shame, the susceptibility of the parties

---

34. Above, note 4 at 484.
35. Ibid.
36. *Canadian Broadcasting Corp.* v. *New Brunswick (A.G.)*, above, note 10 at 504; *Southam inc.* v. *Brassard*, [1987] R.J.Q. 1841 at 1848 (Que. Sup. Ct.).

involved,[37] and/or the nature of the offence[38] are not sufficient grounds in and of themselves for ordering a publication ban on the parties' identities during a criminal trial. These criteria have been developed mainly in response to motions made by the accused in criminal proceedings, which demand a much heavier burden of proof than civil actions. Mr. Justice La Forest in *Canadian Broadcasting Corp.* v. *New Brunswick (Attorney General)* justified the refusal to order *in camera* criminal proceedings, even where the situation is shocking, embarrassing, or sexual in nature: "It must be remembered that a criminal trial often involves the production of highly offensive evidence, whether salacious, violent or grotesque. Its aim is to uncover the truth, not to provide a sanitized account of facts that will be palatable to even the most sensitive of human spirits. The criminal court is an innately tough arena."[39]

Despite this statement, Mr. Justice La Forest invoked the right to privacy as a means of tempering this rule, a right that has gained in importance. An *in camera* hearing will be ordered where the right to privacy affects other societal interests, or where the victim or witnesses, if not adequately protected, will be significantly harmed—as in sexual abuse actions. Further on in the same decision, the judge admitted that in the interests of the orderly administration of justice, fear of undue harm (including embarrassment, unease, shame, the susceptibility of persons involved, or the type of offence) can constitute a legitimate ground for excluding the public.[40] Such a fear must be justified by the circumstances of the case and the evidence.

A civil trial seeks to achieve different objectives and involves a lighter burden of proof than a criminal trial. We therefore believe that embarrassment, unease, shame, the susceptibility of persons involved, and/or the nature of the offence *are* sufficient grounds in and of themselves on which to base an order banning publication of the parties' identities during the civil trial.[41] Many victims do experience shame when confronted with the events they have experienced, events that they are incapable of speaking about publicly. Protecting their identities allows them to overcome this emotion and institute proceedings. The victim's dignity is further violated by

---

37. See *A.G. (Nova Scotia)* v. *MacIntyre*, above, note 10 at 185.
38. *R.* v. *Lefebvre*, [1984] C.A. 370 at 373 (Que. C.A.).
39. Above, note 10 at 504.
40. Above, note 10 at 520.
41. *Contra: R.K.* v. *McBride,* above, note 4 at para. No. 55.

the humiliation that accompanies the publication of intimate details.[42]

461. *Perpetuating Taboos* – Some plaintiffs who seek to protect their identity refer to the taboos associated with sexually violent crimes. They dread the reaction of family, friends, or workplace colleagues. Does this ground deserve consideration? Are not taboos perpetuated by the parties' anonymity? This issue was addressed in *Monsieur X v. Société canadienne de la Croix-rouge,* a case involving AIDS.[43] The appellant made a motion to protect the identity of the representative of a group of hemophiliacs and for the proceedings to be held *in camera*. Among the arguments raised was his fear of harassment and the publicity surrounding his condition. The judge dismissed the motion for several reasons. First, the judge pointed out that the Canadian Red Cross, a public institution, and the Attorney General of Quebec were both parties. The proceedings were, in his view, not strictly private. The judge then went on to explain that "allowing the applicant's motion would perpetuate a retrograde attitude towards this disease."[44] We are of the opinion that fear of taboos is sufficient grounds for ordering that the parties' identities be protected, whether it concerns AIDS victims or sexual abuse. The plaintiffs should not have to pay the price for changing society's attitudes.

b)   In Camera *Proceedings*

462. *In Family Matters* – In family law proceedings, not only are the parties' identities protected (article 815.4 C.C.P.), but proceedings are held *in camera* (paragraph 2 of article 13 C.C.P.).[45] As indicated in the parliamentary debates, the legislature's objective was to ensure respect for the parties' privacy and dignity while at the same time encouraging a more propitious climate for settlements:[46] "*In camera* proceedings confirm the private nature of the disputes . . .

---

42.   See Madam Justice Wilson's opinion in *Edmonton Journal* v. *Alberta (Attorney General)*, above, note 11 at 1364.
43.   [1992] R.J.Q. 2735 (Que. C.A.).
44.   Ibid. at 2738 (our translation).
45.   *An Act to Provide for the Carrying out of the Family Law Reform and to Amend the Code of Civil Procedure*, S.Q. 1982, c. 17. See Jean-Pierre Senécal, *Droit de la famille québécois*, Farnham, CCH/FM, vol. 1, No. 34-150 at 34-160; *Droit de la famille—1473*, [1991] R.D.F. 691 (Que. Sup. Ct.).
46.   Dominique Goubau, "Incidences de la réforme du droit de la famille sur le rôle des juges au Québec," (1988) 19 *Revue générale de droit* 393, 410.

and guarantee that every citizen's right to a private life is respected at a moment when their life is experiencing turbulence and is exposed before the court. . . . The *in camera* rule assists in keeping to a minimum the trauma and upheaval that necessarily accompanies families in distress."[47]

463. *In Matters of Sexual or Spousal Abuse* – For various reasons, we propose that the rule on *in camera* proceedings should also be applied to civil actions for sexual or spousal abuse. First, this type of litigation often occurs within the family setting and thus necessarily involves families in distress. As with family matters, the right of citizens to public hearings must cede to the right of the parties to privacy. Moreover, it is definitely in the public interest for such proceedings to be held in private: the interests of society will in fact be better served because some victims will be reassured at the prospect of closed hearings and will be encouraged to launch actions for damages. All victims will thus enjoy improved access to justice. The best interests of society are served by *in camera* proceedings: it encourages denunciation and reparation of the injury caused and avoids subjecting the plaintiff to a second victimization.

464. *Irrelevant Grounds* – As with publication bans,[48] we believe that *in camera* proceedings should be ordered to avoid feelings of embarrassment, unease, shame, the susceptibility of persons involved, or simply due to the nature of the offence.

c) Protecting the Defendant's Identity

465. *Complete Protection* – In certain cases, such as incest, in order to protect her own identity the plaintiff must include in her motion a request that the identity of the defendant also be protected.

466. *Protecting the Defendant's Reputation* – In other situations, in particular where criminal proceedings have not been instituted or where no conviction has resulted from criminal proceedings, the defendant will want to protect his reputation or his career. He will then make a motion to protect his identity, arguing that the allegations are as of yet unproven, that the trial is only in the preliminary stages, that he is still innocent, and that he will be irreparably

---

47.Quebec, National Assembly, *Journal des débats* (11 June 1982) at 4702 (our translation).
48.See above, at §460.

harmed by the publicity surrounding the trial.[49] In response, the victim can argue the public's right to know and be protected from the abuser. Moreover, the publicity may alert other victims to the proceedings, causing them to emerge from the shadows.

467. *Criteria of the "Innocent"* – The question of the criteria of the "innocent" was raised in *Dr. "A" v. Mr. "C".*[50] The defendants were sued for defamation by the doctor against whom they had instituted an action for having sexually abused their young daughter. After he received an order protecting his identity, the defendants appealed this decision. In granting the motion for the doctor's anonymity the judge ruled that the applicant was "innocent"[51] at this stage of the proceedings, given that the police had not continued investigating the parents' complaint and that the College of Physicians had not suspended his licence to practice, and because of the potentially devastating impact of the allegations should they prove unfounded.

In *J. Doe* v. *T.B.H.*, the judge granted the victim's motion seeking permission to use a pseudonym.[52] The identity of the defendant, the abuser's employer, was protected only during pre-trial procedures. The defendant was a charitable institution that housed and counselled adolescents. The allegations were unproven at this stage of the proceedings and could have caused irreparable harm to the defendant and its role as protector of the adolescents.

468. *Conclusion* – It is our opinion that, in light of these considerations, the courts should be more inclined to order publication bans and *in camera* proceedings for actions in sexual or spousal abuse, at least where the victims are concerned. As demonstrated, it is possible to circumvent, without necessarily betraying, the principle of public legal hearings by issuing such orders. Moreover, the information to be protected must be relevant. Judicial transparency does not require that the public have access to the identity of the parties or the details of their sexual lives. As to the rest, it appears undeniable to us that "the interests . . . of public order," stipulated in article 13 C.C.P. and section 23 of the Quebec Charter, amply justify exceptions to the rule on public disputes. Encouraging victims

---

49. See *T.H.* v. *C.D.G.*, [1997] M.J. No. 273 (Man. Q.B.) (Q.L.).
50. (1994) 113 D.L.R. (4th) 726 (B.C. S.C.).
51. Ibid. at 738. The judge makes reference here to the criterion elaborated by Mr. Justice Dickson in *A.G. (Nova Scotia)* v. *MacIntyre,* above, note 10 at 187.
52. Above, note 4.

of sexual or spousal abuse to denounce their abusers is certainly in the interest of public order. Moreover, the rights to privacy and integrity of the person are fundamental rights, just as much as freedom of expression. When balancing these rights, the scales must be weighed in favour of the lesser inconvenience.

II. THE EVIDENCE

Having settled the issue of a public hearing, the plaintiff must present "her evidence." We will begin our discussion by examining the problems that may arise.

469. *Contestation on the Merits* – An interesting phenomenon has evolved in civil sexual abuse actions:[53] numerous actions go uncontested. The defendant has already been found criminally responsible and either does not appear or does not enter a defence.[54] Yet, it is highly improbable that the judgment will be executable. This phenomenon, which leads one to conclude that proceedings are instituted primarily for symbolic or therapeutic rather than monetary reasons, appears to have been curtailed in the common law provinces.[55]

Where the action is uncontested, this section on problems in the presentation of evidence obviously has less application.[56] Where the abuser does enter a defence, one must expect the contestation to be tough. The defendant may still be in denial or may feel that he holds power over the victim: he does not believe that she will go the limit. In these cases, particular attention must be paid to problems in the presentation of evidence. Thus, we will first clarify some of

---

53.   See Bruce Feldthusen, "The Civil Action for Sexual Battery: Therapeutic Jurisprudence?" (1993) 25 *Ottawa L. R.* 203.

54.   See the report wherein abusers will often confess after having watched and listened to the videotaped testimony of the abused child: Nicholas Bala, *Bill C-15: New Protections for Children, New Challenges for Professionals* (Toronto: Institute for the Prevention of Child Abuse, October 1988) at 18, cited by the Ontario Law Reform Commission, *Report on Child Witnesses* (Toronto, 1991) at 83.

55.   The number of contested actions has increased in the common law provinces between 1993 and 1996.

56.   Evidence in this case can be made by detailed affidavit (art. 196 C.C.P.); see Jean-Claude Royer, *La preuve civile,* 2nd ed. (Cowansville, QC: Les Éditions Yvon Blais, 1995), No. 714 at 419.

the uncertainty surrounding the degree of proof required, followed by a look at evidentiary procedures that may be used at trial.

A. Degree of Proof Required

470. *A Higher Degree of Proof?* – The plaintiff to any action must prove the facts upon which the cause of action is based (article 2803 C.C.Q.). These facts must be proved on the preponderance of evidence. Article 2804 of the *Civil Code of Québec* specifically states that the required standard of proof is the preponderance of evidence "unless the law requires more convincing proof." Certain analysts have suggested that proof of criminal offences requires a higher burden of proof than the preponderance of evidence.[57] The decision generally referred to in support of this proposition is *Mutuelle du Canada* v. *Aubin*.[58] The Supreme Court dismissed an appeal by one of the insurance companies that sought to invoke an exclusionary provision in a life insurance policy. The insurance company argued that at the time the deceased insured was killed in an automobile accident, his blood alcohol level was well above the level permitted under the Criminal Code. Both the Superior Court and a majority of the Court of Appeal considered that the insurer had not successfully proven the blood alcohol level, and they allowed the widow-plaintiff's action. The probative value of the blood test submitted by the insurance company was scientifically doubtful. Within the context of this case, the court suggested that proof of an allegation of a criminal nature, such as drunk driving, must be supported by extremely conclusive evidence.[59]

471. *The Preponderance of Evidence* – The Civil Code Revision Office recommended rejecting a higher standard of proof.[60] The lan-

---

57.　Léo Ducharme, *Précis de la preuve*, 5th ed. (Montreal: Wilson and Lafleur, 1996) Nos. 163–72 at 54–8, suggests that a higher degree of probability is sometimes demanded by the courts in criminal trials or for suicide, No. 172 at 57. He admits, however, that the new wording of the *Civil Code of Québec* does not leave much room for a "scale" of preponderance. For his part, Royer, above, note 57, Nos. 181–4 at 104–6, suggests not that the standard of proof be higher but that the proof be more severely evaluated. According to him, this requirement is justified by the "principle of normality," which explains certain legal presumptions (such as good faith).

58.　[1979] 2 S.C.R. 298.

59.　See above at §243 and note 214, where the case law considers impaired driving to be gross negligence.

60.　See Quebec, Civil Code Revision Office, *Report on the Quebec Civil Code, Draft Civil Code*, vol. 1 (Quebec: Éditeur officiel, 1977) Book Six, chap. 1, art. 3; see

guage used by the Supreme Court in *Aubin* imposed on the insurance company the burden of proving the facts supporting the application of the exclusionary provision. In addition, it involved evaluating circumstantial evidence capable of rebutting presumptions of fact in the absence of testimonial evidence. It is incorrect, in our opinion, to extrapolate the language used in *Aubin* to proof of all criminal acts: such an interpretation presupposes the rejection of earlier established Supreme Court rulings. In fact, Justice Fauteux unequivocally stated in the 1954 decision of *Industrial Acceptance Corporation* v. *Couture*: " . . . in civil proceedings where evidence of a crime is material for the action to succeed, the applicable rule is not that which prevails in criminal proceedings, where one seeks the penalties imposed by the criminal law, but that which governs the determination of civil actions."[61]

472. *Applying the Rules of Evidence More Strictly?* – In spite of such considerations, some people want to continue to evaluate criminal allegations raised in civil trials more strictly. The Superior Court decision in *Bentata* v. *Compagnie d'assurances Missisquoi*[62] is a good example of the reluctance a judge may feel when asked to rule on the commission of a criminal act by one of the parties. The court explained the following:

> " . . . while the civilian philosophy is repelled by the idea of two levels of preponderance of evidence, it is obvious that the judge presiding in Civil Court is uneasy at the prospect of declaring a party guilty of a criminal offence. . . . Without being capable of expressing it simply, it is obvious that the preponderance of evidence must be subjected to a detailed, in-depth study."[63]

---

also *Report on the Quebec Civil Code, Commentaries*, vol. 2, t. 2, Book Six, chap. 1, art. 3.

61.   [1954] S.C.R. 34 at 43 (our translation); see also *American Home Assurance Co.* v. *Auberge des Pins inc.*, [1990] R.R.A. 152 (Que. C.A.).

62.   [1996] R.R.A. 94 (Que. Sup. Ct.).

63.   Ibid. at 100 (our translation). Judge Denis then referred to the common law principle to this effect and the famous decision by Lord Denning in *Bater* v. *Bater*, [1950] 2 All E.R. 458, which explains: "In criminal cases the charge must be proved beyond a reasonable doubt, but there may be degrees of proof within that standard. Many great judges have said that, in proportion, as the crime is enormous so ought the proof to be clear. So also in civil cases. The case may be proved by a preponderance of probability, but there may be degrees of probability within that standard. The degree depends on the subject-matter. A civil court, when considering a charge of fraud will naturally require a higher degree of probability than that which it would require if considering negligence were established. It does not adopt so high a degree as a criminal court, even when considering the charge of a criminal nature, but still it does require

According to Professor Royer, the presumption of normality explains the reaction of the courts. It requires greater effort to convince someone of facts that fall outside the ordinary, assuming that the perpetration of the criminal act in question satisfies this criterion.[64]

473. *Proof of Criminal Acts by Presumptions of Fact* – Note that the majority of decisions favouring a scale of preponderance or a more severe application[65] of preponderance of evidence involve the assessment of presumptions of fact. In *Bentata*, for example, the plaintiff insurance company sought to establish by presumption of fact that the defendant acted fraudulently in willingly setting his house on fire. There were no eyewitnesses to the events.[66]

474. *Application in Cases of Spousal and Sexual Abuse* – In actions for sexual or spousal abuse, the victim is generally available to testify. Thus, there is always at least one "eyewitness" to the abuse. In addition, proof of spousal or sexual abuse is no longer considered to be proof of "exceptional" facts.[67] The applicable standard remains the preponderance of evidence. It is important not to re-create the myths surrounding proof of sexual offences under cover of a stricter application of the criminal law rules of evidence.[68]

B. Proof

The present section proposes certain avenues that may be taken to avoid the pitfalls that plague the presentation of evidence

---

a degree of probability which is commensurate with the occasion" (at 459, cited on page 100 of *Bentata*). In our opinion, it is not appropriate in this context to refer to the common law. There is no mention of a scale in article 2804 C.C.Q., which reformulates the rule on weighing evidence. The legislature could have expressed itself otherwise, but did not. We can only conclude that it did not intend to incorporate varying degrees into the ponderation of evidence.

64. Above, note 56, No. 183 at 105.
65. This distinction is suggested by Professor Royer, above, note 56, No. 183 at 106.
66. This was also the case in *Aubin*, above, note 58.
67. See above, at §2. Also, for an application of this principle in youth protection cases, see: *Protection de la jeunesse—329*, [1988] R.J.Q. 1739 (Que. Trib. jeun.); *Protection de la jeunesse—207*, J.E. 86-384 (Que. Trib. jeun.); *Protection de la jeunesse—468*, J.E. 91-154 (C.Q.). For instances where the court considers that the gravity of the allegations influences the degree of proof required: *Protection de la jeunesse—584*, [1993] R.J.Q. 274, 278-280 (C.Q.); *Protection de la jeunesse—558*, J.E. 92-1123 (Que. Sup. Ct.).
68. See below, at §501.

in an action for spousal or sexual abuse. These pitfalls are a result of the continuing exceptional nature of this type of trial and the ongoing ignorance of the courts in matters of spousal or sexual abuse. The different evidentiary methods applicable in a trial for spousal or sexual abuse will be examined: testimonial evidence and evidence by means of written documentation, by presumption, or by admission (article 2811 C.C.Q.).

1. *Testimonial Evidence*

The heart of a trial for spousal or sexual abuse is the testimonial evidence presented by the parties. Most of the time, it consists of irreconcilable, opposing versions given by the plaintiff and the defendant. The probative value of their respective testimony will often determine the trial's outcome. Because their testimonial evidence is important in the assessment of damages for spousal or sexual abuse, evaluating the witnesses' credibility will be discussed at length below. We will first discuss witnesses to the facts,[69] followed by expert testimony.

a) *Witness to the Facts*

475. *Questions Studied* – In this section we will attempt to answer certain questions that may arise during a trial for spousal and sex-

---

69.   The qualifier "ordinary" is generally applied to these witnesses. See J.-C. Royer, above, note 56, No. 451 at 258ff. In this chapter, we prefer to identify this testimony by its essential trait: testimony to facts known personally by the witness. In fact, the qualifier "ordinary" supposes that the expert witness is "extraordinary." Several authors have denounced this hierarchy because it devalues the surviving plaintiff. See, among others, Kate Sutherland, "Measuring Pain in Sexual Assault Cases," in Ken Cooper-Stephenson and Elaine Gibson, eds., *Tort Theory* (Toronto: Captus University Publications, 1993) 212 at 229; Melanie Frager Griffith, "Battered Woman Syndrome: A Tool for Batterer?" (1995) 64 *Fordham Law Review* 141; Katherine O'Donovan, "Law's Knowledge: The Judge, the Expert, the Battered Woman, and Her Syndrome," (1993) 20 *Journal of Law and Society* 427; Elizabeth Comack, *Feminist Engagement with the Law: the Legal Recognition of the Battered Woman Syndrome*, ICREF Document No. 31 (Ottawa: Canadian Institute for the Advancement of Women, 1993). Note that, in practice, the plaintiff should be the star witness during the trial. The expert should be viewed only as an interpreter who is there to translate the emotional content of the plaintiff's testimony for the judge. See, on this subject, Nathalie Des Rosiers, Bruce Feldthusen, and Olena Hankivsky, "Legal Compensation for Sexual Violence: Therapeutic Consequences and Consequences for the Judicial System," (1998) 4 *Psychology, Public Policy and Law* 433.

ual abuse. For example, what are the safeguards available to protect the witness, wife, or child terrorized by the defendant/abuser? When can the child witness testify? How much weight does her testimony carry? Can an adult woman testify from behind a screen? What other witnesses can be heard? What criteria should be used when determining the admissibility of post-abuse confidences, or proof respecting other abuse committed by the defendant/abuser?

i) The Victim's Testimony

476. *Psychological Effects of Testimony* – In some instances, it can be therapeutic for the victim to find the "words to say it,"[70] and it may be beneficial for her rehabilitation to actually "say" what happened.[71] Yet, the victim can suffer the harmful effects of a voyeuristic cross-examination. The victim is forced to recall sordid events and can be questioned at length on details that may seem unimportant to her, or she may be re-victimized by the story's reconstruction.[72] A majority of studies show that it is crucial for the victim's well-being that others perceive the story as valid.[73] Victims who are believed recover more quickly. This is obviously one of the more serious risks for the victim who institutes legal proceedings: the dismissal of the action and the public disbelief of her story.

In this section, we will explore those strategies that facilitate testimony offered by a victim of sexual or spousal abuse. To start, we will examine issues specific to testimony given by children, followed by the difficulties relating to the testimony of women who have been victims of violence.

---

70. Marie Cardinal, *Les mots pour le dire* (Paris: Grasset, 1975), available in English under the title *The Words to Say It* (Paris: Women's Press, 2000), is a discussion about a young woman filmed as a child by her father when she went to the toilet. She told of the psychological difficulty she experienced before she could find the "words to say it," as implied in the title of her book.

71. See Des Rosiers, Feldthusen, and Hankivsky, above, note 69.

72. The participants are sensitive to the language used in court. See, for example, the sexual abuse victim who was asked, "Is that where you had sex with him?" to which the offended victim responded: "HE had sex with me." Example cited in Des Rosiers, Feldthusen, and Hankivsky, above, note 69.

73. Louise Dezwirez Sas and Alison Hatch Cunningham, *Tipping the Balance to Tell the Secret: Public Discovery of Child Sexual Abuse* (London, ON: Family Court Clinic, 1995).

(a) Child Sexual Abuse Victim

Children who have been sexually abused can be summoned to testify where their parents have instituted proceedings against the abuser on their behalf.[74] They must also testify if they have been witness to sexual or spousal abuse, or where they have been indirectly harmed.[75] This section explores the difficulties encountered by children who have themselves been victimized, either directly or indirectly. Our interest focuses on three aspects of child testimony: capacity to testify, credibility, and safeguards required for the protection of the child.

The Child's Capacity to Testify

477. *Capacity* – The child's capacity to testify must first of all be determined by the court. A child who understands the significance of being under oath testifies in the same manner as an adult. A child who does not appreciate the nature of the oath can testify if she is capable of relating the facts of which she has knowledge and if she understands the duty to tell the truth (paragraph 2 of article 2844 C.C.Q.).[76] Experts may be summoned to assist the court in evaluating this capacity.[77] The court will consider the child's age, level of functioning, and emotional state when determining capacity to testify.

---

74. *Gagnon* v. *Béchard*, [1993] R.J.Q. 2019 (Que. C.A).
75. Above, at §§337ff. See *S. et al.* v. *Clement et al.* (1995), 22 O.R. (3d) 495 (Ont. Gen. Div.), where the children of a sexually abused woman received significant damages. See also *Roberge* v. *Carrier,* REJB 1997-03743 (Que. Sup. Ct.), where the abused spouse's children were awarded damages.
76. Article 2844 (2) C.C.Q. replaced former article 301 C.C.P., repealed during the Civil Code reform (S.Q. 1992, c. 57, in force 1 January 1994). See Ducharme, above, note 57, No. 503 at 152. For examples of decisions in which unsworn children testified, see *De Grosbois* v. *Commission des écoles catholiques de Ville St-Laurent*, [1974] C.S. 292 (Que. Sup. Ct.) and *Guénette* v. *Lapierre*, [1976] C.S. 1786 (Que. Sup. Ct.). See also Christianne Dubreuil, *Le témoignage des enfants en droit pénal et en droit civil* (Montreal: Les Éditions Thémis, 1991) at 19.
77. Louis Gélinas and Bartha Maria Knoppers, "Le rôle des experts en droit québécois en matière de garde, d'accès et de protection," (1993) 53 *Revue du Barreau du Québec* 3 at 54.

478. *Need for Corroboration* – In contrast to criminal[78] and youth protection law,[79] unsworn testimony given by a child must be corroborated (paragraph 2 of article 2844 C.C.Q.).[80] In light of developments in international law[81] and in certain Canadian common law provinces, the rule requiring corroboration appears archaic.[82] It seems strange that this rule has been abandoned by the criminal law but maintained in the civil law of evidence. If the goal of this rule is to avoid injustices that may occur due to the "fragility" of a child's testimony, it would then be particularly important to maintain it in criminal law, where the accused's liberty is at stake.[83] It is fitting that this obsolete rule be eliminated; however, until that happens, we must consider the requirements respecting corroboration.

479. *Nature of Corroboration Required* – The criminal law used to require corroboration of testimony given by children or accomplices, or by women in sexual abuse hearings.[84] This corroboration had to

---

78. *Canada Evidence Act*, S.C. 1987, c. 24, s. 18.

79. Section 85.2, *Youth Protection Act*, R.S.Q., c. P-34.1, amended by S.Q. 1994, c. 35, s. 52.

80. The wording of article 2844 C.C.Q. essentially reproduces former article 301 C.C.P. The two articles allow the unsworn testimony of children to be admitted but stipulate: "a judgment may not be based upon such testimony alone."

81. See the Ontario Law Reform Commission Report, *Report on Child Witnesses*, 1991, recommending that the rule under section 18(2) of the *Evidence Act*, R.S.O. 1990, c. E-23, be repealed. This recommendation was adopted by Ontario lawmakers in 1995: see S.O. 1995, c. 6, s. 6. The report by the Law Reform Commission discussed similar recommendations made by other law reform commissions: see the Law Reform Commission of Ireland (*Report on Child Sexual Abuse*, 1990), the Law Reform Commission of Western Australia (*Discussion Paper on Evidence of Children and Other Vulnerable Witnesses*, Perth, Australia, 1990) and of Victoria, Australia (Victoria Law Reform Commission, *Sexual Offences Against Children*, 1988). Several American states have also abolished this rule: see John R. Spencer and Rhona Flin, *The Evidence of Children: The Law and Psychology* (London: Blackstone Press, 1990) cited by the Ontario Law Reform Commission, at 43.

82. New Brunswick no longer requires corroboration of children's unsworn testimony: see N.B.A. 1990, c. 17, s. 5. See also amendments to the British Columbia law: S.B.C. 1988, c. 46, s. 25, and in Ontario, *Evidence Act*, R.S.O. 1990, c. E-23. See John Sopinka, Sidney N. Lederman, and Alan W. Bryant, *The Law of Evidence in Canada* (Toronto: Butterworths, 1992) at 584.

83. See, for an explanation of the different objectives underlying the laws of evidence in criminal cases and child protection laws, Dubreuil, above, note 76.

84. See below, the commentary by Lord Diplock in the text accompanying note 125.

come from independent testimony linking the accused to the crime.[85] Abuse of this rule is well documented.[86] As noted above, testimony given by children in criminal matters no longer needs to be corroborated. Rules applying to testimony given by accomplices have also been relaxed.[87] What about the Civil Code requirement that unsworn testimony given by children be corroborated? Relying on a 1982 Superior Court decision, Dubreuil concluded that corroboration in civil proceedings includes evidence that "supports" the testimony[88]—that is, evidence that generally supports its truthfulness. It does not mean, as it once did under criminal law, that the abuser need be connected to each aspect of the crime. Royer has adopted a similar definition, adding that the corroboration must always address essential issues relevant to the trial's outcome.[89]

480. *Application to Instances of Sexual Abuse* – Unsworn testimony given by a child can be "supported" by several types of evidence: testimony of a parent or a teacher regarding the child's behaviour,[90] a medical report documenting anomalies,[91] or even the abuser's refusal to testify or to summon witnesses.[92]

The Child's Credibility

481. *A Debated Question* – Once admitted, testimony—sworn or otherwise—must be credible in the eyes of the court. The reliability of children respecting the occurrence of sexual abuse has been debated by numerous observers.[93] Jurists as well as child and memory psy-

---

85.See *R.* v. *Baskerville* (1916), 12 Cr. App. R. 81 (Cr. App.) and the analysis by Dubreuil, above, note 76 at 21–30.

86.See Dubreuil, above, note 76 at 21–30.

87.*R.* v. *Vetrovec*, [1982] 1 S.C.R. 811.

88.Above, note 76 at 32. See *St-Pierre, ès qualités "Personne autorisée par le Directeur de la protection de la jeunesse"* v. *G. (L.)*, REJB 2000-20184 (C.Q.).

89.Above, note 56, No. 177 at 101.

90.See Judge Warren's decision, cited by Dubreuil, above, note 76 at 33.

91.Ibid. See also Jacques Ulysse, "La Loi sur la protection de la jeunesse et l'abus sexuel," in Hubert Van Gijseghem, ed., *L'enfant mis à nu. L'allégation d'abus sexuel: la recherche de la vérité* (Montreal: Méridien, 1992) 191 at 221.

92.Royer, above, note 56, No. 177 at 102. See *Middleton* v. *Bryce* (1931), 40 O.W.N. 583 (Ont. C.A.); *Moran* v. *Richards* (1974), 38 D.L.R. (3d) 171, [1973] 3 O.R. 751 (Ont. Sup. Ct.).

93.See in Quebec, among others, Luc Morin and Claude Boisclair, "La preuve d'abus sexuel: allégations, déclarations et l'évaluation d'expert," (1992) 23 *Revue de droit de l'Université de Sherbrooke* 27 at 36; Hubert Van Gijseghem, "L'enfant témoin: facteurs cognitifs," in Continuing Education Department of the Barreau, *L'enfant abusé: psychologie et droit* (Cowansville, QC: Les Édi-

chologists have been and continue to be preoccupied with certain aspects of these debates, to which we now turn.

482. *Moral Capacity to Tell the Truth* – The historical fear that children are morally incapable of telling the truth appears to be unfounded. Generally speaking, no existing scientific study has established that children are less morally capable than adults of telling the truth.[94] Studies have shown that, to the contrary, children rarely lie about sexual matters, especially when the abuse has been spontaneously revealed.[95] Research has shown that the rate of false allegations stands between 1 and 3 per cent.[96] False allegations or, more frequently, false retractions, occur primarily after an adult has intervened. False allegations appear to occur almost exclusively during conflicts over child custody.[97] False retractions occur once the child has ascertained, after having been examined, re-examined, and examined yet again on the same facts, that she will not be believed. Hubert Van Gijseghem explains:

> The child could no doubt 'survive' a single examination . . . however, she will interpret each additional request to 'recount' and each new examination as an indication that she has not been believed the first time. Moreover, she will become convinced that the adults (the abuser and the examiner) are 'sticking' together and will stop at nothing to prove that she is lying.[98]

483. *Capacity to Remember* – Testimony given by children was once inadmissible because it was believed that, under a certain age, chil-

---

tions Yvon Blais, 1992) at 27; Van Gijseghem, "Particularités du témoignage de l'enfant victime d'abus sexuel," in Van Gijseghem, ed., above, note 92 at 17. In Canada, John C. Yuille, "L'entrevue de l'enfant dans un contexte d'investigation et l'évaluation systématique de sa déclaration," in Van Gijseghem, ed., above, note 91 at 67; John C. Yuille, Mary Ann King, and Don Macdougall, *Child Victims and Witnesses: The Social Sciences and Legal Literatures* (Ottawa: Department of Justice Canada, 1988). On the international scene, see also Spencer and Flin, above, note 81; Inger J. Sagatun and Leonard P. Edwards, *Child Abuse and the Legal System* (Chicago: Nelson-Hall Publishers, 1995); Cathy Cobley, *Child Abuse and the Law* (London: Cavendish, 1995).
94. See the Ontario Law Reform Commission Report, above, note 81 at 13–14.
95. See, for a summary of the more interesting studies conducted recently, Van Gijseghem, "Particularités du témoignage de l'enfant victime d'abus sexuel," above, note 93 at 19–20.
96. Ibid. at 19.
97. Ibid.
98. Ibid. at 20 (our translation).

dren were not intellectually capable of remembering the facts and acts they witnessed. Yet, recent studies demonstrate that children as young as three can remember traumatic events they have experienced. Children obviously do not remember the same things as adults. Temporal memory is not organized by date or hour, but possibly according to special events—a birthday or holiday, for example. Temporal perception is particularly deficient in children and leaves the person doing the examining with the impression of incoherence. King and Yuille comment: "The child will most probably remember the *context* within which the abuse took place, as opposed to specific incidents. The interviewer, aware of this distinction, could adapt the examination in such cases and examine the child as to the general context of the abuse rather than what happened on precise dates."[99]

In addition, children may not remember details that an adult would consider important, such as the exact location or how long sexual contact lasted. Note, however, that studies seem to indicate that children remember more than they are capable of spontaneously communicating.[100]

484. *Intellectual Capacity to Distinguish Fact from Fiction* – Jurists used to believe that children lived in an imaginary world and were incapable of distinguishing fact from fiction. Because it was impossible to separate fact from fiction in the story they told, their testimony was therefore considered worthless. Once again, prevailing presumptions by the legal system appear to have been contradicted by research. In fact, while children often create imaginary worlds, they are not likely to imagine the types of incidents at the basis of legal proceedings, such as automobile accidents or sexual or physical abuse.[101] This is particularly true where the nature of the sexual touching surpasses the child's understanding of adult sexual activity.

99. Mary Ann King and John C. Yuille, *L'enfant comme témoin* (Ottawa: Ministry of Health and Welfare Canada, 1986) at 5, cited by Van Gijseghem, "Particularités du témoignage de l'enfant victime d'abus sexuel", above, note 93 at 31 (our translation).

100. Gail Goodman, an author who has written extensively on this subject, concluded that errors in memory by children are errors of omission rather than commission. Children say less than they know. See Gail Goodman and R. Reed, "Age Difference in Eyewitness Testimony," (1986) 10 *Law & Human Behavior* 317 at 329; Gail Goodman and V.S. Helgeson, "Child Sexual Assault: Children's Memory and the Law," (1988) 12 *Prov. Judges J.* 17, cited by the Ontario Law Reform Commission, above, note 81 at 11.

101. Ontario Law Reform Commission Report, above, note 81 at 13.

485. *Susceptibility to Conditioning* – How is it that false allegations occur, given that children do not lie, have the same level of memory difficulties as adults, and do not willingly invent sexual abuse? In reality, cases of false allegations are rare and arise mainly in instances of disputes surrounding child custody where one parent, innocently or not, accuses the other of sexual abuse.[102] Children are more susceptible to conditioning than adults,[103] and this remains the weak spot in their testimony. A child is more likely than an adult to be manipulated by an adult. Her parent, the interviewer, the social worker, or the lawyer all exercise power over her. The child may adapt her testimony in order to satisfy the more or less obvious needs of the questioner because the child wants to please the adult.

486. *Consequences on the Civil Trial* – In conclusion, research into the credibility of abused children has provided the courts with at least three guidelines. Firstly, a child should be spared the repetition of difficult testimony so that the child does not conclude with quasi-certainty that she was not believed. Secondly, testimony given by a child should never be discredited because time and spatial references do not satisfy the credibility criteria applicable to adults. Madam Justice Wilson in *R. v. B.G.*[104] endorsed this flexible attitude towards testimony given by children: "While children may not be able to recount precise details and communicate the when and where of an event with exactitude, this does not mean that they have misconceived what happened to them and who did it." Hesitation by the court as to the credibility of testimony given by children should be restricted to situations where it could have been manipulated by an adult, where the child did not spontaneously offer the information or where it appears that the child could have fashioned the story according to the expectations of adults. Psychologists have recommended certain safeguards for the child-witness designed to ensure that testimony given by the child is the most credible possible.

---

102. For an interesting discussion of the dynamics this creates, see: Van Gijseghem, "Les causes de divorce ou de droits d'accès comme contexte de la fausse allégation d'abus sexuel," in Van Gijseghem, ed., above, note 91 at 117–52.

103. Note, however, that weaknesses in adult testimony are also well documented in psychological studies. See Elizabeth Loftus, *Eyewitness Testimony* (Cambridge: Harvard University Press, 1979) cited by the Ontario Law Reform Commission, above, note 81 at 8.

104. [1990] 2 S.C.R. 30 at 55.

Safeguards for the Child Witness

487. *Safeguards* – Safeguards are both a means of protecting the child from the trauma of the trial and—a point not to be forgotten— a means of ensuring truthful testimony from a shocked and stressed child possibly incapable of answering questions asked of her. The protection offered by the *Code of Civil Procedure* in this regard will now be examined.

488. *Provisions of the* Code of Civil Procedure – Articles 394.1 to 394.5 C.C.P. were introduced during the Civil Code reform,[105] and are meant to guarantee adequate representation of a minor's interests. The provisions focus on the right to representation by a lawyer where the child's interests are in issue (articles 394.1 and 394.2 C.C.P.), accompaniment of the child in court (article 394.3 C.C.P.), and her examination outside the presence of the parties (article 394.4 C.C.P.)[106] and outside the courtroom (article 394.5 C.C.P.).

489. *Accompaniment to Trial* – At the very least, the child, when testifying, should be supported by someone she knows. Article 394.3 C.C.P. stipulates that the minor can be accompanied by a person "capable of assisting or reassuring him." It is possible that the persons most likely to offer such support (i.e., parents, tutors, or psychologists) have been excluded from the courtroom, given that they are themselves often witnesses who will subsequently testify.[107] They are thus unable to fulfil their role as protector of the child if

---

105. S.Q. 1992, c. 57.

106. It appears that a legislative amendment was necessary to allow out-of-court examinations. In fact, in a decision later reversed on appeal for procedural reasons, Judge Mayrand of the Superior Court suggested that the legislation itself must specifically mention the possibility of testifying in the absence of one of the parties and that the court has no power to create procedures, even where it would mean that a child avoids confronting his abuser: *Protection de la jeunesse—226*, [1987] R.J.Q. 326 (Que. Sup. Ct.). The decision by the Court of Appeal, rendered on 29 April 1989, is reproduced in Appendix 3 of Professor Dubreuil's book, above, note 77. Note that Judge Mayrand addressed this issue within the context of a criminal proceeding under the *Young Offender's Act*. He overturned Judge Ruffo's decision whereby an eleven-year-old child who was sexually abused by an adolescent was allowed to testify by closed-circuit television. Judge Mayrand concluded that it was the accused's constitutional right to directly hear the testimony in order to assess its credibility.

107. See the Ontario Law Reform Commission Report, above, note 81 at 93, which recommends that the support person be allowed only when not required to testify later on. See also, to the same effect, s. 486 (1.2) Cr.C., also discussed in Schabas, above, note 17 at 250–2.

they are to respect the order excluding witnesses. Therefore, the solution of accompanying the child witness in court can be of little utility in protecting the child.

490. *Examination outside the Presence of the Parties* – Another protection mechanism consists of allowing the child to testify out of the presence of the parties, "where his interest requires it" (article 394.4 C.C.P.).[108] Van Gijsehem explains that a child's fear of the abuser, especially if it is a parent or a loved one, can lead to a retraction.[109] We suggest that the interest of the child requires that she testify out of the presence of her abuser. Confrontation with the abuser is always troubling for the child.[110] Testifying out of the presence of the parties should therefore be the rule in sexual abuse actions, as should permission to be examined by the judge in a place other than the courtroom.

491. *Examination outside of the Courtroom* – Article 394.5 C.C.P. permits the examination of a child by the court at the child's residence or another appropriate place. The need for flexibility is necessary to minimize any trauma experienced by the child when testifying in an overly formal setting imbued with rites foreign to the child.[111]

492. *The Extent of Paragraph 2 of Article 396 C.C.P.* – Despite the important improvements to the protection of children's rights brought about by the possibility of testifying out of the presence of the parties or outside of the courtroom, the most acute problem still exists for the child: the constant repetition of testimony and examinations.[112] In addition, under paragraph 2 of article 396 C.C.P., a party can always request that a witness be re-examined if the witness is in Quebec. It does not appear that the judge has any discretion to refuse the party's request. In our opinion, even though the language of paragraph 2 of article 396 C.C.P. is unclear, it is up to the judge to interpret this provision in accordance with the spirit of

---

108. See the possibility in criminal law under s. 486 (2.1) Cr.C. of testifying via closed circuit television. See Schabas, above, note 17 at 246–50.
109. See "Particularités du témoignage de l'enfant victime d'abus sexuel," above, note 93 at 22–3.
110. Ibid.
111. More and more Crown attorneys are offering accompaniment services for children in criminal proceedings, which often include advance courtroom visits: see Schabas, above, note 17 at 250–2.
112. See above, at §482.

the reform and require that cogent reasons be provided before victimizing the child anew.[113] It is contrary to the legislature's objective of protecting the child to allow the defendant to re-examine the child during the trial once she has been duly examined by the court out of the presence of the parties.

493. *Testimony Not Subject to Judicial Control?* – Aside from the fact that paragraph 2 of article 396 C.C.P. gives the parties the discretion to re-examine the child in the courtroom, criticism can also be levelled at the absence of provisions allowing the child's testimony to be replaced by a videotaped examination, which is not subject to judicial control and is conducted by experts. Admitting this testimony early on and one single time would eliminate the traumatic consequences mentioned by psychologist Van Gijsehem.

494. *Role of the Court* – Given that it is not possible completely to eliminate the need for children to testify in court, we can only recommend that judges be sensitized to the impact of repetitive examinations on children, and that they provide as much reassurance as possible. Ideally, children need to hear that they are believed, which is difficult for a judge to do because she or he is obliged to weigh the evidence prior to arriving at a conclusion and to maintain her or his impartiality as between the two parties. Perhaps incompatibility between the roles of impartiality and reassurance is the reason why testimony not subject to judicial control should replace testimony given before a judge.[114]

Several aspects of testimony given by children deserve the attention of the legal system: from the assessment of the child's credibility to the introduction of effective safeguards that permit the child to be truly understood. There may also be a need to re-evaluate certain legal practices if adult victims of sexual or spousal abuse are to be heard and understood. These concerns are addressed in the following section.

---

113. The Court of Appeal in *Dans l'affaire de: L.(J.)*, REJB 1997-03240 (C.A.) overturned the decision of the Superior Court and rejected the request by the respondent (father) for an expert evaluation.

114. See Des Rosiers, Feldthusen, and Hankivsky, above, note 69, for a description of the judge's symbolic role in the victim's rehabilitation. It is understandable why the judge cannot immediately accept the story of an adult victim. It is, perhaps, possible for an adult victim to wait for the decision before being heard and believed, but this waiting period can have devastating implications for a child.

(b) Women Victims of Violence

495. *The Problem* – The search for the truth is a complex process. So little is known about memory and remembering the necessary items required to testify before a court.[115] Who are the "good" witnesses? Do they really tell the truth? A growing number of studies reveal the difficulties encountered by certain social groups in persuading legal authorities to believe them.[116] The goal of the present section is to discover how the victim should testify in order to receive justice. We hope to convey a greater understanding of the context that may influence the victim's behaviour and the manner in which her testimony is perceived. We will examine the impact of certain emotions on the victim's ability to testify: her fear of the abuser ("the safeguards"), her modesty in the face of the facts alleged, and the myths that continue to influence the manner in which the testimony is perceived.

The Witness's Safeguards

496. *The Goal of Safeguards* – As with children,[117] safeguards for women victims of violence are meant to ensure that the witness can testify in total security and recount "the whole truth." They are not wrenches thrown into the contradictory system of the administration of evidence, but rather adjustments that enable the person to be understood and heard. They are no different in this respect from other measures employed to assist the court in understanding persons who are mute or have language difficulties.

497. *Fear of the Abuser* – A first factor meriting examination is the victim's fear of the abuser, which can prevent her from talking or force her to censure certain parts of her testimony. It has been established that an abusive spouse frequently commits retaliatory acts, particularly where spousal abuse is concerned.[118] It is obvious that the danger of the witness being subjected to physical abuse must be eliminated.

---

115. See Loftus, above, note 103.
116. Louise Mandell, "Native Culture on Trial," in Sheilah L. Martin and Kathleen E. Mahoney, eds., *Equality and Judicial Neutrality* (Toronto: Carswell, 1987) at 358; Joan Brockman, Denise Evans, and Kerri Reid, "Feminist Perspectives for the Study of Gender Bias in the Legal Profession," (1992) 5 *Canadian Journal of Women and the Law* 37.
117. See above, at §487.
118. See above, at §56.

498. *Safeguards against Intimidation outside the Courtroom* – A court's general power over the trial gives it the authority to order measures aimed at physically protecting the witness. It can order that the defendant be prohibited from communicating with the victim, with his children, or with his spouse. Other measures are also available, such as an order to stop following the victim or to stop having the victim followed, or to stop harassing or approaching the victim at her workplace.[119]

499. *Safeguards against Intimidation inside the Courtroom* – The presence of the parties during the testimony of the witnesses is a basic principle set out in the *Code of Civil Procedure* (article 204 C.C.P.).[120] Can the court permit the victim to testify by closed-circuit television or from behind a screen? We believe that it is possible to testify from behind a screen. This method does not violate the principle that the parties be present during the testimony and is frequently used in criminal law.[121] This safeguard, minimal though it is, does nonetheless increase the victim's level of comfort.

500. *Testifying by Closed-Circuit Television* – The option of testifying by closed-circuit television offers the victim much greater protection. This safeguard, however, can be considered to be a violation of the rule requiring that all parties be present during the hearing. Indeed, in a case involving an eleven-year-old girl abused by an adolescent, Judge Mayrand of the Superior Court held that the option to testify in the absence of the parties needed to be clearly stated in the law.[122] Article 404 C.C.P. allows the court to order a witness to be heard out-of-court "if it sees fit to do so." This "exceptional" proceeding[123] has been used primarily where the witness was absent or very ill.[124] In our opinion, it might be appropriate for the court to exercise the discretion conferred by article 404 C.C.P. in favour of the victim's protection under certain conditions—for example,

---

119. See Alberta Law Institute, *Protection against Domestic Violence*, Report No. 74 (1997).
120. See *G.K.* v. *D.K.*, [1994] O.J. No. 31680 (Ont. Gen. Div.) (Q.L.), where based on this principle, the court refused to bar the defendant abuser from the plaintiff's pre-trial examination despite evidence that he had followed her and harassed her children.
121. See s. 486(2.1) Cr.C., which allows testimony in sexual abuse proceedings to be given from behind a screen.
122. See above, note 106.
123. See Royer, above, note 56, No. 638 at 379.
124. See *Wohl* v. *Marché Théberge inc.*, J.E. 92-815 (Que. Sup. Ct.); *Lamarre* v. *Hôpital du Sacré-Coeur*, J.E. 90-461 (Que. Sup. Ct.).

where the victim has already been threatened by the defendant. It is important for the court to hear "the whole truth," and it is with this goal in mind that the victim should be allowed to testify outside the defendant's presence.

Testimony

501. *Myths Regarding the Hearing of Testimony* – As recently as 1973, Lord Diplock required corroboration of testimony given by a sexual abuse victim before condemning the abuser. He stated: "But common sense, the mother of the common law, suggests that there are certain categories of witnesses whose testimony as to particular matters may well be unreliable either . . . through defect of intellect or understanding or, as in the case of those alleging sexual acts committed on them by others, *because experience shows the danger that fantasy may supplant or supplement genuine recollection.*[125]

Although it is true that the need for corroboration in criminal law has disappeared, it is not certain that the attitudes that supported it have likewise evolved. The evaluation of the credibility of testimony given by women on the abuse they have suffered is rife with myths. An examination of the indicators generally used to evaluate a witness's credibility will assist us in identifying those aspects that can influence how testimony given by a victim of sexual or spousal abuse is negatively perceived.

502. *Silence Explained* – The former common law rules requiring a spontaneous complaint,[126] although abolished, still persist in the minds of many lawyers and judges. They may think, though not say, that the "normal" reaction of a victim would be to file a complaint with the police as soon as possible. It is essential to explain to the judge that the first reaction of a woman who has been raped or battered by her husband may not be to turn to the police.[127] Such behav-

---

125. *D.P.P.* v. *Hester* (1973), 57 Cr. App. R. 212 (H.L.) at 242, cited by Dubreuil, above, note 76 at 23.

126. See Schabas, above, note 17 at 184–8; Jean-Guy Boilard, *Manuel de preuve pénale* (Cowansville, QC: Les Éditions Yvon Blais, 1991) at 5-8.2 to 5-10.4.

127. See, as regards the context of spousal abuse that leads the woman to believe that she is herself capable of controlling the abuse, above, at §§61ff. Sexual abuse victims may hesitate to file complaints if they have no moral or therapeutic support. See Holly Johnson and Vincent F. Sacco, "Researching Violence against Women: Statistics Canada's National Survey," (1995) 37 *Can. Journal of Criminology* 281; Roberts, above, note 16. See the comments in *Roberge* v. *Carrier*, above, note 75, where the judge, having reviewed the evi-

iour does not necessarily mean that a victim who has kept quiet for years is inventing the abuse.[128] The victim must at least be given the opportunity to explain her silence.

503. *Different Versions of the Abuse* – Courts view consistency in the narrative of the abuse as an indicator of credibility. A strategy often used in cross-examination is to demonstrate that the victim has most likely invented the story, given that new or different details are described with each new narrative. In an action for spousal or sexual abuse, especially where the violent acts occurred over several years, it is highly possible that certain details will have been forgotten or minimized during earlier testimony. Therapy often assists the victim in remembering specific events that have been suppressed in her memory.[129] In addition, the victim could have censured the testimony depending on the circumstances under which it was first given. Complaints lodged with the police are often lacking in detail because the victim is reluctant to reveal the more intimate aspects of the incident. Revelations made to therapists may also have been confused if the victim did not feel completely at ease in telling her story[130] or if the relationship between the therapist and the patient was in any way difficult. Before concluding that contradictory narrations are an indication that the event probably did not occur, the court should offer the survivor the opportunity to explain any contradictions. She may explain that she did not want to reveal particularly cruel or sordid details of the abuse to the police in the presence of her spouse.

504. *The Victim's Morality* – The defence can attack the victim's morality in an effort to discredit her testimony. The defendant's lawyer can try to depict a victim who has a criminal record for fraud[131] or prostitution as someone likely to invent the event. The court must recognize that inconsistencies are often a consequence of

---

dence, indicates that he found it difficult to understand why the woman stayed with the man for so long, given her financial independence.

128. The plaintiff must explain her delay in suing, especially if her remedy is "apparently prescribed." See above, at §§85ff.

129. See the controversy surrounding the extent of this phenomenon, above, at §§36ff.

130. See, for example, the decision in *M. (K.)* v. *M. (H.)*, [1992] 3 S.C.R. 6, where the plaintiff failed to reveal the incest to her first therapist, a male. She confided several years later to a female therapist.

131. Fraud that is considered as a sign of dishonesty should also be systemically evaluated: fraud is more of a female crime than breaking and entering. Identifying fraud, in contrast to violent crimes, as an obvious sign of the ten-

sexual abuse and that it would be unjust to deny the victim's story due to the consequences of the wrongful behaviour.

505. *The Witness's Behaviour* – Finally, the courts often say that the behaviour of a witness is a factor in assessing her credibility. Witnesses who speak frankly, who look the judge directly in the eyes, and who express themselves unhesitatingly are favourably judged, while those who perspire, appear fearful, and prefer to avoid questions rather than answer them directly are considered to be "bad witnesses." Once again, it is essential that a survivor's low self-esteem not be negatively interpreted: it is, after all, frequently caused by the abuse.

ii)   Other Witnesses to the Facts

The experience of the plaintiff, whether adult or child, with the Quebec legal system will no doubt be traumatic, despite all the support she may receive. It is likely that, based solely on the testimony of the child or adult, the judge will not be convinced that the allegations are founded. Therefore recourse can be had to other testimony supportive of the victim.

Three types of testimony often presented by the victim's friends, members of her family, neighbours, or work colleagues, and even made to the police, will be examined in this section. We will first examine the admissibility of extrajudicial statements made by the plaintiff in support of her version of the facts. Second, we will focus on testimony aimed at demonstrating changes in the plaintiff's personality, possibly due to the abuse. Finally, we will examine testimony by persons as to the abuser's typical method of committing the crime. This evidence can confirm some of the evidence introduced by the victim.

(a) Extrajudicial Statements Made by the Victim

506. *The Problem* – Consistency in the narrative of events is an indicator of the credibility of statements made by the plaintiff.[132] The

---

dency to lie before the courts must be avoided. This can reproduce a certain systemic inequality.

132. See above, at §503. See, among others, the decision by the Ontario Court in *Strong* v. *M.M.P.* (1997), 31 C.C.E.L. (2d) 47, 50 O.R. (3d) 70 (Ont. C.A.), for an illustration of the impact of standardization in the recounting of events, where the judge admitted into evidence testimony given by a confidante of the

plaintiff often wants to introduce previous statements made to the police, family, or friends, or during the criminal trial, in order to establish consistency in the different versions of events. Can she have her confidantes testify, or can she simply file the transcript of testimony given before the criminal courts? In order to answer this question, two tenets of the law of evidence must be discussed: the rule on inadmissibility of previous consistent statements and the principle of the inadmissibility of extrajudicial statements.

507. *The Rule on Inadmissibility of Previous Consistent Statements* – Where the sole purpose is to confirm her version of events, common law generally refuses to admit earlier statements made by the witness. However, it is clear from the *Civil Code of Québec* that civil law differs from common law on this point.[133] Article 2871 C.C.Q. cannot be any clearer on the issue of previous statements made by a witness: they are admissible if their reliability is sufficiently guaranteed. This guarantee exists, in our view, where sworn testimony has been given before the criminal courts.[134] In our opinion, a transcript of the plaintiff's sworn testimony given during the criminal trial or before the Commission de la santé et de la sécurité au travail (C.S.S.T.) during a hearing for benefits under the *Crime Victims Compensation Act*[135] is admissible and is proof of its contents. What is the situation for unsworn statements made to the police or to family and friends? Are these statements sufficiently reliable?

---

victim on the grounds that the confidante's version of events supported the victim's version.

133. The former law was more compatible with the common law: former article 320 C.C.P. provided for admissibility of testimony given in another proceeding in exceptional circumstances. This article was narrowly interpreted and did not admit transcripts of testimony given before criminal proceedings: *Société canadienne des métaux Reynolds* v. *C.S.N.*, [1980] R.L.N.S. 253, 276 (Que. Sup. Ct.); *Caisse populaire de Saint-Raymond* v. *Boily*, [1974] C.S. 74 (Que. Sup. Ct.); *Commission municipale du Québec* v. *Saint-Léonard (cité de)*, [1972] C.S. 827 (Que. Sup. Ct.); *Arbour* v. *Dunn*, [1967] C.S. 691, 695-696 (Que. Sup. Ct.); *Bélanger* v. *Comtois*, [1980] C.S. 891 (Que. Sup. Ct.). According to Royer, the repeal of article 380 C.C.P. and the adoption of articles 2870 and 2871 C.C.Q. suggest that this testimony should be more easily accepted by the courts because the circumstances under which it was given increases its credibility: see above, note 56, No. 678 at 399.
134. See Royer, above, note 56, Nos. 763–7 at 449–50.
135. See above, at §365.

508. *Inadmissibility of Extrajudicial Declarations* – In principle, extrajudicial or hearsay statements made by a witness or a person not summoned to testify during the trial are inadmissible under the *Code of Civil Procedure*, which stipulates that the witness must be present in court (articles 294, 299, 317 C.C.P.), and pursuant to article 2843 of the *Civil Code of Québec*.[136] Nonetheless, where sufficient guarantees exist as to the reliability of the extrajudicial statements, exceptions to this principle have been developed by the jurisprudence.[137] Some of these are particularly relevant to the civil actions by victims of sexual and spousal abuse. We will now examine the admissibility of statements made contemporaneously to the event, "spontaneous complaints made by a victim of a sexual offence," confidences made by a child regarding sexual abuse, and statements as to the abuser's identity.

509. *Statements Made Contemporaneously to the Event* – Article 2870 C.C.Q. admits into evidence "spontaneous and contemporaneous statements concerning the occurrence of facts," provided such statements are sufficiently reliable.[138] In sexual or spousal abuse actions, witnesses are permitted to testify to spontaneous statements issued contemporaneously to the abuse that serve to explain, for example, the source of the plaintiff's injuries[139] or the abuser's mental state.[140] The spontaneity and contemporaneousness of the statement must be appreciated according to the particular circumstances. Thus, the plaintiff's statement to a neighbour that she was being abused should be admitted as a statement made contemporaneously to the incident. In addition, a later statement made to this same neighbour can be admitted as a "spontaneous complaint," even where it was not contemporaneous to the abuse.

510. *The Crime Victim's Spontaneous Complaint* – In criminal law matters, the common law rule requiring that a sexual abuse victim's complaint be spontaneous before a conclusion of abuse could be

---

136. See Royer, above, note 56, No. 673 at 396. They are inadmissible only where offered as proof of the truth of their contents.
137. The *Civil Code of Québec* is not meant to amend the jurisprudential rules: see the comments by the minister to this effect: *Commentaires du ministre de la Justice*, t. 2 (Quebec: Publications du Québec, 1993) art. 2843 C.C.Q., cited by Royer, above, note 56, No. 689 at 406.
138. See the recent analysis of this provision by the Court of Appeal in *Services de santé du Québec* v. *Manoir du Fleuve inc.*, REJB 2000-19941 (Que. C.A.).
139. See *Beaumont-Butcher* v. *Butcher*, [1982] C.S. 893 (Que. Sup. Ct.).
140. See Royer, above, note 56, No. 702 at 413.

drawn has been repealed.[141] The victim's disclosure can now be introduced as evidence by the Crown, but only where the accused suggests that the abuse is fabricated or when the statement was made contemporaneously to the abuse.[142] Proof of a spontaneous complaint is also admissible where it is integral to the victim's story and can be used to explain, for example, the manner in which the police were involved. Remember that the objective sought by the amendment was to prevent negative inferences from being drawn in the event that the victim failed to file a prompt complaint following the sexual abuse. Its goal was simply to recognize that not all victims react similarly[143] and that it is erroneous and stereotypical to presume that the victim's failure to disclose is indicative of fraud. As noted by Judge Kerans in *R.* v. *M. (T.E.)*, " . . . there is no inviolable rule how people who are the victims of trauma like a sexual assault will behave. Some will want to raise a hue and a cry, some will want to crawl into a hole and die. Reactions vary."[144]

Greater flexibility than in criminal proceedings is imperative in civil proceedings. Statements supporting the plaintiff's testimony are admissible because they are relevant, especially where the abuser alleges that the plaintiff has invented the entire story[145] or that she is merely relating memories created by a therapist.[146] Disclosure can also be useful when determining the exact moment

141. S.C. 1980–81–82–83, c. 25, s. 19; R.S.C. 1985, c. 19 (3rd suppl.), s. 11; see also Schabas, above, note 17 at 184ff.

142. See Boilard, above, note 126, Nos. 5.012–5.014 at 5-8.2 to 5-8.10; see also, for a summary of the actual law on this issue: *R.* v. *F. (J.E.)* (1993), 85 C.C.C. (3d) 457 at 476 (Ont. C.A.). See also, among others, *R.* v. *F. (H.P.)* (1995), 39 C.R. (4th) 80 (B.C. C.A.); *R.* v. *B. (O.)* (1995), 103 C.C.C. (3d) 531 (N.S. C.A.); *R.* v. *Ledinski* (1996), 106 C.C.C. (3d) 287 (Sask. C.A.); *R.* v. *M. (T.E.)* (1996), 110 C.C.C. (3d) 179 (Alta. C.A.).

143. See the decision by Judge Kerans of the Alberta Court of Appeal in *R.* v. *M. (T.E.)*, cited by Boilard, above, note 126 at 5–10, No. 5 014[3].

144. Above, note 142 at 183. See also the comments by Madam Justice McLachlin in *R.* v. *W.(R.)*, [1992] 2 S.C.R. 122, 136: " . . . victims of abuse often in fact do not disclose it, and if they do, it may not be until a substantial length of time has passed."

145. See, among others, the admissibility of a statement made to a friend the day following the abuse in *Strong* v. *M.P.P.*, above, note 133. See also *J.M.T.* v. *A.F.D.*, [1995] S.J. No. 210 (Q.L.), (1995) 130 Sask. R. 270 (Sask. Q.B.), where the child, then eleven years old, revealed during a meeting with a social worker, who was investigating physical abuse, that sexual abuse had taken place.

146. *M.E.D.K.* v. *Delisle*, [1996] A.J. No. 318 (Alta. Q.B.) (Q.L.).

when prescription began to run.[147] Incidentally, the only criterion of admissibility referred to in article 2871 C.C.Q. is the probable reliability of the statement. It should be left up to the court to determine the plausibility of the disclosure or confidence, given the particular circumstances.[148] Circumstances should be similarly assessed where the disclosures stem from children.

511. *Admissibility of Statements Made by Children* – A statement made by a three-year-old girl to her mother was admitted by the Supreme Court of Canada in *R.* v. *Khan.*[149] The Court held that the statement was "necessary" and "reliable." The necessity of the statement must be realistically appreciated, including taking into account any trauma the child may suffer when testifying. The Court noted that the determinative criteria used to assess the statement's reliability are its spontaneity, "the child's demeanour and personality, intelligence and understanding and the absence of any reason to expect fabrication in the statement." The criteria of necessity and reliability are flexible.[150] The Quebec legislature adopted the essence of these criteria in article 2870 C.C.Q. It therefore appears that statements made by children that satisfy the conditions imposed in *Khan* are admissible in civil law.[151]

512. *Statements as to the Abuser's Identity* – Finally, it is possible that, prior to the trial—during the police investigation, for example—a victim was capable of identifying her abuser, where the abuse was perpetrated by a stranger. Can the plaintiff rely on the earlier identification when she is unable to certify that the defendant was her abuser with the same degree of certainty during a trial held five years later? The British Columbia Court of Appeal in *R.* v. *Swanston*[152] admitted the testimony of a police officer to the effect that the witness had previously positively identified the thief. The witness had in good faith admitted to now being unable to identify

147. See above, at §§85ff.
148. See, as an example, *J.M.T.* v. *A.F.D.,* above, note 145.
149. [1990] 2 S.C.R. 531.
150. See *R.* v. *L. (D.O.),* [1993] 4 S.C.R. 419 at 456–7.
151. This is the opinion of Royer, above, note 56, No. 748 at 443. See also section 85.5 of the *Youth Protection Act,* above, note 79, which admits such statements where the child is unable to testify or is exempt from doing so. This type of statement must be corroborated if a conclusion is to be drawn that the child's security or development is likely to be compromised.
152. (1982), 65 C.C.C. (2d) 453; see also *R.* v. *Tat,* [1997] O.J. No. 3579 (Ont. C.A.) (Q.L.).

the accused. It is, therefore, not unthinkable that testimony as to previous identification should be admitted where the plaintiff is no longer able to identify her abuser, but had done so earlier under circumstances that left no doubt as to the reliability of the identification.

513. *Conclusion* – In our opinion, the rationalization by the *Civil Code of Québec* of the rules of testimonial evidence clarifies the issues before the civil courts. Reliability criteria developed under articles 2870 and 2871 C.C.Q. enable a better understanding of the many rules and exceptions to hearsay. While it appears that the legislature merely intended to codify these rules, the clarity of the language used is an invitation to the courts to innovate[153] and to develop a more flexible attitude towards the concrete examination of circumstances surrounding disclosure or previous statements in order to determine whether or not they offer guarantees of reliability. This evolution may prove to be advantageous for victims of spousal and sexual abuse.

Flexibility in evaluating the evidence should also apply to the appreciation of other types of testimony, including those attesting to changes in the plaintiff's personality or behaviour.

(b) Describing the Victim's Behaviour

514. *Opinion Evidence?* – "Ordinary" witnesses normally relate facts of which they have personal knowledge. Except in specific circumstances, witnesses to the facts, or ordinary witnesses,[154] may not proffer their opinion. It is, nonetheless, admitted that witnesses are able to testify as to the emotional state of a person,[155] even though strictly speaking this constitutes opinion evidence.

515. *Circumstantial Corroboration* – Although spousal and sexual abuse remain essentially private matters, it happens that brothers

---

153. See above, at §500, our suggestion that the courts occasionally permit the plaintiff to prove her case without having to testify if she is extremely worried or fearful of the abuser.

154. See our explanation as to why we prefer the expression "witness to the facts," above, note 69.

155. See *R.* v. *Graat*, [1982] 2 S.C.R. 819 at 835. See, in civil actions for sexual abuse, the decision in *C.L.B.* v. *F.J.B.*, [1995] B.C.J. No. 965 (B.C. S.C.) (Q.L.) at para. Nos. 16 and 17, where the judge took note of the testimony given by the plaintiff's boyfriend to the effect that his girlfriend cried following sexual relations.

and sisters are witness to the abuser's unusual behaviour: he arrives nude at the breakfast table or can be found in the victim's room upon the brother's return from school. Such testimony can be introduced in support of the victim's claim—for example, that the abuse took place after school while the mother was at work.

516. *Behavioural Changes as Corroboration* – A child's testimony can also be corroborated by evidence of changes in the child's behaviour. Abuse is possible where a child exhibits fear of the abuser, demonstrates advanced sexual behaviour for her age,[156] or is depressed. A witness to the facts can often introduce evidence of behaviour. This admissible evidence corroborates statements made by the child and is required if the child gave unsworn testimony.[157]

517. *Evidence of Injury* – Testimony about the behaviour of the victim, whether a child or an adult, is also relevant when determining injury. Family members will often be called upon to describe to the court the impact of the trauma: nightmares, irrational fears, feelings of isolation, or agoraphobia. All of this evidence should be admitted.

(c) Similar Fact Evidence

It happens, at times, that the testimony given by sisters or brothers may not establish that the victim was abused, but rather that the sisters or brothers were themselves abused. Should this testimony be admitted into evidence?

518. *Distinction between Criminal and Civil Evidence* – Similar fact evidence is admitted in criminal law, subject to qualifications.[158] These qualifications are, in our opinion, inapplicable in a civil trial. Similar fact evidence is relevant, which is the fundamental criterion for admissibility.[159] The probative value of similar fact evidence varies according to the level of similarity between the type of abuse

---

156. See *Protection de la jeunesse—323*, [1988] R.J.Q. 1473 (Que. Trib. jeun.), where the exaggerated tendency to masturbate is viewed as evidence corroborating the extremely explicit statements made by the child.
157. See above, at §478.
158. See Schabas, above, note 17 at 202–6.
159. See Royer, above, note 56, No. 975 at 594 and No. 980 at 598, where the author criticizes the rejection of evidence because of its "weak probative value." This criterion, along with prejudice to the accused, is used in criminal law to bar admission of similar fact evidence.

described by the witness and the abuse alleged by the plaintiff.[160] Evidence of collusion between the complainants will lessen the probative value of similar fact evidence without necessarily rendering it inadmissible.[161] Thus, evidence by the sister as to sexual touching beginning at the age of nine and progressing to a full sexual relationship by the age of twelve, under circumstances similar to those alleged by the victim, should be considered cogent. Note that, in this regard, there is no need for separate trials; the sisters' claims should be joined in one liability action (article 67 C.C.P.).[162] The entirety of the evidence respecting the defendant's sexual or aggressive behaviour should be weighed.

519. *Jurisprudence* – On the subject of the defendant's sexual behaviour, evidence has been admitted regarding the abuser's sexually deviant behaviour or his inability to recognize appropriate limits on sexual behaviour, even where this behaviour was not directly related to the victim or similar victims.[163] The courts appear to recognize that the exhibition of disturbed sexual behaviour can be associated with the perpetration of sexual abuse, especially where children are involved. However, the absence of sexually deviant behaviour should not be seen as confirmation of an absence of violent tendencies. As Kimberly Crnich so aptly notes, "besides the fact that they like to have sex with children, sexual abusers look

160. See *T.P.S.* v. *J.G.*, [1995] B.C.J. No. 1650 (B.C. S.C.) (Q.L.) and *R.* v. *Kenny*, [1996] N.J. No. 180 (Nfld. C.A.) (Q.L.), regarding abuse that took place at the Mount Cashel reform school in Newfoundland, motion for leave to appeal to the Supreme Court denied, [1996] S.C.C.A. No. 482 (Q.L.).

161. See *Doe* v. *Hirt*, [1995] B.C.J. No. 273 (B.C. S.C.) (Q.L.), where the judge was of the view that similar fact evidence should be rejected only if the similarity between the so-called similar facts was too tenuous, if it was introduced without the defendant having had the opportunity to present contradictory evidence, or if the evidence overly complicated matters for the jury. This last motive is irrelevant in Quebec since juries in civil proceedings were abolished; *contra*: *W.P.* v. *H.B.D.*, [1995] O.J. No. 605 (Ont. Gen. Div.) (Q.L.), where the court ruled that similar fact evidence was inadmissible because the facts were not sufficiently similar to those alleged by the plaintiff. The action against the doctor was dismissed. The court suggested that similar fact evidence "is admissible if it is relevant to an issue in the case other than relevance that derives simply from showing that the party is a bad person" (para. No. 37 (Q.L.)).

162. See *Jacobi* v. *Griffiths*, [1995] B.C.J. No. 2370 (B.C. S.C.) (Q.L.), overturned regarding the employer's liability, [1997] 5 W.W.R. 203; (1997) 89 B.C.A.C., [1999] 2 S.C.R. 570, where the actions for abuse perpetrated on both the sister and the brother were heard in the same proceeding.

163. See *Strong* v. *M.M.P.*, above, note 132.

like normal persons."[164] There exist in the jurisprudence numerous examples of married men who appeared on the surface to have led healthy sexual lives, but who have been found guilty of sexual abuse.[165]

Because appearances can often be deceiving, it is on occasion essential to introduce expert testimony.

b) Expert Witnesses

We will discuss two types of expert testimony relevant to a trial for spousal or sexual abuse. We will first examine evidence supporting the victim's testimony on the perpetration of abuse. This evidence can be introduced either to corroborate a child's unsworn testimony or in general support of the allegations. Second, the role of expert witnesses in explaining the nature of the injury suffered and the impact of the abuse on the victim's life—that is, the damages incurred—will be evaluated. The latter type of evidence is well established and has been used for years to determine bodily and moral injury. The former type of testimony, however, deserves further attention in the context of a trial for sexual or spousal abuse.

i) Corroboration by Experts

520. *Admissibility of Testimony* – Although the jurisprudence attested to the court's initial reluctance to accept expert testimony on the question with which it was seized,[166] it is now generally accepted that such witnesses can testify on issues ultimately falling within the jurisdiction of the court. The court can and must be aided by experts in order to better determine whether spousal or sexual abuse has occurred.[167]

---

164. See Kimberly A. Crnich, "Redressing the Undressing: A Primer on the Representation of Adult Survivors of Childhood Sexual Abuse," (1992) 14 *Women's Rights Law Reporter* 65 at 65.
165. See, among others, *Colquhoun* v. *Colqhoun* (1994), 114 D.L.R. (4th) 151 (Ont. Gen. Div.).
166. See, among others, J.H. Wigmore, *Evidence in Trials at Common Law*, vol. 8 (Boston: Little Brown, 1961), revised by John T. McNaughton, who talks about "encroaching" on the jury's role (para. 1920). The Supreme Court, in *R.* v. *Graat*, above, note 156 at 837, appears to have established once and for all that the exclusion of opinion evidence on the ultimate issue is a "fetish."
167. See, among others, in the context of a youth protection hearing, *Protection de la jeunesse—323*, above, note 156 at 1476 and 1477.

(a) Medical Evidence

Medical evidence of physical symptoms consistent with abuse is often sought. However, the absence of a medical report detailing the physical after-effects of the abuse is not always determinative in matters of sexual or spousal abuse.

521. *Physical Symptoms of Spousal Abuse* – Damages awarded in Quebec cases for injuries resulting from spousal abuse have been based on medical reports detailing the extent of the injuries suffered. For example, in *Beaumont-Butcher* v. *Butcher*[168] the medical evidence indicated cerebral shock. This evidence supported the plaintiff's contention that she was abused by her husband, and not his version of the facts, that the injuries were caused by an accident. A victim who does not immediately seek medical assistance can be disadvantaged because contemporaneous medical evidence is then unavailable at trial. It may be sufficient, in these situations, to enter into evidence photographs detailing the extent of the injuries[169] or descriptive testimony to this effect. The plaintiff who declines invasive medical examinations following a humiliating abuse should not be inordinately punished.[170] Sexual abuse victims are entitled to refuse re-victimization by the medical profession.

522. *Physical Symptoms of Sexual Abuse in Adults* – Certain sexual abuse leaves identifiable physical signs: bruises around the genital area or the breasts, abrasions or cuts to the anus or vagina, or even symptoms of venereal diseases. However, due to the delay between the abuse and the exam, or the particular physical make-up of the victim, much sexual abuse does not display the same physical symptoms. It is, in our opinion, improper to insist that the plaintiff introduce conclusive medical evidence of the abuse. It is more important to evaluate the circumstances surrounding the abuse and the credibility of witnesses. This applies equally to medical evidence of sexual abuse against children.

523. *Physical Symptoms of Sexual Abuse in Children* – Medical evidence can be inconclusive as to sexual abuse against children. Physical indicators include inflammation of parts of the vagina[171] or

168. Above, note 139.
169. Ibid., the judge concluded that the photos were "eloquent" evidence of the abuse.
170. *Contra*: *J.C.C.* v. *Keats*, [1995] S.J. No. 390 (Sask. Q.B.) (Q.L.).
171. See *Protection de la jeunesse—233*, [1987] R.J.Q. 2701 (Que. Trib. jeun.),

abnormal configurations of the anus, hymen, or vagina. Neither the absence nor the presence of physical symptoms justifies a finding of sexual abuse.[172]

Few civil trials for injury caused by sexual or spousal abuse are concluded without expert psychological testimony.

(b) Psychological Evidence

524. *Need for Expert Testimony?* – One might think that expert psychological evidence, except as corroboration of unsworn testimony by children required under the Civil Code (paragraph 2 of article 2844 C.C.Q.), should be unnecessary. The victim's testimony is often the only evidence required to establish a cause of action in, for example, an insurance claim for theft of property. It all comes down to a question of credibility, and it would be unthinkable for lawyers to introduce psychological evidence confirming that the claimant's behaviour was consistent with that of a person who had been robbed as opposed to someone acting fraudulently. In sexual abuse cases, however, the courts are very reluctant to believe the victim, and reliance upon expert evidence is frequent.

This technique is not without disadvantages. It could have negative symbolic implications for the party who sees her story recounted, rewritten, and reformulated by the expert in order that it may be better "digested" by the courts.[173] Also, it often invites discussion as to the type of therapy deemed acceptable. It is recommended that this type of psychological evidence be used after much reflection and once the court has been amply instructed as to the two purposes served by psychological evidence: to prove wrongful conduct and, in particular, to establish the extent of the injuries.

---

where the court did not consider conclusive the irritated vulva noted by the mother: this could have been caused by a long bath or the application of baby oil just as probably as by sexual abuse.

172. See Morin and Boisclair, above, note 93 at 33; M.A. Reinhart, "Medical Evaluation of Young Sexual Abuse Victims: A View Entering the 1990s," (1991) 31 *Med. Sci. Law* 81, who also suggests that children have little knowledge of sexually transmitted diseases.

173. See, on the need for lawyers to discuss the role of experts in the civil trial, above, at §72.

525. *Expert Qualification* – Psychiatrists, psychologists,[174] and social workers[175] are deemed qualified to testify in civil court on the existence of sexual abuse. It is not so much the expert's technical qualification that solicits debate as much as his or her adherence to specific schools of thought. More and more, experts are developing a reputation based on their total support of the false memory syndrome movement[176] or their absolute rejection of memory's fragility. Evaluation of the expert's predispositions is accompanied by a critique of the therapy adopted. This is particularly the case with expert testimony in sexual abuse actions involving children.

526. *Psychological Evidence of Abuse towards Children* – Great caution is demanded when introducing psychological evidence on the occurrence of sexual abuse, especially where children are concerned.[177] The trial puts into issue the psychological technique used as much as the actual cause of action. Before the court will even consider, much less adopt, the expert's conclusions, it seems that the therapy must be "validated." It is therefore important not only to prove the therapist's qualifications, but also that the interview method used was reliable.

527. *Therapies Considered "Dangerous"* – The courts have classified different therapies as "unreliable and dangerous." Therapies or opinions issued by therapists are deemed to be unbelievable or unreliable where:

- an overly favourable bias exists respecting the veracity of testimony given by children (for example, children never lie about sexual abuse);

- the interview presents a truncated version of the events, where the circumstances in which the child finds herself are neither discussed nor considered, in particular hostility between separated parents;

---

174. *Protection de la jeunesse—323*, above, note 156.
175. *Protection de la jeunesse—233*, above, note 171.
176. See *T.K.S.* v. *E.B.S.*, [1995] B.C.J. No. 1542 (B.C. C.A.) (Q.L.), where the Court of Appeal ordered a new trial because the trial judge erred regarding the evaluation of the abuser's testimony. The Court of Appeal did not address the issue of false memory syndrome raised by the appellant. See also *D.M.M.* v. *Pilo*, [1996] O.J. No. 938 (Ont. Gen. Div.) (Q.L.), where the judge criticized the abuser's expert, previously reprimanded by a judge for lack of objectivity and his tendency to defend his client's rights.
177. See Morin and Boisclair, above, note 93 at 29.

- rewards are offered to children who confirm the existence of sexual abuse;

- the adult asks suggestive questions.[178]

528. *False Memory Syndrome* – False memory syndrome has already been discussed above.[179] Developed in reaction to treatments practised by certain therapists, false memory syndrome, misnamed and misunderstood, can justify a negative attitude towards non-traditional therapies.[180] The lawyer should first explain to the court not only the type of therapy followed by the victim, but that this is a personal choice independent of the civil action.

Certain experimental techniques have been recognized by the courts. Thus, a youth protection hearing admitted a reconstitution on video.[181] Use of anatomically correct dolls has also been permitted, although it is never determinative. However, psychological tests aimed at establishing pedophilia have had little impact. Psychological tests indicating an absence of pedophilic tendencies are of little significance, given that sexual abusers of children need not be pedophiles.[182]

529. *Therapeutic Context* – It must be remembered that psychological evaluation is not a perfect science. Sometimes the techniques employed by therapists and other participants will be seen as reprehensible by the courts. This does not mean that all the evidence offered by the therapist should be discredited. The technique, and the reasons for its use, should be explained to the court.[183] Expert evidence is only one aspect of the evidence introduced to establish the occurrence of sexual abuse. It is probably wise to point out the

178. *Protection de la jeunesse—233*, above, note 171, where the responses suggested by the social worker during a videotaped interview were judged to be of little probative value.
179. See above, at §§36ff.
180. See *S.M.* v. *D.D.R.*, [1994] B.C.J. No. 2243 (B.C. S.C.) (Q.L.), overturned on appeal, under the name *S.H.V.* v. *D.D.R.*, [1997] 2 W.W.R. 370 (B.C. C.A.).
181. *Protection de la jeunesse—233*, above, note 171.
182. Other types of abusers exist. See above, at §7. See also *Protection de la jeunesse—323*, above, note 156.
183. See the decision by Judge Bertrand Laforest of the Youth Court, (Que. Trib. jeun. Kamouraska 250-41-000002-860) cited in *Protection de la jeunesse—233*, above, note 171 at 2709: "The methodology employed and the social worker's professional training in the application of this method must be presented to the court" (our translation).

chosen technique's weak spots, thus minimizing any negative effects resulting from a cross-examination strategy seeking to discredit the therapist's use of this technique.

ii)   Expert Evaluation of Injury

Eminently valuable testimony offered by the expert as to the evaluation of injury and the impact of the abuse on the victim should not be discredited by the adverse party's attacks on the choice of therapeutic method.

530. *Well-Established Role in the Jurisprudence* – Expert testimony is generally admitted with the goal of establishing causation between the wrongful behaviour and the injury, or to measure the extent of the injury. With this objective in mind, the plaintiff can summon economists and actuaries as well as psychologists to testify.

531. *Symbolic Dangers of Overstatement* – The victim can, however, find herself painted as a sick woman incapable of realizing her potential by her own expert witnesses.[184] This could be shocking for her, and it is suitable to discuss the strategy to be employed with the plaintiff.

2.   Written Evidence

In addition to testimonial evidence presented by witnesses to the facts or by experts, the plaintiff can also enter written evidence in support of her allegations.

532. *Types of Written Evidence Introduced* – Generally, written evidence in a spousal or sexual abuse trial comprises expert reports that precede the oral testimony of the expert (article 402.1 C.C.P.). The defendant will often enter into evidence other documents designed to serve three particular objectives. First, documents created by third parties such as school counsellors, psychologists, hospitals, and the like, will be introduced attesting to *their silence* regarding the mention of sexual abuse. The defendant will try to show that the plaintiff never complained before about the abuse.[185]

---

184. See Sutherland, above, note 69.
185. It appears that the aim of this evidence is to support the myth of the spontaneous complaint: see above, at §510.

Other documents can be entered to discredit the plaintiff's testimony by undermining her present or past morality. This is the case with the introduction of documents that tend to identify the plaintiff as hysterical, as being prone to fantasies, or as a liar. Finally, the defendant can also try to introduce the plaintiff's personal documents describing her feelings towards the defendant. The infringement of the right to privacy caused by this last type of evidence has already been discussed.[186]

533. *Silence Established by Documents* – Proof of a negative fact is difficult to make. It is important that the court not presume, for example, that those involved possessed general knowledge concerning the impact of sexual abuse when, during the 1970s, those persons might have minimized the importance of the abuse or felt that it was not their place to intervene in tricky family matters. These documents should be appreciated separately, as should those created by the defendant or his employer.

534. *Documents Created by the Defendant* – It often happens that the defendant-abuser or his employer has created documents relevant to the inquiry. If it is alleged that a teacher abused a child, how much weight should be afforded to school reports that suggest the plaintiff was a child who lied? Each case must be determined on the basis of the facts in evidence. However, we should mention here various concerns regarding the use of documents that have been created either by the abuser or his employer. It is our opinion that it would be erroneous to presume their good faith or their accuracy. The teacher/abuser would certainly never indicate in his academic records that he has had a sexual relation with one of his students. What conclusion should be drawn where the adolescent is identified as a "liar"? One could argue that the identification of specific characteristics generally not found in an academic record make such remarks suspect, an indication that the teacher fears the child. It is our view that the same can be said for remarks of the same nature made by other teachers. It is highly probable that a child who is being sexually abused by one of her teachers regularly "lies" at the behest of the abuser.

535. *Documents Created by the Plaintiff* – Personal letters or diaries kept by the plaintiff are often of interest to the defendant. It is recommended that these types of private documents remain inadmis-

---

186. See above, at §§435ff.

sible, given that their publication infringes the plaintiff's right to privacy.[187] If, despite everything, they must be produced in court, it is essential that the range of emotions experienced by a victim be explained to the court so that the reading of private documents is not without context. The defendant will often attempt to rely on strong uncensored language used in private diaries when insinuating that the plaintiff is seeking revenge and is suing him because she is "crazy" or needs a scapegoat towards whom to direct her hatred of the human race. It is essential, however, that this emotional discharge be used, instead, to support the plaintiff's theory. The personal diary reveals feelings of revenge? Normal. Feelings of guilt or a desire to be loved by the abuser, despite everything? Normal. Profound loathing towards the defendant or men in general? Once again, a normal reaction.

Testimonial and written evidence often play a key role during a civil trial for spousal and sexual abuse: most of the energy during the trial is directed towards the testimony and writings of the victim, the abuser, and his experts. Nonetheless, the plaintiff's case can be greatly simplified by the use of evidence by presumption, if, for example, the abuser has already been found criminally responsible.

3. Presumptions

The relationship between a judgment in criminal proceedings and the civil trial is best understood within the context of proof by presumption. Indeed, the defendant's guilty conviction should give rise to a factual presumption that the acts did occur.

536. *Civil Not Bound by the Criminal* – It is often said that, in contrast to French law,[188] "the civil is not bound by the criminal" in Quebec civil law. It is true that a criminal conviction does not have the force of final judgment in the civil trial because the objectives differ.[189] Nonetheless, a criminal conviction is factually authoritative.

---

187. See above, at §435.
188. See Geneviève Viney, *Introduction à la responsabilité*, 2nd ed. (Paris: L.G.D.J., 1995) No. 131ff. at 234ff.
189. See *Prévoyants (Les) du Canada* v. *Poulin*, [1973] C.A. 501 (Que. C.A.) and also *Laverdure* v. *Bélanger*, [1975] C.S. 612 (Que. Sup. Ct.), upheld on appeal, J.E. 77-75 (Que. C.A.); Jean-Louis Baudouin and Patrice Deslauriers, *La responsabilité civile*, 5th ed. (Cowansville, QC: Les Éditions Yvon Blais) Nos. 59ff. at 37ff.

537. *Criminal Conviction as an Assumption of Fact* – Quebec jurisprudence recognizes that a criminal conviction raises a factual assumption that the events occurred.[190] Given that the criminal burden of proof is heavier than the civil burden, a judge presiding over a civil trial based on the same facts would be hard put to ignore his or her colleague's conclusions. Indeed, civil courts often admit the criminal conviction into proof as corroboration of the victim's testimony that has been contradicted by the defendant[191] and this is also now the case in Canadian common law.

538. *The Common Law Solution* – In the United Kingdom, the House of Lords in *Hollingworth* v. *Hewthron & Co.*[192] held that proof of a guilty plea is not admissible in civil proceedings based on the same facts. This decision, however, has been criticized in England.[193] A decision rendered by the New Zealand Court of Appeal is often cited when circumventing the principle expressed in *Hollingworth*:

> In my opinion a finding of guilty after a trial in which one of the parties to the subsequent civil action had every opportunity of defending himself cannot possibly be regarded as being of no greater weight than the opinion of a witness. There is, I think, force in the observation of Mr. Wright in the Canadian Bar Review that "To state that a civilized community is willing to see a man hanged on such a finding of fact but to treat such finding as a mere opinion in a subsequent case involving a matter of dollars and cents is a reflection on the administration of justice as well as an offence to common sense."[194]

In English Canada, the *Hollingworth* rule was completely discarded by *Demeter* v. *Pacific Life Insurance Co.,*[195] in which a man found guilty of having murdered his wife tried to collect on her life insurance policy. The Ontario Court relied on the guilty plea to dis-

---

190. See *Lapointe* v. *Équitable, Cie d'assurances,* [1979] C.A. 8 (Que. C.A,); *McClish* v. *C.A.T.,* [1982] C.A. 473 (Que. C.A,); *Meilleur* v. *Morin,* [1988] R.R.A. 89 (Que. Sup. Ct.).
191. See *Beaumont-Butcher* v. *Butcher,* above, note 139; *Pie* v. *Thibert,* [1976] C.S. 180 (Que. Sup. Ct.).
192. [1943] 2 All E.R. 35.
193. See also *McIlkenny* v. *Chief Constable of West Midlands et al.,* [1980] 1 Q.B. 283, and *Hunter* v. *Chief Constable of West Midlands Police,* [1982] A.C. 529. (H.L.), which appear to support the rejection of this principle.
194. *Jorgensen* v. *News Media (Auckland) Ltd.,* [1969] N.Z.L.R. 961 (C.A.). The court referred to the case commentary by Cecil A. Wright, (1943) *Can. Bar Rev.* 653, 658.
195. (1983), 43 O.R. (2d) 33 (C.A.).

miss the murderer's action against the insurance company. This Ontario decision appears to have had an influence on the law throughout Canada and corresponds to the legislative language used in British Columbia and Alberta.[196] We consider that the introduction of the certificate of conviction is *prima facie* proof of the accused's guilt.[197]

539. *Guilty Plea* – In our view, a guilty plea should also support the presumption of fact that the events occurred. The defendant may be able to rebut this presumption by explaining the reasons for which he entered a guilty plea in spite of the inaccuracy of the facts: to avoid embarrassing his family, or to "get it over with." The judge must then weigh the facts in accordance with article 2849 C.C.Q. In this respect, legal treatment of the guilty plea resembles the extrajudicial admission.[198]

4.   Evidence by Admission

540. *Types of Admissions* – Admissions can be judicial or extrajudicial. They are judicial if made during the proceeding in which they are invoked, such as admissions made during the pleadings or during the defendant's discovery. Admissions made during other trials or outside legal proceedings are extrajudicial, and their appraisal is left to the discretion of the court (paragraph 2 of article 2852 C.C.Q.).

541. *Frequent Occurrence* – Extrajudicial admissions of sexual abuse are rather frequent. Numerous abusers believe themselves to be invulnerable and easily discuss past abuse with the victim. The

---

196.   See *Alberta Evidence Act*, R.S.A. 1980, c. A-21, s. 27, and *British Columbia Evidence Act*, R.S.B.C. 1979, c. 116, ss. 80–81.

197.   See *Simpson* v. *Geswein* (1995), 25 *Canadian Cases on the Law of Torts* (2d) 29 (Man. Q.B.).

198.   A guilty plea is an admission because it is the "acknowledgment of a fact which may produce legal consequences against the person who makes it" (art. 2850 C.C.Q.). In our opinion, it should have greater probative value than an extrajudicial admission made outside a criminal proceeding. In fact, in order to protect innocent individuals from pleading guilty to crimes that they did not commit, the criminal court must be convinced of the truthfulness of the plea before it can be accepted. The Crown attorney is also bound by an ethical duty to prevent innocent persons from entering guilty pleas. It must be remembered that the guilty plea was obtained under circumstances that, at first glance, guaranteed its credibility.

circumstances surrounding these admissions must be noted and argued.

* * *

The civil trial can be empowering for the victim, a time for her to establish a more egalitarian relationship with the abuser. From victim she becomes a plaintiff seeking justice. Yet, the civil trial is both psychologically and legally taxing. Myths surrounding spousal and sexual abuse continue to have an impact, however involuntary. This could lead to the rejection of the testimony's probative value. The accused's denial is often encouraged by social or family institutions that push him to respond using the courts. He can decide to sue for defamation. It is essential to prepare the client for this eventuality.

Chapter 7

The Defendant's Response:
Action for Defamation

542. *The Problem* – In the United States,[1] Canada,[2] and Quebec,[3] some men who have been tried in criminal court for acts of sexual or spousal abuse, or against whom such complaints have been filed, will respond by suing the victim for defamation. A lawsuit of this type can arise at two different points in time. First, the presumed abuser can file suit as soon as he knows that the victim has filed a complaint or has launched proceedings. For example, the presumed abuser can file a cross-claim in response to the victim's action for extracontractual liability. This action for defamation is often meant to intimidate the victim: she must cope with another trial, the costs, the examination, and so on. She may decide to abandon her criminal or civil complaint, or to settle out of court in order to avoid these upsets. The presumed abuser may also institute an action for defamation against the victim once the criminal or civil action has been dismissed. The victim's lawyer, as well as the victim, may also

---

1. See Eric T. Cooperstein, "Protecting Rape Victims from Civil Suits by Their Attackers," (1989) 8 *Law and Inequity* 279.
2. See *Newhook* v. *Smith and Mackenzie* (1993), 120 N.S.R. (2d) 228; 332 A.P.R. 228 (N.S. S.C.), action for defamation dismissed; *Khalsa* v. *Bhullar*, [1992] B.C.J. No. 378 (B.C. S.C.) (Q.L.), action for defamation dismissed; *Pangiligan* v. *Chaves and Chaves* (1988), 52 Man. R. (2d) 86 (Q.B.), action allowed; *Frigault* v. *Bartram, MacNeil and Goss* (1995), 167 A.R. 216 (B.R.), action for defamation dismissed; *Swerid* v. *Swerid* (1995), 103 Man. R. (2d) 81 (Q.B.), action dismissed; *Karpati* v. *Sherman*, [1997] O.J. No. 3303 (Ont. Gen. Div.) (Q.L.), action for defamation allowed, the plaintiff received $7,938 in general damages, $15,000 in special damages, and $10,000 in punitive damages; *Strong* v. *M.M.P.*, (1997), 31 C.C.E.L. (2d) 47, 50 O.R. (3d) 70 (Ont. C.A.), action dismissed; *L.E.* v. *W.P.*, [1998] B.C.J. No. 1250 (B.C. S.C.) (Q.L.), action allowed; *M.J.M.* v. *D.J.M.*, [1998] S.J. No. 668 (Sask. Q.B.) (Q.L.), aff'd by [2000] S.J. No. 300 (Sask. C.A.) (Q.L.), action dismissed.
3. See *Nadeau* v. *Beausoleil-Lefrançois*, [1994] R.R.A. 798 (Que. Sup. Ct.); *Walker* v. *Singer*, [1997] R.R.A. 175 (Que. Sup. Ct.); *Michaud* v. *Québec (Procureur général)*, [1998] A.Q. No. 2399 (Que. Sup. Ct.) (Q.L.); *André* v. *Québec (Procureur général)*, [1999] J.Q. No. 4213 (Que. Sup. Ct.) (Q.L.); *D.F.* v. *A.S.*, [2001] Q.J. No. 3273 (Que. Sup. Ct.) (Q.L.).

be sued for defamation based on the allegations contained in the pleadings. The objective of these actions is often to discourage the victim, who can reply with an action for abuse of process. In this chapter, these remedies will be studied with special attention paid to the victim's defence. As will be seen, the actions for defamation stand little chance of success if minimum precautions are taken by the victim and her lawyer.

I. ACTION FOR DEFAMATION AGAINST THE VICTIM

543. *Elements of Proof* – In Quebec law, in an action for defamation the plaintiff must establish the defendant's fault—that is, the plaintiff must prove that his reputation was harmed as a result of the defendant's negligence (intentional or otherwise)[4] (article 1457 C.C.Q. and section 4 of the Quebec Charter).[5] Defamation can occur even if the defendant did not have an intent to harm, if there has been negligence, recklessness, or carelessness.[6] In addition, defamation can occur where the sole purpose of the publication or the disclosure is to harm the plaintiff in the defamation suit, even where the facts published or disclosed are true. This contrasts with common law, where it is sufficient for the defendant to prove the truth of the facts in order to defeat an action for defamation.[7] Thus, in a plaintiff's action for defamation against a work colleague who had filed a sexual harassment complaint with the employer,[8] the judge

---

4. See *Radiomutuel inc.* v. *Carpentier*, [1995] R.R.A. 315 (Que. C.A.).
5. See Jean-Louis Baudouin and Patrice Deslauriers, *La responsabilité civile*, 5th ed. (Cowansville, QC: Les Éditions Yvon Blais, 1998) No. 476 at 301.
6. See *Piquemal* v. *Cassivi-Lefebvre*, [1997] A.Q. No. 1509 (Q.L.), R.R.A. 300, 303 (Que. C.A.).
7. See *Congrégation des Soeurs de la charité de Québec* v. *Radio Beauce inc.*, [1996] A.Q. No. 355 (Que. C.A.) (Q.L.); Nicole Vallières, *La presse et la diffamation, rapport soumis au ministère des Communications du Québec* (Montreal: Wilson and Lafleur, 1985) at 10; James W.W. Neeb and Shelly J. Harper, *Civil Action for Childhood Sexual Abuse* (Toronto: Butterworths, 1994) at 243. See *Hill* v. *Church of Scientology of Toronto*, [1995] 2 S.C.R. 1130; *Newhook* v. *Smith and Mackenzie*, above note 2; *Khalsa* v. *Bhullar*, above, note 2; *Pangiligan* v. *Chaves and Chaves*, above, note 2; *Strong* v. *M.M.P.*, above note 2.
8. *M.M.* v. *P.Y.*, [1992] R.R.A. 333 (C.Q.). The action for defamation was dismissed and, although the judge recognized that the defendant had suffered sexual harassment, the plaintiff was not condemned for sexual harassment. See on actions for loss of reputation caused by false accusations of sexual harassment, *Darke* v. *Moullas*, [1999] R.R.A. 527 (Que. Sup. Ct.); *Williams* v. *Arthurs*, [1998] J.Q. No. 3235 (Que. Sup. Ct.) (Q.L.); *N.A.* v. *C.R.*, [2000] J.Q.

remarked: "However, such defamation could result not necessarily from the disclosure or publication of information that is false or erroneous, but where the defendant's sole objective in *publishing true facts* was to harm the defendant [sic]."[9]

544. *An Additional Requirement?* – Thus, the victim could be liable not only where she intentionally defamed the plaintiff by falsely accusing him, but also where he was unintentionally defamed—for example, where the accusations were negligently made in spite of their veracity. This additional requirement in civil law is more theoretical than real in cases of defamation brought against those who have made accusations of sexual or spousal abuse. In fact, it would be surprising for the plaintiff in a defamation action—that is, the presumed abuser—to argue that the victim wanted to harm his reputation by launching proceedings based on well-founded allegations. The presumed abuser will generally try to prove the falsity of the victim's allegations.[10] It is also difficult to imagine a court, faced with truthful allegations, holding a sexual abuse victim liable for defamation because she supposedly filed a complaint or instituted an action out of vengeance.

545. *The Victim's Defences* – In reply to an action for defamation, the victim can raise various defences, depending on the point at which the defendant launches his action. If the presumed abuser files his defamation action as soon as the victim files a complaint or institutes civil liability proceedings, the victim must prove the truth

---

No. 700 (C.Q.) (Q.L.). See Josée Bouchard, "L'indemnisation des victimes de harcèlement sexuel au Québec," (1995) 36 *Cahiers de Droit* 125, 137.

9.   *M.M.* v. *P.Y.*, above, note 8 at 358 (our translation; emphasis added).

10.   See *Nadeau* v. *Beausoleil-Lefrançois*, above, note 3. This case involved an action for defamation launched following accusations of sexual abuse. The court tried to verify whether the complainant's allegations were well founded. After being searched at a police station, Mrs. Beausoleil and her daughter filed a sexual abuse complaint against Officer Nadeau with the police and the Comité de déontologie policière and sought compensation under the *Crime Victims Compensation Act*. They stated that the search conducted by Officer Nadeau was tantamount to sexual abuse. Once the complaints had been dismissed, the accused policeman, Nadeau, launched a successful action for defamation against them. The judge concluded that there had been a plot to harm the officer. The falsely accused policeman received $5,000 for trouble and inconvenience, $3,000 for moral injury, $4,000 for loss of reputation, and $2,000 in punitive damages. See also *Walker* v. *Singer*, above, note 3, where, following a difficult relationship, the plaintiff was accused of sexual abuse by the defendant. He received $5,000 in damages for loss of reputation, $2,000 for psychological injury, and $3,000 in punitive damages.

of the allegations and that her motivation is not based on vengeance.[11]

Once the presumed abuser institutes his action following the dismissal of the criminal complaint or civil action, the victim must prove that she honestly believed that her allegations were well founded, even though she was unable to convince police or civil authorities to this effect.[12] She must also prove that it was not her intention to harm the presumed abuser's reputation. In *Hade* v. *Dumont*,[13] a complaint by an educator was filed with the employer about sexual touching supposedly inflicted on a client by another educator from the same institution, a rehabilitation centre for adolescents. Following an internal inquiry, the file was closed by the centre's administration due to insufficient evidence. The educator against whom the complaint was filed instituted an action for defamation against his colleague, whom he accused of acting out of vengeance. After analysing the facts, the court found defamation to have occurred[14] because the educator had not shown the sufficient degree of discernment, discretion, and prudence required by the situation. He had acted more out of anger. Had the judge been convinced that the complainant had verified his sources and had taken all necessary precautions, he would not have found him liable for defamation, even though his allegations were not well-founded. In *Cassivi-Lefebvre*,[15] the owners of a day-care centre sued two supervisors and the president of the Parents Committee for defamation for having filed a complaint with the police and the Office des services de garde de l'enfance respecting physical abuse inflicted on the children. The Court of Appeal overturned the trial court's finding of defamation on the grounds that the defendants' statements had been justified. It is imperative that the person who files a complaint

---

11. See *Newhook* v. *Smith and Mackenzie*, above, note 2; *Khalsa* v. *Bhullar*, above, note 2; *Strong* v. *M.M.P.*, above, note 2.

12. In *Newhook*, above, note 2, the plaintiff's father, a religious minister, sued her for defamation after she told several family members that he had sexually abused her. The judge dismissed the victim's cross-claim for damages on the grounds of insufficient evidence. This is not to say that the victim's accusations were false. The judge stated thus: "I do not make a finding that Sheila has been untruthful as to her beliefs as to what occurred when she was a child. Instead the evidence as presented at trial on this subject was not of the clear and cogent nature that is necessary in these circumstances" (at 250). Note that the plaintiff was not represented by counsel.

13. [1995] R.R.A. 792; J.E. 95-1493 (Que. Sup. Ct.).

14. The court awarded $10,000 in moral damages and $2,500 in punitive damages.

15. Above, note 6.

with the authorities, whether or not she is the victim, act prudently and with discernment, regardless of the complaint's outcome.

546. *The Witnesses' Defence* – The apparent abuser may also sue the victim's witnesses for defamation. They are protected by a qualified privilege because their testimony was not intended to harm the abuser, but to disclose information about the fault and resulting injury suffered by the plaintiff. In 1939, Justice Rivard defined qualified privilege in *Corporation du village de St-Félicien* v. *Tessier*[16] as follows: "This is the defence of he who commits a fault, but who is not at fault for having done so because he was exercising his right, he acted in good faith as a reasonable person would have done, with the appropriate degree of discretion."[17]

This privilege has been granted to several categories of individuals: to the witness for statements made in good faith relevant to the examination,[18] to the employer for letters written about the employee within the context of disciplinary proceedings,[19] and to public officers in general.[20]

547. *Countering Perverse Effects* – The perverse effects of defamation actions must be well measured by victims of sexual or spousal abuse who institute actions for defamation. The accused abuser can institute an action for defamation against the victim if the Crown attorney does not follow up on the victim's complaint, if the criminal trial results in an acquittal, or if the civil action is dismissed, for whatever reason. This sword of Damocles hanging over victims' heads may be sufficient to discourage them from filing complaints. In these highly particular circumstances, it is essential that the courts, when making their determination as to the existence of defamation, apply the criterion of intent to harm the victim regardless of whether or not they believe the victim. While it is true that the abuser's reputation may be blemished following the dismissal of an action for civil liability for sexual or spousal abuse, the victim is but exercising her right. In addition, the defendant is also entitled

---

16. (1939), 67 K.B. 456.
17. Ibid. at 458 (our translation).
18. See Baudouin and Deslauriers, above, note 5, No. 493 at 313. See *Nolin* v. *Baron*, [1992] R.R.A. 318 (C.Q.).
19. See *Van Den Hoef* v. *Air Canada*, [1988] R.R.A. 543 (Que. Sup. Ct.).
20. See *Mathieu* v. *Lavoie*, [1975] C.S. 1239 (Que. Sup. Ct.) (appeal dismissed 6 November 1981, C.A.Q. 200-09-000472-750); *Blais* v. *Lemieux*, [1976] C.S. 1376 (Que. Sup. Ct.), (appeal dismissed [1980] C.A. 170).

to costs if the victim's action is dismissed (article 479 C.C.P.). An action for defamation should not be used to punish the victim of violence who fails to prove her cause of action.

II. ACTION FOR DEFAMATION BASED ON THE ALLEGATIONS IN THE PLEADINGS

548. *The Plaintiff's Burden of Proof* – It may happen that the presumed abuser will join an action for defamation against the victim with an action for defamation against the victim's lawyer based on the allegations and proceedings.[21] In order to succeed, he must establish that the defamatory allegations were false, were irrelevant to the proceedings, and were made with malice, or a recklessness equivalent to malice, because there was neither justifiable nor probable reason for making such defamatory allegations.[22] Baudouin and Deslauriers summarized the criteria thus: "It is necessary to determine whether the allegations or comments made were (even if they later prove to be unfounded) made in good faith, with the goal of promoting the client's rights or, to the contrary, with a recklessness or intent to harm the person against whom they were directed."[23]

549. *Privilege for the Victim's Lawyer* – In defence, the victim's lawyer may invoke her or his privilege covering statements or allegations made during legal proceedings. Strong debate on the absolute or qualified character of this privilege was resolved in Quebec in favour of the latter in the 1986 decision *Pearl* v. *Byers*.[24] Judge Gratton remarked: "Quebec civil law, combining both the *common law* and the French civil law, is different from the two, a unique system that is complete yet distinct. I do not see how we can

---

21. See Odette Jobin-Laberge, "La responsabilité civile des avocats pour diffamation dans les actes de procédures," in *Développements récents en droit civil (1993)*, Continuing Education Department of the Barreau du Québec (Cowansville, QC: Les Éditions Yvon Blais, 1993) at 21.

22. See *Daoust* v. *Bernier*, [1992] R.J.Q. 1868 at 1872 (Que. Sup. Ct.); *Borenstein* v. *Eymard*, [1992] R.R.A. 491 (Que. C.A.); *Juneau* v. *Taillefer, Pigeon, Bernier, Sheitoyan*, J.E. 88-694 (Que. Sup. Ct.); *Bilodeau* v. *Cutler*, [1985] R.D.J. 139 (Que. C.A.); *Selig* v. *Coallier*, [1997] R.R.A. 1052 (Que. Sup. Ct.); *Hamel* v. *Turcotte*, [2000] J.Q. No. 1399 (Que. Sup. Ct.) (Q.L.).

23. See Baudouin and Deslauriers, above, note 5, No. 1502 at 910 (our translation); see also Pierre Beullac, *La responsabilité civile dans le droit de la province de Québec* (Montreal: Wilson and Lafleur, 1948) at 113.

24. [1986] R.J.Q. 1194 (Que. Sup. Ct.); to the same effect: *Juneau*, above, note 22.

decide that the lawyer enjoys an absolute privilege for his statements or writings made during legal proceedings."[25]

Qualified privilege was recognized by the Supreme Court in a
recent common law case.[26] This case unequivocally confirms that
this privilege is "not absolute and can be defeated if the dominant
motive for publishing the statement is actual or express malice. . . .
Qualified privilege may also be defeated when the limits of the duty
or interest have been exceeded."[27]

When will a qualified privilege exist? It exists when the person
who provides the information has a legal, social, or moral interest
or obligation in transmitting it to the person to whom it is supplied,
and the person who receives it has a corresponding interest or obligation in receiving it. Reciprocity is essential.[28] Once the privilege is
established, the defendant's good faith is presumed, and he or she is
free to make comments about the plaintiff, even where they are
defamatory and inaccurate.[29]

An action for defamation is subject to a one-year prescription
period; the delay starts running as of the date the defamed person
learns of the defamatory allegations. This rule concerning the
beginning of the delay applies even if judgment on the merits in the
proceedings in which the defamatory comments were allegedly
made has not yet been rendered (article 2929 C.C.Q.).[30]

III. THE VICTIM'S RESPONSE: ACTION FOR ABUSE OF PROCESS

550. *A Complaint with the Bar* – Several remedies are available to
the lawyer and her client who find themselves abusively sued for

---

25.   Ibid. at 1201 (our translation).
26.   *Hill* v. *Church of Scientology of Toronto*, above, note 7.
27.   Ibid. at 1189.
28.   Citation from *Adam* v. *Ward*, [1917] A.C. 309 (H.L.), cited in *Hill*, above, note
       7 at 1189. See also André Nadeau, *Traité pratique de la responsabilité civile
       délictuelle* (Montreal: Wilson and Lafleur, 1971) at 259–62.
29.   Nadeau, ibid.
30.   See *Borenstein*, above, note 22; *Pearl* v. *Byers*, above, note 24; *Bilodeau*, above,
       note 22; *Blais* (C.A.), above, note 20.

defamation.[31] They may invoke section 4.02.01 (a) of the *Code of Ethics of Advocates*[32] against the plaintiff/abuser's lawyer for having instituted an action for defamation that was only meant to "harass."[33] They can also complain about the aggressive behaviour of the presumed abuser's lawyer during cross-examinations rife with stereotypes regarding the victim. A motion requesting that an abusive proceeding be dismissed may also be filed under article 75.1 C.C.P.[34] If, upon examination, it appears that the action is frivolous or clearly unfounded,[35] the court may order the unsuccessful party to pay damages to the victim in compensation for any prejudice suffered, where such amount has been determined (article 75.2 C.C.P.).

551. *An Action Founded on Article 1457 C.C.Q.* – While this suggestion is theoretical, an action for abuse of process based on article 1457 C.C.Q. may also be instituted. The victim must prove the other party's objective fault—that is, that the justice system was abused

---

31. On the subject, see Yves-Marie Morissette, "L'initiative judiciaire vouée à l'échec et la responsabilité de l'avocat ou de son mandant," (1984) 44 *Revue du Barreau du Québec* 397.
32. R.R.Q., c. B-1, r.1.
33. ". . . The following are derogatory to the dignity of the profession of advocate: (a) introducing a demand, adopting attitudes, assuming a defence, delaying a trial or taking any other such measure on his client's behalf when he knows or when it is evident that such action only serves to harass another person or to harm him in a malicious manner . . ."
34. Article 75.1 C.C.P.: "At any stage of the proceedings, the Court, on a motion, may dismiss an action or a proceeding if the examination held pursuant to this Code shows that the action or proceeding is frivolous or clearly unfounded, on a ground other than those provided in article 165, or if the party who instituted the action or filed the proceeding refuses to have such examination. If the proceeding dismissed under the first paragraph is a defence, the defendant is foreclosed from pleading." The same rule applies to appeals: articles 501 (5) and 524 C.C.P.; see Denis Ferland and Benoît Émery, *Précis de procédure civile du Québec*, vol. 1, 2nd ed. (Cowansville, QC: Les Éditions Yvon Blais, 1994) at 113ff; Pierre Larouche, "La procédure abusive," (1991) 70 *Can. Bar Rev.* 650; Denis Ferland, "La nouvelle requête pour rejet d'action ou procédure manifestement mal fondée ou frivole (art. 75.1 C.C.P.)," (1985) 45 *Revue du Barreau du Québec* 607; Pierre Bélanger and Ruth Veilleux, "La responsabilité de l'avocat en matière de procédures civiles," in *Congrès annuel du Barreau du Québec*, Continuing Education Department of the Barreau du Québec (Cowansville, QC: Les Éditions Yvon Blais, 1994) 831 at 846ff.
35. According to statistics for the period from May 1988 to February 1994 compiled by the Fonds d'assurance responsabilité professionnelle du Barreau du Québec, abusive procedures constituted 11.18 per cent of all complaints filed and ranked fourth immediately after late procedures and notices (16.15%), improper execution of mandate (13.15%), and failure to execute instructions (12.16%). See Bélanger and Veilleux, ibid. at 847.

for motives of vengeance or to cause harm. The abusive proceeding must have resulted in an acquittal or a dismissal.[36] In addition, the victim must prove her injury: the costs associated with her defence, the personal consequences due to having to participate in another trial, and so on.

552. *Conclusion* – Due to the nature of the crime, evidentiary difficulties, and stereotypes against women, actions in defamation by the presumed abuser are more likely to occur in response to criminal and civil proceedings for sexual and spousal abuse than in response to other criminal offences. Unrestricted denunciation of this abuse is essential if this type of behaviour is to be eliminated. The efforts of various groups to facilitate the filing of complaints in instances of sexual or spousal abuse must not be frustrated by the presumed abuser's strategy of suing the victim for defamation.[37]

---

36. See Bélanger and Veilleux, above, note 34 at 843; Larouche, above, note 34 at 675.
37. See Madam Justice L'Heureux-Dubé's comments in *R.* v. *Seaboyer*, [1991] 2 S.C.R. 577 at 649–50, where she explained the numerous reasons why female sexual abuse victims do not file complaints.

Table of Cases

Index

(References are to paragraph numbers in the text)

–M–

Master-Servant relationship, 207-208

Medical evidence, 520–523

Medical examination. *See also* **Medical evidence**
Defendant, 417
Relevance, 415, 416

Medical or psychiatric file. *See also* **Professional secrecy**
Privilege, 437
Relevance, 420
Time limit on access, 421

Moratory Damages, 290, 335

Multiple remedies, 154, 368, 380, 381, 389–392

–N–

Nightmare, 52

Non–intervention
Justification, 178

Non–pecuniary consequences
Analysis of the victim's state, 314
Civil Law, 308
Common Law, 309, 310
Factors, 313
Framework, 307
Impact of the Criminal trial, 315
Indemnity ceiling, 312
Out–of–court settlement 441–444

Novus actus interveniens, 274–276

–O–

Occupational Health and Safety Law
Applicablity, 379–382

Opinion evidence, 514

Out–of–court settlement, 441–448
Advantages, 441
Alternative dispute resolution, 447, 448
Conclusion of not financial nature, 445, 446
Deferred payment of the payable sums, 442–443
Objective, 441

Overlap. *See* **Theory of the overlap**

–P–

Parent. *See also* **Family**
Duty to protect, 183–187
Vicarious liability, 221–224

Pedophilia, 7, 192, 193, 528

Personal fault. *See* **Responsibility for personal fault**

Personal injury
Definition, 254

Physical after–effect
Spousal violence, 56, 63

Physical violence, 13, 56

Physician. *See* **Professional**

Plea bargaining, 318

Plaintiff. *See also* **Victim**
Protection of identity, 449–463

Post-Incest Syndrome, 141, 144

Post–traumatic neurosis
Application, 51
Definition, 31
Description, 30
Evolution, 35
Judicial recognition, 31
Limit, 33
Measure, 34

Witness to the facts

Corroboration, 515, 516

Similar facts of the aggressor, 518, 519

Victim, 476–505

Victim's behavior, 514–517

Woman. *See* **Battered Woman Syndrome, Testimony of assaulted women, Spousal violence, Sexual violence**

Workers' Compensation Plans, *See* State indemnification plans

Written Evidence

Document created by the defendant, 532, 534

Document created by the plaintiff, 535

Silence of the victim, 532, 533

Typology, 532